ELECTION NOTEBOOK

www.**transworldbooks**.co.uk

Also by Nick Robinson

LIVE FROM DOWNING STREET

ELECTION NOTEBOOK

The inside story of the battle over Britain's
future and my personal battle to report it

Nick Robinson

BANTAM PRESS

LONDON • TORONTO • SYDNEY • AUCKLAND • JOHANNESBURG

TRANSWORLD PUBLISHERS
61–63 Uxbridge Road, London W5 5SA
www.transworldbooks.co.uk

Transworld is part of the Penguin Random House group of companies
whose addresses can be found at global.penguinrandomhouse.com

Penguin
Random House
UK

First published in Great Britain in 2015 by Bantam Press
an imprint of Transworld Publishers

A CIP catalogue record for this book
is available from the British Library.

ISBNs 9780593075180 (cased)
9780593075197 (tpb)

Typeset in 10.5/14pt Palatino Linotype by Falcon Oast Graphic Art Ltd.
Printed and bound by Clays Ltd, Bungay, Suffolk.

Penguin Random House is committed to a sustainable
future for our business, our readers and our planet. This book
is made from Forest Stewardship Council® certified paper.

MIX
Paper from
responsible sources
FSC® C018179

1 3 5 7 9 10 8 6 4 2

Acknowledgements

I could not have got through the past year, let alone written this book, without the love and support of my lovely family: my wife, Pippa, our children Alice, Will and Harry, my mum, my brother Mark and my sister Debbie; or the care of so many medical staff, especially those at the Royal Brompton and Royal Free hospitals; or the extraordinary backing I've had from my bosses at the BBC and a wonderful team at Westminster. Too many to name, but Jess, Chris, Jon and, above all, Katy deserve a special mention.

Huge thanks, too, to my PA, Karen, and agent, Mary, for making sure I live a full life but not a crazy unmanageable one, and to Caroline North for once again turning a collection of sows' ears into a book which I hope includes the occasional silk purse.

Introduction

It was a year like no other.

A year that ended in a way almost no one saw coming.

A year in which the fate of the nation hung in the balance.

The denouement came on 8 May 2015, when David Cameron stood outside the most famous front door in the world to announce that he was forming a majority Conservative government. Moments later, I was standing in the same place to report, in a scratchy voice, on what the future might bring and on the resignation in a single morning of not just one or two but three opposition leaders.

It began exactly twelve months earlier, when, in the flat above Downing Street, we filmed a prime minister who knew his time at Number 10 might soon be drawing to a close. On that day – 8 May 2014 – I started to keep a notebook, writing down what I saw, what I heard and what I thought.

I planned it as a record of the journey to an election that would decide not simply who would win power but could help determine whether our country remains a United Kingdom and a member of the European Union.

I had no idea then that it would also record another journey: one that would take me from a routine visit to the GP to the surgeon's table to have a cancerous tumour cut out of my lung – an operation that would also rob me of my voice.

My *Election Notebook* begins, long before I had any idea I was unwell, with a series of days spent with each main party leader on the campaign trail in the last UK-wide test of public opinion before the big day itself: the European and local elections. Next came September's referendum on Scottish independence, which was meant to settle the issue 'for a generation' but instead transformed the politics of the UK as a whole and led, almost without a pause, into the longest, most unpredictable, most surprising general election in decades.

A year earlier, David Cameron was all too aware that he'd never won an election; that prime ministers almost never gain votes between one polling day and the next and that the rise of UKIP had inflicted a wound from which his party might never recover.

Labour leader Ed Miliband knew that all too many voters did not believe he was up to the job and blamed his party for the country's economic woes. However, he was confident the electorate shared his view that the rules of the British economy had for years been rigged against the interests of ordinary working people.

Deputy prime minister Nick Clegg could read the miserable opinion polls for both himself and the Liberal Democrats but was convinced they would eventually be rewarded for making the transition from party of protest to party of power.

UKIP's Nigel Farage sensed an opportunity to transform himself from the joker in the political pack to potential kingmaker.

In Scotland, the nightmare back in spring 2014 for first minister Alex Salmond, and his eventual successor, Nicola Sturgeon, was the spectre of defeat in the referendum. The idea that a resurgent SNP might dominate the general election on both sides of the border was no more than a distant dream.

This was to be a year none of them could have predicted. I certainly didn't.

My *Election Notebook* is their story, and mine. And yours.

Author's Note

I have only been in a position to write this book because I am the BBC's political editor. It's a job that gives me privileged access to politicians in all parties. These relationships are built on mutual trust. Politicians know that they must allow me to report with confidence on what they are thinking but they also know that I will respect their confidences.

So, while my notebook pulls back the curtain to reveal more than I can in a short TV or radio report, I still take the old-fashioned view that the substance of what is said 'off the record' stays 'off the record'.

What's more, like all broadcasters, I have a duty to report on politics impartially. So while you'll find in these pages plenty of sharp observations and instant judgements – some right, some quickly proved hopelessly wrong – you will not find my personal political opinions. I'm well used to people telling me they know what I think but tend to find that the fans of political parties are rather like football fans: whatever happens, they are inclined to view it from the perspective that 'the ref' must be biased against their team.

How politics is reported and what impartiality really means are huge subjects in their own right – enough, in fact, for an entire book of their own. Luckily, there is just such a book: *Live from Downing Street*, my first tome, examines both at length.

ELECTION NOTEBOOK

— MAY 2014 —

Thursday 8 May

The flat above the shop

It's almost 6.30am. Work is just beginning. On the kitchen table a box of Weetabix promises to 'fuel your day'. Next to it is a child's toothbrush and a tube of toothpaste. It's organic. The eye is drawn to the details: the immaculate graphite kitchen cabinets, the gleaming coffee-maker, the modern art on the walls. This is a home straight out of the pages of a glossy magazine. At this hour only one of the family is up and awake. And on camera.

He is reading, then signing, a pile of letters, each removed from and put back into a large, battered, red leather box which sits on the kitchen table. 'I normally do this in my dressing gown,' he jokes. Now, that would have made an irresistible start to my report on *BBC News at 10*.

The clock on the wall is a reminder of why we've been allowed a look through the keyhole of 10 Downing Street. It shows not just the time but the date: 8 May 2014. In exactly a year the man with whom I am to spend the day – and will be watching for much of the next 365 days – will know if he will be staying or leaving. David Cameron will be thinking about what to say to the country, to his party and to his family on the morning after the election night before. For most people in Britain what will be at issue is who will be leading the country. For the three young children who live high above the famous black door, it will be whether they need to pack their things and prepare to move out of what has become home.

That day twelve months from now is one I know I won't ever forget, either. Just the thought of it makes me shiver a little. It will begin as the polls close at ten o'clock on 7 May, the start of a twenty-four-hour continuous shift. First I will sit alongside David Dimbleby trying to make sense of the exit polls, the early results, the signs of who might be prepared to do deals with whom. Then it will be on to the breakfast radio and TV programmes. Finally, I'll be back at Downing Street to witness the transfer of power – one family moving in, another moving out – or Cameron's victory speech, or, if the result is uncertain, the parade of officials, advisers, negotiators and takeaway food that marks the process of deal-making.

I will begin this dramatic political year by spending a day on the road with each of the key players – filming, interviewing and chatting with the leaders who will shape our country's future as they campaign in the last dry run before the general election itself.

Few people realize that they have a vote in the European elections in a fortnight. Few will vote and very few will care about the results. Many will vote one way in these elections and another in the local elections being held in some areas on the same day, and perhaps another when it comes to choosing their next government. So you might think everyone could happily ignore the results. Not a bit of it. Politics, like sport, is a team game. Morale and momentum count and party leaders know it. David Cameron fears the Tories could come third in the Euros, not just behind Labour but behind UKIP as well.

Platform 1, Paddington station

The prime minister and I are filmed striding purposefully towards the train, one of the sequences we need to assemble a three- or four-minute TV report on a day's campaigning.

To get the pictures I need I try to make any politician I'm with feel relaxed without giving the impression that we're mates. I like plenty of politicians but you can't do this job and have them as friends. What the prime minister and I say as we walk along platform 1 will scarcely be heard on TV, though a viewer with good hearing, a pause button and the ability to lip-read might pick out a word or two. So it's important to choose the right subject for small talk. 'How was your holiday in Lanzarote?' I ask. 'Great,' he replies, adding that his protection squad had said how much they liked the views.

I giggle, recalling that the *Sun* has shown him lying on a beach surrounded by three beautiful topless girls under the headline 'PM EYES RECOVERY – THE FIGURES ARE LOOKING GOOD.' That's one sequence we won't be using tonight.

The 8.30am to Chippenham

Time for a coffee and a chat. These conversations – away from the office, off camera and off the record – are a chance to test the mood, to get a sense of what's on a leader's mind and what he thinks about the months ahead.

It is a day after Prime Minister's Questions and David Cameron is still smarting from Ed Miliband's accusation that he failed to stand up for British science and British jobs by refusing to intervene in the attempt by Pfizer, the US pharmaceuticals giant, to take over UK-based AstraZeneca. Cameron is all too aware that leaders of the opposition have to seize any moment they can to put the prime minister on the wrong side of public opinion. However, he has never forgiven Miliband for his stance on Syria last year, when the Labour leader first offered support for possible military action against President Assad, then claimed credit for stopping the world taking a dangerous step. Cameron is fond of telling his aides: 'I can stomach opportunism and I can stomach sanctimony, but not both at the same time.'

A garden centre near Stroud

Today's trip is meant to be a charm offensive. David Cameron is trying to heal the rift between himself and his traditional supporters and to woo back those enticed by the amusing, cheeky and rather risqué Nigel Farage.

After a series of recent revelations about the private views of UKIP candidates, the PM is desperate to shout 'I told you so.' But today he will not repeat his scathing dismissal of UKIP as 'fruitcakes, loonies and closet racists'. He will, instead, tell their supporters that he understands 'the things they care about' and shares their 'frustration'.

Where better to do that than over tea and scones in the café of a garden centre? No Tory leader can dream of holding on to office without the backing of Gloucestershire ladies of a certain age who like to check out whether secateurs or begonias are on special offer before meeting up with their friends. With his Home Counties upbringing and Eton education, David Cameron knows exactly how to handle them. He pours the tea, offers his seat to a couple of latecomers and carefully avoids talking about politics. All very polite. All very English.

This, I hiss to my producer, Jess, won't do at all. I march up apologetically, microphone in hand, and ask the ladies whether they've been tempted by that nice Mr Farage. 'Oh no, dear,' say the first three or four, but their leader is made of sterner stuff. 'I'm not committing myself,' she tells the prime minister, fixing him with a gimlet eye before regaling him with a complaint about the number of people coming into the country. That's more like it, I tell Jess. In these elections charm may not be enough.

Stroud rugby club

In steady drizzle in an empty rugby club car park I am about to find out why. The PM has come here to launch an election poster pledging to deliver an EU referendum. Legs planted apart like a second-row forward, his gaze trained firmly on our camera lens, Cameron launches into five minutes of passionate oratory directed at the assembled throng. There is only one problem: 'throng' is something of an over-statement. Almost no one has turned up to hear him save a couple of local hacks and a small gaggle of invited party workers. There is not an ordinary voter in sight. I tell my cameraman to take a wide shot revealing the empty tarmac over which I can add a line of commentary: 'The question is, will anyone be listening?'

Among the Tories here for the photo opportunity is the Olympic rowing hero James Cracknell. Not content with a fistful of gold medals, he now fancies a stab at becoming a Euro MP. What, I ask him, is the key issue he's hearing about on the doorstep? I'm fully expecting him to parrot the party line about the referendum pledge, but he's refreshingly new to this game. What is stirring voters here, particularly the older ones, he tells me, is gay marriage. More votes for Mr Farage.

Renishaw factory, Wotton-under-Edge

The PM is standing in the middle of a circle of workers in a factory down the road. He unveils the soundbite of the day, promising the 'politics of answers' in place of what he dubs the 'politics of anger'.

I put it to him that he has long underestimated, if not dismissed, that anger and that is why, in exactly a year's time, he may have to pack his bags. The prime minister gulps. 'I know who's the boss,' he says. He means it is not him, but the British people.

While we're editing I get a text: 'Did you notice the date on the clock in the Camerons' flat?' Of course, I think, until I read the rest of the message. The year was wrong. It showed 8 May 2013 – a sign, perhaps, that for David Cameron time is passing just a little too quickly.

Monday 12 May

The 8am Euston to Crewe

Another day, another leader, another train ride. Today it's Ed Miliband's turn. In a year from now, he could be drawing up his first Queen's speech.

On any other day I'd be delighted to be heading home to the northwest. This, though, is not any day. Manchester City have just won the Premier League. The streets there will be decked out in blue. I tell Ed and his entourage that although I grew up loathing City and cheering United I will do my best not to allow this to colour my mood. He responds by reading out what he says is to be the opening line of this evening's speech, which will promise to save the NHS from competition, privatization and fragmentation. I want to talk, he says, about 'a much-loved institution ... the envy of the world for so long ... which is going through troubled times'. He pauses theatrically. 'But that's enough about Manchester United.' It could be a very long day.

Publicly Miliband is seen as dry and humourless. Privately he is much more appealing. He tells me about a man who sought him out in Doncaster, encouraging his kids to meet 'the next prime minister'. The Labour leader glowed with pride – until the guy revealed that he wasn't actually planning to vote for his party as he'd decided to back the BNP. Miliband's aides exchange worried looks. He reassures me, and them, that a ten-minute chat was enough to woo the voter back to the Labour cause.

Leighton hospital, Crewe

Rather than talk about UKIP or their issues, Miliband's strategy is to change the subject by making a series of policy announcements – like the one he'll reveal today guaranteeing patients an appointment with a GP within forty-eight hours.

When he first became leader he told me with great firmness that he wasn't going to ape Cameron's obsession with photo opportunities. He singled out the Tory leader's infamous 'husky tour' – the visit by dog sled to the North Pole designed to highlight his green credentials – as precisely the sort of stunt he intended to avoid. I remember pointing out at the time that TV and, indeed, newspapers depend on pictures and not just on the qualities the Labour leader values or the power of words, ideas and policies. As he tours Accident and Emergency it's clear to me that I didn't really convince him.

Miliband can and does engage well with the staff. He is interested in their experiences. He is knowledgeable about the challenges faced by the National Health Service. He wants to exchange ideas. All good qualifications for a prime minister. However, when he chats to patients he is, at times, painfully ill at ease, coming over as solemn and earnest when a smile or a joke is what's needed. I've filmed him so often that I no longer notice this awkwardness but my cameraman – the one who gets up close and personal on these jobs – describes today's encounters as 'awful'.

I had tried to relax Miliband pre-filming by telling him a favourite anecdote of mine about the time the former leader of the Liberal Democrats, Charles Kennedy, visited a hospital, with TV cameras in tow, while on an election tour. Approaching a patient with a bandage on his head, Kennedy asked him whether he intended to vote at the forthcoming election.

'Oh yes,' came the reply from the hospital bed. 'I'm voting Liberal Democrat.'

At this point Kennedy would have been well advised to have thanked the man, beamed appreciatively and continued on his round. Instead he asked what we call in journalism the 'question too far' – the one that spoils the story. 'What', inquired the politician, with the cameras still whirring, 'are you in for?'

The reply was brief but deadly: 'Brain surgery.'

Resuscitation unit

The Labour leader's aides have chosen an interesting backdrop for my interview with him, I remark to my producer, but isn't it tempting fate? Miliband has a similar reaction when he walks in, declaring 'Ah, Dr Robinson will see you now.'

Besides getting him to set out the detail of his new promise on GP access I want to explore whether Labour is preparing to raise taxes to fund a big increase in NHS spending as they did when Miliband was Gordon Brown's adviser in the Treasury in 2001. Before that year's general election Labour had said it had no plans to raise taxes if it stayed in government but soon after polling day an increase in National Insurance to pay for the NHS was unveiled. Now expert opinion predicts a looming NHS funding crisis and some think Miliband would gain credit with the electorate for having the bravery to spell out what is needed to fund the health service properly.

Brown's National Insurance rise was the most popular tax hike in recent British history. Predictably, though, Miliband's answers are non-committal – 'This is not the time to set out our tax and spending plans . . .' and that sort of thing. After the cameras are switched off his team are desperate to ensure I don't report that he is – in the formulaic phrase beloved of my colleagues in the press – 'refusing to rule out a tax increase'. So, I ask innocently, shall I report that he is ruling one in?

No, comes the reply; we have no plans to raise taxes. 'No plans' is the counter-formula beloved of politicians, who are well aware, as are journalists, that whoever wins the election tends to hike taxes in the year after their victory.

Evening train, Crewe to Euston

Twitter is awash with chatter about Miliband, but not about his new NHS policy or my interview with him. Instead the talk focuses on two other interviews with the Labour leader today, both apparently 'car crashes'. My producer, Jess, and I share a bottle of wine and a pair of earphones as we watch the online clips and wince.

On ITV's breakfast TV sofa this morning he was quizzed about the price of his weekly shop. Visibly nervous, he hazarded a guess that it was £70 to £80 a week. Susanna Reid pounced, informing him that the average family spent well over £100 and suggesting that this only went to show how out of touch politicians were. Ouch.

Worse was to come. Speaking to Radio Swindon as part of Labour's campaign to win control of the council there, Ed was asked what he made of Jim Grant. It was clear that he had no idea who Jim Grant was. It had to be explained to him that Jim was the Swindon Labour leader.

Miliband replied that Jim was 'doing a good job as leader of the council'. The presenter, on a roll now, pointed out that the town was not run by Labour but by the Conservatives. Double ouch.

None of this should matter, I try arguing to Jess. After all, Clement Attlee and Winston Churchill wouldn't have had a clue what their groceries cost or who local council leaders were. She sets me straight. The problem is not so much what Ed did and didn't know as that he pretended he knew, and that he didn't laugh when pulled up on his mistake. Politicians are terrified of appearing human, but isn't that precisely what the public are screaming out for them to be?

Monday 19 May

Ramsgate

'I'm Millwall and UKIP,' says the man who has just been greeted by Nigel Farage. The UKIP leader laughs appreciatively. He knows what Millwall's fans chant at the Den: 'No one likes us, we don't care.' It could almost be the slogan for the party that seems to be on the brink of breaking the mould of British politics.

Farage is among friends here on the south coast. Lots of friends. In over an hour walking around the harbour and the local cafés not a single person fails to greet him warmly. I've never seen that before. Except perhaps with Boris Johnson.

Last night hundreds crowded into the Winter Gardens, an old sea-side theatre up the road in Margate, to hear their hero declare:

> Now we're small-minded little Englanders, we're xenophobes, we're bigots, we're homophobes, we're the nastiest people who exist in the country. It reminds me of the tale that Gandhi used to tell. He said, 'First they ignore you, then they laugh at you, then they attack you and then you win.' Well, they're attacking us now and we're about to win.

I've not seen numbers like this since the creation of the SDP in the early eighties, even if many of those Farage attracts don't seem that far off their early eighties themselves. He calls them 'the people's army' and claims the establishment is terrified of them.

Today, with the sun shining brightly, the sky blue and the water sparkling, he jests: 'It's like the Med. If we left the EU it would be like this every day.'

Laughter is Farage's secret weapon. It disarms people. It makes interviewers drop their guard and it makes the general public warm to him as a human being rather than listening to his political evasions.

This is my first outing with Farage since the 'German wife' affair – the day I asked him whether the German woman he employs as his secretary, who just happens to be his wife, was depriving a British person of work. I did so as he launched a campaign poster featuring a large, pointing finger alongside the message: '26 million people in Europe are looking for work. Whose job are they after?' Nigel tried to laugh off the question, reasoning that no one other than his wife could be in his house in the early hours to get everything done.

I long ago decided that it was time the media stopped falling for the pint, fag and cheeky grin routine and started testing the UKIP leader as the serious player he aspires to be. So I accused him of always trying to make a joke of everything and asked if he was seriously suggesting that no Brit could do his secretary's job. This briefly made me a hero of anti-UKIP types on Twitter and Facebook. But it was followed by a 4 per cent rise in UKIP's poll ratings. Farage is a man rewriting the rules.

The harbour wall

Today's interview, like that one, will focus on immigration. The Farage non-stick coating seemed to wear a little thin last week when he tried to defend his suggestion that people were right to be worried if Romanians moved in next door.

Last night Farage said his choice of words had been wrong and blamed tiredness. This morning the party was sufficiently worried to take out a full-page advert in the *Telegraph* explaining what he had meant. The *Sun*, meanwhile, has done what Messrs Cameron, Miliband and Clegg have studiously tried to avoid. They've branded his comments racist.

Again and again I give him the opportunity to apologize. Every time he insists he was right to point out that the UK's borders are open, right to say that nothing can stop even known criminals coming here and right to say that there is a particular problem with organized Romanian gangs.

It is only when I ask him if he would tell people they were right to be worried if Nigerians or Jamaicans or Irish people moved in next door that his position starts to shift. Prospective landladies, I reminded him, had once put up signs reading 'No blacks, no Irish'. Was he saying 'No Romanians'?

'No,' he tells me. 'If I gave the impression in that interview that I was discriminating against Romanians, then I apologize, certainly for that.'

An apology for giving an impression. Mmm.

Farage has more to concern him than his own choice of words. Yet whatever his party has thrown at him in the past few weeks – the candidate who thinks Lenny Henry should be sent to Africa; the star of an election broadcast whose anti-Semitism led him to conclude that Ed Miliband isn't really British; the former British Asian youth leader who left claiming that UKIP is now peddling 'a form of racist populism' – seems to have bounced off the ever-smiling personification of 'none of the above'.

Hotel bedroom/temporary edit suite, Ramsgate

It may look like the Côte d'Azur today, with the yachts bobbing around on a sunlit sea, but Ramsgate has been in long, slow, painful decline for years. The port where the 'little ships' began their voyage to Dunkirk in 1940 once boasted over 250 fishing boats. Now there are just twenty-five. And even these might soon be gone, according to the fishermen, thanks to new EU regulations banning drift nets, designed, they say, to save Mediterranean turtles. 'We haven't seen a turtle here for thirty years,' one told me.

The ferry to Calais closed a while back and the town's airport shut last week. Hotels that were once the preserve of the wealthy are now filled with residents claiming benefits, many of them new arrivals from eastern Europe. As I recall the mixture of pride and anger in the voices of the locals, I am reminded of a focus group of UKIP supporters who, after itemizing a seemingly endless list of grievances about the state the country was in, were asked by the young market researcher logging their responses: 'Is there anything you *like* about Britain?' After a pause the answer came from first one and then all the assembled group: 'Its past.'

Evening train, Ramsgate to St Pancras

A friend texts to ask me if Nigel stormed off after our interview. Not a bit of it. We chatted amiably as he lit up yet another fag. My encounters with him during this election campaign may have garnered lots of praise from those who dislike him but it's clear they haven't ruffled him one bit. On the contrary, he explained that he wanted a row at the start in order to dominate the news when people are filling in postal votes. The row about Romanians gave him a platform to highlight the scale of the crime perpetrated by the country's organized gangs. You know what? This one-man party leader/campaign strategist/spin doctor might well prove to have a better idea of what people want to hear than either his political enemies or his media interrogators.

Tuesday 20 May

Clegg family home, Putney

What's good enough for David is clearly good enough for Nick. My day's filming with Nick Clegg begins in his kitchen.

'I've got my own homework to check now,' he says on camera as he stops packing schoolbooks into one of his children's backpacks and turns to his red box, embossed in gold with the words 'Deputy Prime Minister'.

The greatest crime a politician can be found guilty of in the court of public opinion is being 'out of touch'. Clegg's unspoken message is: I have kids, I start the day with the school run, they eat Weetabix (there's a box on the table), just like yours.

His problem is that the British electorate has made itself resistant to his undoubted charm. The public fell for him once and is absolutely determined not to do it again. So much so that people simply won't listen to what he's saying even when they agree with it.

He and his party have become victims of a phenomenon demonstrated by a fascinating piece of market research. Voters were shown a photograph of the Downing Street cat. Some were told that it was Margaret Thatcher's and others that it belonged to Tony Blair. Tory supporters who thought it was Maggie's cat liked it a lot more than those who believed it belonged to Blair. Labour voters, too, preferred the moggie – which I have no reason to suppose was anything other than unaffiliated and entirely impartial – when they were under the impression it was owned by their leader and not by 'that bloody woman'.

The conventional wisdom is that Cleggophobia stems from that broken promise on tuition fees. My hunch is that the problem is much more fundamental. For years the Lib Dems wooed those people who felt they were to the liberal left of Labour: anti-war, pro-tax rises to pay for better public services, less hard-line on law and order and immigration. But then they got into bed with the Tories, and these supporters were left feeling not just conned but humiliated. They will never, ever forgive Clegg, in part because they can't forgive themselves for believing in him.

He has paid a heavy price. He is now more of a public hate figure than any Tory. Here at his family home people have pushed dog shit through the letterbox. No one deserves that.

Methodist church hall, Oxford

Clegg is trying to rebrand himself as the leader of the 'party of In' – the man brave enough to take the fight over Europe to his rival Nigel Farage, whose party has replaced his as Britain's favourite protest party.

Today, in front of the altar and a stained-glass window, he tries to answer those who accuse him of blind faith in Europe. He attacks the isolationists and narrow nationalists who, he says, are stuck in the past and don't live in the real world.

I remember when I first heard this idea. It sounded a good one: convince pro-European voters who backed other parties to lend their support to the Lib Dems to keep UKIP out, while at the same time motivating party activists by leading them into a fight they could really feel good about.

The trouble is that there's not the slightest sign of it working. Clegg's two TV debates with Farage resulted in Mr Anti-Europe being proclaimed the surprise victor, with even those who didn't agree with him thinking that he had made the better arguments.

University of Oxford science park

Why, I ask Clegg, do you insult those who disagree with you? He looks surprised at the question. For him, belief in Europe is not just common sense. It runs through him like the letters in a stick of rock. A man with a Dutch mother and a Spanish wife, who has worked and studied in Brussels and Bruges and speaks a handful of European languages, he struggles to comprehend those who regard Europe as a threat rather than a blessing.

Late evening train, Oxford to London Paddington

I have long believed – as has Nick Clegg – that the Lib Dems will eventually bounce back, at least a little, as voters reward them for their staying power and for proving that they are a party of government. But for the first time I'm beginning to have my doubts.

Wednesday 21 May

Home, the garden

Every year I swear I won't do this. I promise myself that I won't leave everything to the last minute. By tomorrow night – the night the votes are counted in the local elections – I need to know the significance of such exciting phenomena as Three Rivers council changing hands. Come to think of it, I have to know where Three Rivers is. I tell Pippa, my wife, that I am anxious. She is unsympathetic. She recalls that ever since she first met me at Oxford I have lived from one 'essay crisis' to the next. I turn for solace to Sam. My dog always thinks I'm right. Sam and I sit in the sun surrounded by a sheaf of papers on vote shares, swings and council compositions. The truth is that I will scarcely remember a single one of these facts but appearing on TV is 10 per cent knowledge and 90 per cent confidence.

Tomorrow the country goes to the polls. Everyone has a vote for their Euro MP and many people in England will be electing local councillors. If UKIP top the European poll it will be the first time in a hundred years any party other than Labour or the Conservatives has won a national election. If they also do well in the locals it will send tremors through both big parties as well as compounding the Lib Dems' misery.

The results are a chance for the BBC to give our general election team, computers and on-air look a run-out – on not just one night but two. The local results come in tomorrow night; the Euros not until Sunday, once all the countries in the EU have voted.

Election rehearsal, Elstree studios

My car takes me through the gates, past the waiting autograph-hunters towards the election studio. A high fence bars those tempted to pry. Signs upon it warn that this is a 'Total Exclusion Zone' protected by 'Forces Personnel'. Can all this be for David Dimbleby, Emily Maitlis and Jeremy Vine? The producer who greets me has a stern warning: 'Don't even think of taking a photo. And anyone who walks on to the *EastEnders* set will have their BBC pass removed.' Election night might feel like the Oscars of my world but as I stride past the signs for Holby City hospital I am reminded that millions will sleep their way through our programme.

Yet as I walk into studio 4 I feel the hairs on the back of my neck twitch. A slight chill runs up my spine as memories of general election night 2010 flood back.

The set is the same as it was then. I am to sit, as I did then, next to the man who has held the nation's hand through every election since 1979. I am reliving the moment when David Dimbleby and I were handed the results of the exit poll – the first indication of whether Gordon Brown or David Cameron would occupy Number 10 for the next few years. They showed an election too close to call and the Lib Dems losing seats despite a campaign in which Nick Clegg had been the undoubted star.

'This can't possibly be right,' I muttered. Our credibility was on the line. David and I agreed to treat the exit poll with a degree of scepticism – an approach that, I'm told, led to us giving a good impression of two men holding their noses with one hand and a piece of rotting fish in the other. The poll, as it turned out, was a near-perfect forecast of the final result. That night brought it home to me that the real luminaries of election broadcasting are the scores of number-crunchers, data-processors and analysts the viewers never see, as well as the one they do: the king of psephologists, John Curtice. It is the people who provide the data on our screens, and the team of producers who whisper in our ears, that make the presenters look clever. I should know – one of my first jobs in television was being the voice in David's ear.

On set the master of election ceremonies is entertaining himself with a list of mystery councils whose names give no clue as to where they actually are. He decides to turn this into a quiz for me. I fail miserably with the first two. Aiming for a hat-trick, he presses on. 'What about Three Rivers?'

'Ha!' I exclaim jubilantly. 'I know that. It's in Hertfordshire.' Sam would have been very proud.

Since the last time we presented results together I have turned fifty. As if that weren't enough to make a man feel old, I have also been forced to acquire a pair of varifocals. I confess this to my colleague and mentor, twenty-five years older, hoping, perhaps, for a reassuring word or two. He thinks for a moment, grins and then advises, 'It's time you retired.'

Car home from Elstree studios

Back in the car I catch up with the extraordinary speech home secretary Theresa May has just made to the Police Federation. No minister has ever talked to them like this. No one has dared. Today May spoke as the shop steward for the trade union of home secretaries taking on what is, in effect, the bobbies' trade union. It's something ministers, whether Tory or Labour, have dreamed of doing for years as each has taken their turn to face humiliation at the Fed's conference.

Some have been heckled, some slow-handclapped, others heard in orchestrated silence. All have been told they have betrayed police officers who have died or been injured in the line of duty. Two years ago Theresa May was forced to stand in front of a conference slogan which called her policies 'criminal'.

Today was payback time. She stunned delegates by criticizing some officers for showing 'contempt for the public' in their handling of sensitive cases, citing the Hillsborough disaster, corruption in the investigation of the murder of black teenager Stephen Lawrence and the death of newspaper vendor Ian Tomlinson after becoming caught up in a demonstration and struck by police. She pointed out that deep cuts to police budgets and numbers have not led to the surge in lawlessness they predicted. She highlighted how the Plebgate affair – the row that cost Tory Andrew Mitchell his Cabinet job for allegedly calling Downing Street police 'plebs' – had revealed to the public gaze the misconduct politicians had suspected for years.

And you know what? They simply had to suck it up.

For months Theresa's allies have been lining her up as David Cameron's successor. This is the day many in the Tory party will finally start to take that idea seriously and be thinking, 'I wonder. I wonder.'

Thursday 22 May

Home, the kitchen

Polling day. I pack my election-night survival kit after taking advice on how to sustain myself through the all-nighter to come. Manchester United have Jaffa Cakes at half-time so perhaps I should do the same.

No, says the guy at the gym. They only need to keep going for ninety minutes; you have to stay alert and awake for at least eleven hours. We agree a shopping list: fruit (healthy), nuts (protein), chocolate (emergency sugar rush), plus porridge (slow-release energy) for after the results programme ends at 5am and before the *Today* programme and breakfast update begin.

Pippa and our younger son Harry, thirteen, agree to do the shopping. On their return he tells me: 'I got you some Freddos.' Great – nothing can go wrong. Unless I get caught on camera eating a chocolate frog.

Dressing room, Elstree studios

My dressing room feels like a prison. The heating's on so high that I start to sweat. The windows won't open. The TV won't work. The blue, plastic inflatable bed is a reminder that I am not going to get any proper sleep for a very long time. My head is racing. Why didn't you rest? Why didn't you swot up more? Why is it so bloody hot in here?

The balcony above the BBC election studio

I am about to go live on *BBC News at 10*. There's only one problem. I have no idea what I'm going to say. None at all. My mind is so full of election facts and clever analytical observations that I've forgotten the basics. Why the hell do these elections matter? It's too late: I am on air and launching into the opening thought I had planned. I have rehearsed a flourish in the middle, in which I gesture towards our impressive studio set, but no conclusions. I do what I always do when lost for words: over-emphasize in a broadly non-specific way. The elections will change everything, I say, or something like it. What do I mean? Who on earth knows? Only another twenty-four hours to go before this shift ends.

At my desk in the studio

Ten, nine, eight . . . the countdown is in my ear. The live results programme for the local elections is about to begin. 'Good luck, everyone,' says a voice trying to sound reassuring. Luckily, by the time David Dimbleby asks me a minute or two later why these elections matter, I have remembered. His introduction has given me the inspiration I needed. David spoke of the dreams of each of the main party leaders a year before the general election. I say that these elections might confirm their nightmares. David Cameron's centre on the fracture in the Conservative family that might make victory unattainable, Ed Miliband's on the danger that the anger of the electorate has bypassed the official opposition and found another outlet. Nick Clegg, meanwhile, is facing up to the likelihood that a large number of voters will never forgive him for forming a coalition with the Tories.

The first results come in

At every election there is one consistent winner – of the race to declare the first result, that is. I have no idea whether the good burghers of Sunderland beam with pride at the idea that theirs is the town that can open a ballot box and count its contents faster than anyone else, but I for one am grateful to them. They always give us something to talk about early on and, of course, to extrapolate wildly from. Tonight the first few wards in the first council to declare indicate that UKIP are on the up – not only in their share of the vote but in geographical terms, too. They take ten seats from Labour in Rotherham and deny Ed Miliband's party victory in key target seats in Swindon and Tamworth.

Next Mrs Thatcher's old favourite, Essex man, shows signs of transforming himself into UKIP man. As the night wears on and the UKIP gains mount, the guests from the main parties wrestle with what has been happening. Labour's John Healey, speaking from Rotherham, comments that voters told him they wanted to give politicians a kicking. The Tory Bernard Jenkin praises Nigel Farage for being 'refreshingly authentic'. It is, though, the Lib Dems' Lynne Featherstone who sums it up best: they 'speak human'.

Friday 23 May

Still at my desk in the election studio

At 1.30am the guests on the panel change. Slightly better-known politicians are replaced by 'I'd-really-like-to-be-better-known' ones. Results are coming in painfully slowly. On Twitter a series of messages announce, 'I'm off to bed.' I'm tempted to reply: 'It's all right for you,' but reach instead for a Freddo bar. In this age of austerity many councils save on their staff overtime bill by counting in normal office hours rather than overnight. I wish they'd all agree to do the same thing so that we could cover the results in one exciting, fast-moving show, either in the traditional overnight slot or in a new daytime format. Perhaps if we offered a cash prize to the returning officer who counted quickest we could have the whole country behaving like Sunderland.

Car from Elstree to Westminster

Its 4am. Sleepily, I ponder how to sum up the events of the night for the morning news bulletins. Every bump in the road knocks my iPad off my keyboard. 'Nigel Farage predicted an earthquake,' I write, with some difficulty. 'From the very first result the tremors could be felt.'

BBC Westminster

After two-and-a-half hours' sleep and a quick shower I re-engage with the results, which are only now coming in from London. It is clear that the capital really isn't in love with UKIP. What's more, Labour are having their best performance here in decades, winning councils they haven't controlled for years. The country, though, is reacting to the story to which it woke up: Nigel Farage is celebrating victory by pulling a pint in a pub in Essex. David Cameron and Nick Clegg are conceding their losses. Even Ed Miliband is talking of the need to win back people lost to UKIP. His shadow Cabinet are making coded criticisms of a campaign that failed to communicate Labour's message on immigration or Europe.

Labour has not learned the lessons of Ken Baker, the Tory party chairman who brilliantly spun the local election results for Margaret Thatcher in 1990. Baker, knowing that the Tories faced electoral melt-down in London, except in two Tory flagships, Wandsworth and Westminster, arranged for their counts to be completed as early as possible. The *Sun* was given a sneak preview of the result and splashed their first edition with news of the Tories' triumph. Baker invited the cameras to film him walking into Conservative headquarters carrying the paper with the headline visible. He set the narrative before anyone else could. It worked, but not for long. Six months later, Thatcher was ousted from office.

Car home

As my shift clocks up its twenty-fifth hour I am texted by an ally of Ed Miliband's. Would you, he asks reasonably, have reported things in the same way if you'd known at the start of the day that Labour would make so many gains and the UKIP success would peter out? I answer, equally reasonably – or so I hope – that I can only report what is happening at the time and neither I nor he could have known what would unfold. Perhaps I should have told him the story about Ken Baker.

It's the use of the word 'earthquake' that has upset people. Some complain it's hyperbole, others that it's a description of a phenomenon we in the media have created.

I beg to differ. From the very first result it was clear that tectonic plates were shifting. UKIP were emerging as a fourth national political force capable of disrupting the hopes and plans of each of the big three parties. Or, as Farage himself puts it rather more memorably, the UKIP 'fox' is now in the 'Westminster hen house'.

That said, once every vote is counted UKIP will not run a single council. They will still have far fewer councillors than their rivals and they will not have an MP. But, in the words of one Labour council leader, they will have caused mayhem.

And that's before the first vote has been counted in the European elections.

Sunday 25 May

BBC election studio, Elstree

I walk into the studio as David Dimbleby is rehearsing his opening to our second results programme in four days. His script includes an introduction to me. Without pausing or blinking, he ad-libs '. . . the man who stole my research file, leaving me without notes, having lost his mobile phone leaving anyone to find the prime minister's numbers.'* I had accidentally picked up David's election file at 4am after the locals. I'm now on standby for the killer on-air question that might well be my punishment.

We are briefed that the exit polls show the right-wing Front National has won in France. Marine Le Pen has achieved something her father Jean-Marie, the party's first leader, never dreamed of. She has turned his creation – for so long shunned as beyond the mainstream – into a challenger for power. Syriza, on the radical left, are performing well in Greece with comedian Beppe Grillo's anti-establishment Movimento 5 stelle (Five Star Movement) coming second in Italy. Even Germany has elected anti-EU candidates; what's more, there's a possibility of a German neo-fascist making it to Strasbourg. The peoples of Europe – or, to be more precise, around a quarter of them in many countries – have blown a bloody great raspberry in the direction of their ruling classes and Brussels.

---

* A few weeks earlier I caused a security panic when I lost my mobile, complete with the numbers of most leading politicians.

Frustratingly, we are prevented by law – British law, as it happens – from announcing the results of exit polls while anyone in the EU is still voting. The law, however, does not trouble Twitter.

David Dimbleby has one last rehearsal of his introduction, which includes the explanation that if he gives out results before the last EU citizen votes he will have to pay a £5,000 fine and go to prison.

'Enough UK people have been to prison already,' he observes. He is not amused.

Neither am I. It is absurd that people can read news on their phones which they can't pick up on the telly.

10.12pm

The first region to count its votes is the north-east. Labour surge, UKIP come a remarkably strong second, the Lib Dems are wiped out and the Tories lose their only MEP. When David introduces Martin Callanan – the leader of the Tories' group in the European Parliament – as 'a senior figure', he interrupts to say, 'Not any more, I'm not.'

This short exchange brilliantly captures the precariousness of the position of a politician facing the electorate. There are not many jobs in which every few years you face being publicly sacked and humiliated by people who barely know who you are. It's what gives election nights their human drama.

12.40am

Jeremy Vine's magic studio floor, which projects the results on to a map of Britain, is now flashing UKIP purple.

This is the moment Nigel Farage has been preparing for. The moment he has dreamed of. The moment UKIP stops being a fringe pressure group and becomes a player in national politics. He's already boasting of the consequences of tonight's results. He says that Clegg will fall before the general election, Miliband will do a U-turn and back an EU referendum and Cameron will come under pressure to harden up his policies on the EU and immigration.*

---

* He will be proved right only on the last point.

Bank holiday Monday, 26 May

BBC election studio

Every election our producers line up the plotters, the whingers and the attention-seekers in the party that looks set to lose. At 1am it is the Lib Dems who help to fill the small hours with recriminations. A spokesman for their MEPs is sanguine, blaming the tide of history and what he calls 'the strongest anti-European feeling since the Napoleonic wars'. But a party hack (of whom I confess I'd never heard before he popped up on screen) sums up the message he says voters have sent out that they are 'no longer prepared to listen to our leader'. He is shown on a split screen with a grim-faced Danny Alexander. 'You can't lose all bar one of your MEPs and pretend nothing's happened,' the guy tells the chief secretary to the Treasury. He might have added '. . . and come fifth behind the Greens.'

The Lib Dem leadership are not pretending nothing's happening. Rather they simply can't believe it and don't know what to do about it. No one will be feeling the losses more than Nick Clegg. These are his old friends and colleagues in the European Parliament. Europe is the issue he is most passionate about. It was a gamble to rebrand his party the 'party of In' and to challenge Nigel Farage to debate publicly. Clegg's hope – his belief, damn it – was that he'd be rewarded for his courage and supporters of other parties would lend him their votes. It didn't happen. Failure doesn't come much more complete than this.

Car home

Heading home at 4am for an hour or two's kip, I tap out my WDIAM for this morning's news. WDIAM is the lovely acronym the radio newsroom gives to the analysis pieces they ask those of us with 'editor' in our job titles to write from time to time. It stands for 'What Does It All Mean?'

> . . . It's a hundred years since a national election has been won by a party other than the Conservatives or Labour. What's more, the UK Independence party did it by winning seats not just in every region of England but in Wales, where they almost topped the poll, and in Scotland, too.

That UKIP gain in Scotland and their 10 per cent vote share will undermine Alex Salmond's argument that the values and politics of his country are fundamentally different from those of the rest of the UK. During the night I watched the camera feed and saw how Salmond switched from off-air grimace to on-air grin. Although the SNP have topped the poll he knows that their vote is not strong enough to suggest they're heading for success in the independence referendum in September.

Number 4 bus

'You haven't had much sleep recently,' remarks a cheery woman on the bus. The morning after my marathon on-air shift, I'm on my way to work. My favourite restorative – a long soak in a hot bath, radio on one side, pile of papers on the other – was my first chance to pause and digest the full horror of the election results from the rest of Europe.

Twenty-five per cent for Marine Le Pen's Front National is the low-light. There is also a new Polish MEP who is anti-women ('women are dumber than men and should not be allowed to vote'), anti-democracy ('the stupidest form of government ever conceived') and anti-EU ('a communist project') persuading more than a quarter of young people to vote for him. I find myself getting angry with the young for ignoring the lessons of history – the lessons I learned from my grand-father, a German Jew who fled the Nazis. My seventeen-year-old son Will, the only person on hand first thing this morning, had to suffer a brief lecture on the perils of a repeat of European extremism.

My Twitter feed reveals that the *Guardian*'s acerbic and scatological cartoonist Martin Rowson has me in his sights today. Amid a grey wasteland I am portrayed saying: 'And another frankly CALAMI-TOUSLY disappointing night for ED MILIBAND as LABOUR WIN NO VOTES WHATSOEVER' and below, in tiny print, 'in the Ukrainian election'. My caricature continues blithely: '. . . while UKIP SURGE AHEAD TO ANOTHER LANDSLIDE after winning no votes whatsoever in the Ukrainian election.' I text Labour headquarters a copy of the cartoon for their amusement.

It seems that the BBC is, once again, being attacked in two contra-dictory ways. First we are alleged to have exaggerated UKIP's success and secondly to have created that success by giving them too much air-time. They can't both be true. Nevertheless, the criticism worries me. I e-mail colleagues to see if they think we overdid UKIP's results and under-did Labour's. A consistent view comes back. All respected psephologists have reached the same conclusion over the past few days: UKIP have made a significant breakthrough to emerge as the fourth party of the UK while Labour have made gains, but not on a big enough scale to inspire confidence anywhere that they will win the next election. They still can.

The leaders of the other parties emerge to say they've listened to the voters and then simply repeat whatever it was they thought before the votes were cast.

Intercontinental hotel, Westminster

A dozen TV cameras and even more snappers are waiting for the arrival of the leader of the self-proclaimed 'people's army'. UKIP's commander-in-chief has lined up his 'infantry' – twenty-four newly elected MEPs – to parade before the world's media. Nigel Farage boasts that they are no longer a party of retired generals who want to birch people (though UKIP certainly has more than its fair share of those). He claims that they now represent all social classes and all parts of the UK.

The poster boy for the non-posh, non-southern, non-Tory-in-all-but-name section of UKIP is its Scouse skinhead deputy leader, Paul Nuttall, who asserts that 'this is probably the most exciting moment in politics since the birth of the Labour party'. Keir Hardie must be turning in his grave.

Farage likens the three main party leaders to 'goldfish that have been tipped out of their bowl on to the floor and are gasping for air', adding, rather confusingly, that they are 'clinging on to the comfort blanket that this was a protest vote'. A goldfish with a blanket? Well, it has been a long night.

His closing flourish is to promise to unveil new policies at his party conference in . . . wait for it . . . wait for it . . . Doncaster. Ed Miliband's constituency.

Farage insists he'll be stepping out of the limelight a little from now on but without his personality, his bonhomie and his phrase-making the UKIP balloon could rapidly deflate. For all the talk of the people's army marching into Westminster they face formidable obstacles. The first-past-the-post voting system will require them to build a far bigger coalition than they have so far. Parties that spread a lot of votes thinly win very few seats.

They will also face searching questions about those policies that remain undeveloped and on which their members disagree. Nuttall has championed the privatization of NHS services while Farage says he disagrees with the idea.

Farage knows that to break through they have to tackle the fear factor – the belief that they're too extreme. In a snatched interview in a mêlée of cameras and balloons I suggest to him that armies, even so-called 'people's armies', tend to scare people. He replies: 'I don't think anyone should be scared of UKIP.'

They are, Nigel. They are.

Wednesday 28 May

I have a bad case of what apparently we must now call 'social jet-lag'. To you and me that's 'not enough sleep'. The problem with having done two twenty-five-hour shifts on two election nights in four days is that my brain has got used to being awake and able to calculate differential vote shares in the middle of the night. At 4am I woke from a dream about the council results in Thurrock. Sad. Very sad. Time for a day off.

— JUNE —

Monday 2 June

Outside the Lords

I bump into a mate of John Prescott's, who tells me about a phone call the former deputy PM had with Ed Miliband. Prescott says he told Miliband not to worry about how the party would react to the election results. 'They won't get rid of you with only a year to go.' Apparently, Miliband didn't so much as crack a smile. Even after being told it was a joke.

Prescott's serious point was that the party has to stop acting as if it is scared of an EU referendum and as if defeat is inevitable. It is time to admit that Europe must change and to challenge the rules on freedom of movement of labour. Will Ed listen?

Quirinale restaurant, Westminster

How will the Tories deliver their oft-repeated, crowd-pleasing, head-line-generating promise to 'stop foreign judges telling Britain what to do'? That's what I try to discover over lunch with a minister who is closely involved with the discussions.

My guest says there is, to use Tony Blair's favourite phrase, no 'third way' between being in or being out. The PM's idea of scrapping the Human Rights Act and replacing it with a new British bill of rights that will assert Parliament's sovereignty is a 'recipe for a car crash with an in-built time delay'. Sooner or later there will be a clash and Britain will face an uncomfortable choice: try to persuade Strasbourg to change its judgement (often tried and, so far, never achieved) or withdraw altogether. This, he continues, will attract international opprobrium, undermine Britain's ability to criticize any other country's human-rights record and invite the judges on another European court (the EU's European Court of Justice) to attempt to fill the vacuum.

Foreign secretary William Hague describes Europe as an 'unexploded bomb' that Tory party leaders have to carry around. He, Cameron and Osborne have spent years trying to avoid setting it off by mistake. If they listen to my lunch guest and admit there's little they can do, the bomb will go off. If, on the other hand, they choose confrontation with Strasbourg, it may go off just the same.

Everyone finds it very easy to agree what they're against: the European Court of Human Rights in Strasbourg ordering the government to give prisoners the vote or risk having to make hefty compensation pay-outs to those serving time. The difficulty comes when anyone tries to decide what to do about it.

London Business School

He's back and, I confess, I've missed him. Tony Blair is, despite everything, simply the best there is at leading a political debate. You don't have to agree with him to relish the well-practised precision with which he makes an argument. It's like watching David Beckham judge the perfect cross.

Blair very rarely gives public speeches in his home country but today he is talking about the EU to the CBI. He's timed it well. According to German press reports, David Cameron has warned Angela Merkel that Britain would drift closer to the EU exit if the wrong candidate is chosen to replace José Manuel Barroso as the top Eurocrat. The leading candidate is Jean-Claude Juncker, the ultimate Brussels insider – loathed by Eurosceptics, seen as insensitive to British politics even by Euro-enthusiasts and – as was confirmed to me recently by a big player in Brussels – a notoriously heavy boozer.

This morning's *FT* reports that Blair met Germany's chancellor last week and told her he wanted a role in Europe. Could he be an alternative to Juncker? I speak to his office and they deny it. Taking questions after his speech, he insists that he's not angling for any job, but I can't resist. The possibility of President Blair in Europe is a perfect hook into a story that otherwise risks being impenetrable to most viewers.

I start my piece for the ten o'clock news with pictures of a chauffeured limo pulling to a stop and the line: 'Wanted – a big hitter, someone who can speak for Europe but who needs to understand Britain.' As the former prime minister is seen getting out I add: 'Oh, look! Here's Tony Blair, who just happens to be giving a speech about – guess what? The EU.'

For good measure I remind viewers that the memories are long in Westminster of the last time Blair was talked of for a top job in Europe, back in 2007, after he'd handed the keys of Number 10 to Gordon Brown. William Hague, then the shadow foreign secretary, delivered the funniest speech I've ever heard in the Commons.

> Picture the scene at a European Council some time next year. Picture the face of our poor prime minister as the name 'Blair' is nominated by one president and prime minister after another; the look of utter gloom on his face at the nauseating, glutinous praise oozing from every head of government ... Then the awful moment when the motorcade of the president of Europe sweeps into Downing Street. The gritted teeth and bitten nails ... The prime minister emerges from his door with a smile of intolerable anguish; the choking sensation as the words, 'Mr President' are forced from his mouth.

Blair's argument today was striking for such a passionate advocate of the EU. The victories of UKIP and the Front National in France 'signify something ... deep anxiety, distrust and alienation from the institutions and key philosophy of Europe,' he said.

What he did not do was as interesting as what he did. There was no criticism of David Cameron's promise to renegotiate Britain's relationship with the EU or his plan to hold a referendum in 2017. Instead Blair came up with a negotiating strategy for his Tory successor: persuade the leaders of the EU's twenty-eight countries of the need to agree a common agenda to reform Europe, do it before any names are talked about for any jobs, and then hand it down to the EU Commission as a mandate rather than waiting for them to come up with their own centralizing plans.

The question is, is it too late for Cameron? Has what the German press has written up as a threat – 'We'll quit if you choose Juncker' – destroyed any hopes of winning allies?

Wednesday 4 June

Home, bed

A buzz. I turn over and groan slightly. It's 6.15. Too early for the alarm, surely? It's a text message. There are only two sorts at this time: stories (good and rare) and complaints (bad and common).

This one's a complaint. My morning radio report on the Queen's speech, due to be delivered at the state opening of Parliament today, isn't fair, says the man at Number 10. I have half a mind to write back: 'Just because you can hear me on air it doesn't mean I am awake.' But I think better of it, roll over and close my eyes again. It's taken me a long time to learn that the best way to deal with trivial complaints is to ignore them.

Another buzz. What, asks someone at the BBC, do I think of the extraordinary row between Michael Gove and Theresa May? The honest reply would be 'What row?' My phone contains the answer to that question. *The Times* reports a fierce spat between the education secretary and the home secretary on how best to combat Muslim extremism, not least in Britain's schools. It comes just days before a report is due to be published into allegations of a plot by extremists to take over schools in Birmingham.

A source close to Michael Gove has attacked the Home Office for failing to 'drain the swamp' of extremists and instead simply waiting to fight off 'the crocodiles once they reach the boat'. The language is a giveaway. The source is clearly someone very close indeed to Michael Gove. None other than Mr Gove himself, in fact. In response, in the early hours of this morning a private and highly critical letter from May to Gove was released on the government's website. This is unheard of. The letter suggests – and I paraphrase liberally here – that he knows what he can do with his fucking crocodiles.

A note from my BBC colleagues who worked late last night tells me that the home secretary's fiery and combative adviser, Fiona Cunningham, was on the phone just before midnight slagging off colleagues at the Education Department.

My basement study

I had been expecting to spend the day talking about the Queen's speech. Instead I pad downstairs to the basement, firing off a series of texts to Gove's and May's fellow ministers and spin doctors designed to find out more. The confrontation matters because Theresa May has been positioning to replace David Cameron, an ambition not calculated to endear her to Michael Gove, his good friend and supporter.

All replies confirm the row but add little detail. Then one minister says, infuriatingly: 'Will ring in few mins.' I reply: 'Going on air in 5.'

I am able to broadcast my reports on Radio 4's *Today* programme from home, thanks to an ISDN box – a digital phone line that comes with a studio-quality microphone and pair of headphones – which turns my basement into a radio studio. Hazarding a guess at what lies behind the row, at 7.58 I begin to dial up *Today*.

My mobile rings.

'Do you want to know what this is really about?'

'Yes,' I respond breathlessly, 'but it'll have to be quick as I'm on air in a moment.'

The story is a good one. The ministers have openly rowed at meetings of the prime minister's extremism task force, not just about the so-called Trojan horse plot to take over schools – he is convinced there is one, while she wants to tread carefully until a 'smoking gun' is found – but about something rather fundamental: how to actually define extremism. Gove is said to be pursuing an 'aggressive neo-con agenda'. Having lost the argument with fellow ministers, he went behind their backs to get the support of his chum the prime minister. Theresa May is sick of the continuous sniping and is 'going for the kill'.

'That'll do,' I say, and seconds later I'm repeating the minister's words to listeners across the country.

Kitchen

Heading back upstairs for a much-needed coffee, I find my son having his breakfast. Will, who has just sat his politics AS-Level, asks a penetrating question. 'Why do people tell you stuff like that? What's in it for them?' That, I reply, is a question with many answers, and I begin an impromptu seminar about journalists and their sources.

Victoria line tube

My morning report causes a stir and leaves Team May fuming. I suggested that 'a complicating factor' in the row is the fact that Fiona Cunningham, the home secretary's adviser, is in a relationship with one of the targets of Gove's ire: Charles Farr, the head of counter-terrorism, or chief spook, at the Home Office. This is no secret; indeed, it caused controversy a few months ago.

It is clear to me that overnight Fiona has exploded. Her fingerprints are all over an extraordinary series of briefings, including the one made to my BBC colleague in the early hours. In an e-mail he sent at the end of his shift he joked that she'd never returned one of his calls before but it had been worth the wait.

The quote that call produced, from an unnamed Home Office source, was: 'The Department for Education is responsible for schools. The Home Office is not. They have got a problem and they are trying to make it someone else's problem.' Another extraordinary quote, again from an unnamed source, was published by *The Times*: 'Lord knows what more they have overlooked on the subject of the protection of kids in state schools. It scares me.'

It is these statements, together with the posting of May's letter to Gove on the government website, that led me to conclude that Fiona is fighting like a tigress to protect not just her boss but her lover, too. I had sent her a text asking her whether she was 'trying to put Michael back in his box'. I added a PS: 'Shout if you think this personal or inaccurate, but you are still in a relationship with Charles Farr, aren't you?' It was not my most subtle attempt to flush out a story.

There's no denial in her reply. It's clear, though, that she thinks her relationship is irrelevant to the matter and should play no part in my coverage.

For the rest of the day I ignore the personal and report the account of someone I describe as a 'source familiar with the row but who is not in either department' – the minister who called me seconds before my *Today* broadcast this morning.

The bubble, College Green

Here we are again. Whenever anything big happens in politics the BBC bubble is brought out of storage and erected on the little patch of grass opposite the House of Commons.

It was here that I sat in 2010 for what seemed days after the general election produced no clear winner. It is here, today, that I am watching the state opening of Parliament – the start of the coalition's final year. When Black Rod knocks three times on the door of the Commons to summon MPs to hear Her Majesty he is greeted by something almost as traditional: the heckle from Dennis Skinner. 'Coalition's last stand!' he booms, to laughter on all sides.

All my adult life politicians have talked of doing away with the pomp and the flummery. The ceremony has, though, remained virtually untouched, even while so much has changed around it. Alongside Black Rod – who, I fear, must sound like some porn star to many teenagers – are the lord great chamberlain and the earl marshal, each performing their carefully rehearsed roles. The Queen's enormous and heavy train is carried by young, smooth-skinned aristocrats. If you were writing a satire you might hesitate to christen one of them Hugo Bertie, but that was, indeed, the name of one today. Television viewers see an elderly lady in an enormous and obviously painfully heavy crown read out a series of absurd political slogans – 'My government will continue to deliver its long-term plan' (apparently the Palace vetoed the full Tory catchphrase, 'long-term economic plan') – 'and convey a promise to boost "Eesas"' (I suspect the Royal Household don't put their savings in what most of us call ISAs).

Labour's Jack Straw, who has played just about every role in this pageant apart from the Queen's, is sitting alongside me in the studio. He makes a stout defence of the whole affair as a symbol of the stability and continuity provided by our constitutional monarchy. On arriving at the studio he asked to sit with his good ear next to the presenter, Huw Edwards. He is pretty much deaf in the other. I joke that it must have been interesting serving with Gordon Brown, who only has one functioning eye.

'It was worse than you think,' he says. The official Cabinet seating plan, based on status, not personal preferences, required that Jack sat on Gordon's blind side, which meant Gordon was on his deaf side. As a result they were never able to exchange a discreet word about what others were saying, being forced instead to swap notes written in the fat, bold, black felt-tip pen Brown always used to ensure he could read them. The only problem was that everyone else nearby could read them as well.

Penguin Books offices, the Strand

After the six o'clock news I rush off to Tristram Hunt's book launch. The shadow education secretary is a rather distinguished historian who has somehow found time, as well as doing his day job, to write an impressive and original tome on ten cities that made the Empire.

He jokes that as the 'incoming education secretary' he's looking forward to putting his own book on the national curriculum. He quotes from Michael Gove's review, which begins with almost gushing praise for the brilliance of his rival and ends by noting that the book features a series of basic factual errors that might need to be cleaned up before the paperback is published. Classic Gove.

The guest of honour is Ed Miliband. In contrast to Hunt he speaks about what will happen 'if' a Labour government is elected. An exasperated supporter utters 'WHEN!' in a stage whisper. We chat afterwards. He is anxious to know what I made of his speech in the Commons. Aware that at the same time I was preoccupied by the Cabinet row, he asks me to explain what's going on there. I try to encapsulate the story concisely. When another person in our company kindly compliments me on a brilliant summary, I quip that I could have been doing this for Ed if he'd taken up my offer to be his adviser. To my amazement, the Labour leader responds as if I were being serious. 'But you never offered, did you?'

I am left with a sense that he is feeling vulnerable. When things aren't going well for a political leader there are few jobs that are more lonely.

Thursday 5 June

The *Daily Mail* has picked up my on-air reference to the 'complicating factor' in the May–Gove row. Its headline, 'THE DISCREET AFFAIR BETWEEN TWO OF THE HOME SECRETARY'S CLOSEST ADVISERS WHICH MAY BE THE REAL REASON FOR HER BITTER SPLIT WITH CABINET COLLEAGUE MICHAEL GOVE', is, of course, precisely what Fiona was so desperate to avoid when I texted her yesterday morning. After our exchanges I certainly didn't need the *Mail* to tell me that my report 'caused outrage in the Home Office, which is convinced he was put up to it by Mr Gove's officials'. I'm only surprised they didn't blame Number 10 as it's a well-known fact that the PM's director of communications, Craig Oliver (who was a colleague of mine at both ITV and BBC News), loathes Fiona and would be delighted to see her go.

It is often assumed that reporters have been put up to say something by somebody else. The truth is usually much more dull. The affair was public knowledge and seemed relevant. But I'm still worrying about whether I should have talked about it. Everyone with whom I've checked insists that it was germane to the story. The people who disagree are, of course, the ones who don't respond to your texts.

Friday 6 June

Home, bed

I awake in the small hours and reach for my phone. The result from a by-election in Newark, traditionally a safe Tory seat, is just in. The Conservatives have won, and won comfortably.

A year or two ago UKIP's result – a good second – would have seemed extraordinary. Now, though, it hints that there may be a ceiling to their potential vote of around 25 per cent. The Lib Dems have come a humiliating fifth behind the Greens and not that far ahead of the Monster Raving Loony party. Labour will comfort themselves that they were never the real challengers here but, remembering that this was a seat they won when Tony Blair swept to power in 1997, the result should worry them.

No UKIP victory, and therefore no astonishing upset, means there is no call for me to go on the news tonight. Phew.

The country is rightly much more absorbed by the seventieth anniversary of the D-Day landings. I find the emotion of the veterans very affecting. Even all these years on, the memory of the brothers-in-arms they lost still moves them – and me – to tears. At eighteen, around the same age some of these survivors would have been then, I lost two good friends. The pain dulls but it never disappears.

Saturday 7 June

Outside the Mildmay club, Stoke Newington

'Why are you out here on the pavement?' ask friends heading into a party. I explain that there's a news story breaking. Fiona Cunningham, Theresa May's adviser, has been forced to quit and Michael Gove has written not one but two letters of apology for briefing against the home secretary, the first to the PM and the second to Fiona's lover Charles Farr, the Home Office counter-terror chief.

The partygoers seem less than interested. 'It's a big deal in my world,' I explain.

I text Fiona to say I'm sorry. Her reply is short and pithy. She doesn't believe me. Oh, well.

Close associates of hers are more forthcoming. They believe Cameron has punished Team May much more severely than his friend Michael Gove. The bad blood created by this row will not pass quickly.

Sunday 8 June

Broadcasting House

Radio 4 has asked me to put Michael Gove in the 'psychiatrist's chair'. This morning I'm presenting *Broadcasting House* (the programme, not the building) and they've asked me to analyze the education secretary's almost unrivalled capacity to both impress and infuriate people. How is it that a man so unfailingly polite can inspire such fury and hatred?

The answer is simple. He is a softly spoken revolutionary, a genuine radical and an outsider (the adopted son of an Aberdeen fish trader) who sees his mission as smashing the educational establishment. For a long time many ears were tuned only to the elaborate, old-world courtesy and failed to hear his arguments. As long as he was getting his way, that suited him just fine. However, the passing of time, the fiery briefings of his Rasputin-like adviser Dominic Cummings and his own ill-discipline have ensured that more and more people have cottoned on.

Michael has also made a fatal mistake. His own colleagues have begun to realize that he treats them with the same contempt previously reserved for those in the education establishment, or what he calls 'the Blob'.

Monday 9 June

Home, the study

'We'll be talking about the substance later but first here's our political editor . . .' says Justin Webb on the *Today* programme.

'Yes, I'm here for the trivia,' I say, trying not to sound touchy. I then earnestly attempt to explain why there really is a link between the politics of the May–Gove row (the turf war, the jockeying for position and the personality clash) and the substance (how to combat Islamic extremism in schools). It frustrates me that the current all-pervasive, anti-politics mood persuades people that all political arguments are rooted in the base and selfish instincts of politicians whereas other 'real' people exist in a world where issues are always judged on their merits and their own interests are put to one side. The truth, of course, is that everyone – even nurses and doctors and human-rights lawyers – does what they do as a result of a mixture of motives.

Breakfast table

I turn to the *Mail* again this morning. It has concluded that I was a pawn in a Downing Street plot to clip the wings of the Cabinet's rising star, Theresa May. Someone with a long memory has told them how, a year ago, I revealed that David Cameron regarded Theresa May as 'grotesquely naïve' for allowing herself to be touted as his successor. 'Barely an hour before,' continues the paper, 'Robinson was spotted deep in conversation with Craig Oliver, an old friend, at Westminster.' I confess that I can't remember the story, let alone the meeting. Either Theresa or Fiona obviously can.

The *Mail* shrewdly observes that May 'will sorely miss her Rottweiler adviser'. The home secretary, 'who is seen as cold and aloof by some of her colleagues, has lost the one person who could make her seem more human'.

House of Commons gallery

Really big moments in politics have to be experienced inside the House of Commons. They're not the same on television. It's like the difference between watching a match in the stadium and watching it at home. The small screen shows you only part of the action. In Parliament the microphones are designed to pick up the sound of the person speaking and to screen out background noise. The cameras can show the odd brief reaction shot, but they do not allow you to see both sides at once. In politics, as in football, only a select handful get a touch of the ball but the responses of both team-mates and opponents, as well as the morale of your supporters, is crucial.

Theresa May has been summoned to the Commons to explain how and why her private and none-too-complimentary letter to the education secretary found its way on to the government website and stayed there for three whole days. She is to be followed by Michael Gove, who must deal with 'the substance' of how and why extremists have taken over the running of some of Birmingham's schools.

The home secretary is at her most imperious. An inquiry by the Cabinet secretary has found that she did not authorize the leaking of the letter. An interesting choice of words, I thought. They have not excluded the possibility that she wrote the letter expecting it to be leaked, knew it would be leaked and did nothing after it was leaked to remove it immediately from the website. Once Labour MPs spot these gaps in the armour of the Tory ice queen they try again and again to draw blood, succeeding only in provoking her to proclaim her record as a home secretary who – unlike her Labour predecessors – has ensured the deportation of extremist Muslim clerics Abu Qatada and Abu Hamza and seen off every criminal this side of Gotham City (or something like that).

The only person to take a chip out of the ice is Dennis Skinner. 'If the home secretary's case is so convincing, why didn't you manage to convince the education secretary? Is it because there is an alternative agenda in the Tory party, which is that, post-election, the nasty party is getting ready for a succession battle and you are battling it out with the education secretary?' May sits there shaking her head before rising to spit out her reply: 'I do not think that question should be dignified with a response.'

The Tories know Skinner has a point and that she is being evasive but nevertheless they roar her on. Michael Gove nods along, like one of those dogs you used to see in car rear windscreens. He is separated from May by a human shield – the imposing form of Eric Pickles – but reaches across to pat her arm at the end of her statement. She sits down impassively.

When Gove gets to his feet Theresa finds herself exactly where she doesn't want to be: alongside her tormentor from the Education Department. In a dramatic change of tune he is soon insisting that no government – and, indeed no home secretary – has as good a record on combating extremism. There are no nods from Theresa, no smiles, no encouraging pats of the arm. She sits there stony-faced, looking rather like a crossed mafia boss. I don't think she will ever forget, let alone forgive.

Maybe Justin Webb had a point after all.

Tuesday 10 June

Home, the kitchen

Over breakfast Will tells me that he's just caught up with *The Thick of It*, the brilliant BBC political satire. He has been devouring whole series in a single sitting. 'You're in it a lot, Dad,' he says.

'Am I?' If that is the case, I have genuinely forgotten.

Looking ever so slightly proud of his father, he quotes an inept Cabinet minister in an early series: 'There's more to life than drinks parties at the Foreign Office and having Nick Robinson's number on your fucking BlackBerry.' Will hesitates before adding, 'And then there's that other bit . . .'

A suppressed memory slowly begins to resurface. The memory of a parting shot to his team from Malcolm Tucker, the foul-mouthed, testosterone-fuelled Glaswegian spin doctor played by Peter Capaldi: 'I'm away to wipe my arse on pictures of Nick Robinson. I'm getting good at giving him a quiff.'

There is absolutely nothing I can say.

Harry, our youngest, grins.

Wednesday 11 June

Commons gallery

Normally I cover Prime Minister's Questions from the *Daily Politics* studio but today I have the chance to watch it from the gallery. It's the first time the PM and the leader of the opposition have faced each other since the elections. When Ed Miliband stands up there is a huge cheer and shout of 'More!' The noise is all coming from the Tory benches.

Miliband does his best to salvage the substance from the May–Gove clash. His best is simply not good enough. He tries to use the row over extremism in schools to make the argument that parents need to know schools are being monitored and that someone can be held to account for what goes wrong in them. He reasons that not all schools can be run from a desk in Whitehall. So far, so good, but none of it would be comprehensible to anyone without extensive and detailed knowledge of school governance. Surely, I say to the man from the *Mirror* who's sitting next to me, he's got a decent soundbite to capture what he's talking about? 'Isn't it time,' the Labour leader asks, for 'a proper system of local oversight, separate from councils, responsible for standards at all schools?' My fellow hack turns to me and says, 'That's why we often have to rewrite their press releases to get them in the paper.'

Miliband has failed what I call the 'my mum' test. Put simply, can you sum this up in a way that my mum will grasp instantly? I have often apologized to my mum for the mildly patronizing and sexist nature of this rule of thumb but she knows what I mean. The other test I occasionally use is the 'Turkey Twizzler test' as in ''Ere, luv – put them Turkey Twizzlers back in the oven and look at this. They're talking about ... the need for a proper system of local oversight, separate from councils, responsible for standards at all schools.' Quite.

A good, old-fashioned administrative cock-up, one that means many people may not get their passports in time for their hols, makes for richer pickings for the Labour leader but it is too little, too late. Cameron points out that once again he has ignored good economic news. There has been another big rise in the number of jobs being created, announced this morning. The PM then turns a question that refers to the World Cup to his advantage: 'If you have a strong team with a strong plan, stick with them, and keep on putting it in the back of the net.' Crass. Meaningless. Effective.

Moments later, the man who won the Newark by-election for the Tories is signed in. His side can scarcely believe how good things feel. Labour look on in stunned silence.

It's faintly depressing that this tribal warfare is raging just as the real war that never seems to end in Iraq is flaring up again. Forces regarded as too extreme even to be allied to Al-Qaeda have overrun cities in the country and are even said to be contemplating making a move on Baghdad. Not a single question is asked in the Commons about it.

BBC Westminster, Millbank

The jury at the Old Bailey has just retired to consider its verdict in the phone-hacking trial.

Before it began I fully expected to be in court for this moment but, as things have turned out, over the past eight months I have not once reported on the trial. The judge achieved what I would not have thought possible at the outset. He kept politics out of the case – despite the fact that the two key defendants were at one time two of the most powerful people in Britain. A former editor of the *News of the World*, Andy Coulson went on to become an official spokesman for David Cameron, hired on the advice of his co-defendant, News International chief executive Rebekah Brooks, the PM's friend and confidante.

Five of their former colleagues have pleaded guilty to conspiracy to hack the phones of celebrities, politicians and others whose lives had already been blighted by appalling, high-profile crimes in pursuit of stories for the Murdoch-owned tabloid the *News of the World*, the country's biggest-selling paper until it was closed down three years ago.

I didn't know Andy when he was at the *News of the World*. I didn't like the paper and felt ever so slightly ashamed on the few occasions I bought it (even though its political coverage was often excellent and written by people I like and respect). I got to know him when he became Cameron's spin doctor and I dealt with him virtually every day during the 2010 election. Whisper who dares, I found him straight, professional and likeable. I took a decision not to ask him about hacking on the grounds that he was never going to tell me anything in private that he hadn't said in public. To do so would have been to admit to a crime.

As the allegations of hacking mounted I faced some criticism for continuing to deal with Coulson. When we had lunch together to discuss the prime minister's forthcoming plans, another diner took a photo and posted it on Twitter. It was presented as evidence of some sort of conspiracy. I regarded it then, and do now, as evidence of me doing the job I'm paid to do.

Coulson believes that if he'd never crossed the threshold of Number 10 he might not now be facing prison. Without the Downing Street link, the hacking scandal might never have become front-page news and the police would never have launched the massive investigation currently being played out in court. Now he looks certain to go down, according to reporters who've sat through the whole trial. The revelation of an e-mail from him concerning the celebrity Calum Best, which told a reporter simply to 'do his phone', changed the whole atmosphere in court.

No one is certain about Rebekah Brooks's fate. The elaborate stories offered by her and her husband as to why huge quantities of paperwork and computer hardware were destroyed or disposed of in the bins of an underground car park seem laughably incredible to many. However, that does not add up to proof that she knew of, let alone sanctioned, phone-hacking. The one person who surely knows what she knew is Andy Coulson, and he's not saying.

Old shadow Cabinet room, Commons

Another Labour MP has a book to launch this evening. Jim Murphy's *The 10 Football Matches That Changed the World . . . And the One That Didn't* combines his fascination with the beautiful game and his devotion to politics. Jim's fellow shadow Cabinet author, Tristram Hunt, is also present. One of their colleagues mutters resentfully, 'I don't know where they find the time.'

Over a glass of warm white wine, one senior figure from the Blair era laments: 'There are three very weak leaders in politics at the moment.' This does not feel like a room filled with people who believe that they are about to return to government.

A Westminster restaurant

Dinner with a senior Liberal Democrat close to Nick Clegg. He argues that Labour can't win with 'the leader they do have and the credible economic policy they don't have'. Nevertheless he believes the electoral arithmetic may still ensure that Ed Miliband becomes prime minister. This is exactly my view. Labour's underlying problems mean they shouldn't be able to win the next election, yet they very well might. People forget that opposition leaders are routinely seen as less prime ministerial than the person in office at the time. Thatcher was far less popular than Callaghan in 1979, and the economic policies of Blair and Brown were thought less credible than those of Major and Clarke in 1997. What's more, it's hard to see the Tories gaining votes compared with last time, when UKIP are an open wound for them.

Thursday 12 June

'CAMERON: WHAT PASSPORT CRISIS?' screams the *Mail*. It's a deliberate echo of something another prime minister never actually said. The retort 'Crisis? What crisis?' was erroneously attributed to Jim Callaghan on his return from a summit in sunny Guadeloupe in 1979, while the UK was in the throes of the so-called 'winter of discontent'. It was in fact written by a sub on the *Sun*.

The current 'crisis' was all caused by some leaked photographs of boxes of unopened passport applications and stories of long and anxious waits endured by people who need their travel documents in time to go on holiday. If there wasn't a crisis before there sure as hell will be one now, as everyone will bring forward their applications and/or start panicking about where their documents have got to. Theresa May has been summoned to the Commons to explain.

Rumour has it that Number 10 has ordered May to take the bull by the horns rather than leave the matter to her junior immigration minister. This could be because they want the government to be seen to be 'getting a grip' on the backlog; alternatively, they might simply be enjoying the spectacle of the home secretary wallowing in the soup. This is precisely the sort of problem that can haunt ministers. Back in the late 1990s, as people queued in their thousands outside passport offices, Labour home secretary Jack Straw contemplated resignation.

Teflon Theresa fronts up, announces a set of new measures to ease delays and survives a storm that might well have brought down somebody else.

Grosvenor House hotel ballroom

I'd been dismayed to find a prize-giving commitment at the annual Charity Awards clashing with the opening night of the World Cup, which I was hoping to spend with a beer and my boys, watching Brazil play Croatia. But once the ceremony has got underway, I'm uplifted by the atmosphere and the reminder brought by each award of the extraordinary work charities – often small, very niche charities – do to change lives: the text helpline for deaf people who are victims of domestic abuse or the basketball club that has attracted 2,000 young people in east London to play against each other rather than stab each other.

When I present the award for outstanding achievement (which goes to Michael Norton, founder of the Directory of Social Change), I point out the difference between the people off the telly invited to give the prizes and the audience here. I share with the audience the opinion of my niece, twelve years old at the time, that all I do is 'burble for a living'. The people in this room, on the other hand, give not just their time, energy and money but also their passion, commitment and idealism. They seem pleased. Who needs to watch another game of footie, anyway?

Friday 13 June

Proof once again of David Cameron's limited control of his 'plan' to renegotiate Britain's relationship with Europe. Tory MEPs have just done what he begged them not to do. They have joined forces with Angela Merkel's new Eurosceptic rivals in the German AfD (Alternative for Germany) party. Their excuse is Merkel's continued backing for Jean-Claude Juncker to be elected president of the European Commission. Cameron has been privately claiming that Merkel has her doubts about Juncker but has to be seen to be pushing him until the moment he can be dropped in the face of opposition from the Brits, Swedes, Hungarians and others. I think it's the PM who might find himself dropped by his German friend. Gone are the days when prime ministers could simply do deals behind the scenes with fellow leaders. Today they can't even rely on doing deals with their own parties.

Meanwhile, as the World Cup kicks off in Brazil, Ed Miliband has just apologized for a photo of himself cheerily holding up a special World Cup edition of the *Sun* which has been distributed free over the past two days to 22 million homes across the country. Excluding, that is, homes in Liverpool, where the paper has been boycotted since 1989 for its much-criticized coverage of the Hillsborough disaster.

Or rather, he hasn't apologized, exactly; his spokesman has said that he 'understands the anger that is felt towards the *Sun* over Hillsborough by many people in Merseyside and he is sorry to those who feel offended'. Translated, this means he's sorry that you're sorry.

The condemnation from Liverpool Labour folk has been widespread. Associating yourself with a *Sun* marketing exercise, not only while the latest Hillsborough inquest is ongoing but in the week when the jury in the trial of two of Rupert Murdoch's former newspaper editors on phone-hacking charges has retired to consider its verdict, was neither a sensitive piece of politics nor terribly bright for a man who has boasted of standing up to Murdoch.

It might arguably have been worth risking in the interests of appearing to back the national team in a free edition of the country's most popular paper. But doing it then semi-apologizing for doing it would seem to be the worst of both worlds.

Monday 16 June

Lib Dem headquarters

I have that Monday morning feeling. How many other days in the next year will start like this? A handful of hacks drift into a gloomy room in an anonymous building somewhere in Westminster. The presence of a lectern and its brightly coloured backdrop reminds us that the man we've come to hear will try to persuade us to report his promises to the electorate. We, on the other hand, will take the opportunity to ask about whatever else in the news we believe will interest our viewers, listeners and readers rather more. The run-up to the election will be filled by endless news conferences like this.

When Nick Clegg steps up to tell us that the Lib Dems would protect education spending if they were in government after the next election, even he seems a little less than enthused. In fact, he looks weary and pale. Quentin Letts, the *Daily Mail*'s irrepressible sketch-writer, clearly feels the same as I do about what he calls 'this melancholy event'. He tells Clegg that instead of looking 'Tigger-ish', as politicians normally do on a Monday morning, he resembles a 'spat-out Smartie'. Clegg smiles wanly and insists that his is 'the pluckiest, toughest, bravest party in British politics'.

I remember seeing him on the morning after the European election results when he told me that he felt as if the entire country had become his mother, worrying about how he looked and how miserable he was. In his television interviews he looked pale, drawn and distressed.

It seems that one of the roles of the Westminster media pack is to assess the health of the nation's leaders in the manner of a witchdoctor, slicing open politicians to examine their entrails and holding them up to the electorate for inspection before declaring the patient to be not in the best of health.

House of Commons gallery

This afternoon William Hague reveals that the official estimate of the number of Brits fighting in Syria and Iraq is 400. The worry is that these people might bring home their hatred, extremism and violence. Earlier Nick Clegg told me the advice ministers had (from the spooks) was that this is the 'number one security threat facing the country' as such jihadists pose 'a direct threat to citizens here'. He and his party would not, he went on, stand in the way of well-targeted military action by the Americans.

Hague reassures MPs that the UK will play no part in military action and, to emphasize the point, insists that there will be no 'boots on the ground'. At the same time he says there are already British 'counter-terrorism experts' in Iraq. That's normally code for special forces. Perhaps they don't wear boots?

Tuesday 17 June

Studio 23, Broadcasting House

I never do this. I do not come to the BBC studio when I'm broadcasting on the *Today* programme. I sit in my basement, wearing a pair of headphones and talking into my microphone with a steaming cup of coffee close at hand. Wife, dog and occasionally children are upstairs waiting patiently to offer me a brief glimpse of normality. But a late text last night pleaded with me to come in because the director general would be paying a visit to watch the broadcast. I protested that Tony Hall knows how news programmes are made. After all, he used to make them himself. 'Please,' begged another text. So I'm here but he is not. He's late.

'Ah,' says John Humphrys with a grin, 'what an honour.' He notes that I am not wearing a tie (neither is he, I might add). I promise that next time I will wear evening dress like the news announcers of old, who kept on their dinner jackets even as the German bombs were falling on Broadcasting House.

I wonder if all visits by the director general are like this. Are walls freshly painted as they are for the Queen? One producer tells me that they're under pressure to make sure every guest possible has been brought to the studio. 'We've turned down an offer of an interview with Obama,' she says, adding sarcastically, 'as he wasn't able to come in.'

Predictably enough, when he does arrive, Tony Hall simply wants a gossip about how things are going.

House of Commons gallery

Once again the real world is a damn sight more interesting than the day-to-day goings-on in the Westminster bubble. Almost unnoticed by anyone, the West is chumming up with Iran. The foreign secretary has just announced that the 'circumstances are right' to reopen our embassy in Tehran. Time to bring out those clichés about my enemy's enemy.

The circumstances are that the land of the ayatollahs and the country they call the Great Satan – respectively Iran and the United States to you and me – suddenly find themselves on the same side against the strengthening forces of 'Islamic State', the extremist jihadist rebel group and self-proclaimed 'caliphate' based in Iraq and Syria.

What a difference three years can make. Back in 2011 a mob ransacked the embassy, smashed pictures of the Queen and chanted 'Death to England'. At around the same time I was making a radio programme about the likelihood that the US and/or Israel would bomb Iran to stop them developing nuclear weapons.

The great thaw has been helped by the election of a former Glasgow university student – a man who tweeted a photograph of himself watching Iran playing in the World Cup on TV with the message 'proud of our boys'. President Rouhani is, as Margaret Thatcher famously said about the young Mikhail Gorbachev, 'someone we can do business with'.

Home, in front of the telly

I settle down to watch Jeremy Paxman's last-ever *Newsnight*. It involves a tandem ride with Boris Johnson and Michael Howard, in the studio, offering to be asked the same question twelve times (as famously happened some years ago when Paxo became exasperated with the then home secretary's evasiveness). Fittingly, another question put to another political figure elicits a news-making answer. Paxo asks Peter Mandelson whether Ed Miliband is the best leader Labour could have. Peter's carefully calibrated and revealing response is that he is the leader Labour *does* have and, therefore, has his support.

Monday 23 June

London St Pancras

Now arriving from Brussels: a slow-motion political train crash. When Herman Van Rompuy, the president of the European Council, gets off the Eurostar he's greeted by my colleague Gobby* shouting 'What have

---

* Paul Lambert, or 'Gobby', as he is better known, was at the time the member of my BBC team who stood outside 10 Downing Street shouting questions at those entering or exiting. If a politician was in big trouble, Gobby would be found outside his or her house shouting, 'Are you going to resign?'

you come to tell Mr Cameron? Is Juncker the best man for the job?'

The man who'll be in the driver's cab at this week's EU summit has arrived in London to try to stop it being derailed by an argument about who gets the top job in Brussels.

Downing Street

There's no news conference after the meeting – too risky – but hacks are briefed that Van Rompuy and the prime minister have had 'full and frank talks', a phrase so overused that it now barely qualifies as a euphemism for a mighty great row.

Cameron knows he has already lost but he has decided to be seen to be going down fighting, not just with the man but with the process by which Jean-Claude Juncker will be appointed as the head Eurocrat in Brussels. He didn't plan this row. He didn't want it. He didn't expect it. But he is trying to snatch some sort of moral victory from diplomatic defeat.

He believed that Merkel would dump Juncker for him. He thought the Swedes, Danes, Dutch and Italians would follow suit. But she dumped Cameron instead, and so did they, leaving him isolated.

This might seem like an old-fashioned Euro-squabble about who gets what job but it is, in truth, a very modern power struggle between national governments and the European Parliament in Brussels.

At issue is the vexed question of whether it should be the prime ministers and presidents of the twenty-eight EU countries that decide who runs the EU day-to-day or the 751 recently democratically elected members of the European Parliament, which claims to represent the views of European voters.

Juncker's supporters say he has the backing of the people. After all, they contend, he was chosen by a meeting of Europe's biggest political bloc, the centre-right European People's Party (EPP), and then took part in live TV debates with his socialist and green rivals. There is just one problem with this argument: even in Germany, the country where it is made most vigorously, only 7 per cent of voters actually knew that Juncker was the guy being backed by Merkel's party.

BBC offices, Millbank

Perfect timing. A secretly made tape of the Polish foreign minister declaring that Cameron has 'fucked up' his handling of Europe has emerged just before the news at ten.

Radek Sikorski, an old Bullingdon Club mucker of Boris Johnson's, has helpfully been recorded doing to Cameron's reputation what he may once have done to Oxford restaurants.

Smash! 'It's either a very badly thought-through move or, not for the first time, a kind of incompetence in European affairs.'

Crash! 'Remember? He fucked up the fiscal pact. He fucked it up – simple as that.'

Bang! 'He is not interested. He does not get it. He believes in the stupid propaganda. He stupidly tries to play the system.'

It transpires that this is a mere amuse-bouche. The entrée is an assault on the PM's entire tactic of appeasing the Eurosceptics. Cue the sound of sirens as Cameron is detained and found guilty. 'You know, his whole strategy of feeding them scraps in order to satisfy them is, just as I predicted, turning against him; he should have said, "Fuck off," tried to convince people and isolate [the sceptics]. But he ceded the field to those that are now embarrassing him.'

The assumption is that the Russians have been taping the Poles as part of their diplomatic war over Ukraine. I do hope they record the next Sikorski–Cameron encounter.

Tuesday 24 June

The Old Bailey

Having walked into Court 12 a free man, Andy Coulson is today facing prison. His former boss – and, as it has turned out, former lover – Rebekah Brooks leaves a free woman after 138 dramatic days of evidence.

This is the first and last day I've reported on the trial. There is a political story to tell now: of how a politician who vowed to keep his distance from the most powerful media magnate in Britain ended up befriending his most senior executive and, on her recommendation, employing the editor of his bestselling paper to spin for the Tories. As the man who helped to get him into Number 10 awaits sentencing, David Cameron is left to make his plea in the court of public opinion.

Downing Street

There is to be no interview. No questions. Just a swift and abject apology made straight to camera.

David Cameron says he was wrong to give Andy Coulson 'a second chance' and to accept his 'assurances' about what had happened at the *News of the World*.

This implies that the only problem was the prime minister being too trusting or too naïve. What it ignores is why Cameron hired Coulson in the first place and was so resistant to firing him, even as evidence of the true scale of the phone-hacking scandal emerged.

When Coulson was first taken on by the Tories in opposition in 2007 it was possible to argue that phone-hacking was limited to the 'one rogue reporter' who had gone to jail for it. However, in the year before the general election both the *Guardian* and *The New York Times* produced evidence that it had been far more widespread.

David Cameron could have chosen not to ask his spin doctor to enter government with him but he opted to ignore the flashing red lights, despite the warnings of the press pursuing the story, his colleagues, his coalition partners and, of course, the Labour party.

He argued that this was because Coulson had proved himself to be competent and trustworthy. It was only part of the story. Team Cameron came to learn, like so many before them, that it is much easier to say you'll shun the Murdoch press than to actually do it.

In a country where politicians can't buy advertising, as they do in the States, and where so much of broadcasting is controlled by the BBC, they crave the partisan cheerleading of papers like the *Sun* and the *News of the World*. Coulson knew how to deliver that support. But he had one other quality that was nothing to do with his connection to Murdoch. As the product of an Essex comprehensive he knew, as so many senior Tories do not, how to connect them to parts of the electorate they struggled to reach. Ever the pragmatist, the prime minister put his own need for Coulson ahead of all the reasons why he should have let him go.

That's why Ed Miliband can today attack David Cameron for bringing a criminal into Downing Street.

It's a charge that will pain the prime minister but one which, I suspect, will do him little damage with voters who've never shared the media's obsessive interest in how the newspapers got the stories they loved to read.

Wednesday 25 June

Prime Minister's Questions

As so often when the goal appears wide open it is mighty hard for the leader of the opposition to slot the ball into the back of the net. Yes, Miliband is able to list the warnings about Coulson that Cameron ignored but no, he is not able to tell us anything we didn't already know or to land a killer blow.

The truth throughout the hacking scandal has been that while it gripped the media and political classes, it simply did not move others in the same way. It confirmed what most voters think: that tabloid journalists don't respect people's privacy; that politicians suck up to the owners of newspapers and that spin is a murky business. People may well have been angry but they weren't madly surprised and don't expect anything very much to change, whoever's in power.

River Room, Savoy hotel

The Savoy is swimming in champagne, courtesy of Sky. They've thrown a lavish bash to celebrate Adam Boulton's twenty-five years as their political editor and his departure to the place where old reporters prepare to die: the studio. A video charts Boulton's life and times covering five prime ministers, five US presidents, five Labour leaders, six Tory leaders and four Lib Dems. And counting.

This could be me next, I tell a passing BBC boss. I am in my tenth year as political editor and before that I had three as chief political correspondent of BBC News 24 (as it was then) followed by three at ITV. She replies: 'You can make the sandwiches and I'll brew the tea.' Ah, the joys of working for a public-service broadcaster.

Thursday 26 June

Ypres

I've been waiting for what feels like an hour in the garden of a hotel in Belgium, wondering how the PM will try to snatch political victory from negotiation defeat, when he walks up to my camera. He is in no mood for small talk. My attempt at a joke falls flat. He adopts his second-row forward's stance, stares straight ahead and waits for the inevitable question on why, at tomorrow's summit, he will force a vote which it is clear he has already lost by 27 to 1. 'What I say is what I do,' he tells me, adding that this is just the 'start of a long campaign'.

It is a message directed as much at voters back home as at fellow European leaders. It's meant to declare: 'I will not compromise on my principles, I will not do last-minute deals, I will not back down, even when facing isolation.'

A number of the Tory voters who have defected to UKIP tell pollsters that they don't trust Cameron to hold a referendum, let alone to get a better deal for Britain in Europe. After all, they say, doesn't the prime minister keep telling people that he really wants to stay in the EU?

Although this is a crisis he didn't anticipate, he is now using it to try to earn credibility with those Cameron-sceptics, many of whom contend that the complete failure of his negotiating strategy proves you can never win in Europe while everyone believes you are determined not to leave. What will be fascinating to see is whether he will be tempted to take the next logical step, one he has so far resisted, by declaring that if the EU will not reform in the way he wants, he would be unable to recommend that Britain should stay in.

It would be a public version of what Germany's Angela Merkel called his private threat that Britain would be more likely to leave if Mr Juncker is chosen as the next president of the European Commission. It would be a huge diplomatic and political gamble. Other European leaders might react by treating Britain as if she is already on her way out. Some businesses may reconsider their investments in the UK.

The pre-summit leaders' dinner, which follows a moving ceremony at the Menin Gate, finishes early. After all, there's only so much you can say to commemorate a hundred years since the start of the Great War.

Friday 27 June

VIP entrance, Justus Lipsius building, Brussels

Since Gobby is rarely sent abroad I have to do my own shouting at European summits. As each car pulls up I shout a question at every president or prime minister who steps out on to the red carpet. There is, of course, one small problem: knowing which of the EU's twenty-eight countries these dignitaries represent. I usually recognize a handful – President Hollande of France, Chancellor Merkel of Germany, Harry Potter of the Netherlands (or Prime Minister Rutte, as he prefers to be known, but he really should change those small, round glasses) and Denmark's Gucci Helle (Thorning-Schmidt, who earned her nickname for her expensive taste in clothes). That still leaves a couple of dozen to identify. No matter. I have come prepared; arming myself before squeezing into a packed press pen with a printed list of names and photographs of each nation's leader.

It is not, however, as easy as that. In the few seconds between a chauffeured car door opening and the politician it has disgorged disappearing through the doors of the EU summit there isn't time to check the mug shot, run through the twenty-eight options on the list, look up at him or her again to be sure, position the microphone in the right place, ask the security guy to get out of the way and then put your question. So instead I shout first and work out who I was shouting at later. This is a policy with risks attached. I do a long-distance shout to a woman I know is the leader of a small East European country: 'Is Britain isolated?' Keen to be helpful, she puts a thumb up before realizing she has just confirmed that Britain is indeed isolated and promptly turns it downwards instead. Just enough for a script line saying that EU leaders are tired of uncertainty about Britain's role in the EU.

As I jab out a tweet describing her as the Latvian prime minister, someone looks over my shoulder and says, 'No, that was the Lithuanian.' As more and more leaders come and go, my cameraman, a veteran of the Brussels bureau, demonstrates an unerring knack for knowing who's who. I explain to a colleague that this is the result of years of experience. Disarmingly, he points out that the motorbike outriders who precede each car carry a sticker identifying the country of the dignitary they're escorting.

This may not strike you as grown-up journalism. But it is the only access we get to the leaders before the summit ends. No shouts, no package for the TV news.

Sometimes, by uttering three magic letters when we shout – 'B' 'B' 'C' – we succeed in getting a president or prime minister to come over to our camera and microphone for a proper interview. Our own prime minister tends to stride up, stick out his chest and deliver a defiant soundbite. It is his one chance to shape the news that day. He tells me this morning that he knows the odds are stacked against him but nevertheless it is right to stand up for what you believe. If only he had a handbag to swing, his message would have required no amplification.

The woman who's caused Cameron such nightmares, Angela Merkel, marches into the summit without saying a word. One of those on whom Cameron was counting, but who has switched to Merkel's camp, is Helle Thorning-Schmidt. She tells me she is sure Britain will 'get back in the game' once today is over, thereby confirming that this is a day David Cameron is not going to enjoy one little bit.

This is turning into the sort of week when columnists will reach for the overworked superlative 'the PM's worst week ever' (Alastair Campbell once added up all Tony Blair's 'worst weeks ever' and got to a whole year's worth). And things aren't getting any better.

The basement, European Council headquarters

This must count as one of the most demoralizing places for a journalist to be. We are in the same building as the EU summit, but it is taking place eight floors above us and we have almost no way of finding out what is going on. Hundreds of hacks fortify themselves with subsidized coffee and cake while speculating idly.

Some trade their knowledge of the micro-details of Europe's top table like kids swapping Top Trump cards. Prime ministers and presidents occasionally send a text or an e-mail to their staff updating them on what's happening but most of the time our usual sources are no better informed than we are and, quite often, just as bored. If every EU leader speaks at the summit for just two minutes, a mere throat-clearing for your average politician, that's an hour gone.

Occasionally the odd titbit will seep out. The lunch menu is always seized upon by journalists as a source of irrelevant details that give the erroneous impression they are privy to inside information. It offers a chance, too, to recycle the old jokes about the PM being served a helping of hard cheese accompanied by sour grapes.

We TV reporters watch and re-watch the few pictures we're provided with in the hope of finding something we can write to that lifts the story. Every summit has the same set of pictures: the arrivals (with shouts), the 'family photograph' (which we scrutinize to pick out who looks unhappy) and the *'tour de table'* (the leaders milling around and taking their seats for the summit proper). Today our trawl is not in vain. In the *tour de table* David Cameron is the last to take his seat. He stands alone, surveying the other leaders who are about to outvote him. It's the image of the day. There is only one question: is that why he did it?

The British briefing room

In the event, Cameron was not alone. He got the support of Hungary. 'It is a sad day for Europe,' Cameron tells his packed close-of-summit news conference. No other leader has attracted as many journalists. The defiance he showed on his arrival has gone. This is a much more subdued prime minister than the one we saw eight hours ago. He talks of being prepared to 'lose a battle' in order to win the war but he doesn't look entirely convinced. His acknowledgement that it has just got harder to persuade the British people to vote to stay in the EU is guaranteed to produce headlines about Britain heading towards the exit.

Pondering what to ask him, I try out a thought on colleagues waiting next to me. 'When Mrs Thatcher wielded her handbag she was isolated, but she won. You're now isolated and you've lost . . .' That'll work, says the shrewd and well-informed man from the *Guardian*. Moments later the prime minister says 'Nick,' and points in our direction. I clear my throat in anticipation but the mic is given to the *Guardian*'s excellent Nick Watt, who promptly delivers my question almost word for word. Being a man of generous spirit, I assume that he wasn't planning on asking one himself and, when picked out, found mine popping into his head. That has certainly happened to me. I once delivered the whole of ITN's opening script on *BBC News at 10* before realizing it was what I'd just heard them rehearsing.

Undeterred, I simply rephrase my question and repeat it so that it can be used in my TV report. Cameron's reply is telling. Since the days of Mrs T. a series of treaty alterations has made it harder for Britain to veto or block changes we don't like. That may be true, but it is also ammunition for those who think the only way is out.

The balcony above the press room

Below me are row upon row of empty journalists' desks. The floor is strewn with papers in a dozen or more languages. The press boys filed their stories within an hour of the summit's end and ran for the last Eurostar home. The coffee bar has long since closed and the security has been lifted. I am the last man standing. All that remains is to decide what to say. I've been to many summits where Britain has been isolated – over the Euro and the social chapter and the sale of British beef – but this feels different. In just over two years we may all be voting on whether to stay in or get out. I conclude my live report on the ten o'clock news by saying that Britain's place in the EU looks more uncertain than it has in a very long time.

— JULY —

Tuesday 1 July

Airedale factory, Leeds

So nearly right and yet so disastrously wrong.

I am sitting on a factory floor watching a party leader speaking about the need to rebalance the economy; the need to ensure that there's growth here in the north and not just in the south. He's talking of people's worries about where the good jobs of the future are going to come from and explaining that politics cannot address this problem.

But, and it's a mighty big but, he – and we're talking about the leader of the Labour party here – is saying all this to a group of bosses in suits with his back to the hundred or so workers dressed in company polo shirts who've been placed there for the cameras. Not once does he turn to face them.

Ed Miliband is making the sort of speech he'd deliver to a think tank, not to a bunch of guys who've just downed tools at the country's largest air-conditioning factory and missed their tea break to listen to a bloke up from London. Their rolling eyes and suppressed yawns suggest they've concluded that all he has to offer is what they already earn a living dealing with: hot air.

At the end of his lecture Miliband compounds his mistake by taking questions from the suits and hacks like me before belatedly turning to the workers and beseeching them to ask something, about this or anything else. He is met by silence and not a single raised hand.

Afterwards I ask one woman, now back at work, why he'd been given that reception. She admits she found it hard to follow what he was saying. 'They don't speak to the public, do they? It's all for t'media, i'n't it?'

The truth is that the Labour party leader has been unveiling an important and thoughtful report by Lord Adonis about how to give so-called city regions incentives to invest in improved skills and infrastructure.

Interesting policy. Lousy PR. Again.

Thursday 3 July

The Spectator *offices*

A never-ending supply of free champagne and the chance to glimpse what passes for celebrity in SW1 – a minister or even a moderately well-known TV presenter – is enough to attract the hordes to Westminster's annual round of summer parties.

The *Spectator*'s is among the most sought-after summer invitations. The prime minister usually turns up, as he has tonight. This year he has been joined by the home secretary and the defence secretary. Oh, and Joan Collins.

At these shindigs I have learned to beware charming, flattering young people who ask questions about the BBC and laugh at my jokes. They are almost always diary columnists. The solution, I've found, is not to engage in casual conversation before proper introductions have been made. I offer a hand, announce my name and company and then invite them to do the same. I can then reply: 'The *Daily Mail*? And what do you do there?' before making my excuses and heading off in search of my own sources of printable gossip.

The best story at this year's party comes from a successful businessman and Tory donor who was at the Conservatives' summer fund-raising dinner at the Hurlingham club last night. Images of the two Eds, Miliband and Balls, were apparently pasted on the walls to loosen people's wallets.

The auctioneer at the event, Foreign Office minister Hugo Swire, donated a jar of honey produced by the bees on his own farm, declaring that he wanted it to become the most expensive pot of honey ever sold. It went for a staggering £15,000. The star lot was the chance to play tennis with Dave (the prime minister to you and me) and Boris

(Johnson). That allegedly fetched £160,000. To make matters more murky, the winning bidder, a Russian banker, is married to a former ally of Putin's.

The sale of the 'ultimate tennis match' is likely to give rise to more questions about the Tories' dependence on the super-rich. Like every political leader I've known, David Cameron swore that he would clean up party funding. He did try, at first, but as has happened so often, the need to keep the coffers supplied has outweighed most scruples about where funds come from.

Friday 4 July

Home

Tonight Andy Coulson will spend his first night in prison. I am forced to do what I avoided doing as the phone-hacking allegations gathered momentum: to reach my own verdict on a man I haven't seen for three years. The judge was clear that 'Mr Coulson . . . has to take the major share of the blame for the phone-hacking at the *News of the World* . . . he knew about it and encouraged it when he should have stopped it.'

For the first time in my life I have read every word of a court judgement and I agree with all of them.

> The true reason for the phone-hacking was to sell newspapers. In an increasingly competitive market, the editor wanted to make sure that it was his paper that got the stories which would create the biggest headlines and sell the most newspapers and he, and others at the newspaper, were prepared to use illegal means to do that. No doubt Mr Coulson was under considerable pressure to maintain, if not increase, market share. He had been appointed as editor at a very young age. He was ambitious and it was important for him to succeed. He, amongst others, passed that pressure down to their subordinates. There was great competition between the various desks . . . They all knew that it was contrary to the PCC [Press Complaints Commission] code which governs the conduct of journalists and they all knew it was morally wrong.

The judge went on to note that Coulson and those facing charges with him 'have said that they did not realize that it was a criminal offence' but added, 'ignorance of the law [is] no defence'.

So why do I still feel some sympathy for Coulson? Phone-hacking was merely one method – as it turns out an illegal one – of intruding into the private lives not just of the rich, the famous and the attention-seekers but of those who found themselves in the public eye as a result of a mistake, an accident or a tragedy. It is the public who made the paper that printed the fruits of those intrusions the bestselling news-paper in Britain. Among its readers were many who added the *News of the World* to their order for 'quality papers': an interest in politics and highbrow culture does not preclude a taste for the salacious, the invasive and the prurient. Politicians and many others in public life queued up to feature in its pages. Is it surprising that Coulson, along with plenty of others who have escaped prison, concluded that he was doing something that a large section of society, including some of the most powerful people in the land, at worst tolerated and at best secretly approved of?

Phone-hacking is wrong except when it is used to expose some-thing that journalists have a duty to expose and the public has a right to know. So, too, is raiding people's bins, paying their friends or bribing public officials. A braver man than Andy Coulson would have refused to go along with it or would have spoken out.

He was, though, very far from being the only one who ignored the fact that these activities were unethical and accepted the 'way things are done'.

In that sense phone-hacking is no different from the abuse of the parliamentary expenses system. In the wake of that scandal a few MPs ended up in prison. Many others, people who were in all their other dealings straight, professional and likeable, effectively colluded with the exploitation of the system by doing nothing about it.

Monday 7 July

Home, the kitchen table

I hate conspiracy theories. I loathe the unthinking certainty of those who peddle them. I instinctively resist the way they assemble a bit of gossip here, an allegation there and the inevitable 'list of unanswered questions' to suggest that the whole is much bigger and much more sinister than the sum of altogether unconvincing parts. The papers – and, to be fair, our own BBC news bulletins – are full of this stuff this morning.

For five days now the media has been gripped by the latest 'scandal' to hit Westminster: an alleged conspiracy to cover up the sexual abuse of children by the powerful and the well connected. It all began with the revelation that a 'dossier of evidence' handed to the Home Office three decades ago has gone missing. The man who handed it over – Tory MP Geoffrey Dickens, who used to wow his party conference with calls to castrate offenders – is long since dead. The man to whom he handed it, the then Conservative home secretary Leon Brittan, now faces allegations, strenuously denied, of a sexual assault many years ago (not, I should add, on a child). Home Office officials have admitted that they have lost or destroyed not just the dossier but 114 files connected to it. Proof, surely, of a conspiracy and a cover-up? Or will it prove to be another monstrous administrative cock-up at the Home Office?

It could be that Dickens produced allegations but no actionable evidence; that Leon Brittan did what he was meant to do, and passed it to officials and the police to assess; that the missing files were destroyed as part of the usual departmental clear-outs or by mistake. These wouldn't be the only documents to have been lost: it turns out that 36,000 other files from the pre-digital era have also gone.

However, after the child-abuse cases involving Jimmy Savile, Rolf Harris and Stuart Hall, no one dares say, 'Let's not jump to con-clusions.' Just as after the MPs' expenses scandal, no one is prepared to put anything other than the most negative gloss on allegations against politicians as a class.

This morning's top line to the story sums it up. The former Conservative Cabinet minister Norman Tebbit has said he believes there 'may well' have been a political cover-up. In other words, he has no evidence there was a cover-up, he isn't in a position to know whether there was one but, shucks, there might have been. I'm not clear why his view matters much more than that of any guy down the pub.

The whole thing depresses me.

I send an e-mail to a few BBC folk I trust to check if they see it as I do. 'This may be beginning of Savile-style revelations or, er, nothing very much at all?'

The study

Having calmed down a little I realize that my reaction is, in part, down to panic. I am rushing too fast to catch up with the story. When the Labour MP Tom Watson first used PMQs to make the charge of a paedophile ring with connections to Number 10 I was happy to leave it to Home Affairs colleagues to dig into. Their patch, not mine. When the story re-emerged last week I was taking a day off to watch Andy Murray's Centre Court humiliation at Wimbledon. Then I had a proper family weekend: no watching news bulletins, no digesting papers, no more than a scan of the headlines on my iPad. A mistake.

Since the moment I woke up I've been sitting here with a pile of papers, the iPad, my phone and an endless stream of coffee trying to bring myself up to speed. I've been spraying out text messages to people asking for the latest.

At 7.34 a reply: 'May statement significant.' The home secretary is due to make a statement to MPs. It will go much further than they expect, I'm told. She will do what ministers have resisted doing for months: set up an over-arching inquiry into child abuse.

I go on to the *Today* programme to break the news. Now, that feels better.

House of Commons gallery

Over the Commons hangs an air of solemnity. For all the talk of this place as a children's playground or a bear pit, MPs still have a collective sense of when it's time to behave. Wars, tragedies and statements about failing hospitals or, in this case, child abuse.

Only a few weeks ago the home secretary was content to send her junior Lib Dem minister to meet the child-protection officer who first told Tom Watson about allegations of a powerful paedophile network. Now Theresa May is promising what that whistle-blower was demanding: a Hillsborough-style inquiry. The signs that this is a rushed change of mind are all here: there's no named chair for the inquiry and no terms of reference.

Shadow home secretary Yvette Cooper responds positively but can't resist observing that eighteen months ago she'd called for such an inquiry and been blocked by the government.

What's interesting is that Tom Watson and his fellow campaigner

Simon Danczuk, Labour MP for Rochdale – who has written a book exposing the child abuse perpetrated by his Liberal predecessor, the late Cyril Smith – do not say, 'We told you so.' Instead they magnanimously praise the home secretary, who returns the compliment.

Theresa May shows once again why she is the longest-serving home secretary in fifty years. She is doing something she has long resisted but she is doing it with apparent conviction, professionalism and efficiency.

Edit suite, Millbank

Some stories tell themselves. Others I agonize over as I wrestle with what should go in and what should be left out. Tonight's is one of those.

My producer, Chris, proposes that we use the latest news on Cyril Smith as a way into the story. The Greater Manchester Police have called for wider inquiries into a possible cover-up of the former Liberal MP's history of abuse. Chris has unearthed black-and-white footage of the beaming, 29st Mr Rochdale towering over a small group of children and shaking their hands. But will the lawyers let us use it? The short and firm answer is 'No!' We'd be suggesting that the children in the images were victims of abuse.

I start the piece with duller shots of Smith and a line designed to grab the attention of those who may be tiring of endless reports of abuse. 'How did he get away with it?' I ask. The lawyer warns my producer that I am implying that Smith was guilty when that has yet to be proven. 'You can't libel the dead,' I protest.

'You still need to be fair to the dead,' is the response.

Earlier I read the latest reports into Smith. There was sufficient evidence to prosecute him when he was still alive in the late 1990s but prosecutors believed that his lawyers could use legal arguments that would enable him to evade justice. I include this in my report and decide that, unless and until I'm told to remove the point, it stays in.

Also in is an extraordinary interview from a twenty-year-old BBC documentary in which a Tory whip, now dead, talks about the notorious 'dirt book' used to keep a record of the personal failings of members of Parliament. This information can sometimes be used to offer an MP support but its ultimate purpose is to keep rebels in line. In the interview the whip says the failings noted could include being in debt, alcohol, marriage difficulties or 'problems with small boys'. At the time the documentary was broadcast no one batted an eyelid at what would now be seen as the cover-up of child abuse.

With so much to squeeze in I manage just the slightest hint of my earlier worries about a possible witch-hunt. Over shots of the gargoyles that cover the Palace of Westminster, I say that 'Westminster is full of gossip and innuendo but short of facts'.

Tuesday 8 July

Old Palace Yard, House of Commons

Walking to my office I bump into one of the MPs who pushed hardest for an inquiry into allegations that child abuse was both committed and covered up by the establishment. 'Do you really think there is a conspiracy with links to Number 10?' I ask him.

The answer is more nuanced than might be expected from this campaigner and certainly more nuanced than the headlines. There was, he suggests, no single organized conspiracy but the Paedophile Information Exchange (PIE) – a now defunct activist group that campaigned for the abolition of the age of consent – allowed child-abusers in Whitehall and Westminster to network, to exchange information and to cover for each other. He relates the story of one abuser, now in prison, who'd got himself the job of advising ministers on who should and, crucially, who should not be on a list of adults barred from working with children. This man, my source claims, cunningly told his minister that they ought, of course, to get a second opinion. He had just the chap. Another member of PIE.

Although I have no means of verifying such evidence personally (the BBC has a separate team working on this), when it is put this way, I find the notion of abuse by the powerful much more convincing than the overblown conspiracy theories that fill the blogs and Twittersphere.

Inn the Park, St James's Park

Over lunch a friendly member of Team Miliband and I chew over his leader's gruesome couple of months. I pass on my view that it is no use him blaming his aides if he doesn't follow their advice. It's not their fault that he gives cameramen a shot of him failing to wrestle a bacon sandwich past his molars when he has just been told that the first rule of photo opportunities is 'Don't eat on camera.' It's not their fault that he speaks in front of a group of factory workers but forgets to talk to them about their concerns in language they can engage with. Ed, I'm told, is considering a speech or an interview which addresses the 'leadership issue'. I can hear the clunky soundbite now . . . 'I may not be good at photo opportunities but I do know how to fix Britain.'

Labour are also pondering how to deal with the other elephant in the room: their argument that austerity would fail when it seems to many to have worked and, in the words of my source, the widespread view that their attitude to public money is like that of a drunk towards alcohol – they can't resist reaching over to grab the bottle for another slug. The two Eds, I'm told, haven't changed their minds on this. They are unshakeable in their belief that it was the banking crisis, not excessive spending, that caused the deficit and that spending was cut too far, too fast by the coalition, choking off the recovery.

Apparently, they are considering making clear where they disagree with Gordon Brown, as they already have with Blair. Brown, they will argue, allowed the City of London to grow unchecked, seeing this as the way to pay for investment in schools and hospitals and huge cash transfers from the rich to the poor, largely in the form of tax credits. The Eds will say this cannot be repeated and that they will need to change the way markets work, rather than relying on cash from the City, to deliver social justice.

I somehow doubt this will do the trick but as I watch Germany thrash Brazil 7–1 in their World Cup semi-final I can't help noticing that another poll gives Labour an election-winning, German-size lead. They have been 7 per cent up in several polls which, with the current boundaries, would place them comfortably in government next May.

BBC, Millbank

There's more than one way to put pressure on an organization like the BBC. One method is to shout, whinge and lodge formal complaints. Another is to put an arm round us, sympathize with the position in which we find ourselves and express total confidence that, being the BBC, we won't give in to the ranting and railing of the other side.

So it is today, during a background chat with one of those leading the fight for a No vote in the Scottish referendum, who expresses his hope that we are withstanding the pressure from those he memorably describes as the 'swivel-eyed, hairy-kneed zealots on the banks of the Clyde'.

So far I've had only a brief, though memorable, glimpse of such pressure as the BBC's coverage of the campaign is, quite rightly, being led by colleagues based north of the border. Back in January the governor of the Bank of England warned of the 'clear risks' of an independent Scotland trying to share the pound with the remainder of the UK. Robert Peston and I regarded the speech as political dynamite. On air the BBC economics editor called it a 'stink bomb' thrown into the debate. I reported that even the merest mention of the dangers of replicating the chaos in the Eurozone was toxic for those attempting to persuade voters to take a step into the unknown.

Our contributions were not welcomed by those who have become known as the 'cybernats'. Ever since the Yes campaign has been keen to keep us in London and the No campaign to get us up to Scotland as often as possible. Awkward. Very awkward.

I'm not due to cover the referendum race day-to-day until its closing weeks. That's in no small part because it's not running high on news bulletins since it's widely believed among politicians to be as good as over. Not a single senior figure in any of the pro-union parties expresses any doubt that the No vote will prevail. Support for independence has rarely topped a third of the population and the future of the pound is only one of the many unanswered questions facing Alex Salmond.

Our guest today is less worried about the outcome than about the wounds being opened up by the campaigns. Divisions are, he says, cutting through families and communities. Politicians are like 'kids in the playground having a massive brawl now, but once the vote is over we must all sit together with cardboard, glue and scissors and make a rocket together'. That may prove easier said than done.

Just one thing makes me question the conventional wisdom. It is Salmond himself. The man who turned round a big Labour lead to win a majority in the Scottish Parliament is the great defier of odds. He has shaped himself into 'Mr Scotland' by embodying the optimism, the defiance and the independence of spirit he wants for his country.

And that's a damned sight more inspiring than warnings from

men in Westminster concerning unanswered questions about the pound.

My office

Lady Butler-Sloss has just been unveiled as the woman to assess why not enough was done to protect children from abuse. It is for the police, of course, to weigh up the competing claims of a conspiracy and alleged lack of evidence. Formerly Britain's top female judge, president of the family division and the chair of the inquiry into the Cleveland child-abuse scandal, she seems well qualified. She is, though, a member of 'it' – you know, 'the establishment' – once a Tory candidate, the sister of a former attorney general and the woman trusted by the Palace to conduct the inquiry into the death of Princess Diana. For that she may not be forgiven.

Wednesday 9 July

House of Commons office

Splendid. Rising – and thus much-resented – Tory star Matt Hancock, the business minister, has just been photographed on the South Bank, posing on one of Boris's bikes for hire against a backdrop of the graffiti-covered concrete skateboarders love. One slogan, by his head, is particularly visible: 'Sack Cameron'. I text one of his chums, who replies: 'He's making light of it but inside he's screaming.' With just a few days to go before a reshuffle that could see Matt elevated to the Cabinet, there will be many of his colleagues who will struggle to suppress a smile tonight.

Bored snappers whose creativity is too rarely challenged by day after day of filming men in suits in front of podiums or getting out of cars delight in these moments. Spin doctors are paid to look out for and avoid them. A trawl of the archives for other humiliating backgrounds to politicians' photo ops would yield Gordon Brown in front of a swastika; Nigel Farage, a short, black microphone covering his top lip, evoking another Nazi image; and my favourite: David Cameron standing in front of a Peacocks clothing store, whose logo features bubbles. Thanks to the masking effect of a strategically placed campaign balloon, a thought bubble appears to be emerging from the prime minister's head containing the word 'cocks'.

I once came back with a piece to camera filmed on the graffitied mean streets of Brixton. My producer and I were congratulated for getting out of Westminster and producing a report 'from the real world' until a colleague, with the insouciant air of the little boy pointing out that the emperor is wearing no clothes, had the temerity to ask: 'Why did you stand in front of that bit of graffiti that said "Fuck You"?'

My office, Millbank

The door is closed. I am looking round in disbelief. If only someone else had been there to hear what I just heard.

There was, though, no mistaking the purpose of the phone call I've had from what, in the customary code, I must call 'a senior Labour figure'. This would be easier face to face, I was told, but the caller ploughed on regardless. The party knows it has a problem and is determined to fix it. The leader needs advice, and it has to come from someone with sufficient stature to ensure he'll listen to it. On a rather bad mobile line I was sure, at first, that I was being asked if I could recommend anyone to take charge of Ed Miliband's presentational difficulties. I began to rack my brains until it began to dawn on me that I had misheard. I was being asked whether I would consider taking on the job, with a role at Number 10 to follow, naturally. That's right – me.

For the rest of the conversation I had to resist the urge to roar with laughter and inquire whether the caller had got the wrong number. Instead I politely expressed my thanks for being considered and explained that I remained committed to journalism (just as I did when the papers reported a long time ago that I'd been approached to work for 'the other side').

I hustle my bureau chief, Katy, into the office, swear her to secrecy and tell her the whole extraordinary tale. I have no idea whether this approach was made with Ed Miliband's knowledge or, as is more likely, by someone freelancing to try to be helpful, but as I walk down Whitehall I phone my wife and say 'You'll never guess what . . .'

The gardens, Downing Street

The annual Number 10 drinks party for political journalists. For the dozens who turn up it's a chance to name-drop to their news desks; for others it's simply an irresistible opportunity to take a snoop behind the most famous black door in the world and to see the Cameron family climbing frame.

The PM is on good form, laughing about some absurd photographs published last month of himself, Angela Merkel and Dutch premier Mark Rutte being rowed across a lake by Sweden's prime minister, Fredrik Reinfeldt. It was during this sojourn at Reinfeldt's summer residence that he realized he'd lost his battle to stop Juncker. At 2am, after many drinks had been served and consumed, Merkel admitted that she couldn't deliver what she'd promised.

Just as we are about to learn more, Ed Llewellyn, the PM's chief of staff, interrupts. 'Netanyahu's on the phone.' As Cameron excuses himself I remark to the group left behind mid-anecdote, 'Ah, the old Israeli PM ruse.' In Gordon Brown's day, someone I know was initially impressed and then horrified when, four times in twenty minutes, Brown was told the Israeli prime minister was on the phone and responded that he would have to wait. Only later did he discover that this was the code used by the staff at Number 10 to give Brown an excuse to bring a meeting to an end.

This evening, however, on my way home I receive an e-mail from the Downing Street press office with a 'read-out' of Cameron's phone call with his Israeli counterpart. Either the code has changed or the bluff has become even more elaborate.

Thursday 10 July

Studio 23, Broadcasting House

A rare early-morning visit to Broadcasting House. I am here to break a story on both *Breakfast* and *Today*. At last night's Downing Street party I was taken to one side and asked to come through to Number 12, headquarters of the prime minister's press team, where I was briefed that emergency legislation is to be introduced in the House of Commons next week. The story was given on a strict no-approach embargo of eight o'clock this morning. In other words, not only must I not report it before then but there could be no calls to anyone for a reaction, either.

The government wants to force phone and internet companies to log records of their customers' phone calls, texts and internet usage and, in the wake of a legal ruling in the European Court of Justice which has declared existing powers invalid, to clarify the legal basis of the warrants currently used to intercept the content of calls and e-mails.

The proposed new law has the backing of Labour as well as the coalition parties, who have been told by the security services and the police that without it they will no longer be able to access the data they need.

As I enter the *Today* studio Justin Webb turns to John Humphrys and remarks dryly that this is how martial law will one day be imposed in Britain – by Nick Robinson walking in here with a piece of paper.

10 Downing Street

My next stop is what is now an uncommon event: a joint news conference with both the prime minister and his deputy. They seek to justify their rush to pass this controversial new law with only one day's scrutiny in the Commons and another in the Lords. We would not be standing here, they assure us, unless the country were at risk from terrorists, organized criminals and paedophiles.

In the time we have been given it has been impossible to call round civil-liberties campaigners, lawyers and telecoms companies to get their reactions. Even if I'd been able to do so, they'd have had no time themselves, and very little information, to form a judgement. So I decide to ask a question which sums up why they might be worried. Does history not warn us to be wary of politicians who pass emergency legislation on the basis of a generalized threat and seek to reassure us that, because they all agree, everything will be fine?

Cameron tells me that the public ought to be worried if the government *didn't* act and he and Clegg insist that they're simply restoring powers the spooks and the cops already have 'to keep us all safe'.

Mmm. In other words, 'trust us', and 'we trust the spooks'.

My office, Millbank

I have been looking forward to a working lunch today rather more than I usually do. It was guaranteed not to be the bland, low-calorie, 'I'll stick to tap water' affair so beloved of many of the new generation of politicians. Breaking bread with Boris Johnson couldn't fail to be fun, could it? Alas, the mayor of London has cancelled. I'd been warned in advance that he would have no light to shed on his parliamentary ambitions (will he stand as an MP and if so, where?). I'm sure his sudden change of plan can have had nothing to do with the *Evening Standard* splashing on the decision of the Tory MP for Uxbridge to retire, creating the perfect vacancy for you-know-who. But Boris has clearly followed the advice of the paper's editorial to 'make his mind up'. If only not to have lunch with me.

I am determined not to repeat the mistake I made a few years ago when I was called by a good Tory source with the news that BoJo was planning to run for mayor of London. I put the phone down laughing. Boris as mayor? No one would take this seriously, surely? The following day, quite by chance, I bumped into Boris as we both hopped on the tube at Highbury. We gossiped amiably about this and that but so dismissive of his mayoral ambitions was I that I almost forgot to raise the subject at all. It was only as we rode the escalator into Westminster station that I remembered the call from the night before. 'You'll never guess what someone told me yesterday . . .' I began with a grin.

Boris didn't laugh. He didn't even smile. Instead he trawled his hand through his blond mop, muttered 'Oh, God' a couple of times and then begged me to hold the story for a couple of hours so he could make a few calls before it went public. That was the last time I underestimated Johnson's ambition or potential.

It's not so long ago that Boris declared himself more likely to be 'decapitated by a frisbee, blinded by a champagne cork, locked in a fridge or reincarnated as an olive' than to become prime minister. I'm no believer in reincarnation but I may yet have to change my mind.

Friday 11 July

Home

I've been asking questions about when Ed Miliband will get to the White House. I've heard he's desperate for a meeting with Obama before the election. His office think they're about to get a slot but they're nervous that they may be running out of time. The White House don't want it next year, when they could be accused of taking sides in our election campaign. They don't want it this autumn, either, with the Scottish referendum and the US mid-term elections taking place.

It's obvious why Team Ed hanker for the Obama photo op but those who know their history are well aware that it's a huge gamble. For a start there is the risk that they will be granted a dismissively brief meeting or the dreaded 'brush-by'– White House-speak for a planned meeting that is not in the official published diary as a planned meeting. Instead it is arranged that the president will just happen to drop in on another meeting – with the vice-president or national security adviser – where he 'brushes by' the visitor from Blighty. What's the point? you may wonder. It's to ensure that no precedent is set that allows every other European party leader to demand equivalent access.

When John Major went to Washington as prime minister he didn't get a meeting at all. Bill Clinton, then president-elect, who hadn't forgiven him for helping the Republican election campaign, gave him not a brush-by but the brush-off, granting him a mere twenty-minute phone conversation.

Gordon Brown's encounters with President Obama were excruciatingly awkward in spite of Obama being a Democrat and no lover of the Tories. The reporters who travelled with Brown to the United Nations will never forget the famous White House 'snub', or what the *Sun* dubbed 'Gordon's kitchen nightmare' – a brush-by in the kitchens of the UN headquarters in New York.

But the nadir of such meetings, and one that still haunts Labour, was the visit paid to Ronald Reagan in the run-up to the 1987 election by party leader Neil Kinnock. Despite being allotted barely half an hour with the president – during which Reagan apparently read from prompt cards and managed to mistake shadow foreign secretary Denis

Healey for the British ambassador – Kinnock professed himself pleased with the way the meeting had gone. He hadn't even reached the airport before Reagan's people, in a calculated snub, issued a statement expressing deep concerns about Labour's nuclear disarmament policy. It was a gift to Reagan's dear friend Margaret Thatcher.

So much to gain by being seen with the globe's most famous politician. And so much to lose.

Monday 14 July

House of Commons

Make pledges in haste, repent at leisure. The woman appointed in a rush to head an inquiry the government didn't plan to stage, with terms of reference they had not worked out, has quit.

Given the reason why Lady Butler-Sloss has had to go it's hard to see who on earth will be able to replace her as chair of the child-abuse inquiry. The specific complaint is that her late brother was attorney general in the 1980s, when the alleged cover-up occurred. But if the bigger charge the former judge faced – that she is a 'member of the establishment' – rules out judges, lawyers, parliamentarians and civil servants, the list of qualified candidates could be very short indeed. Even heads of charities would be deemed by many to be members of the establishment. Once those approached realize that the victims have effectively been given a veto they may think very hard about whether they want the job at all.

The government announced this inquiry in a desperate attempt to regain control of a story that had potential to do them real damage. The attempt has failed.

New Palace Yard, House of Commons

A ministerial reshuffle is underway but little news is seeping out. Before the six o'clock news I spend a few minutes chatting to the people who are often first to know what's going on – the ministerial drivers waiting in a Commons car park for the return of their bosses or a call to say that their bosses are now no longer their bosses as they've been fired. One jokes that the first sign a minister gets that he or she has quit is when they spot an Oyster card sitting on the prime minister's desk pointing in their direction.

Reshuffle day is one day when ministers and their advisers pick up the phone instantly. They are well aware that often we know more than they do about what's afoot. The chatter today is that someone unexpected will retire, creating a significant vacancy in the Cabinet. Philip Hammond's people insist it's not him. William Hague's do not answer my texts or calls, a sure sign that something's up.

It is a golden rule of reshuffles that those who stop responding to you are the ones on the move. Years ago when David Blunkett was rumoured to be heading for the chop at the hands of Tony Blair I was greeted with radio silence from all his closest advisers and friends. I rang his private office and, putting on my most innocent voice, asked whether the home secretary had left yet. 'Oh, no,' came the reply from a hapless official to whom I'd never spoken before. 'But he's doing his leaving speech now.' I ran on to the news channel to break the story.

No such trick works with William Hague's people before we're all officially alerted that he is quitting as foreign secretary, though not leaving the government. He is to become leader of the Commons, unofficial deputy prime minister and Tory cheerleader in the north.

We expected him to quit after the next election. George Osborne has been angling to replace him but neither he nor the other obvious candidate, Theresa May, are moving to the Foreign Office. Stand up the man my producer used to call sarcastically 'Box Office Phil': Philip Hammond.

Surveying the resignation or sacking of a string of ministers at Cabinet level and just below, this looks like a purge of middle-aged white men to help make way for the women David Cameron has long promised to promote. If a woman doesn't get the job of defence secretary it may all seem, well, a bit cosmetic.

By the end of tomorrow the question will be not which names and faces have come and gone but the political impact of the changes. We may have a new foreign secretary who has said he'd be ready to contemplate leaving the EU if changes are not made and an attorney general who, unlike his predecessor Dominic Grieve, would not oppose threatening to withdraw from the European Convention on Human Rights.

Tuesday 15 July

Downing Street

I count them out and I count them in: the reshuffle losers, mostly men, and the winners, a few of them women. Reshuffles are now a 'made-for-television' event. Every move is choreographed. One by one, ministerial cars are instructed to drive through the Downing Street gates and drop off their passengers well short of the door of Number 10 to allow the cameras to get their shots and the hacks to shout their questions –'Got your wellies?' to the woman tipped to be the new environment secretary or 'What you got?' to people whose future is not known. The promoted and the demoted are told by the spin doctors not to answer the questions so that Number 10 can control the flow of information.

Years ago, the first lady of off-camera shouters, the BBC's Joy Johnson, came up with the idea of calling out 'Are you happy?' at everyone who came in or went out. It never failed to produce a grin on the faces of those on the way up and a grimace from those who could see their political careers spinning down. Then Number 10 took steps to ensure we'd see only the faces guaranteed to be happy – those of the newly hired or promoted. Those demoted would be told by phone or seen in the Commons away from the cameras.

The purpose of today's photo-call is to suggest that Team Cameron is being feminized. Half of Labour's shadow Cabinet are women but David Cameron has struggled to meet his own limited target of having a third of his ministers look like half the population. The PM is promoting women into three senior roles – in Education, Environment and as leader of the House of Lords – but the biggest moves, into Foreign and Defence, are still made by men.

I do not help my own feminist credentials by accidentally tweeting that Nicky Morgan has become Education Sexretary. Nor by another tweet that reads: 'Esther McVey makes her way up the Downing Street catwalk as the camera bulbs flash.' Actually, the second is deliberate. McVey, a former television presenter, arrives looking as if she's spent two hours in wardrobe and make-up for a night out at an awards ceremony. When she emerges after being told she is merely keeping her junior ministerial job, and will be allowed to attend (as opposed to being a member of) the Cabinet, she poses on the step of Number 10 as if she has just won an Oscar.

Reshuffles always go wrong. The only question is how. Every move impacts on the next one like a series of interlocking cogs. One cog fails and the whole machine grinds to a halt. During one reshuffle years ago an MP called Davies (or maybe it was Davis) was ushered in to the prime minister's office to see Harold Wilson and hear his good news. As he entered the PM seemed surprised. His aides looked alarmed. This was the wrong Davies (or Davis), a man who would have been at the bottom of any list of MPs fit for office. After a brief pause Wilson smiled broadly, shook the hand of Davies (or Davis) and told him how pleased he was to have him on the team.

'What on earth were you thinking of?' Wilson's aides demanded a few minutes later. The PM explained that if he'd told Davies (or Davis) the truth the man would never have forgotten the humiliation and would have become an enemy for life. On the other hand, the government could cope with one more useless minister.

Today's broken cog is the new leader of the Lords. The appointment of Tina Stowell, unveiled as the third new woman to join the Cabinet, doubles the number with which the government started this morning . . . until it doesn't. Halfway through the day the official press release is amended to reveal that she won't be a full member of the Cabinet, merely an attendee. There is a legal limit on the number of full Cabinet ministers and on the bill for their pay, and Team Cameron have just discovered they've appointed too many. The difference between being a Cabinet minister and just going to meetings may appear to be cosmetic but it also involves Baroness Stowell being paid less than her male predecessor. Not in the script. When journalists point this out, Tory HQ suddenly discover their feminist credentials and have to find £22,000 to top up Tina's salary.

BBC Westminster

'Greater love hath no man than to lay down his friends for his life,' a wit remarked after Harold Macmillan's cull of his Cabinet, or what became known as the Night of the Long Knives. And that turns out to be the real story of this reshuffle, too.

To the joy of teachers and their union leaders, Michael Gove has been defenestrated by his own close friend David Cameron. Michael himself tries to put on a brave face when he does a round of TV interviews, batting back my repeated and rather ungenerous assertions that he's been demoted. He insists that he's delighted with his new job. It is a line of questioning he quickly grows weary of. A few minutes later, on Radio 4, he says, 'Demotion, emotion, promotion, locomotion, I don't know how you would describe this move, though move it is. All I would say is that it's a privilege to serve.'

He is not out but he is certainly down. His new job is chief whip, a more junior role which means that he, too, will only 'attend Cabinet' and thus take a pay cut of over £30,000 a year, for which the Tory party will not be compensating him.

The prime minister's spokesman insists that this 'is not a demotion'. I am told I am confusing rank with influence. Gove will, it is explained to me, be at the centre of political events and present at all the key meetings.

Chief whip, the man in charge of discipline, is a curious choice of position for a man whose downfall is connected with a lack of it. He was allowed to keep his previous job as long as his acerbic tongue was only deployed to take on the educational establishment, or those he called 'the Blob'. However, his growing unpopularity with teachers and his behind-the-scenes outbursts with his Liberal Democrat deputy David Laws, Nick Clegg and Theresa May proved too much for David Cameron to stomach.

Gove may have been a friend of the PM's and one of this government's few real radicals, but he became an obstacle to David Cameron's re-election so he had to go. Another reminder of just how ruthless the prime minister is and how much he wants to win.

Wednesday 16 July

Victoria line tube

The clearest possible sign this morning that Michael Gove may not be quite so enthusiastic about his new job as he has been suggesting. His wife, the *Daily Mail* columnist Sarah Vine, has had her own say in a tweet this morning: 'A shabby day's work which Cameron will live to regret.' It is, strictly speaking, a retweet of a link to an article by her fellow *Mail* columnist Max Hastings, who avers that her husband has effectively been sacked in a move that 'has shocked Middle England'. She adds no words of her own. There is no need.

Daily Politics *studio, Millbank*

With all this ammunition at his disposal, you might expect Ed Miliband to find it easy to hit the target, but no. Once again David Cameron is ready for him, deploying a quote from Harriet Harman which proves, he says, that Labour want to put up taxes on those on middle incomes.

I'm instantly suspicious that this has been taken out of context. Ed is not assisted, though, by the fact that while he's shaking his head Harriet is unhelpfully nodding hers. With a bit of help from the BBC's behind-the-scenes sherpas I find the context of the quote and say on air that Harriet doesn't seem to have been saying what she, well, actually said. Off air, a huddle of half a dozen colleagues debate whether I am being too generous to her. This even after they've had a chance to listen to the quote in question.

From David Cameron's perspective, this is, once again, job done.

College Garden, Westminster Abbey

My last port of call today is one of the Westminster summer drinks parties, where I'm assured by a close ally of the prime minister's that the new chief whip genuinely relishes the move. Perhaps he is right. Some years ago Michael Gove turned up at a fancy-dress party got up as Cardinal Richelieu, Louis XIII's infamous fixer, apparently enjoying the inevitable comparisons. Richelieu it was who consolidated the king's power and crushed rival factions by deploying a large network of internal spies. In short, an ideal role model for a chief whip.

Thursday 17 July

Home, the study

Got it. The other reason for the reshuffle. Cameron has cleared away the barriers to fulfilling the oldest of all unfulfilled Tory promises: to curb the power of the European Court of Human Rights. I spell out my analysis on the *Today* programme after digging into my old notebooks to find just the quote, given to me by that minister over lunch last month, to make the story come alive. It was Dominic Grieve, just sacked as attorney general, who told a meeting of Tory ministers that the manifesto plan drawn up for the PM for a so-called British bill of rights would be 'a legal car crash', albeit one with 'a built-in time delay'.

Grieve was not the only Tory minister to challenge colleagues who fuelled 'human rights gone mad' headlines. Three years ago Ken Clarke, then justice secretary, declared that the home secretary was talking 'nonsense' after she delivered a party conference crowd-pleaser about how a cat had stopped a man from being deported. Now he's gone, too.

There was one other voice who raised doubts about the plan for confronting the Strasbourg court. It was that of the foreign secretary, or rather, the now ex-foreign secretary, William Hague.

I point out to listeners that for a long time the PM has been demanding, 'Who will rid me of this troublesome court?' This week some of the remaining obstacles to that plan have been removed or, conveniently, have stepped aside.

There is, of course, a pretty big gap between what David Cameron tends to say he wants on Europe and what he actually delivers. A vivid reminder of that comes with the striking image of him high-fiving the man he vowed to stop becoming the chief Eurocrat in Brussels, Jean-Claude Juncker.

BBC offices

It's all too easy to forget the unexpected consequences of a reshuffle: the fact that the new faces in the big jobs could at any time be required to make momentous decisions for which they may be little prepared and to which no one, least of all them, can be sure how they'll react. This is never more true than today. The new foreign secretary, Philip Hammond, and his successor as defence secretary, Michael Fallon, now face an extraordinary first few days in their jobs.

A Malaysia Airlines plane en route from Amsterdam to Kuala Lumpur has come down on Ukrainian territory. All 298 passengers and crew have been killed. It is presumed to have been shot down and the signs are that the atrocity was carried out by the pro-Russian separatists controlling the area using Russian kit and Russian know-how. President Putin denies this, not surprisingly, but it may not be long before the evidence is clear and irrefutable.

The question now is how the world will respond. In America, says Senator John McCain, there will 'be hell to pay and there should be'. Of course, the man who beat him to the White House, President Obama, does not share his hawk-like tendencies, but if it is not hell that has to be paid it is going to be Russian cash and contracts. Since the annexing of Crimea in March, the United States has been far tougher on Russia than Europe has, much of Europe being more dependent on Russian oil and Russian trade. Surely that cannot continue after a day like today?

With nine British people among the casualties, the UK may soon have decisions to make on sanctions and, who knows, military action, too.

House of Commons

Other reshuffle movers have rather less important decisions to worry them. Ever since the vote not to take military action against Syria for using chemical weapons, the Commons has seemed somehow insulated from world events.

Questions to the new leader of the Commons focus on the much more substantial issue of Michael Gove getting stuck in the toilet on his first full day as government chief whip. William Hague, who just three days ago would have been the man on the phone to Moscow, Kiev and Washington DC, offers a lighthearted defence of Mr Gove's predicament, pointing out that 'knowledge of who is in the toilets in whatever lobby is a very important piece of information for any chief whip, and I take this as evidence that he was carrying out his duties very assiduously'.

Sunday 20 July

Home

I've cancelled plans to fly with Ed Miliband to the White House. He has secured the meeting with Obama he wanted but not the pictures or the words his advisers dreamed of. It will take place too late to make tomorrow's ten o'clock news and there will be no moving pictures of it, only stills, and therefore no broadcastable words from the president.

I'm simply not prepared to jet across the Atlantic just to film a man walking into an important building, especially when the news from the Ukraine is so grave.

I text Ed and his team to apologize and explain my reasons. Their disappointment is palpable. This was a big moment they've spent weeks hoping and dreaming about and it risks passing virtually unnoticed.

Monday 21 July

BBC, Millbank

I am in my edit suite watching pictures and reactions to the downing of flight MH17 coming in from all over the world. The challenge is pulling it together into a lead piece for *BBC News at 10*.

By now the rhetoric from Westminster and Washington sounds familiar. The PM's Commons statement is heavy with hints that the West is, once again, guilty of appeasing a dangerous tyrant. 'Those of us in Europe should not need to be reminded of the consequences of turning a blind eye when big countries bully smaller countries.'

The president calls on the Russians to stop Ukrainian separatists tampering with the evidence at the crash site. He demands to know, 'What exactly are they trying to hide?'

Strong words, but there are few signs that tough actions will emerge from the EU meeting in Brussels tomorrow. The reasons are oil (Italy, which continues to hover close to recession, is very dependent on Russian energy), trade (6,000 German firms do business in Russia) and arms (France has resisted pressure to halt delivery of two Mistral helicopter-carriers to Russia).

You might think that the Netherlands, the country that has lost the most in the MH17 tragedy – the plane flew out of Amsterdam and two-thirds of those on board were Dutch – would be leading the way in taking on Russia. They are also, though, the country with the largest trade deficit, spending €16 billion more in Russia last year than Russia did with them.

And what about us? Some EU countries argue that the most effective sanctions would be financial – stopping Russia accessing the City of London. In March I reported the contents of a document a senior official was seen carrying into a meeting in Downing Street which said that 'the UK should not support for now trade sanctions or close London's financial centre to Russians'. Nothing has changed since then.

The other reason, of course, why Europe is afraid to upset Vladimir Putin is that his assistance is needed to get the bodies of loved ones home. No one wants to offend him so much that he refuses to co-operate at all.

Tuesday 22 July

Home, the kitchen

Consequences. That's the word diplomats like to use when they call in the man from Moscow or the woman from Beijing to express the displeasure of Her Majesty's government. Naturally, they rarely spell out what those consequences will be or link them explicitly to whatever has offended them.

So it is this morning when the Home Office announces a public inquiry into the murder of the former KGB man whose tea was poisoned by radioactive polonium-210 in 2006. Alexander Litvinenko's widow has long called for justice to be done. Events in Ukraine have brought her a little closer to getting her way.

The security services have for years been telling anybody who would listen that Litvinenko was poisoned by agents working on behalf of the Russian state 'with their direct involvement'. But until today Theresa May has always said that a public inquiry would not help Britain's international relations. Translated, this meant that no one wanted to annoy former KGB chief Vladimir Putin by delving too deeply into his old outfit's methods of silencing his critics. Why has she changed her mind? To put it bluntly, Britain no longer cares if it upsets the Russian president.

It's a poke in the eye for the Russian bear, though one that's unlikely to make it do much more than blink.

*

Summer is here. Holiday time! Oh no, I'm sorry – that should read 'MPs head back to their constituencies to do vital work'. It would be no use. No one would believe me. The truth is that although, yes, MPs do get long holidays, many of them work very long hours, including evenings and weekends. Just like teachers – and, indeed, political journalists.

So this diary is taking its cue from the House of Commons and pausing until the political season kicks off again in September. Unless, of course, something happens in the meantime . . .

— AUGUST —

Tuesday 5 August

Montgomery, Alabama

A pit stop on the Robinson family tour of the American South, from Washington DC to New Orleans. I'm catching up with news from home and, boy, is there a lot of it.

Baroness Warsi has resigned over Gaza. It's the first ministerial resignation over a matter of policy in four years. The conflict has been raging bloodily for weeks and the Tory foreign office minister has clearly had enough of Cameron's policy of not condemning the Israelis. She says the government's position is 'morally indefensible . . . not in Britain's long-term interests and will have a long-term impact on our reputation internationally and domestically'.

That last bit is code for 'You're losing support in the Muslim community and now you've lost me – your most prominent Muslim frontbencher.' Ed Miliband has praised her decision. No wonder. Labour are desperate to woo back those Muslim voters they lost after the Iraq war.

George Osborne is publicly dismissive, calling Warsi's resignation 'unnecessary'. The truth is that he and David Cameron wanted her blend of plain-speaking northern and Asian credibility but never took her seriously. She's been fuming for months and now she has paid them back. Big time.

Having said that, it should not be forgotten that they do, of course, in fact disagree on the not insignificant matter of life and death in the Middle East.

The kids are munching popcorn and nachos, supplied gratis during

What on earth could it be? My first thought is UK and US air strikes on ISIS forces in Iraq. *The New York Times* has just reported that, according to White House sources, the president is trying to assemble an international 'coalition of the willing', including the UK, Australia and the Gulf states, to stop the creation of a caliphate in the Middle East.

A Sunday newspaper journalist once remarked that his job was to spot the 10 per cent of the iceberg above the water and guess what the 90 per cent we couldn't see looked like (we journalists are fond of percentages). This is a risky business, as anyone reading some Sunday stories and comparing them to what actually happens will be all too well aware.

On the streets of Govan

I am knocking on doors in the Glasgow suburb which gave us the man I once hyperbolically dubbed 'the greatest living Briton', Sir Alex Ferguson. Like so many people here, Sir Alex is a loyal Labour man. I've come to his birthplace to test Alex Salmond's hope that he can persuade voters who've never liked him or nationalism to lend him their vote just once to see the back of the 'hated Tories', or, as exhorted by a sticker we film on a bin, 'Vote Yes to end London rule'.

A car drives up. A hefty guy sporting a Ryder Cup cap gets out and is obviously keen to speak. He confirms he's a Labour man but says he doesn't trust Salmond and thinks independence is too much of a risk. He adds, securing his place at the top of my piece for the news at ten, 'You wouldnae jump into a shark pit to see if you got bit.'

Moments later a young guy stops his bike to ask what we're doing. The bike carries a sticker that reads: 'Sack the Tories! Vote Yes'. He says that independence is a way not only of getting rid of the Tories but of building a fairer society.

The interview over, he walks into the same house as my buddy in the golf cap has just entered. The cameraman tells him we've interviewed his dad. Angrily, he turns and retorts: 'He's not *my* dad.'

As has been warned, this referendum is dividing not just a country and communities but families and stepfamilies too.

Thursday 28 August

BBC Scotland, Pacific Quay, Glasgow

I am on a conference call with Broadcasting House discussing what to ask David Cameron in my interview with him later. 'Oh look,' someone says, catching sight of a breaking-news strap on the television screen. 'Douglas Carswell is defecting to UKIP and standing down to force a by-election.'

What?!

I am in the wrong place but at least I am with the right man.

I rush on to the news channel to talk about my third subject in the past twelve hours. Then I bash out a blog.

> This is a body blow for David Cameron.
>
> When he became Tory leader he told his party that they needed to stop obsessing about Europe. This defection . . . this by-election will revive that obsession.
>
> Conservative MPs and activists as well as the Tory press will angst and speculate about who might follow Douglas Carswell into UKIP's ranks. They will debate and argue about whether their leader now needs to threaten to leave the EU and spell out his full negotiating demands. They will disagree and fall out about whether and how to control immigration.
>
> Their coalition partners in the Lib Dems will do nothing to ease their plight and Labour will claim that every new Tory election promise is being dictated by Nigel Farage.

I end with a flourish: 'One of Cameron's predecessors compared the issue of Europe to an unexploded bomb. Not any more. It just went off.'

It's a line I end up repeating all day.

Malcolm Logistics, Glasgow

One of the skills required of any political leader is the ability to live up to the wartime slogan now seen on millions of mugs, towels and key rings: 'Keep calm and carry on'. Your mind may be racing – how are you going to deal with the defection of one of your MPs, stop others following him and prevent this crisis bringing your career to a premature end? – but you have to carry on with the day that was planned for you and look calm, particularly when you're on camera.

David Cameron is just in front of me, talking to a Glaswegian mechanic repairing a van. The only sign of the tension he must be feeling, or what poker-players call a 'tell', is that habit he has of planting his legs several feet apart as if to ground himself. Looking up, I notice that one wheel is off the van and lying on the floor. I whisper in the cameraman's ear. He grins knowingly. He too can hear the line of script in his head: 'The wheels are coming off.' Tempting but, on second thoughts, too obvious, too cheap.

Briefly, I wonder whether this is the secret statement I was tipped off about but the Downing Street team assure me that the first they knew of Carswell's defection was the announcement at a news conference.

Even without the resignation of the MP for Clacton Cameron would have reasons aplenty to be distracted, if not tense. I tell my news desk that I simply will not have the time to ask him about the new immigration figures, which show that he has a snowball's chance in hell of meeting his target, as well as speculation that the United States has asked the UK to take part in military action against Islamic State forces in Iraq and the fact that Russian forces have, in all but name, just invaded Ukraine. Not to mention Cameron's failure to find anyone to chair the inquiry into child abuse which has been high-lighted by horrific revelations about the rape of underage girls on an industrial scale in Rotherham.

I mention this list when I snatch a brief word as the prime minister moves from one part of his visit to the next. He replies wryly, 'Well, it was never meant to be easy.'

When he was still running for the job I remember him telling me that what mattered was whether you had the character to be the nation's leader. He clearly felt he had and Gordon Brown hadn't.

That faith in himself, that he's the 'right sort of chap' to be in charge, and relative lack of belief in a set of ideas, let alone a fully fledged ideology is, of course, precisely why instinctive 'believers', whether on the right like Douglas Carswell or on the left like Ed Miliband, hold him in contempt.

He handles my interview with infuriating ease, batting away my invitations to say he would recommend leaving the EU if he doesn't get the deal he wants; to admit that he has no chance of meeting his pledge to cut immigration and to acknowledge that his party's position on the EU creates at least as much investment-killing uncertainty for business as the possibility of Scottish independence. He looks discomfited only once, when I put it to him that his decisions to hold referendums on Scotland and the EU have fuelled the very uprisings they were meant to quash, which some will see as two 'dreadful miscalculations'. I detect a slight twitch in his face as he replies emphatically, 'That is completely wrong.'

Outside the Hilton hotel, Glasgow

Inside David Cameron is making a rather bloodless appeal to Scottish businessmen to back the union. Outside, speaking on the news at ten, I hear myself say, once again, that this is the day the Tories' European 'bomb' went off. Am I right, though? The problem with instant news is that it requires instant judgements. It's all too easy to hyperbolize in haste only to repent at leisure.

But no, I think I am right. This is a judgement formed not in an instant but over a quarter of a century – ever since Margaret Thatcher said 'No, no, no' to Europe and was, very soon after, ejected from Number 10. Back then I wrote a memo for my bosses at the BBC saying that Europe had the potential to split the Conservatives as comprehensively as the corn laws did in the 1840s. The issue helped finish off Mrs T. and proved utterly debilitating for her successor, John Major. Now it may ensure that David Cameron goes down as the Tory leader who never won an election.

The names Carswell and Clacton may be long forgotten by polling day 2015 but if UKIP take this by-election, which surely they will, they'll have increased the likelihood that Ed Miliband will be moving into Number 10 in a matter of months.

Carswell is one of that most dangerous breed of politicians: so-called 'men of principle'. In an era when politicians are almost universally regarded as grubby, biddable and out for themselves, these people draw their strength from standing aside from the pack. They are often loathed by their colleagues for refusing to see politics as a team sport; they are resented by party leaders for sneering at the compromises necessary to achieve and hold on to power, for refusing to 'play the game', and, above all, for being immune to the patronage that tames so many others.

By resigning his seat and triggering a by-election rather than just switching parties, Carswell has ensured that his decision cannot be dismissed as one day's bad headlines. He has forced his party into precisely what they wanted to avoid: a head-to-head electoral contest with UKIP in an area of Essex full of angry white marginalized voters, or those the academics who study these things have dubbed 'the left behind'.

Friday 29 August

Radio car, Glasgow airport

'There's a technical term for that, John,' I say, pausing theatrically. 'It's tosh.' John Humphrys has just asked me about the *Mail*'s splash suggesting that another eight Tory MPs may be about to defect to UKIP. Actually, as so often, if you study the paper carefully you can see the truth for yourself. The *Mail*'s headlines state that eight MPs 'have been "in UKIP talks"'. It is the quotation that is the giveaway. It indicates that someone – just possibly from UKIP? – has claimed this but that there is no other evidence for it whatsoever.

In fact, in this instance there is a good deal more evidence against it. My team have spoken to ten Tory 'better off out-ers' who, in the past, have talked of running on a joint ticket with UKIP. They all insist they are staying put. Many of them are furious that Carswell has jumped ship and, they fear, killed the chances of a Tory victory and with them the hope of an EU referendum.

The truth is much more mundane. Tory MPs worried that they're heading for certain electoral defeat will wait and watch. If Carswell wins they may be tempted to follow him but what might well put them off is the fact that they will have to stand down and fight a by-election. MPs who lose their seats at a general election get 'redundo', a few thousand to ease the pain. If they lose a by-election brought about by standing down they get no pay-off as they have resigned rather than being sacked by the electorate.

House of Commons

Back in London, the mystery is solved. It feels a very long time since Wednesday, when I was tipped off about a major announcement, but it has just been made. Dressed in a black suit, a sombre Theresa May has declared that the terror threat level is being raised to 'severe' which, just in case we weren't alarmed enough already, means an attack by international terrorists on the UK is 'highly likely'.

We are then called in to Number 10 to hear the PM say a great deal, though none of it is very new. 'The murder of the American journalist James Foley is clear evidence that the conflict in Iraq is not one we can ignore . . . this is a generational struggle . . . the root cause is a poisonous ideology . . . it is a battle between Islam and a perverted form of it . . .' And so on.

One thing has changed. He told me when I interviewed him last week that he'd asked the police and security services if they needed new laws and they'd said no. Apparently they've now identified 'gaps in our armoury', including one that prevents them from stopping murderous jihadists returning home using British passports.

The cynics and conspiracy theorists believe this was all cooked up to distract attention from Carswell. Given that I was told a big announcement was coming some days ago, I know the truth is rather different. It may not, though, reflect that much better on the PM. He was alarmed at the prospect of leaving four days between announcing the raising of the terror-threat level (a decision taken by counter-terrorism experts) and speaking in the Commons, which reopens for business next Monday. So he wanted to look as if he'd got a grip instead of waiting for the three horsemen of the Cameron apocalypse – Farage, Boris and Miliband – to fill the hiatus for him.

At least he didn't do what Obama did last night when he held a press conference at the White House. Asked about his plans for combating Islamic State he replied, 'We don't have a strategy yet.' He probably meant that he was still taking advice, analyzing evidence and making sure that the US Doesn't Do Stupid Shit, but as he headed off for a long weekend away it didn't sound good. Not good at all.

— SEPTEMBER —

Monday 1 September

House of Commons

On its first day back after the summer the Commons is packed for a statement by the prime minister on wars past (Gaza), present (Ukraine) and future (if, as seems increasingly likely, Western forces bomb Iraq again). The PM is asked for an assurance that he will consult MPs before using British forces. His answer – 'I reserve the right to act immediately and inform the House of Commons afterwards' – unnerves some MPs, even when he explains that he is simply ensuring he can take decisions at speed if necessary to 'defend Britain's national interest' or to carry out a humanitarian mission.

A senior minister who'll be in the war Cabinet, if there is one, tells me afterwards that there is both a legal and moral case for military action to support the new Iraqi government, providing they ask for such support. What's more, he says, he senses that the mood has changed in the Commons since last year's vote against bombing Syria. He insists no decision has been taken, confirming that the PM said what he said to avoid being boxed in by any notion that he could act only with Parliament's prior agreement. Normally, the minister explains, these things would be discussed in confidence with the opposition but after Miliband withdrew his support for military action a year ago Cameron simply doesn't trust him any more. He is convinced that he will say one thing in private only to come out with the opposite in public a few days later.

Flight from London to Edinburgh

An e-mail drops in my inbox as the flight from London to Edinburgh taxis down the runway. A poll in tomorrow's *Sun* reveals that the referendum race just got close. Very close. No is still clearly ahead of Yes but the lead has shrunk to 6 per cent with a pollster (YouGov) which has consistently had the lead at more than double that. This is what Sir Alex Ferguson used to call 'squeaky-bum time' for those who want the UK to survive.

The steward asks me what I'm going to be doing in Scotland. When I tell him I'll be interviewing Alex Salmond he drops his voice to a whisper, pulls a 'No Thanks' pen out of his pocket and says that he fears the anger being unleashed by this campaign. He adds: 'You can see how civil wars start.'

He looks over my shoulder at the interview questions I am drafting. My theme is whether the promises made for an independent Scotland – everything you dislike about the UK will change, but everything you like will stay the same – are too good to be true. Can you have a fairer country and keep the Queen, the pound, your favourite shows on the BBC and membership of the EU, all at no cost?

Tuesday 2 September

Eden brewery and distillery, St Andrews

Something's brewing in Scotland. Public opinion is on the move. As the polls show 'don't knows' making up their minds and pouring into the Yes camp, Alex Salmond senses that victory could yet be within his grasp. So do the international media crowding round him as he is presented with an empty barrel which will be filled with a new brand of Scotch once distilling begins on (wouldn't you know it?) referendum day in just over a fortnight. By the time it's ready to drink in 2018, Scotland will either be an independent nation and Salmond its founding father or he'll be the man who nearly broke Britain apart.

'I'll have a lot of friends in four years' time,' he quips to the cameras. 'You'll have a lot in two weeks' time,' one of the hardened Scottish hacks replies.

'Independence might be a disaster,' a local journalist tells me, 'but it would be a bloody amazing story.' He has summed up one huge advantage the pro-independence campaign has had: change is exciting whereas the status quo is not. This dynamic was well known in Northern Ireland. Most hacks thought it was a damned sight more interesting being a correspondent in Belfast during the Troubles, however awful they were, than it was once peace was secure.

When I interview Salmond he tells me that 'independence is closer than ever' and we have been witnessing 'a democratic sensation' as people have queued up to register to vote. After that he and I lock antlers like two stags. I put it to him that his promises are too good to be true. He responds with the old pro's technique – long answers that dispute the premise of the question and correct you for getting your facts wrong. The effect is to render the exchange unusably long for a short news bulletin. He picks me up for misquoting the governor of the Bank of England – 'I would expect a Tory MP to make an error like that, Nick, but for the political editor of the BBC . . .' The clock ticks. We are both bloodied but unbowed. I respect him; he seems to respect me. However, I'm not at all sure the spectacle will make for either interesting or revealing television.

It is on the pound where he seems to struggle most. I point out that the boss of this business – a Yes backer – could not tell me what currency he'd be using in a year's time. Why, I ask Salmond, does he want to copy the Euro and share a currency with a foreign country? Surely it didn't work so well for Greece or Spain? He resorts to a soundbite about 'a common currency making common sense'. The public shows every sign of being bored by this issue but it is where his case appears to be at its shakiest.

After the cameras are off he is keen to try to persuade me and spends ten minutes explaining why 'sterling-ization' can work.

I ask him what could close the gap that remains in the polls. 'A lot can happen in two weeks,' he says. After a short pause he adds: 'There could be a war.' His meaning is unstated but instantly clear. If Britain bombs Iraq again it will remind voters of the 'illegal war' Tony Blair waged a decade ago and which Salmond opposed. It would be a game-changer.

Dundee university freshers' event

Perhaps the talk of a democratic sensation is not as far-fetched as it sounds. The student union president tells me that he's been asked for fifty voter registration forms today alone. The council say they've had queues at their offices.

University car park, St Andrews

'Let's get this finished and treat ourselves to one of St Andrews' famous local lobsters,' I suggest to Jess and Tony, our cameraman. As they wrap up our piece for the six o'clock news a text arrives which dispels all enthusiasm for dinner. A second American journalist has been beheaded by Islamic State militants. The fact that his life was threatened after the barbaric murder of the first hostage raises fears that a British aid worker – a Scot, as it happens – who has also been paraded on camera will become the next victim.

Nick Clegg calls. Sounding cheery, he tells me about a story he hopes I'll cover tomorrow. He gives no sign of knowing about the news that has just broken. When I tell him, there's a brief silence. Neither of us can think of any words that don't sound banal in the face of the horror of it. War has always been governed, in theory at least, by 'rules' about what is and is not acceptable in conflict. So, too, was the terrorism I grew up with – even if the only reason the IRA insisted it targeted 'combatants' or 'collaborators' and not 'civilians' was for its own cynical PR purposes. Now there seems to be only one rule: anyone who isn't 'one of us' is fair game for brutal public slaughter. Reporting the conflict? Feeding the hungry? Treating the sick? None of these offer you any protection.

Wednesday 3 September

Edinburgh airport security

My shoelaces still undone, belt and see-through plastic bag of toiletries in hand, I run out of security in search of a quiet corner where I can talk live to the *Today* programme. The airport authorities very kindly rushed me through so that I have time to both broadcast and make the plane back to London. Now I just have to hope that my portentous analysis of the prospects of British military engagement in Iraq is not interrupted by 'Bing-bong . . . Would all passengers for Malaga now proceed to Gate 8.'

Jack Straw is on before me and, to the obvious surprise of his interviewer, Sarah Montague, declares that his inclination would be for the UK to launch attacks on IS targets in Iraq. The man who was foreign secretary at the time Blair and Bush ordered the invasion of Baghdad asserts that we should 'learn from the past but not be paralyzed by it', before criticizing President Obama as being 'long on analysis' but not so 'fleet of foot on being decisive' – a view I happen to know is shared inside Number 10.

House of Commons

Shared outrage. Churchillian defiance. Sombre determination. You expect all that from the House of Commons on a day like this but beyond the predictable words of condemnation for the beheading of a hostage and the threat that a Brit will be next is something altogether more surprising. It is a change in the mood.

MPs on all sides who, only last summer, seemed set on not re-engaging in military action in the Middle East are now ready to contemplate it. The prime minister tells MPs that all options are open while insisting that there will be no 'Western-led intervention'. No one stands up to warn him not to intervene, not to repeat the mistakes of the past, not to risk Britain getting sucked into a quagmire.

Ed Miliband, who ran for the Labour leadership as a critic of the Iraq war and who a year ago blocked military action in Syria, now states that he will give the government his full support. David Cameron praises both the content of his opponent's response and the manner in which it is delivered.

The prime minister is haunted by losing a vote in 2013 which would have given him the authority to launch military strikes on Syria to punish President Assad for the use of chemical weapons. You can only imagine what it must have been like for him having to phone the White House to explain why Britain would now take no part in attacks he had been calling for month after month.

For many MPs the horror of seeing children frothing at the mouth after being gassed and the exhortations to stand up for international law were trumped by a sense of regret and even shame for their vote a decade earlier that sanctioned the invasion of Iraq.

As I head to Wales for tomorrow's NATO summit, my third

country in a day, I wonder whether the Commons is about to exorcise the ghost of Tony Blair.

Thursday 4 September

Celtic Manor golf course, Newport

What would Colin Montgomerie have thought if you'd told him that the greens and the fairways where he led Europe to victory over the United States in the Ryder Cup, the most famous eighteen holes in all of Wales, would, four years later, become the venue for deciding whether to wage another war?

Celtic Manor is hosting a summit of the most powerful military club in the world. Viewers of news bulletins around the globe must be rather puzzled to see TV correspondents talking about war in the Middle East and Ukraine while standing incongruously in front of the eighteenth green, a series of bunkers and – thanks to the ever image-conscious spin doctors at Number 10 – a selection of NATO's military hardware. The jet fighter, tank and armoured personnel-carrier at the back of our shots make it look as if we're broadcasting from a rather macabre crazy-golf course.

This morning the prime minister joins us on our balcony, moving from camera to camera and microphone to microphone. First *Good Morning Britain*, then *BBC Breakfast*, Sky's *Daybreak*, Radio 4's *Today* and *5 Live Breakfast*. I follow him, coffee in one hand and bacon roll in the other, listening to how he answers questions and noting which ones he carefully avoids answering. Step by step, interview by interview, he is making the case for Britain to take up arms again in the Middle East.

Contrary to what I was told just a day ago by senior ministers, he says that air strikes would be legal as well as moral in Syria as well as Iraq. Assad's war crimes have, he claims, removed his legitimacy. I wonder if the attorney general, the government's top legal adviser, will agree – although, come to think of it, the highly independent holder of that job, Dominic Grieve, has just been sacked.

Cameron goes on to explain that air strikes will not be carried out 'over the heads' of those on the ground. I resist the temptation to point out that, by definition, they certainly will be. What he means, it becomes clear, is that military action will only be contemplated if it is requested by a new broadly based Iraqi government with the involvement of other powers in the region. Cynics will, no doubt, counter that after ten years of war, 150,000 troops on the ground and several billion dollars, such a government has yet to be formed.

This, it seems, is Obama's missing strategy. It feels like back to the future. Not for him a repeat of George W. Bush's 'shock and awe' or Bill Clinton's favoured response of unleashing a few cruise missiles. No, he is copying the approach of Daddy Bush in 1990, the president who assembled an international coalition to eject Saddam Hussein from Kuwait . . . a coalition without any troops.

Friday 5 September

Celtic Manor

No war has ever been paused, no ceasefire declared quite like this. Just after 3.30 this afternoon the president of Ukraine marches on to the fairway to make the dramatic announcement that hostilities between his troops and pro-Russian separatists will stop in half an hour's time.

Earlier the Red Arrows roared overhead, part of a display of military prowess laid on for NATO's leaders or, perhaps in truth, for their enemies. This on the day NATO has decided to deploy more of its forces on the eastern border with Russia. David Cameron has announced that Britain will send troops. At his news conference I put it to him that the ceasefire is a reflection of the fact that the West has done too little, too late and that Russia will get away with its aggression. Unsurprisingly, he doesn't agree but adds that it is very important to focus on the 'pressure that we can realistically effectively bring to bear, and that is economic sanctions pressure'. In other words, there is not the slightest chance of the world's most powerful military club using its weapons to defend the sovereignty of Ukraine. President Poroshenko marched on to that golf course to declare a ceasefire because he knows it and he knows that Putin knows it.

Back in London, the child-abuse inquiry has a new chair. She's a lawyer – good, you might think – who specializes in . . . the energy market.

And the woman chosen to replace another woman deemed too close to the establishment is the holder of one of the most ancient establishment posts in the land. She's the lord mayor of London. Mmm.

Fiona Woolf is by all accounts a clever, committed, thoughtful person but will she be able to silence the critics, let alone the conspiracy theorists?

Sunday 7 September

Home, the kitchen

It's after midnight. On the way back from a night at the Proms I do what I always do before heading to bed: check the next morning's headlines.

It's happened. Just as they said it would. For the first time a poll has the Yes vote in the lead in Scotland. Alex Salmond and his closest allies have always said they'd make up the ground and go ahead just in time for referendum day, precisely as they did before the Scottish parliamentary elections in 2011. Westminster politicians and experienced pollsters and, yes, pundits like me all thought this was little more than wishful thinking and believed that the sizeable gap in the polls could not be closed in time.

I am now forced to think the previously unthinkable: that the United Kingdom really could come to an end in less than a fortnight, triggering a major constitutional crisis which will rock many of this country's institutions – the monarchy, the armed forces, Parliament and my own BBC – as well as shaking both traditional governing parties, the Conservatives and Labour, to their very core.

A Scottish colleague tells me that he is shocked to hear members of his own family, who've always been unionists, now saying that they are backing independence. The reason? They loathe being told repeatedly that Scotland isn't capable of governing herself. Every warning about the consequences of independence – 'You can't share the pound', 'You won't be allowed into the EU', 'The oil will run out' – is being seen as a patronizing put-down by the Westminster political class.

And loathing of that class, whatever your party, is as big a factor in the increase in support for independence as a deepening of the desire for self-government. The Yes campaign has brilliantly tapped into the anti-politics mood that has swept Europe – a mood harnessed by UKIP in England, but which has been combined north of the border with hope for the future. Alex Salmond's success has depended on drawing from a well of optimism that Scotland can be a fairer and better country as well as providing an outlet for the anger and grievance of voters with what they see as an out-of-touch political London elite.

Alex Salmond and Nigel Farage agree on very little. They would be insulted to be compared to each other. Their appeal to the electorate does, however, have real similarities. They are both charismatic, anti-Westminster champions of their people, selling a vision of what David Aaronovitch of *The Times* brilliantly called 'Out-opia' – the idea that if only you were out of the UK or Europe, all the things that anger you would go away. Thus Salmond sells Scottish independence as a means of finally being rid of the Tories, austerity and illegal wars while Farage's pitch for UK independence promises an end to excessive immigration, competition for jobs, lower wages and political correctness.

I still believe that No will win, albeit narrowly; that this poll is likely to make some people pull back as they contemplate the prospect of such dramatic change. This belief, though, is no better than a hunch. It could be that, far from scaring people, the poll will instead encourage undecided voters to join the crowd heading for the door marked 'Exit'.

Monday 8 September

The flat above the shop, 10 Downing Street

Through the familiar black door, down the corridor, up the stairs until we reach the front door of what ten-year-old Nancy Cameron calls the family's 'pretend home'. Inside it feels anything but.

Sam Cam gives her guests – Pippa, me and a couple who write for the papers – a quick tour. We're shown the kitchen, which was rebuilt to give a view of the garden so she wouldn't have to look down on people endlessly babbling about what her husband is up to. The modern art is a legacy of the last residents. Gordon and Sarah have not been back for dinner in their old place, though Brown is a new ally and adviser in the battle for Scotland. But Cherie and Kathryn Blair did recently come for tea.

The PM is remarkably relaxed, despite the fact that on the menu for dinner conversation are the imminent possibilities of the break-up of the UK (he has just been to Balmoral and had the uncomfortable task of explaining to the queen why the referendum no one thought could be lost now might be), war in Iraq and a new cold war with Russia. Not that much further down the track is the prospect of having to call in the removal men and find a real home to live in.

I suggest to him that the first two of these topics could soon become intertwined. Alex Salmond, one of the few political leaders to oppose the Bush–Blair invasion of Iraq, would relish the chance to condemn the return of RAF bombers in the days before the referendum. This thought had clearly already occurred to the prime minister. I make a mental note: no bombing in Iraq before 19 September, then.

Cameron's view of his chances of political survival is no secret. If Labour can hold on to the votes of the former Lib Dems he wooed, and if the Tories can't woo back the roughly similar number who've deserted them for UKIP, his days are numbered.

As we leave I pause to look around and wonder what the Milibands might alter.

Tuesday 9 September

Millbank

'Be in Westminster for 11,' says a text from a man at Number 10. 'Will tell you more later.' So here I am. The news is not the declaration of war but a sign of the alarm sweeping through the London political classes who have just simultaneously reached the same conclusion: the Scottish Nationalists might actually do it. David Cameron and Ed Miliband have agreed to suspend their normal hostilities by skipping tomorrow's Prime Minister's Questions and travelling to Scotland instead. They have issued a joint statement with Nick Clegg, telling Scots, 'We want you to stay.'

At first sight this announcement appears to have been dreamed up by Alex Salmond who, predictably, greets it as a sign of panic in Westminster's out-of-touch elite. The explanation coming from SW1 is that PMQs would have produced TV clips of Cameron and Miliband agreeing on the threat posed by independence. So the lesser of two evils was to let them both be in Scotland while keeping them apart.

I have my doubts.

Broadcasting House

A meeting of senior editorial folk at the BBC consists of people competing to conjure up visions of every possible crisis that could follow a Yes vote: a run on the pound, a collapse in the markets, the drying up of mortgage finance, the resignation of the prime minister. The BBC's splendid arts editor, Will Gompertz, modestly comments that a row about how to separate national art collections would prove a little testing before hastily adding that this is, of course, not quite such big potatoes.

Calton Hill, Edinburgh

The view from the hill above the rooftops of Scotland's capital city is stunning. Will the setting for tonight's *BBC News at 10* soon be the capital of a new independent state?

My job is to analyze an extraordinary day in which the PM, the deputy PM, the leader of the opposition, the governor of the Bank of England and Her Majesty the Queen have intervened in the same political debate. I tell Huw Edwards that we are unlikely ever to live through another like it.

He points out off camera that he's had quite a day himself broadcasting in such a public place. A woman sang her way through the six o'clock news headlines. A man showed up claiming to be Jesus and a Yes campaigner unfurled a banner behind Huw's head. It could have been worse, apparently. Last night a group of satanists arrived in Calton Hill just in time to feature in the back of a live shot.

Strictly speaking, the Palace has intervened to say it will not be intervening. In what we are told we must call 'guidance' rather than a 'statement' the Queen's aides have served notice that she will not be dragged into the debate. A few Sunday papers reported at the weekend that she was very unhappy about the thought of the break-up of Britain, not least because she'd have to cross a border every time she visited her beloved Balmoral. Meanwhile, today's *Telegraph* says she has been under pressure to make her private views public. The 'guidance' makes it clear that won't happen but read it carefully and what you see is that at no stage does the Palace deny that she does not want Scotland to vote Yes.

The PM joked the other night that during his weekend at Balmoral, he tried to hide *The Sunday Times*, which carried the poll indicating that the union was in danger. He quipped that he passed a safer paper over the marmalade and the cornflakes in their plastic Tupperware box and said, 'You really must take a look at the *Express*, Ma'am.'

Wednesday 10 September

Portobello, Edinburgh

We are waiting for the man whose statue could soon start to appear in the public squares of Scotland and whose name might feature on a hundred road signs. A gaggle of happy T-shirted supporters have formed a semi-circle to greet Alex Salmond. In their hands are letters spelling out 'Team Scotland'. The message couldn't be clearer: you're either with us or with what Salmond has dubbed 'Team Westminster'. They burst into song. 'You only smile when you're winning, you only smile when you're winning . . .' The optimism is infectious.

When Salmond turns to the cameras I ask him why he's so obsessed with talking about people from London when those who may deny him victory aren't Londoners but fellow Scots who simply don't share his vision. He doesn't look pleased.

Scottish Widows headquarters, Edinburgh

I am now looking at a man who knows that his tombstone could read: 'The prime minister who presided over the break-up of Britain'. There is a catch in his throat as he makes a plea for Scotland to stay.

David Cameron tells the staff of one of Scotland's biggest financial institutions that it would be 'heartbreaking' to separate 'this family of nations'. To the visible shock of his audience he urges voters not to dismantle the union simply to 'give the effing Tories a kick'. People have whispered in his ear, he adds, that it wouldn't be so bad for him and the Tories if Scotland did go. However, he insists, he cares more about his country than his party.

Many Scots find it hard to believe this but it happens to be true. It is a point I made to Alex Salmond years ago over scrambled eggs and the finest Scottish black pudding you could eat in London. Salmond is one of the most engaging and thought-provoking politicians with whom to chew the political fat. He explained his hope that George Osborne, a politician whose tactical nous he clearly admired, would understand the benefits of easing Scotland's path to independence, allowing the Conservatives to govern England for ever and a day. 'It won't happen,' I told him. Even if Osborne did come to that view, which I very much doubted, David Cameron was an old-school Tory who would put 'Queen and country' first.

Another who found this hard to believe was Gordon Brown, whose great weakness has always been his inability to understand people who don't share his own views. For months after the referendum campaign began, Gordon refused to accept that the Tories weren't secretly hoping for Salmond to win. Now, though, he calls Number 10 to brief Cameron's staff on strategy and the PM openly talks of seeking and getting Brown's approval for his speeches.

Those speeches could, of course, prove counter-productive. I am stopped on the street outside by a guy who tells me that he has just hours to make up his mind as he needs to cast his postal vote before going on holiday. Middle-aged, middle-class, well-educated, he says he thinks that the sight of Westminster's three leaders – or those he refers to as 'three old Etonians' – flying up 'to tell us what we can and cannot do has probably made up my mind'.

Calton Hill, Edinburgh

The ten o'clock news is on air and I am pacing around honing what I'm going to say in my 'live' when a text flashes up. The *Sun* has revealed that Lloyds bank are moving their headquarters down south. Then the phone rings and a Treasury source tells me that the RBS board are meeting tomorrow and likely to follow suit. This is no huge surprise as there has been speculation about it for weeks, but it is news. I stress on air that the story is unconfirmed and that the implications in terms of jobs are, as yet, unclear.

Thursday 11 September

Malmaison hotel, Edinburgh

A week to go until Scotland decides. Over a hundred Labour MPs are travelling up together on the train from London to join their Scottish colleagues in the battle to convince voters here that independence is a risk not worth taking.

Meanwhile, I am about to head to what's being billed as an 'international media' event. A chance for the first minister to show Scots that the eyes of the world are on them. A chance, too, for him to talk of his country joining an international family of independent nations.

This morning's headlines are not the ones Alex Salmond wanted: 'FINANCIAL TURMOIL HITS SCOTLAND', '. . . MORTGAGE RISK . . .', 'BLACK WEDNESDAY'. Yesterday Standard Life became the latest financial institution to confirm that it is preparing to move its base south of the border. BP and Shell joined those saying that Scotland's oil reserves would run out sooner than the Scottish government's optimistic forecasts estimate. Retailers – including, for the first time, John Lewis – are lining up to warn of possible price rises once there is no longer any need to charge the same for goods across stores with very different cost bases. No longer any need, in other words, for supermarkets in the south-east to subsidize prices in the Highlands as they do now.

There is no doubt that the No campaigners are trying just as hard to frighten the voters as their opponents. In the case of the Yes campaign the focus is on the NHS. What matters more than the tactics is whether the claims and threats have any basis in truth.

As I'm mulling on what question to ask Salmond – something along the lines of why voters should believe that a politician like him is right and these successful business leaders are wrong – I get a text from one of his advisers. 'Why did the Treasury alert BBC before RBS alerted markets?' it asks, referring to last night's story. 'This is a clear breach of rules and seems to prove scaremongering, does it not?' Evidently they are itching for a fight with 'Team Westminster'.

Edinburgh International Conference Centre

Funny old news conference, this. It feels more like a rally. Most of the seats are filled by Yes campaigners in the mood to cheer their heroes and hiss at the mention of their opponents. The warm-up man, Canon Kenyon Wright, gets them going. 'It's about power, stupid,' he declares. 'Scotland, not Westminster, must have the ultimate right to decide.' What really stirs the audience is his condemnation of what the Yes campaign likes to call 'Project Fear and Project Fantasy'.

When Alex Salmond marches on he, too, begins with a message of hope and optimism but swiftly moves on to his favourite theme: condemning the 'blatant bullying and intimidation of the Westminster government'.

He then turns to what he says is a 'matter of extraordinary gravity'. It is the story I reported last night about RBS. The first minister declares that he is writing to the Cabinet secretary to demand an official inquiry into the leaking of market-sensitive information. Flourishing an A3 print-out of the story from the BBC's website, he says the Treasury 'have now been caught red-handed scaremongering', adding theatrically: 'I know the BBC, in its full, impartial role, will want to co-operate fully.'

Cue derisive laughter from Salmond supporters.

The villain of the piece briefly considers toning down his question before thinking, 'Sod that. I'll be damned if I'm falling for this.' Instead I ask two: the first concerns the tax consequences of RBS's move and the second is the question I'd originally planned, about why voters should believe Alex Salmond rather than the business bosses warning of some of the commercial and economic consequences of independence.

Question number one is greeted by heckling from the audience which the first minister ostentatiously silences, asking the crowd to let him answer while signalling his real intention by declaring that he wants to 'do a reverse question to the BBC's role in these matters, which I'm sure Nick will be perfectly happy to explain'. I begin to feel that I am in one of those episodes of *The Sopranos* where a foot soldier is being lined up to be ritually humiliated (though, happily, not shot) for daring to cross the boss.

On RBS Salmond is scathing. He reads out a letter from the chief executive stating that there would be no loss of jobs or tax revenues as a result of the bank moving its brass plate to London. If it doesn't matter a damn where companies are based it's curious that Salmond himself has tried so hard to persuade firms to move their headquarters north of the border.

In response to the second question the first minister attacks the reporting of the metropolitan media who, he claims, are reheating old stories fed to them by the Westminster parties.

I once remarked on air that Alex Salmond was the canniest player of the political game on these isles. He is now employing the 'attack is the best form of defence' gambit. Every camera not trained on him is now pointing at me, to capture my reaction to his strike against the BBC. I can sense his pleasure that he's switched the story from 'Salmond on the back foot' to 'Salmond comes out fighting'.

Irritated, I shout out that he hasn't really answered. He accuses me of heckling him. Cue more laughter from the crowd. Cue more words from the first minister.

We've been at this for nearly seven minutes. Time to move on. Fortunately, the questions put by my colleagues from ITV, Sky, Channel 4 and Channel 5 are just as probing.

At the end it is clear that the crowd regard this as a great victory over the newsman from down south while the assembled hacks see it as merely yet another example of a politician choosing to dodge awkward questions.

I'm too close to it to have any idea what a neutral observer will think.

BBC news bureau, Edinburgh

Editing my row with Salmond is a nightmare. So much to fit into so little time: his positive message, his fightback over RBS, the warnings from business leaders and the reaction of the No campaign.

After more than two hours of experimenting with different ways to cut the piece I decide. I'll run a series of clips of his 'one week to go' pitch to the voters and his attacks on scaremongering. I'll also feature my question on business and point out that he didn't really answer it. The surest sign that I'm not happy with how any of this is going is when I start shouting down the phone at colleagues in London.

I finish the piece just in time to leap into a cab, get driven to the foot of Calton Hill, run to the top, pause to stop wheezing and take up position next to Sophie Raworth to be interviewed for *BBC News at 6*. My brain still whirring with the day's events, I start my answer on air by calling her Katy. Oh, God.

The only note of cheer is the news that a Russian reporter at this morning's international media event has told STV he was 'disappointed' by 'the master of Teflon answers'.

The bar

In need of a glass or two of liquid relaxant before the news at ten, we head to the bar. Plans for a post-match bitch are interrupted, though, by the presence at the next table of Angus Robertson, the SNP's likeable Westminster leader and an ex-BBC reporter. I invite him over to tell us why he still thinks he's going to win. What we're not picking up, he says, is that whole estates and tower blocks and workplaces have turned to Yes as a result of their two-year grass-roots campaign. And the pollsters aren't getting to the never-voted-befores.

He doesn't mention my news conference clash once, even though Twitter is starting to hum with unpleasant and personal abuse. There are complaints that I claimed Salmond hadn't answered when, in fact, he had. I tweet that he answered one question but not the other and then, perhaps as a subconscious security measure, I post a selfie of Angus and me smiling together at the end of a tough day.

Friday 12 September

Princes Street, Edinburgh

A phalanx of cameras, an army of onlookers and a mere handful of shoppers are following Ed Miliband as he walks up Princes Street. He and his office have moved here lock, stock and barrel since that poll. This is Labour country and for them saving the UK is not a matter of patriotism or emotion. It is a matter of survival.

I am just pondering how to turn this into a news story when the phone goes. Ian Paisley has died. Can I go on air to talk about the legacy of the larger-than-life former leader of the Ulster unionists?

BBC newsroom, Edinburgh

In the cab to the BBC newsroom I scribble out a few key recollections that capture how Ulster's 'Dr No' became Dr Yes and embodied Northern Ireland's transition from violence to peace.

'Never!' Rarely spoken, usually bellowed. The 'man of God' standing at the top of a hill surrounded by hundreds of followers waving gun licences. The contrasting memories of 'the Chuckle Brothers', Paisley and Sinn Féin's Martin McGuinness, sharing a smile and a laugh while running a power-sharing executive in Stormont which both had tried to block and then destroy.

My favourite, though, is a personal one which captures the gulf between the private Paisley and the public figure. I once met him on a plane where he was studying his book of daily scripture readings. He was so softly spoken I could barely hear a word he said. Once we landed he was confronted by another reporter with a camera. The old man screamed defiance into the lens and then turned round, looked at me and winked.

Pacific Quay, Glasgow

After editing my piece it's time to get the sleeper home for a break. Having scarcely had time to catch up with the brewing row about my report on the Salmond news conference, I am stopped on the street by a fellow journalist who wants to congratulate me for not allowing myself to be bullied. A somewhat less supportive passerby who recognizes me hisses 'Liar!'

A pro-independence website is accusing me of telling 'a brazen and quite spectacular lie' in claiming that the first minister didn't answer my question. The author of the accusation, the Reverend Stuart Campbell, says I am guilty of 'a mindboggling reversal of the plainly observable facts'.

The Scottish *Daily Record* (anti-Salmond) says he was 'rattled' and trying to 'shrug off dire warnings about the economic dangers of independence'.

The *Herald* (pro) says he 'answered the question at length' but 'only partially'.

The *Guardian*'s Andrew Sparrow, as so often, has the sharpest analysis:

> Salmond did not just play the time-honoured 'demand a leak inquiry' card to turn a headline. In a classic Mandelsonian flourish, he also

wrapped that up with an attack on the BBC. As well as making count-
less jibes about the BBC's reporting of the RBS story, he also started
laying into Nick Robinson. There's nothing actually wrong with that
per se – Nick makes a living winding up politicians, and every time
they deride him, I presume he gets a pay rise – but it was contrived,
and part of his diversionary strategy.

My view entirely. Except, believe me, there has not been and will
be no pay rise.

Sunday 14 September

Taxi to Heathrow airport

'Do you feel the love on the streets of Glasgow today!!?? Not in my
name.' It's an intriguing text but I have no idea what it means. Another
sheds a little more light: 'Anti-BBC protests again. You get a special
mention :).'

It's the third that finally reveals what's going on. This includes a
photograph of an enormous banner, bearing a mugshot of me, on
display amid a crowd, apparently 4,000 strong, that has converged on
the BBC's Glasgow headquarters. The good news is that it's a rather
flattering photo of a smiling yours truly. The bad news is the slogan:
'Sack Nick "the liar" Robinson. A totally corrupt journalist. These days
typical of the British Biased Corporation.'

Other placards protest against 'the British Brainwashing
Corporation', 'Auntie Beeb, Anti-Democracy, Anti-Truth' and call for
viewers to 'Boycott Biased Coverage'.

Most of them look like standard protest banners made in someone's
garage with a bit of hardboard or an old sheet and a pot of leftover
paint. Not mine, though. It is glossy and professionally produced. It
will have cost someone not just a few bob but, I suspect, many hundreds
of pounds.

The question is, who?

Monday 15 September

En route to Aberdeen

A spectacular train journey to Aberdeen for the prime minister's final campaign speech. The views of Scotland's coastline are jaw-droppingly beautiful. Memo to self: come back when not working.

When not distracted by the view I read about what I missed in Glasgow yesterday. The *Daily Record*'s front-page headline is 'ANTI BEEB'. Inside there's a double-page spread entitled 'The Beeb under Siege'.

I have received some heartwarming replies to an e-mail I wrote apologizing to those trying to get to work through that mass protest who might 'want to curse me under their breath or, indeed, out loud'. One tells me the demonstrations aren't new. The protesters have been coming for about the last eighteen months, so 'u keep on doing exactly what u are doing'.

Back in Edinburgh, that's not quite the tone the first minister is striking. He tells reporters that the BBC is guilty of 'institutional bias' and maintains that my report wasn't fair, though he insists he doesn't want me to be sacked. As for those protests calling for precisely that, he avers they were 'peaceful and joyous'. I must explain that to the security guard who, I'm told by the BBC, will now have to accompany me when I'm out filming.

I text one of Salmond's advisers to make peace and receive a nice reply – Alex and his team see me as a fair and professional journalist, apparently – and a promise of a beer on Friday.

My guess is that their anger is rooted in worry that last week's crucial poll putting the Yes vote in front came too early for them. It had the effect of panicking the No campaign, business leaders and some wavering voters and driving the story to the top of UK news bulletins. Up until then viewers and readers had shown every sign of being bored by it.

BBC newsroom, Aberdeen

Gordon would like to talk to you. Those are words I have not heard in a very long time. The potential saviour of the union wants to brief me on his speech calling for three 'guarantees' for Scotland to be 'locked in' before voting takes place on Thursday, namely 'extensive new powers' for Scotland, the 'equitable' sharing of the UK's 'resources', and Scotland being allowed to raise the funds it needs for the NHS by preserving the Barnett funding formula.*

When he rings it's just like the old days. He tells me what he wants me to know. I admire his strategic thought. I then think of some questions. He ignores them and repeats what it is he called to tell me in the first place.

The question he particularly doesn't want to address is whether these measures have been agreed with David Cameron. It is obvious that they have, but Gordon is desperate that this should be seen as a plan made in Scotland, and made by Labour, not an element of what Alex Salmond wants to present as a stitch-up by the Westminster parties.

The British constitution may now be being rewritten in response to a misplaced fear that Scotland is about to vote for independence. Imagine if they'd had online polls in 1832.

Aberdeen city centre

We are on our way to find the saltire-waving protesters lining the streets of Aberdeen. I know they're there as I've seen a video of them on Twitter.

My camera crew, producer and I discuss how we will handle a potentially lively situation, particularly if the crowd take against me. If we can find the crowd, that is. They are not where we are expecting them to be. Indeed, when we finally make it to where the epicentre of the action is supposed to be there's not a protester or a saltire in sight. In their place is a small stall with two very polite ladies leafleting on behalf of the Yes campaign. It turns out a video of a demonstration that happened last night had been tweeted by mistake.

The ladies courteously explain why they're in favour of independence. A number of people sidle up to me and tell me that they're voting no but, no thank you, they'd rather not appear on camera as they don't want to fall out with their staunchly pro-independence neighbours.

---

* The mechanism used by the Treasury to adjust levels of public expenditure in Ireland, Scotland and Wales.

My so-called bodyguard has been given a new role. He looks after the camera tripod and gets in the teas.

Aberdeen conference centre

Protesters may be hard to find but Team Cameron are taking no chances. They are desperate to avoid any image that suggests he's an unwelcome foreign visitor to Scotland, let alone a chance encounter with a real voter who might mention the bedroom tax or suggest that an English Tory toff is not exactly wanted round here.

So Cameron's audience consists of invited Conservatives only. The venue is outside the city centre on a main road not easily accessible to anyone without a car and has no real space for people to gather. Nevertheless the prime-ministerial car is driven at high speed into the basement car park. Not a single ordinary Aberdonian will have had a glimpse of their distinguished visitor.

Nothing must distract from his carefully honed final message to the Scottish people, which he delivers in a voice breaking with emotion. 'Don't think, "I'm frustrated with politics right now, so I'll walk out the door and never come back,"' he tells the crowd, who have been warmed up by a video of Churchill and the patriotic atmosphere. 'If you don't like me, I won't be here for ever. If you don't like this government, it won't last for ever. But if you leave the UK – that will be for ever.'

It's all leading up to the No campaign's big play: 'the vow', which is splashed on the front of tomorrow's *Daily Record*, signed by David Cameron, Ed Miliband and Nick Clegg. It looks a big deal. I wave the front page on camera. In fact all it consists of is the three guarantees that Gordon called about earlier. I wonder how many viewers will really understand what they mean.

Tuesday 16 September

Train from Aberdeen to Glasgow

I've been given a breather – a chance to mug up for election night, to study the polling numbers, think through scenarios and to familiarize myself with the differences between North Lanarkshire, Clackmannanshire and East Renfrewshire.

The row about my news-conference clash with Salmond rumbles on. Unpleasant abuse continues to fill my inbox and my Twitter feed. By generously coming to my aid, fellow political reporters have made themselves targets for abuse as well. My oppo on ITV News, Tom Bradby, commented in a blog:

> I'm not going to suggest that this bears comparison with really bad places, but it is certainly highly unusual in the democratic world.
>
> For example, my first major job as a correspondent was in Ireland in the early nineties and, despite the fact that there was a bitter war going on all round me that took many lives, I experienced virtually no personal hostility at all from anyone. They didn't lob accusations of bias around every time you asked a question, either.

BBC newsroom, Glasgow

Things can only get worse for Ed Miliband's Scottish campaign, it seems. I take a call from one of our team with the Labour leader in Edinburgh. He's had to abandon a walkabout after being mobbed by both pro- and anti-independence supporters. He has scarcely met an ordinary voter. Such was the scrum that planned media interviews had to be scrapped and Miliband eventually had to be escorted out of the rear exit of a shopping centre. These are not days on which he's going to look back fondly.

There's a rumour that the Scottish *Sun* is finally going to declare its hand. Rupert Murdoch has spent months flirting with independence – which, he has tweeted, 'would mean a huge black eye for the whole political establishment' (or should that be translated as: those bastards who used to creep to me and then forced me to close down my bestselling paper and watch my staff being arrested?) – and the man he has dubbed 'clearly the most brilliant politician in UK' (possible translation: the man who still creeps to me, despite the phone-hacking).

It's clear what's in it for Salmond – beyond, that is, the appeal of getting close to a global media magnate who's knowledgeable, well connected and stimulating company. He craves media support in a country where most papers are still backing No and in which, as another Murdoch tweet revealed, he believes that the 'most powerful' medium, 'the BBC', is 'totally biased for No'.

Murdoch flew to Scotland for this moment but the old boy has bottled it at the last minute. Tomorrow's front page is one of the worst the *Sun* can ever have produced. 'YES OR NO', runs the headline. 'TODAY SCOTLAND STARTS WITH A BLANK PAGE'. The paper has lamely decided just to tell its readers to make up their own minds.

Wednesday 17 September

Eve of referendum day, Glasgow Community Central Hall

I've been trying for days to find out what the No campaign's last big rally will be to make sure I can get to events on both sides if at all possible. There was talk of a big gathering involving Ed Miliband. I've just been told by the Better Together organizers that it will take place late this evening. 'But it will clash with the Yes rally in Perth, and might be too late to get on to the ten o'clock news at all,' I protest. The reply is telling. 'Oh, you spotted that, did you?'

So instead I'm in Glasgow, waiting for the real leader of Labour in Scotland, Gordon Brown, and Alistair Darling, the official leader of the No campaign, official Scottish party leader Johann Lamont and the leaders of the Scottish Tories and Lib Dems as well. Oh, and some young people who end up outshining them all.

A young trainee surgeon called Vicky gets the crowd to their feet. She tells them she was born in the NHS, treated as a child in the NHS and now works in the NHS, a service that helped and supported her mother through cancer, enabling her to attend Vicky's wedding last weekend. It is a story that moves her audience first to tears and then to anger as she turns on the SNP, calling them liars for claiming that only independence can save the NHS.

The No campaign has finally discovered its passion, its self-belief and its defiance here. Gordon Brown, so long a tense, brooding presence on the sidelines, roars back into action, reclaiming the country, the flag and patriotic pride from his nationalist opponents.

> Tell the nationalists it's not their flag, their culture, their country or their streets.
>
> Tell them it's everyone's flag, everyone's culture, everyone's country and everyone's streets.

And tell them that our patriotic vision is bigger than nationalism; we want Scotland not leaving the UK, but leading the UK, and through leading the UK, leading in the world.

When I speak to him afterwards he tells me that Scots are hungry for change. The implication is clear. What has gone wrong for Labour in this campaign is that many people have concluded that they and their leader cannot or will not deliver it.

Largs

At an art-deco ice-cream parlour at the seaside resort of Largs, we await the man who has convinced many that he can deliver that change.

A crowd is gathering to greet Alex Salmond at one of a series of stops he's making on a helicopter tour of key locations. The streets of Scotland belong to him. He is greeted like a pop star wherever he goes by people who see him as their liberator.

He is, though, almost always late, which gives me the chance to talk to the crowd. Here, as everywhere I've been, there's a mix of life-long nationalists, left-wingers who crave escape from what they see as the neo-liberal, neo-con consensus and those who simply view independence as the chance of a fresh start, to write on a clean sheet, to discard at a stroke the grimy compromises and bitter disappointments of the recent past.

The energy is infectious and like nothing I've experienced in politics since the birth of the SDP in the early 1980s. Yet beneath the surface there are some uncomfortable currents.

One woman tells me that for her independence is a matter of 'blood and history'.

'Blood?' I inquire, wondering if I've heard correctly.

'Oh yes,' she replies. 'Blood has always been spilled in countries that struggle for freedom.'

I resist the temptation to tell her that my grandparents fled Nazi Germany in 1933 thanks to people who believed in blood and history.

Alex Salmond's genius has been first to assemble and then to hold together this extraordinarily broad coalition. When he finally arrives in Largs everyone wants a selfie, everyone gets a smile. Even me. When he hears my question and spots my camera he turns very deliberately to shake my hand and, having answered, pats me on the shoulder before moving on.

So it's not my turn to sleep with the fishes just yet.

Perth concert hall

Outside the crowd wave huge saltires and sing pro-independence songs. Inside they talk excitedly. They believe this is their time. Their moment in history. The atmosphere is more like that of a rock concert than a political rally.

Until, that is, someone spots the political editor of the BBC standing on the balcony. What begins with a hiss turns into one or two boos and then the entire crowd – 1,500 or so – joins in. For a while I stand motionless, staring at the screen of my iPad, determined not to be seen to react. It's a bit sinister but more than anything else it is absurd. It seems I have become the pantomime villain of this campaign.

Realizing that my BBC colleague James Cook, a few feet away from me, is about to appear live on the news channel, I have no option, to stop the noise, but to beat a retreat, to the cheers of those below. I wait long enough for James to finish his live and then return to a rather less visible position.

Salmond, like Brown earlier in the day, gives a belter of a speech. This, he tells a rapturous throng, 'is our choice, our opportunity, our time . . . we must seize it with both hands'. They respond with Obama-like chants of 'Yes we can!'

The warm-up act was, if anything, even better. Nicola Sturgeon, Salmond's deputy, is a woman to watch.

Moments after the rally ends two new polls put the No camp ahead – just. My own gut says, as it always has, that Scotland will vote no. Privately, the No campaign's confidence has grown in the last few days. My head says, 'Remember how wrong they've been. Remember Salmond has defied the odds before. Remember polls can be wrong.'

Thursday 18 September

Glasgow

It's here. D-Day.

While Scotland casts its votes, I have time to read up and rest before my twenty-four-hour shift begins. It will take me from the ten o'clock news, when Scotland will still be part of the UK, through a long night of results to the ten o'clock news tomorrow when . . . who knows.

For days I have kept my silence despite being called a liar, abused online and hissed at and booed in public. I allow myself one small, low-key act of defiance which, I suspect, no one else will notice. I put on a T-shirt my kids bought for me in Washington DC's splendid Newseum, a museum that chronicles the history of the news business. Its galleries celebrate the bravest of reporters, the men and women who brought into people's homes the stories of war, tragedy, debate, division and democracy. It reads simply 'Trust me, I'm a reporter'.

Matt's cartoon in the *Telegraph* raises the spirits while making an acute observation. His sketch of the Battle of Bannockburn 700 years ago shows one sword-bearing soldier in mid-battle saying to another, 'I've noticed a slightly intimidating and bullying atmosphere creeping into this battle.'

If this is the day a new self-governing nation is born it will be remarkable that the worst that has happened has been a bit of jostling, booing, heckling and calling the man from the BBC a liar.

Pacific Quay, Glasgow

A last word on the news at ten before the results of the referendum come in. How to capture the excitement, the drama, the sheer sense of moment for those not here in Scotland? The words come into my head just before I turn to face Huw on the set. It is not often, I tell him, you can say that if you go to sleep now you could wake up and find yourself in a completely different country. The hairs on the back of my neck stand up. Bloody hell, it's a privilege doing this job.

Scotland Decides, *referendum results programme*

Banana – check. Chocolate – check. Nuts – check. Notes on South Ayrshire and East Renfrewshire – check.

I'm ready. Just nine hours or so to go. All the signs point to No. A final YouGov poll gives a pretty clear margin: No 54 per cent, Yes 46 per cent. The texts from Labour and the Tories sound pretty confident.

But, but, but ... neither the pollsters nor the politicians have a baseline against which to measure what they're hearing. There has been no vote like this before, no turnout like it, no precedent for the level of political engagement. So until I see real results in real ballot boxes, I'm not calling it.

Friday 19 September

1.09am

The first real sign that it's No. Pro-union campaigners in East Lothian have told the BBC they believe 62 per cent have voted against independence. Twenty minutes later, the first result is in. Clackmannanshire votes No by 54 per cent to 46 per cent. The Yes votes will have to stack up very, very high in the strongly pro areas, Dundee and Glasgow, if they're to outweigh results like this.

Around 3am

A snapper has captured an image of a despondent-looking Alex Salmond slumped in the back of his car as he arrives at Aberdeen airport to fly to Edinburgh. He knows he's lost. In the next hour the Nos begin rolling in steadily – East Lothian (+23), Stirling (+20), Falkirk (+6), Angus (+12), Aberdeen (+18), Dumfries (+28) . . .

4.57am

It may be a consolation prize for Yes, but boy, it is some consolation. Glasgow, once the second city of the Empire, has voted for independence. It won't be enough. The UK will survive but it will now have to change.

5.14am

The BBC officially forecasts a No decision.

6.08am

The result in Fife makes this a mathematical certainty. The people have spoken and Scotland has rejected independence.

More Scots cared, more believed in it and more voted for it than ever before, but now that dream is dead. It will be dead for a generation, Salmond said before the ballot, but a resurrection sure doesn't feel that distant now. This debate is very, very far from over. How can it be, when more than 1.5 million British citizens voted not to remain part of the UK, when a majority in Scotland's biggest city backed independence, when the Westminster establishment briefly thought this vote was lost?

7.05am

David Cameron strides out of the door of Number 10. Not for him Churchill's maxim 'In defeat, defiance; in victory, magnanimity'. He is using his victory to defiantly play the English card. 'We have heard the voice of Scotland and now the millions of voices of England must be heard. The question of English votes for English laws, the so-called West Lothian question, deserves a decisive answer.'

The idea of EVEL will play well down south – in England – but it resonates very differently here, in a city that has just voted to break up the UK.

Edit suite, BBC

I am halfway through my edit for the news at six when the phone rings. Salmond is quitting, I am told. He's having a news conference. You are not invited. I switch on the TV to watch with everyone else the announcement by the soon-to-be ex-first minister from his official residence at Bute House in Edinburgh.

> For me as leader my time is nearly over, but for Scotland the campaign continues and the dream shall never die. We now have the opportunity to hold Westminster's feet to the fire on the 'vow' that they have made to devolve further meaningful power to Scotland.

I can feel the heat from here.

Sunday 21 September

Labour party conference, Manchester

There should be a buzz, a sense of anticipation, a whiff of power in the air. Yet the mood is flat at this, the last conference before the election for the party which – if the polls are right – will be heading back to power in just eight months' time.

The big eve-of-conference policy announcement is, well, not very big. A promise to increase the minimum wage to £8 sounds good, particularly if you're currently toiling for an hour to earn the existing rate of £6.31, which wouldn't buy you three Starbucks cappuccinos. However, the new rate will only apply from 2020 and represents a slower rate of increase than was seen before the Great Crash.

It's symbolic of where Labour is: keen to show it can and will tackle the cost-of-living crisis facing the lowest-paid, even at a time when there's little or no money to spend.

Ed Miliband does his best to sell the proposal on *The Andrew Marr Show* this morning but the entire political class is still nursing a referendum hangover. They've had too much adrenaline and too little sleep to find a routine conference policy announcement anything more than a bit of a yawn.

Miliband argues – rightly, in my view – that the reason so many in Scotland voted for change had more to do with anger at the way the country and the economy have been run than dissatisfaction with the UK's constitutional arrangements. Nevertheless Marr and the hacks who've assembled in Manchester are much more interested in Cameron's 'EVEL' play. Again and again he asks the Labour leader for his view on English votes for English laws. Again and again Miliband fails to commit. Some bright spark goes back over the interview transcript and counts up how often this happened. It was thirteen. Unlucky for some.

Midland hotel, Manchester

Ed Balls is running late for our annual conference chinwag. He finally barrels into the room and asks me with a grin, 'Have you seen the photos yet?' Every year he provides the snappers with an irresistible image at the Labour v Westminster reporters football match. This time he's excelled himself by elbowing the man from the *Northern Echo* in the face, leaving him with blood streaming down his face and his shirt. Not a person known for his public acts of contrition, Ed explains that his opponent's face ran into his elbow (or something like that) and that it's all most unfair, as he had been about to 'score a brilliant goal in the top right-hand corner'.

He's already trying out ways in which he can weave this incident into his conference speech tomorrow. 'How about it's proof that I'm ready to carry out bloody cuts?' he suggests, before thinking better of it.

After we've talked about his conference speech tomorrow and the state of politics, Ed marches me through to his and Yvette's hotel room as there's something he wants to show off. In the middle of the room is an ironing board and on top of that a portable fold-out lectern. He proudly informs me that he found this in an online shop for travelling American preachers. Then, stepping forward to show me how it's possible to practise his speech without ever leaving his room, he knocks it to the ground and breaks it.

The other revelation of the night is that Ed and Yvette and the kids went inter-railing this summer, taking in a *Sound of Music* bike tour in costumes made by the Balls-Coopers themselves from curtain material on the train to Salzburg – lederhosen for the boys, headscarves and neckerchiefs for the girls. Now, if only the snappers had caught that.

I leave thinking, as I always do after an hour with Ed, that there's a vast gulf between the one-dimensional public man and the private football-playing, marathon-running, karaoke-singing, piano-playing, curtain-lederhosen-wearing enthusiast.

Monday 22 September

Midland hotel, Manchester

Hanging over this conference is not just the fall-out from Scotland but the likelihood of Parliament being recalled to approve British military action in Iraq.

David Cameron will not risk a repeat of his defeat over Syria last summer. He won't make a move unless he's certain that this time Ed Miliband is going to stick with him.

A chat with some of the Labour leader's team reveals that there has been careful choreography to avoid a rerun of what happened in August 2013. Miliband's chief of staff was called in to Downing Street last Friday to meet his opposite number. They agreed that Team Cameron would keep schtum during the Labour conference, instead of trying to draw attention away from Labour by stoking up talk of air attacks on Iraq, in return for a guarantee that Ed would deliver the votes for air strikes this Friday.

Public opinion has moved a long way. A recent poll showed majority support for the RAF to mount attacks on both Syria and Iraq. Just a month ago, before the video emerged of IS beheading a British hostage, it was just 37 per cent.

Behind the stage

A discussion with Ed Miliband over a cuppa on what he hopes to achieve this week. The slogan on the back of the stage here – 'Labour's Plan for Britain's Future' – says it all. Voters think he has lots to say about what's wrong with the government and he does have some attractive individual ideas, like last year's headline-stealing energy-price freeze. But he lacks a convincingly coherent plan. So he's about to launch one.

It'll have six points in it. 'Six? Not five or ten?' I ask with a puzzled frown, showing myself to be entirely superficial. Ed looks worried. I tell him the favourite anecdote that prompted this frivolity, about the time Michael Heseltine was positioning himself to succeed Margaret Thatcher. He called to tell me that he was about to unveil a 'ten-point plan to clean up Britain's waterways' (people cared about that sort of thing back then).

'How interesting,' I replied. 'What are the ten points?'

Hezza paused, sighed and said that it didn't matter what the points were. What mattered, he explained none too patiently, was that his plan would clean up Britain's waterways, and, then with added emphasis, he said: 'There won't be nine points and there won't be eleven!' And with that he put down the phone.

Ed's plan sounds as if, like so many of his plans, it is based on a great deal of thought about the policy and very little about how to sell it.

Conference hall

I watch Ed Balls deliver his ironing-board speech. The effort to assure his party that the next Labour government will bring about radical change while reassuring the party's critics that they're serious about the deficit produces a speech that is, well, a little flat.

There's an intriguing wrinkle buried away in what he says, though. When he spells out which tax rise will pay for which spending commitment, what he says is different from what was said in previous speeches. The 'mansion tax' on high-value homes is, all of a sudden, not apparently paying for anything unless, of course, it's paying for an increase in NHS spending which the other Ed can announce in his speech tomorrow.

I make a mental note to keep asking people and see if someone gives the game away.

Midland hotel briefing room

It wasn't only me being superficial. The hacks being briefed with the detail of the six-point plan are struggling with how to summarize a mixture of worthy but somewhat vague goals – 'giving all young people a shot in life' and 'tackling low wages', for example – and hard policy specifics: increasing the number of apprenticeships to match the number of university places and doubling the number of first-time buyers getting on to the housing ladder annually.

There is a collective sense in the room that this is going to be a hard sell to news desks. What has captured attention is the fact that these are goals not for one Parliament but for two; ten years, not five. The man from the *Sun* is beginning to play with the idea that the party leader they like to call 'Red Ed' is twice as ambitious as Stalin or Mao.

Feeling virtuous, I spend a good deal of time trying to encapsulate the plan for my piece on the news at ten and then go back to asking people what the mansion tax is going to pay for.

Conference newsroom

Got it. Finding out things before you're meant to know them is a childish thrill, but it is a thrill nevertheless. I break the story that Labour will pay for an increase in health spending by raising £1.2 billion from a tax on homes over £2 million.

Tuesday 23 September

My hotel room

I wake to the news that the US has launched the first air strikes in Syria against IS targets. They've done it with the support of Bahrain, Jordan, Qatar, Saudi Arabia, the United Arab Emirates and France but without, of course, Britain – and, more surprisingly, without any consultation with the United Nations.

The UN general assembly opens in New York tomorrow so it's quite something for the man elected to end Bush's wars in the Middle East to embark on another one – albeit from the air, not on the ground – as world leaders arrive in the US.

Midland hotel lobby

Team Ed are depressed. First Scotland and now Syria have threatened to overshadow their man's big speech. When I bump into one of his advisers I try to cheer him up. Surely, I argue, this is an opportunity for Ed to look prime ministerial; to address the biggest foreign-policy crisis of our age? After all, I go on, Cameron has agreed not to steal your thunder, so the national stage is waiting to be filled. The eyes of the man I'm speaking to say it all. This story is seen as a problem, not an opportunity.

The reason becomes clear later. Miliband has decided to speak without notes again. He believes this allows him to talk directly to those watching at home. The trouble is that it involves learning the text and he is therefore more reluctant to make late changes. To make matters worse, he lost his planned preparation time when he chose to go to Scotland to try to save the union.

Conference hall

Miliband defines his own speech as the start of an eight-month job application. If that is what it turns out to be, he'll wish he could tear it up and start again.

It is a speech built on a single word – 'together' – repeated over fifty times and a single theme, the claim that Labour, unlike the Tories, will not allow people to struggle on their own.

There is also a single new policy announcement meant to capture it all: extra funding for the NHS paid for not by extra borrowing or extra taxes on ordinary people but by the mansion tax, as I reported yesterday, plus a tax on tobacco firms and an effort to target tax-avoiding hedge funds.

The party love this but they are unmoved when their leader outlines those six ten-year goals. My cameraman rushes up to tell me he has shots of a series of people dozing off.

Not only does Miliband scarcely address the threat of IS – not declaring whether he would back RAF strikes on IS forces in Iraq or Syria – he also fails to once mention the deficit.

When this is pointed out to his aides they take the utterly bizarre step of confirming that he intended to mention the deficit but has forgotten to do so. Before he stood up they'd distributed a few copies of the speech he was meant to give, so perhaps they felt they had no choice.

The result, though, is dreadful for Miliband: he will be dubbed 'the man who forgot the deficit' and his speech will be remembered for what it didn't say, not what it did.

Maybe now it will come as a relief that there is other news competing for the front pages.

Wednesday 24 September

Salford Royal hospital, Manchester

Poor Ed Miliband. Why on earth do they let him do this? The morning after forgetting the deficit he has to face a dozen or more interviews. Every breakfast outlet, every TV channel's political editor, plus the regions, too. He's at a hospital to talk about the announcement he did make but no one is interested in anything much beyond the words he did not utter.

I've already heard his explanation for why he 'forgot the deficit' again and again so I try a different approach. 'How big a problem is it?' I ask.

'It's a big problem . . . a significant one,' he replies cautiously.

I try to help. 'It's the biggest in the G7, almost £100 billion and almost as big as when Britain went to the IMF in the 1970s,' I prompt. So, never mind forgetting a couple of paragraphs, why wasn't it front and centre of his speech?

I have one other question. 'How big a dent will the one new spending cut you announced make in the deficit?'

Limiting child benefit will, he tells me, raise hundreds of millions of pounds.

'Yes,' I say. 'That's a thousandth of the annual deficit.'

His problem is not that he forgot a few words. It is that he risks looking as if he wants to forget the problem altogether.

Friday 26 September

Home

If it weren't for the Commons voting on military action in Iraq I would be at the UKIP conference in sunny Doncaster, listening to a 'bloke who tells it like it really is' and who has produced the most inspired bit of pre-conference propaganda I have ever seen. It doesn't mention politics or UKIP once. It's a video of Nigel Farage on a golf course giving his vocal support to 'Team Europe' in the Ryder Cup.

I text him to explain why I won't be at the conference and to jokily suggest we swap jobs as he's so good on the telly. His reply is a classic. 'You're bloody welcome to it. 24/7 and no money.'

House of Commons

The PM is in full consensus-building, reassurance-maximizing mode. He wants MPs to know that this is not Iraq War 2: The Sequel. What's more, it is not Syria War: The Prequel.

There is, he says, 'a strong case for us to do more in Syria' but he has no plan to do more. He knows that it is not only Ed Miliband who wouldn't wear it. Neither would many Tory backbenchers.

He assures MPs that there will be no 'mission creep' and insists that 'the hallmarks of this campaign will be patience and persistence, not shock and awe'.

Perhaps that should be a wing and a prayer. The wings of just six

Tornado bombers – that's a third of the aircraft that flew over Libya and fewer than the number sent by the Danish, Saudi and UAE air forces – and the prayer that somehow everything will turn out OK in the end.

The House votes overwhelmingly for limited military action. Very few MPs are prepared to argue that we should do nothing as we might make things worse. Very few argue that we should go much further. So Britain will send half a dozen planes. Like Belgium.

The great untold story of the past few years is Britain's diminishing significance on the world stage. Many would argue that it was a statement of post-imperial arrogance and extravagance to claim, as Douglas Hurd did when he was foreign secretary, that we should 'punch above our weight' in international affairs. Others would say that to do anything else is to abdicate our historic and moral responsibilities.

What stuns me is that we are watching this happen with barely a word being said about it.

Saturday 27 September

Home, the kitchen

Nigel Farage is again proving his ability to talk fluent human. In an interview on the *Today* programme he is asked to confirm that a new UKIP promise to cut taxes (by increasing the personal allowance and cutting the 40p rate to 35p for 'middle earners') will help millionaires. There is only one truthful answer. It is 'yes'. Most politicians would avoid giving that answer at all costs, even if it made them sound evasive and unconvincing. Their aim would be simply to avoid handing their opponents and the press a quote to justify the headline 'Tax policy helps millionaires, admits X'. Farage, though, concedes that this would be one consequence of the policy before going on to insist that that is not its overall purpose.

If only more interviews could be like this. Of course, Farage has the luxury of being able to live by different rules because few expect him ever to get the chance to implement his ideas.

The sitting room

A break to watch the Ryder Cup is interrupted by a news alert. Another Tory MP is defecting to UKIP. It is the delightfully named Mark Reckless, whose actions are anything but. This is a cold, calculated act of revenge against David Cameron on the eve of his party conference. Reckless it was who led the Tory backbench rebellion that forced Cameron to secure a cut in the EU budget. When the PM came back from Brussels with the cut agreed, he informed Reckless that his rebellion had made absolutely no difference as the decision would have been taken in any case. Reckless was told that he was pointless, and now he has decided to show that this was a terrible miscalculation.

To lose one MP on the eve of your conference may be regarded as misfortune; to lose two looks like carelessness, as Lady Bracknell might have said. A minister has quit his post asking for privacy for him and his family while they deal with the fall-out of a Sunday newspaper story. That can only mean one thing: a sex scandal. But which kind? Prostitutes, rent boys, S&M parties? The truth is much more banal and much more pathetic. The member for Braintree has sent a photograph of his own member, via social media, to a blonde, twenty-something PR girl called Sophie whom he'd never actually met and who turns out to be not just a tabloid reporter but a man. On one hand this self-harming, career-ending online flashing is hilarious, not least given the revelation that the MP was wearing paisley pyjamas at the time. On the other it is truly sad. Brooks Newmark is a bright and successful guy with five children who's been entrapped. And for what?

Sunday 28 September

Conservative party conference, International Convention Centre, Birmingham

Fury. Rage. A desire for retribution. More than panic these are the emotions in the air when I arrive at the Tory conference. It is only days since Mark Reckless denied both publicly and privately that he would follow his friend Douglas Carswell out of the Tory party. His old colleagues have decided not just to get mad but to get even. They have dubbed him a liar and a traitor.

David Cameron begins the day with a very English display of understatement. It was, he says, 'frustrating'. By the time he tours the conference receptions he has turned up the volume. At one event he tells Tories that Reckless only got 'his fat arse' on the Commons green benches in the first place thanks to the efforts of the Tories and it is now their duty to make sure he never does so again. He vows to ensure that Rochester, the seat Reckless represents, is won back for the Conservatives. He is as good as conceding that the by-election triggered by the first UKIP defector, the one in Clacton next Thursday, is a lost cause.

I'm told the joke going round the PM's suite is that even on the day of Reckless's 'treachery', the honourable member for Rochester is 'not the biggest prick on the front page of the Sundays'. History will record that he was overshadowed by those paisley pyjamas.

Monday 29 September

Hyatt Regency hotel, Birmingham

My annual breakfast with the chancellor. He gets the chance to put his spin on what he's going to announce and to ensure that it's circulated throughout the BBC's many outlets. I get a sneak preview of his party conference speech, which gives me a bit longer to prepare tonight's evening-news bulletin.

Five years ago, just before the last general election, I remember George Osborne proclaiming an impending 'age of austerity'. What's more, to underline his point, he was preparing to tell the country that we would all have to work two years longer before we could draw a pension.

Today the message is much the same. Osborne is determined to get the political debate back on to 'the economy, stupid' and to put the deficit at the heart of it. His centrepiece this time is a pledge to freeze all working-age benefits for two years, saving £3 billion. With the economy growing and polling day just months away, you might think that this would be the time for a pre-election giveaway. Think again. George Osborne seems convinced that a pre-election takeaway is the key to a Tory victory. He believes that it will put Labour on the spot, forcing them either to defend unpopular welfare benefits and explain where they would find other savings or to admit that they are committed to higher spending and higher borrowing.

Another appeal of the benefits freeze for the Tories is that it doesn't involve actually taking money away from people now. Instead, it cancels future increases. The much-hated 'bedroom tax' raised just £400 million and caused huge resentment and anger. Compare that to changing the pension age, which saved half a trillion pounds, or up-rating benefits by the CPI rather than the higher RPI measure of inflation, which also saved a small fortune. In both cases people didn't miss what they hadn't yet got.

To lessen accusations that this is another example of Tory injustice Osborne is also preparing to unveil what he knows will be dubbed a 'Google tax' – an effort to force Google and other high-tech firms to pay their fair share of taxes.

It is clever. Osborne always is. Yet I can't help wondering whether it isn't too clever by half. Benefits cuts have proved to be popular but they involve taking money away from 5 million of the working poor. It will look tough but will it look fair?

One thing has changed in the years that we've been having these breakfasts. George Osborne is about two stone lighter and our plates of bacon, sausage, egg, bread, mushrooms, beans and tomato have been replaced by frugal bowls of porridge with a dribble of honey. This is indeed the age of austerity.

Tuesday 30 September

Hyatt Regency hotel

I sit down in front of the prime minister and notice, to my irritation, that my hands are shaking slightly. Perhaps I simply haven't had enough sleep; perhaps it is because I have come determined not to allow David Cameron to sail through another interview unruffled.

On the morning after George Osborne's announcement that the benefits of the working poor must be frozen for two years, the prime minister has succeeded in breezily suggesting that this is just one of those difficult but inevitable decisions and is perfectly fair, because the rate of increase of benefits in recent years has outstripped the increase in wages. I put it to him that this is a justification only a policy-maker would offer. The man or woman on the street is worried about how to meet the gas bill or pay for a school uniform, not the relative position of two lines on a graph.

He often talks about benefits as if they were paid to people who don't work and paid for by people who do. The truth is that the benefits freeze will affect more than twice as many working families as those without work – 7 million compared with 3 million.

I put it to him that the £500 loss for a single household on £25,000 a year would be spent by some at this conference just on dinner. Cameron keeps his cool and continues calmly to make his point. Look closely though, as I always do, and you can see him swallow hard. That's the clip for tonight's news.

Earlier a copy emerged of a guide given to senior Tories advising them to ignore any difficult questions and talk instead about the 'long-term economic plan'. All cuts are referred to as 'difficult decisions'. Cameron is the expert at this. I cannot force him to answer; I cannot control what he says. What I can do is ensure that my questions punch through.

For a long time I've wanted to ask the prime minister to explain what he intends to do if he is not able to deliver the renegotiation with the EU pledged before the promised referendum. He ignores the question: 'My view is I will succeed in this renegotiation.' I point out that his refusal to talk about a plan B is precisely what he criticized Alex Salmond for in the Scottish referendum. He ignores that prompt, too. The truth is there is no plan B.

— OCTOBER —

Wednesday 1 October

Birmingham ICC

David Cameron as Julia Roberts. That's the curious image which pops into my mind as I watch the prime minister plead with the British public not to dump him, to give him a second chance. Remember the scene in *Notting Hill* where Roberts's character, the rich, privileged, spoiled superstar, tells Hugh Grant, the poor, bruised, hurt Mr Ordinary, 'I'm also just a girl, standing in front of a boy, asking him to love her'? The Cameron version doesn't ask the country to love him but to trust him. 'I'm not a perfect leader,' he says. 'I am your public servant, standing here wanting to make our country better.'

The plea to 'trust me' is the thread running though every word and every promise of his party conference speech – undoubtedly his best ever in terms of delivery but one that none the less raises many more questions than it answers.

Gone are the warnings of more pain, more spending cuts, more austerity. In their place is a promise of better times ahead and a pledge of cuts of another kind – to working people's taxes.

I'll deliver £7 billion in tax cuts, he promises. How will they be paid for? What will be cut to pay for them? Why should the working poor – or those he likes to call 'hard-working families'– see their tax credits cut in real terms while those earning much more enjoy an increase in their post-tax income?

I'll do 'what Britain needs' on curbing EU immigration, he says. But what exactly does Britain need? He doesn't say. How will he persuade twenty-seven other EU leaders to give us whatever it is? No answer.

The most powerful section is the PM's righteous indignation in the face of allegations that he can't be trusted with the NHS. How dare they suggest that I, who have carried a child in my arms into the care of doctors and nurses, will do anything other than protect the NHS? he demands. His voice breaks at the memory of his lost son Ivan. His wife Samantha sheds quiet tears. No one can doubt their sincerity but that is not enough in itself to answer the independent report warning that the NHS could be £30 billion short of the funds it needs by the end of the next Parliament.

As I spin up and down the tape of the speech I notice that every so often Cameron pauses and then stares straight down the lens of the TV camera to speak directly to voters at home. Although it is his most self-assured performance in years, the shift in message betrays a lack of confidence that the public are ready to vote to extend the age of austerity and for more 'difficult decisions'.

Sunday 5 October

Liberal Democrat party conference, Glasgow, Crowne Plaza hotel

Welcome back to Glasgow. I've just been shouted at and shoved by a man at the bar during the Liberal Democrats' conference. Not a Lib Dem, you understand. Dearie me, no. This is an angry local who spotted me chatting to Danny Alexander and who clearly regards us both as the enemy. After some fairly innocuous pushing I end the evening with half a pint of beer down my shirt and an unwelcome reminder that the anger I experienced here a couple of weeks ago has not subsided. Someone calls the police – an overreaction, as it turns out – but what is worrying is the sense that you just can't be sure.

Ironically, I spent the journey here examining how the BBC's independent complaints process is dealing with complaints about the way I reported my run-in with Alex Salmond at his pre-referendum news conference. I have told the BBC that I am perfectly happy to put my hands up to choosing my words badly – it would have been better if I had said that the first minister 'did not address those points' rather than the balder 'didn't answer'– but I would be very unhappy if there were to be a finding that my report was inaccurate or unfair.

I have the full backing of my bosses but that is not the same as having persuaded the man who answers the complaints of licence-fee payers. To the BBC's credit, the process strives very hard to hold a large and powerful organization to account, to do so independently and to give aggrieved viewers and listeners a right of appeal. Indeed, several rights of appeal. To its discredit, it is costly, bureaucratic, byzantine and is obliged to take seriously complaints that are politically motivated attempts to bully journalists into submission or caution.

Responses made during the complaints process always include a paragraph informing people that if they are not satisfied they can write back and trigger another review. Then another and then one more. That was the course taken by one outraged viewer after I once, groping for a simile under pressure at the end of a tiring day, said that Peter Mandelson 'attracts trouble rather like manure attracts flies'. Before I'd even finished the sentence, I realized I had just equated the man who was effectively Britain's new deputy prime minister with a steaming pile of horse shit. I instantly texted Mandelson to apologize, wrote a blog pointing out that I'd been a fool and told the BBC press office to point all press inquiries in that direction.

The complainant insisted that my choice of words betrayed a consistent bias against the Labour party. I'm damned if I know how this allegation, without other evidence, could ever be satisfactorily investigated, but three appeals later the BBC Trust did employ someone, at a cost of many hundreds of pounds a day, to watch the tape, transcribe what was said and interview all relevant parties before replying to the effect that 'Nick Robinson chose his words badly, something he himself recognized instantly and apologized for. That apology has been accepted.'

The BBC should of course acknowledge and correct errors it makes quickly and openly but it should resist those who demand trials into alleged 'thought crimes' on the basis of a few words, uttered on the spur of the moment, that could have been more elegantly phrased.

This is a less than perfect ending to an otherwise perfect day. It's my birthday and, more importantly, earlier I took my eldest, Alice, to start her new life studying English at Oxford University. I'm very proud of her; so proud that I can almost forgive her for the birthday present she gave me. It's a T-shirt bearing the message: 'With a body like this, who needs hair?'

Monday 6 October

Portakabin, Scottish Exhibition and Conference Centre car park

'Give him the bullet!' the deputy prime minister barks into his phone. His security detail look on, concerned. Nick Clegg repeats his instruction, this time more insistently. 'Just give him the bullet!' My mind races. Who is it that the DPM is ordering to be taken out? Clegg hangs up, smiles and, turning to the open-mouthed *Today* programme team, explains that his children are having a row about whose turn it is with their toy gun.

Then he settles down for what is his eighth interview of the morning. He tells me and *Today*'s Mishal Husain that they have all begun in roughly the same way: 'You're hopeless, no one likes you, you're going to lose – have you anything to say to that, Deputy Prime Minister?'

His answer is to trumpet the merits of what he calls the 'liberal centre ground' and to promise to moderate the Tories' divisive social policies and Labour's dangerous economic plans. The problem with the slogan 'moderation' is that it's not something anyone would ever stitch on to a banner or chant at a protest.

So instead the Lib Dems have decided to allow their party to let off steam by slagging off their coalition partners. Liars. Arrogant. Absurd. Obsessed by cuts. Those are just a few of the descriptions that have been used by senior Lib Dems. All's fair in love, war and party conferences, but I wonder whether the public will buy the idea that those who have been and remain close colleagues can now legitimately be spoken of in such vituperative tones.

What's more, when you strip away the hyperbole you can see that there's still plenty of scope for the Tories and Liberal Democrats to stay together beyond the next election. Balancing the books on the backs of the poor is immoral, say the Lib Dems, who insist they would never countenance a benefits freeze. They would, however, contemplate – indeed, they've already agreed to – a 1 per cent cap on benefit rises, which is not all that different. They oppose an arbitrary timetable for an EU referendum but are they against a referendum? Not at all – it's just that it must be held in the right circumstances. These are policy gaps just waiting to be bridged by people who have learned to understand and trust each other. What may get in the way, though, is rhetoric used on both sides which will lead both parties' activists and supporters to regard any deal as a terrible betrayal.

Tuesday 7 October

George Square, Glasgow

I've come to George Square, until recently the spiritual home of Yes – the place where, night after night, saltires were waved, protest songs sung, banners held proudly aloft – to record some interviews for a radio documentary on democracy; to ask Sarah and Max, two seventeen-year-olds who took opposite sides in the referendum debate, whether it's possible to bottle any of the excitement and enthusiasm of those weeks and sprinkle it on Britain's flagging political system. Their eyes light up at the memory of what they have lived through. Neither had any political involvement before but neither would give up their interest now. Both display passion and at the same time respect each other's views. The ebullient spirit of George Square and the much quieter passion of the No campaign each depended, it seems to me, on a shared belief that every single person's vote mattered, combined with a real sense of jeopardy on one hand and a belief in the possibility of a completely new start on the other.

This may be impossible, and even unhealthy, to replicate without constantly presenting the electorate with a choice about whether the country should survive in its current form, but surely we have to try to spread the belief in democracy to more Sarahs and Maxes.

The manager's office, Crowne Plaza hotel

'Sorry, I'll be a bit late,' I text Paddy Ashdown. 'Blame the police.'

Actually, it is not the fault of Police Scotland that I am now being asked to give a statement on the alleged assault I suffered in the bar the other night. It was, I explain, just a bit of verbals, or what footballers call 'handbags', during which, as someone tried to intervene, some beer got spilled. I sign a statement that makes it clear I was not assaulted and don't want to pursue the matter further. If someone reported this to the police then my friends in the press won't be far behind.

The bar

When I explain what held me up 'the captain', as Captain Ashdown, formerly of the Special Boat Section, is known to his friends, refrains from remarking that he's faced rather more serious assaults in his day. He is surveying the political terrain for his latest campaign. 'The terms of dialogue have beautifully changed,' he tells me, pointing out the gap into which he believes his Lib Dem troops can march. They will attack the Tories for promising unfunded tax cuts that can only be paid for by the poor or by cutting public services. They will attack Labour for having no plan to rescue the economy.

The Lib Dems have suffered heavy losses, their leader is wounded and bleeding and they are surrounded on all sides with no obvious means of escape but the captain is sure they will get out alive. Like all the best military leaders he is very persuasive – at the time.

All these conference chats – the only real value these events have for me – convince me of one thing. This party's heart may beat on the left but its head tells it that the right is where power still lies. The Lib Dem leadership is mentally preparing for another deal with the Tories, a deal in which they will concede an EU referendum in return for some as yet unspecified concession. They believe that the only way Britain will vote to stay in the EU is if the Tories lead the Yes campaign. They fear that an alliance with Labour would destroy them in the few places, largely in the south of England, where they remain strong.

The Glitter Room, Hummingbird club

Eat your heart out, Freddie! I am singing 'Bohemian Rhapsody', badly and out of tune. Again. This time I am witnessed by only a few colleagues and I am smiling. The first time was just weeks after I became the BBC's political editor, in front of 11 million viewers of *Children in Need*, and it took me years to recover from it.

But karaoke on a smaller scale is now my cure of choice for those end-of-conference, three-weeks-living-out-of-a-suitcase, eaten-too-much, slept-too-little, can't-bear-to-listen-to-another-bloody-speech, missing-my-family blues. Singing raises the spirits, but not half so much as the sight of my BBC colleagues' efforts, notably John Pienaar rapping and James Landale singing a nine-minute version of 'American Pie' without having to look at the words once.

Wednesday 8 October

Conference newsroom, SECC

I am nursing my hangover and sore throat when a colleague asks, 'Do you think Nick Clegg might announce he's quitting?'

'What?' I reply impatiently. 'Of course he's not going to bloody quit. Why on earth would anyone think he would be?'

'You've clearly not been looking at Twitter.'

Twitter is, well, atwitter with rumours (fiction) and speculation (reporting based on fiction) that Clegg is about to resign. And people are staking their hard-earned cash on the notion that there could be something in these 'stories'. The bookmakers Paddy Power have cut the price they are offering on Clegg stepping down before the general election from 13–2 to 2–1.

It's complete and utter, gold-plated, twenty-four-carat nonsense and, God help us, we're bound to get more of it between now and next May.

The executive boardroom, SECC

Are they jeans or are they chinos? The deputy prime minister antici-pates my question as he greets me for our annual conference chat. His wife, Miriam, is delighted, he tells me, that for once it's his clothes that are being talked about. This morning's *Guardian* reports that 'Nick Clegg has attracted mockery for changing into at least four different outfits in one day at the Liberal Democrats' autumn conference in Glasgow'. This, the paper tells us, 'smells of a suit-wearer ill at ease in his weekend clothes, rather than the relaxed, regular-guy look he's going for'. Silly me. Should have included that on last night's news.

Leaders' speeches always have the predictable 'plague on all your houses' soundbites but what can make them interesting is what they tell you about what's going on in the minds of those who are, or want to be, in government. Clegg tells me that he's going to dwell on the rise of what he sees as something very 'unBritish': the rise of the politics of populism, fear and extremism, which he's going to link to the riots of 2011. His belief is that both can be explained by a widespread sense of powerlessness.

Conference hall

It is this theme that shines through the speech when I listen to it in the hall. I may no longer be the fresh-faced outsider, Clegg tells the country, but someone 'has to stand up for liberal Britain'. A man who has been personally vilified and whose party's rating is below 10 per cent in the polls believes there is, that there must be, a space for what he calls 'decent people with decent values'.

Ever since the coalition was formed I have felt that the Lib Dems would pick up eventually as liberal-minded voters contemplate an unpalatable choice between unrestrained governments of the left and right. So far I have been proved comprehensively wrong. Yet, as the conference draws to a close, in my bones I still sense that the Lib Dems will not be wiped out in the way their enemies hope.

Friday 10 October

BBC Westminster

Those David Cameron once called 'loonies, fruitcakes and closet racists' are savouring their revenge today in Clacton. They've elected their first MP.

Back at Westminster, I am assessing the impact of the UKIP landslide in Essex as well as of the terrifyingly near miss Labour experienced in another by-election held yesterday, Heywood and Middleton in Greater Manchester.

In a corridor of the BBC I bump into my favourite professor, John Curtice. Only his hair, which has a habit of pointing in every direction other than downwards, reveals that he has been up since yesterday working on electoral data for the overnight election programme. 'Guess what the projection of the House of Commons would have looked like on the basis of Clacton?' he asks me excitedly. Veteran watchers of BBC by-election programmes may recall that this was the kind of information unveiled in the old days by Peter Snow and his swingometer. 'Just a bit of fun, just a bit of fun!' he'd bark, having predicted the elimination of the Tory party and the arrival of a one-party state. After one set of statistics appeared to suggest that Neil Kinnock would rule for a thousand years this interlude was scrapped as a bit of an editorial nightmare. However, the data-crunchers can't resist secretly making these calculations anyway, and according to John, if Clacton were repeated up and down the country UKIP would form a government with 331 out of 650 seats in the Commons. More important is Curtice's overnight calculation that UKIP is still hurting the Tories much more than Labour, even as it proves able to attract the white working-class voters in northern cities Labour once took for granted. The Farage effect, he believes, gives Ed Miliband a net twenty-seat bonus – enough to see him comfortably installed in Number 10.

On the morning after his victory and near-victory, Farage is talking of holding the balance of power after the next election and of becoming the minister for Europe, having won more Tory seats in the south and Labour seats in the north.

Despite the extraordinary rise of UKIP, I don't buy this. The Tories gave up on Clacton, believing it to be unwinnable. Instead they're throwing the kitchen sink at winning Rochester, portraying Mark Reckless as a lying opportunist. They also believe that, come the general election, there'll be a 'Cameron v Miliband' squeeze, with one committed to holding an EU referendum, the other not. This could work. After all, UKIP did very well in the 2009 European elections but ended up with only 3 per cent of the vote at the 2010 general election.

What's more, the first-past-the-post electoral system used for Westminster elections could be very cruel to UKIP. They could amass an awful lot of votes in an awful lot of places and get very few MPs.

Even the optimists in UKIP have talked only of a handful: Farage, certainly; maybe Carswell again, plus one or two more. With that level of support, they'd be very unlikely to hold the balance of power. Farage will not get to be minister for Europe and the self-styled 'people's army' will not breach the walls of power.

Having said that, I can't help remembering that not so very long ago UKIP were seen as extremists for whom nobody but angry, former Tory, blazer-wearing colonels in the south would vote; who could win only those elections held under proportional representation and who would never top 30 per cent in a poll.

Sunday 12 October

They simply don't know what to say or do.

Speaking from Andrew Marr's sofa, Harriet Harman declares there will be 'no wobble' and no leadership challenge. Hardly a rallying cry. More an uncanny echo of Jim Mortimer's lukewarm backing during the 1983 general election campaign, when the Labour general secretary announced that 'the unanimous view of the campaign committee is that Michael Foot is the leader of the Labour party and speaks for the party', highlighting the very opposite of what he had hoped to convey.

Then Boris takes to the sofa, asserts that UKIP and the Tories are doppelgangers and invites the electorate to vote for the real thing. The man who once highlighted the benefits of immigration, insisting that immigrants work hard, pay their taxes and contribute to London's extraordinary growth, has changed his tune, now saying that it should be curbed.

And this on a day when one poll (probably wrong) puts UKIP support at 25 per cent and pundits' predictions give them anywhere between twenty-five and 128 seats.

I don't believe this. I remember how the SDP's massive poll ratings – above 50 per cent in 1982 – evaporated, producing just six seats in the 1983 election.

Nevertheless UKIP are peaking in the run-up to a general election. They have created, and are very good at creating, a sense of momentum and the electorate can smell the fear emanating from the other parties.

Monday 13 October

House of Commons gallery

I've taken my perch above the green benches to watch UKIP's first elected MP being sworn in. One of the men in tights who run the Commons was laughing earlier at the fact that the Tory whips have punished the 'new boy' by taking away the large, smart office he had as a Tory MP and allocating him a small, poky one instead. No one knows where Douglas Carswell will sit. He'll be no more welcome on the opposition benches than on his old side of the Commons. Nervous Labour MPs mutter, 'Your mates are over there,' as, perhaps wisely, he shakes the speaker's hand and exits without taking a seat at all.

A beaming Farage is here to witness this moment in history. He has every reason to be chuffed, given that UKIP's new status has just been acknowledged by the broadcasters. They say he'll be invited to take part in the leaders' TV election debates, whereas the Greens and the SNP will not. I foresee trouble ahead.

Tuesday 14 October

House of Commons

Gordon Brown is back and doing what he loves best: laying into the Tories. In a debate about what comes next for Scotland, post-referendum, he accuses David Cameron of betraying the Scots by concealing his EVEL (English votes for English laws) plans to down-grade the status of Scottish MPs until after the voting was over.

So Labour are attacking the Tories for being anti-Scots while the Tories risk appearing to suggest that Scottish MPs should be second-class.

Don't the two big unionist parties realize that if they both attack each other as lacking political legitimacy, Scottish voters may agree that they are both right and be driven into the arms of the nationalists?

Wednesday 15 October

The Victoria line

An interesting day ahead. Ed Miliband's first Prime Minister's Questions since that conference speech. The first, too, since Labour's near-death experience at the hands of UKIP in a by-election they won by just over 600 votes. This on a day when unemployment is expected to drop below 2 million. Stand by for the Tories to try to finish him off.

Green room, Daily Politics

Just minutes before PMQs, the phone goes. It's Labour's Bob Roberts.

Ed Miliband has a surprise for the prime minister: a recording of the Tory welfare minister Lord Freud telling a Conservative fringe meeting that disabled people shouldn't be paid the minimum wage. He'll send me the tape, which I can use just before he stands up. Miliband needed something to save him today. This could be it.

Yet I want to see the context. David Freud is an easy target. He can be presented as a wealthy former investment banker who has been rewarded with a Tory peerage for cutting the benefits of the poor. This is to ignore the fact that he works unpaid, could have a much easier life, believes in reforming the system and was first hired to do it not by the Tories but by Tony Blair.

The e-mail Labour send does not give the full context and the recording they forward is hard to hear clearly, but even in the few moments I have it is apparent that Freud was responding to someone arguing that it might be preferable for those with a severe disability who could not otherwise get a job to be paid less than the minimum wage – and to have their income topped up with benefits – than not to have the chance of a job at all. It would at least give them the experience of work and boost their self-esteem.

No matter. Ed is in a hole and Lord Freud is his ladder out of it.

'These are not the words of someone who ought to be in charge of policy relating to the welfare of disabled people. Surely someone holding those views can't possibly stay in his government?' he declares.

David Cameron could defend his minister. He could explain the context. He could ask for time to study what was said. But he dares not give any impression that the Tories are targeting the disabled so he replies that these are not the views of the government.

On air, straight afterwards, I try to explain both what was said and why, but add that Freud's comments will be seen as 'heartless' and will come back to haunt him.

In the studio, the Tory guest is fellow welfare minister Esther McVey. She breaks the first rule of communication by picking up my phrase. These comments, she says, will haunt Freud.

How easily a minister's reputation is trashed.

Edit suite

The pack is in full cry now. Freud has apologized. Labour are demanding his resignation. Disabled campaigning groups, led by MENCAP, are condemning him for suggesting they are second-class citizens.

No one discusses the question he was asked. What if the minimum wage prices some disabled people out of jobs that would enhance their wellbeing? I investigate whether anyone has ever made this case. What do you know? Until a few years back, it was official MENCAP policy to do exactly what they have condemned Lord Freud for having the temerity even to contemplate.

Freud chose his words poorly on a very sensitive subject and I've no idea who's right about whether this is or is not a good idea. But this sort of witch-hunt revolts me. It closes down debate and will merely serve to convince yet more people that they should never, ever risk having anything to do with politics.

A good day for Ed. A terrible one for public life.

Thursday 16 October

Home

Feeling dreadful. I've come down with my annual post-conference, post-adrenaline-rush man flu. I couldn't have picked a worse time to be coughing and wheezing. I'm recording *Have I Got News for You* tonight and need my wits to be sharp. If I pull out the kids will be disappointed. I dose myself with Lemsip and mug up on news trivia: cows wearing nappies in Bavaria and the 50ft giant 'crabzilla' spotted off the south coast.

Dressing room, London Television Centre

First the good: I meet tonight's host, Frank Skinner, and team leaders Paul Merton and Ian Hislop. Then the bad: the hour alone in a dressing room with a pile of this week's newspapers, some lukewarm food from the canteen and my thoughts, which are the same as they always are. Why did I agree to do this? I can never be as funny as the comedians. I'm only here because the tub of lard cancelled. What on earth do I say when they rip the piss out of me?

Tonight they're bound to play the video of the demo outside BBC

Glasgow with the banner calling me a liar. I don't want to get into defending myself as my report is still the subject of an official complaint. And I don't want to wind up the Nats any further as that will look like a declaration of war. I can't afford to appear smug about it. All I can do is keep smiling and put on my best 'Am I bovvered?' expression.

Studio

The audience laugh at my warm-up joke. What actors call 'Doctor Stage' begins to kick in – performing is a great, if temporary, cure for feeling ill. Frank Skinner introduces me as having come from my sickbed tonight, an effort that would in the past, he says, have been cause for admiration but now, in the era of Ebola, creates 'abject terror'.

I sail through questions on UKIP, Lord Freud, Kim Jong-un's cheese addiction and even manage to drop in my favourite recent poll finding: that voters in America rated head lice higher than candidates for Congress. And then it comes . . .

'You got accused of political bias recently,' says Skinner as the picture of that banner fills the screen. 'Yes,' I reply 'there was a warm welcome in Scotland.'

I'm unsure how this is going to play out. Paul, then Ian, come to my rescue with jokey lines, while Frank persists in apparently trying to elicit further comment from me. I laugh nervously until the penny drops. He is aping what I did by repeatedly asking the same question. When the gag gets a response he moves on.

Phew. Survived.

Friday 17 October

Home, the sofa

Watch *HIGNFY* to see how much of the two hours of topical wit we recorded makes it into the twenty-five minutes or so that are aired.

In my case, not much. I check Twitter for reactions. There are complaints. Quite a few. They all accuse me not of lying but of a flagrant display of chest hair.

Monday 20 October

St Pancras International

I've come to the Eurostar terminal to film a piece inspired by yesterday's splash in *The Sunday Times*, which reveals that Cameron is considering making a promise to cap the number of EU immigrants.

It was perfectly timed for the farewell visit to London of the outgoing president of the European Commission, José Manuel Barroso, who assured Andrew Marr yesterday morning that European immigration is not a big problem in the UK given that, after all, unemployment is on the way down; that a cap would be illegal; that free movement of people is a key founding principle of the EU, and, to top it all, that the foreign secretary has made a grave error by talking, as he did last week, of lighting a fire under the EU.

Today, in a speech at Chatham House, the big cheese in the Brussels bureaucracy goes further. The Scottish referendum should have been a reminder to everyone, he warns pro-Europeans, of the dangers of having no positive message. There is a simple rule in politics that the Tories seem to have forgotten: never inflate your party's hopes only to deflate them later. The gap – gulf, to be more accurate – between what the prime minister needs to secure to satisfy his party and what other EU leaders will agree to appears to be getting bigger and bigger.

A restaurant in Mayfair

Just off Park Lane, around the corner from the Dorchester, is the place Ed Miliband has picked for a 'getting-to-know-you-better dinner' with me and our wives. The marble-topped bar, leather chairs and low lighting – not to mention the image, on the door to the men's loo, of a hunter pointing his shotgun at the sky – give it the feel of a gentlemen's club. An unexpected choice, you might think, for a man who stands up to the rich and privileged. 'The owner's a supporter,' Ed explains, ordering a cranberry juice.

His wife Justine, an environmental lawyer, has had a busy day in court representing Colombian farmers in a David-versus-Goliath struggle against the oil giant BP. It's obvious that Ed is immensely proud of her.

The four of us talk about what polite, middle-class couples in smart restaurants tend to talk about – children, holidays, books we've read and, of course, politics. What's striking, though, is that Ed makes no attempt to use this conversation, one of the longest we're likely to have before the election, to make a pitch as to why he's ready to be prime minister.

Indeed, he and Justine are keen to steer the conversation away from what life might be like for them and their family if they get to Number 10. Do they not want to tempt fate or are they wary of seeming to take the result for granted?

I detect, though, something more than natural political caution. It's doubt and uncertainty. Ed, who is a clever, engaging and self-deprecating guy in private, jokes about the time Neil Kinnock was campaigning for him during the Labour leadership election. Neil called on the audience to back Ed for leader . . . 'although I wouldn't wish this job on my worst enemy'. Ed's demeanour suggests that he is thinking, if only I knew then what I know now.

It's all in stark contrast with a dinner I had with the last leader of the opposition. In 2009 David Cameron invited me – no wives – to a restaurant and did everything he could to convince me that he had what it took to be prime minister, inviting me to cross-examine him. In truth, that evening was less enjoyable, even though privately David is also very good company. But it made more of an impact.

Tonight Pippa and I left Mayfair having had a fine meal and pleasant conversation with a couple we both liked, but on the way home we found ourselves wondering whether Ed has one of the key requirements for high office: an apparently never-ending and almost irrational supply of self-belief. On the other hand, perhaps that was the mistake his brother made . . .

Tuesday 21 October

Millbank

Borrowing is going up again, according to the latest figures – 10 per cent in the last year – just as the Tories have been taunting Ed Miliband as 'the man who forgot the deficit'. If he's really gutsy he may be able to turn that insult back on them. To talk of more tax cuts after the next election is to, well, forget the increasing deficit. One senior Tory tells me that, whatever the economics, they have no political worries about this at all because 'we have a twenty-point lead on fiscal probity'.

The thickness of Nigel Farage's Teflon coating is being tested again.

First, UKIP have released a recording of a calypso sung in a mock-Caribbean accent by ageing ex-Radio 1 DJ Mike Read. Its rip-snorting lyrics include a line about 'illegal immigrants in every town'. Read is maintaining that there is 'nothing remotely racist' about the song and has accused critics of losing their sense of humour.

Secondly, the party has made an alliance in the European Parliament with the representative of a party led by a misogynistic Holocaust-denier which even Marine Le Pen, the leader of the French Front National, has shunned as being too extreme.

Farage has been desperate to find someone from another country – anyone, it seems – to join his group in the Parliament to swell the ranks so that it represents enough countries to qualify for millions of pounds of taxpayers' subsidies. Typically, he parries questions with a show of candour. This guy joined their group to save it, he says, and it will ensure that there is at least one group in Strasbourg prepared to be critical of the Brussels bureaucrats.

No one else would get away with it.

Wednesday 22 October

Prime Minister's Questions

An entirely forgettable exchange about the NHS. Miliband asks several variants of 'Does the prime minister accept that the NHS in England is going to the dogs?' and Cameron counters with his favourite riposte: 'Will the leader of the opposition agree to an inquiry into the Labour-run NHS in Wales, which has already gone to the dogs?'

The entire half-hour is memorable only for the angry member of the public who stands up to hurl a bag of marbles at the squabbling MPs below him. Luckily for them, and unfortunately for him, all he hits is the bullet-proof glass screen installed after a protester struck Tony Blair on the shoulder with a bag of purple powder.

As today's demonstrator is bundled away he refuses to explain what he's angry about, other than declaring, 'I'm an English gentleman. I have the right to say my bit.' Quite so. Shame he lost his marbles, though.

Broadcasting House

A sigh of relief ripples round Broadcasting House. No need any more for endless meetings about whether or not Radio 1 should play UKIP's calypso if it reaches number one in the charts. Mike Read, who is still employed by the BBC, has apologized for it and ordered it to be withdrawn from sale just in time to save Auntie's blushes. A party spokesman blames the 'right-on media' and their 'synthetic outrage' for spoiling 'a bit of fun'. Surely this is a time, he says, for a press release condemning 'political correctness gone mad'?

Two new polls confirm the UKIP paradox. The first shows them 13 per cent ahead in the Rochester by-election. The second records support for staying in the EU as higher than it has been in years. Further proof that the rise of UKIP has much less to do with anger at the EU than rage at the political establishment as a whole.

Home

Still struggling with man flu, I head home early to hear the news of an attack – a real one this time – on the Canadian Parliament. Somebody with 'a long gun' has run in through the public entrance and started shooting moments after he, or possibly an accomplice, killed a soldier at Ottawa's war memorial. He was stopped not by the police but by the sergeant-at-arms, the parliamentary official in black robes who carries the ceremonial gold mace into the House of Commons before every sitting. Before Kevin Vickers, a former Canadian mountie, was put in charge of security at the Parliament he said: 'I told them that if they made me their sergeant-at-arms, there would be no walls built around Canada's parliamentary buildings.' I hope he sticks to that view. I hope we do, too.

Thursday 23 October

Outside Moorfields eye hospital

I'm in the radio car listening to the boss of the NHS in England arguing for more money for the health service, more change and a much more aggressive campaign to cut obesity, alcohol abuse and smoking.

He's calling for an extra £8 billion to be spent on the health service each year by 2020. This in the same week we discovered that the deficit is getting bigger, not smaller. The sums are not huge but they may still be very hard to find.

He is seeking an above-inflation, or real-terms, rise of 1.5 per cent, half the rate of increase during the 'Thatcher cuts'. But the funding needed will only be this low if the NHS can make savings at a pace it has never before achieved and if we can all be persuaded, cajoled or forced to eat, drink and smoke less.

This means that politicians and, of course, voters may have to swallow more NHS reorganization, more interference from the 'nanny state' – minimum alcohol pricing, banning smoking in parks, plain packaging of cigarettes and vouchers to reward fat people for taking exercise – and more involvement of the private sector.

There could easily be an all-party consensus on this but the NHS is our national religion and politicians can't resist posing as the only true believers and casting their opponents as heretics hell-bent on the destruction of all that's good and true.

Danny Boyle's Olympics opening ceremony brilliantly captured how the health service represents the very best of British values. However, I worry that the reverence with which it is often treated is the enemy of rational thought. I often hear people argue that the NHS is beyond improvement because it saved the lives of 'my mum' or 'Aunt Bertha'. Saving lives is what doctors and nurses do. They do it within different health systems in France, Germany, Holland and many places besides. As an eighteen-year-old my own life was saved by French doctors in a French hospital after a terrible car crash. I was told I would not have had care like it back home. Perhaps now, after years of higher investment, I would. My experience taught me that statements that the NHS is the best system in the world should be regarded with the same scepticism as any other assertion of national superiority.

I'm struck by how skilfully the new man at the top, Simon Stevens, shapes the debate today. In a manner few other public servants could have got away with he has made a direct pitch for an increase in funding while simultaneously telling his workforce that they're going to have to change.

I knew Simon at Oxford. Unlike so many of our generation he did not go for the riches offered by the City or management consultancy. He chose, instead, the far less glamorous and far worse-paid option of becoming a trainee NHS manager. Despite once being an adviser to a former Labour health secretary, Alan Milburn, and later to Tony Blair, he has been regarded as suspect by some because he went on to work for an American healthcare firm that bid for NHS contracts.

By making the case for more cash and more reform, Stevens may well have saved the NHS for a few more years at least. Stand by, though, for a row about who can really be trusted to spend more on health and who will protect the NHS from an assault by profit-hungry, market-rigging, job-threatening private companies – precisely the message that proved so potent for the Yes campaign in Scotland.

If we get seven months of yesterday's exchanges in the Commons, God help us all.

I am writing this in between a series of appointments in which my eyes are peered into by doctors with lenses and bright lights. I thought I'd come for a routine check-up but am told I have a tear in my retina. One doctor explains that it's like what Gordon Brown had before adding hurriedly, 'but much less serious'. Thank heavens for that. Brown went blind in one eye and lives in constant fear of going blind in the other, a handicap he has rarely talked about but which goes a long way to explain the odd facial expressions and awkwardness with people he can't see properly or recognize.

The first prescribed solution, 'urgent treatment without delay', has just been downgraded to 'probably no need to worry as it looks like an old problem that isn't getting any worse'.

Which prescription for the NHS will our country choose?

Friday 24 October

Home

If there is a God he seems to be smiling on Nigel Farage. First Barroso told Cameron where he could stick his proposed cap on EU immigration. Next his successor, Mr Juncker, declared on Wednesday that freedom of movement is a sacred and unbreakable principle. After all, he explained, with some logic on his side, if we stop it then others will insist on ending freedom of movement of capital. Now this morning comes the *pièce de résistance*.

It's not often I wish I was in Brussels but today is an exception. I decided not to go to the EU summit for all the usual reasons – dull agenda, no access to anyone who matters, hours spent in a lightless basement waiting and waiting, another weekend eaten into – but this one just got lively.

The European Commission has taken another look at the books and concluded that the UK owes them another 2 billion euros, which they'd like before Christmas, please, if that's OK. What's more, a billion of that is earmarked to be paid back to the French. Someone should do an investigation into whether there is a secret unit in Brussels coming up with ideas to drive out 'those dreadful whingeing Brits'.

The prime minister likes nothing better than a good crisis so he takes the opportunity to put on a display of Thatcherite defiance, banging his Euro-lectern to underline his each and every phrase: 'I'm not paying that bill.' Thump. 'It is not going to happen.' Thump. 'They've got another think coming.' Whack.

He clearly remembers the time in 2011 when he snatched a domestic political victory from the jaws of European negotiating defeat, when he somehow turned being outvoted by twenty-six to one into a heroic deployment of the British veto.

The question is, though, whether the electorate will be persuaded by what Boris Johnson recently revealed to be the 'doppelganger' strategy of trying to convince those he calls 'Kippers' that they are blood brothers whose values and views are almost indistinguishable from those of the Tories. What will voters make of being told, 'UKIP is right about the EU and immigration. Whatever you do, don't vote for them'?

Driving on the A12

As the Tories' Euro crisis explodes, Labour's Scottish crisis is beginning to mushroom. Pippa volunteers to drive us to Suffolk for our half-term break while I send texts and make calls to get to grips with a story that has yet to break. I was offered a resignation interview this morning with Labour's Scottish leader, Johann Lamont. She's quitting, she says, because the Labour party in London (i.e. Ed Miliband) treats the Scottish Labour party (i.e. her) as a branch office to be given orders. An alternative view is that she has been comprehensively outmanoeuvred by Alex Salmond and, if it hadn't been for the last-minute intervention of Gordon Brown and those wicked people from London, would have presided over the break-up of the UK.

Jim Murphy is her obvious replacement. His tour of a hundred towns in a hundred days to save the union demonstrated that he had the fight needed to take on the SNP. Though a Westminster politician, he has kept his family home in Glasgow. But, but, but . . . he *is* a Westminster man, a Blairite and a foreign-policy hawk at a time when many in Scottish Labour have concluded that their problem is being insufficiently Scottish and insufficiently left-wing.

I call Jim to chew the fat. To my surprise he appears genuinely stunned by and, initially at least, disbelieving of the news. I tell him, not entirely helpfully, that he now has to decide whether to give up the chance of a seat in the next Labour Cabinet to return home full-time to lead a battle that may be unwinnable.

Saturday 25 October

Suffolk

George knew. David didn't. Oh dear.

It turns out that the Treasury was well aware that a great big Euro bill was looming but took an awfully long time to tell the chancellor, who didn't quite get round to telling the prime minister, who only found out about it in the middle of an EU summit.

Hilariously, it transpires that an underestimate of the size of the British sex trade is partly to blame. Boffins have been scrutinizing Britannia's vital statistics and have concluded that she's bigger and bustier than anyone had previously realized. So we've not been paying our fair share.

Labour have dug out evidence that this revision of the official economic stats has been in the works in London, not Brussels, for months, if not years. Watch out for deputy heads rolling.

Monday 27 October

I feel quite emotional watching the last of 'our boys' leaving Afghanistan. I scan the screen for signs of the places where I stood on many visits to Camp Bastion, once a teeming military metropolis in the desert, now a ghost town. I recall the hope and the commitment of young squaddies, scarcely older than my sons, who risked death and horrible maiming to 'take the fight to the Taliban'. They knew why they were doing it: to make the streets back home safer. They were proud of what they'd achieved – the roads built, the hospitals constructed and the millions of girls they'd ensured would be educated for the first time in their lives. Yet they are returning home to a country where many say they no longer believe any of it was worthwhile. A BBC poll found that less than a quarter of British people feel it was.

Not long ago Afghanistan was widely seen as very different from Iraq. There was no false pretext for war, no 'illegal' invasion, no mass anti-war protests. The fact that both conflicts now seem to have been filed under 'historic mistake' will have a profound impact on what Britain does next in the world – or, rather, chooses not to do.

Tuesday 28 October

Has it really come to this? Britain is opposing search-and-rescue operations which prevent migrants and refugees from drowning in the Mediterranean. An obscure foreign office minister has issued a statement justifying the EU's decision not to continue with the patrols by the Italian navy that have saved an estimated 150,000 lives since the Lampedusa tragedy in which 500 died. Hauling people out of the water is, apparently, 'an unintended pull factor, encouraging more migrants to attempt the dangerous sea crossing and thereby leading to more tragic and unnecessary deaths'.

I wonder if those are words he will come to regret?

Coincidentally, the mayor of Calais is appearing before the Home Affairs Select Committee today. She says it's Britain's fault that her town is filling up with refugees willing to risk death to get to 'El Dorado' and a life on benefits.

Meanwhile, David Blunkett has rushed to the support of Michael Fallon for using the word 'swamped', a term he himself employed twelve years ago to describe the impact of large numbers of asylum-seekers who were being dispersed among northern communities like his own city of Sheffield. Now he says it is right to speak clearly and directly. Back then, when I reported that he had used a word Margaret Thatcher had made notorious, his aides told me he had no idea it was loaded with such toxic political history.

As I watch the immigration debate unfold I have a constant sense of reliving history. Calais is a problem now just as it was when Blunkett was home secretary. The asylum system has a terrible backlog, just as it had when Jack Straw was at the Home Office. Foreign prisoners are not being deported after their sentences, a repeat of the crisis that forced Charles Clarke out of office. Immigration from the EU is soaring, precisely as it did after 2004.

When John Reid took over as home secretary in 2006 he described the system as 'unfit for purpose'. Eight years on I'm not sure it's much better.

Thursday 30 October

Did Alex Salmond lose the battle only to win the war?

A new opinion poll puts support for the SNP at over 50 per cent – not for elections to the Scottish Parliament but to Westminster. If – and it is a mighty big if – that actually happened it would leave Labour with just four MPs north of the border compared with the forty-nine they have now. The SNP is becoming as much of a thorn in Labour's side as UKIP is for the Tories.

It is hardly ideal timing for Scottish Labour's gala dinner. Perhaps it should have been renamed a crisis summit. They have no leader, they're split about who the next one should be and the head of the UK party is now, believe it or not, trusted less than an English Tory toff in another opinion poll.

This, says Ed Miliband in a TV interview, is 'a challenge'. Mmm. Steady on there, Ed. We wouldn't want to exaggerate.

Friday 31 October

Fright night for Theresa May. The woman, or rather the second woman, she chose to chair the child-abuse inquiry has had the smell of political death about her for some time. After being forced to accept one resignation, the home secretary has fought to keep Fiona Woolf, but tonight she quits, not having succeeded in persuading victims that she is the right person for the job. May will have to face MPs on Monday and explain why her officials didn't think of putting Woolf's name into Google to check whether she had any minimal link with any of those prominent individuals alleged either to have covered up child abuse or to have failed to investigate it properly.

Woolf's letter explaining her relationship with the former home secretary Lord Brittan – not a friend, but they had eaten at each other's houses on a number of occasions – was drafted, redrafted and redrafted again by Home Office officials. This was either incompetence or, perhaps, a desire to set up an inquiry which they felt they could limit and control.

The real problem now is that victims have been given an effective veto over who follows Woolf. That means someone who, unlike Woolf, and unlike Lady Butler-Sloss, is deemed not to be a member of that shadowy and fearsome sect known as the 'establishment'.

Some of those who were abused by people in positions of authority are convinced that not only was there a vast conspiracy to abuse children but also an establishment cover-up involving politicians, police officers, lawyers, clergymen and civil servants and, no doubt, the BBC too.

I'm no expert, but there seems a real danger that this inquiry may be set an impossible task: either to find that conspiracy or to prove a negative – that it did not exist. In the process it may ignore what I suspect is the more valuable task: identifying why victims were consistently not believed while paedophiles' denials were, and what processes can be set up to make that less likely to happen in future.

— NOVEMBER —

Sunday 2 November

Frank's Canteen, Highbury

Eggs Benedict, coffee and the Sunday papers. Things, it seems, can only keep getting a little worse each week for Ed Miliband.

The Scottish Labour party is behaving as if it has just lost a referendum while the party that did lose, the SNP, has the confidence and swagger of the victors. Miliband's only hope of averting the loss of dozens of his Scottish MPs and all hope of becoming prime minister now lies with the man who ran his brother's leadership campaign. Jim Murphy has never tried very hard to hide his contempt for the younger Miliband and was, as a result, consigned to the modern political equivalent of Siberia: the post of shadow secretary for international development. Now Ed needs Jim to have any chance of reaching Number 10.

Miliband's personal poll ratings have just fallen below Nick Clegg's – and that was before the photograph that will be added to the bacon-sandwich folder. Ed has been pictured walking past a beggar on a Manchester street before turning round to place a coin in her cup, all the while making no eye contact with her at all. Once the image was blown up, the coin turned out to be a large bronze one: 2p, to be precise.*

Finally, this morning the *Mail on Sunday* has revealed that a T-shirt he sported, carrying the slogan 'This is what feminism looks like' – the same T-shirt David Cameron was attacked for refusing to wear – was

---

* It later emerged that this was just one of a number of coins he'd put in the cup but it didn't suit the papers that ran the picture to point this out.

produced by workers in Mauritius earning just 62p an hour.

In his *Sunday Mirror* column John Prescott complains that party strategy is being driven by 'the pointy-heads, not the lionhearts'. The only reason the party is not in despair is that they just won a contest with UKIP – a by-election for a police and crime commissioner in south Yorkshire – while the polls show that the Tories are on course to lose their parliamentary by-election to Nigel's 'people's army'.

Monday 3 November

Home, the study

I am telling listeners to the *Today* programme something I sense I may end up saying again and again over the next few weeks. Or maybe months. Or even years. David Cameron might struggle to bridge the gap between what voters demand and what other EU leaders will agree to.

Overnight the German news magazine *Der Spiegel* has reported that Frau Merkel is ready to see Britain leave the EU rather than concede changes to one of its founding principles, freedom of movement.

She needn't worry. Cameron won't propose something he knows Angela cannot stomach. George Osborne pops up on breakfast TV seeking to dampen all the speculation on what Merkel might have said about what Cameron may be about to say in his planned big speech on immigration. Osborne, who has just been to Germany, assures us that they understand British voters' worries about people coming here without job offers and claiming benefits. It is time, he declares, to update the principle for the twenty-first century.

What the Tories will end up arguing for – and, interestingly, what quite a few Labour figures support – is the idea of freedom of movement of labour rather than people. In other words, you can go where you like if you've got a job but not if you haven't. Easier said than done. In the meantime, they'll try to curb benefits, in work as well as out of work, for those who come here.

A sign of what they're up against can be seen in a poll of public attitudes. Voters are convinced that there are many, many more EU citizens on the dole than there actually are. Only around 60,000 claim the Jobseeker's Allowance. UKIP supporters believe that the real figure is 500,000.

House of Commons

She says it. The hardest word. And yet often the most effective. Theresa May says sorry to the survivors of child abuse and does it convincingly enough to disarm most of those who have come to complain about her incompetence or gawp at the spectacle of the Teflon coming off Theresa. Jack Straw once told me that the safest place for a minister in trouble was the House of Commons, providing you were contrite. A secret his successor has clearly understood.

The cameras in the House of Commons are slung high over the chamber. As a result viewers often only get to see the tops of the heads of ministers reading their notes. May has thought of this, though, and looks up as she issues what she emphasizes is a direct message to victims:

> I know you have experienced terrible things. I know we cannot imagine what that must be like. And I know – perhaps because of the identity of your abusers or the way you were treated when you needed help – many of you have lost trust in the authorities . . . I am listening . . . I am as determined as you are to get to the truth.

It is four months since this inquiry was announced. There may still be no chairman in four months' time. The home secretary is clearly preparing for that. 'To put it bluntly, Mr Speaker,' she said earlier in her speech, 'it will not be straightforward to find a chairman who has both the expertise to do this hugely important work and has had no contact at all with an institution or an individual about whom people have concerns.'

Things can only get worse, part two: Labour's poll rating has just dropped below 30 per cent for the first time since the days of Gordon Brown.

Tuesday 4 November

Home, the study

Norman Baker's gone. No, listen, Norman Baker has resigned from the government. What do you mean, who's Norman Baker?

The *Today* programme is leading on the overnight resignation of the Lib Dem Home Office minister, but how to make it interesting? The coalition that first bloomed in the rose garden, I declare, has withered and decayed in the Home Office. This is where Baker was sent by Nick Clegg to man-mark Theresa May, who routinely offended Liberal Democrat sensibilities on immigration, civil liberties and drugs policies. She has not taken kindly to him trying to be the Lib Dems' own home secretary. He has been likened to 'the only hippy at an Iron Maiden concert' – apt for a man who's broken new ground by saying that he's quitting to spend more time not just with his family but with his music.

I needn't have worried about how to make his resignation interesting: a few clips of him singing with his band, the Reform Club, a mention or two of his interest in UFOs and his suspicion that the former weapons inspector Dr David Kelly was murdered should do the trick. All in all, the surprise is not that Norman has resigned but that he ever got the job in the first place.

Joining him in the coalition escape club are two Lib Dem whips with small majorities. It's time to stop working with the Tories and start fighting to stop them unseating them in their constituencies.

As for the coalition, so long predicted to fall apart, it will survive this and every other crisis it is likely to face. The reason is simple. The Lib Dems have been desperate for years to kill the idea that a Lib Dem vote is a wasted vote and to prove that they are a party of power and not of protest. Nick Clegg hopes they might just get a little credit for serving in government provided they prove they're in it for the long run.

The problem with this strategy is equally simple. The Lib Dems have made themselves a party of power at the very time when large swathes of the electorate have concluded that a vote for any of the main parties is a wasted vote as 'they're all the same'. Or, as UKIP put it, they're all part of the Lib-Lab-Con, or what the SNP disparage as the 'Westminster parties'.

The Dorchester

Over breakfast I listen to a speech by one of the country's leading spooks. No names, no notes, no reporting permitted. It's a chance to gain an insight into what's concerning the nation's spies. What sticks

in the mind is the description of how ISIS became, apparently overnight, the most feared threat on the planet. After occupying a large
part of Iraq 'they knocked over every bank and withdrew all the funds;
they emptied the prisons and recruited all the inmates; they raided
army bases and stole all the weapons. Now they're even selling oil'.
For months I've been saying that Islamic State are neither Islamic nor
a state. Maybe I was wrong. IS does now seem worryingly close to
being a state.

Government chief whip's office

A first visit to see the 'chief' since Michael Gove took over. I've come
to hear how and when the Tories will handle a looming revolt over
Europe. A hundred Tory backbenchers have threatened to vote against
the government's plan to stay opted in to the European arrest warrant.
The police and the home secretary believe it's vital if the UK is to be
able to deport criminals from other countries. The rebels see it as yet
another power too far for Brussels.

The vote, I later learn, is to be held next Monday, the same day as
the PM is giving two big speeches: his annual foreign policy speech at
the Mansion House and another to the CBI conference. Added to which
the result will not be known until halfway through the news at ten.
They're working very hard to bury their own bad news.

Wednesday 5 November

Coffee shop, Westminster

A cappuccino, a shared almond croissant and a sprinkling of despond-
ency. A senior shadow Cabinet member tells me of his fears that the
public have made up their minds about Ed Miliband and it may be too
late to change them. Miliband's reaction has been to draw up more
and more policy, but that isn't what's needed. His office won't allow
others to share the limelight even though a 'Team Labour' approach
may be the only answer to the party's 'leadership problem'. A 35 per
cent strategy was never very inspiring but a 29 per cent strategy just
won't cut it.

Prime Minister's Questions

It may not be the most edifying of experiences but if you listen hard to PMQs it can be enlightening, at least if you want to get a sense of how either of the two men locked in the struggle for the keys to Number 10 can get the upper hand and how their advisers hope to shape the media narrative.

Today Cameron dubs Miliband 'a dead parrot', dreaming, no doubt, that the *Sun* might reimagine the front page that did so much damage to William Hague when he was the failing leader of the Tories in the late 1990s. His face was photoshopped on to the body of one of our brightly coloured feathered friends, shown hanging upside down from its perch.

Miliband uses his questions to try to pour salt into the Tories' European wounds. He asks the PM to say clearly whether he is in favour of staying in the EU or getting out. The leader's advisers will have told him that this can't fail. After all, if the PM says he is in favour of staying in, it will enrage many Tory MPs and the Tory press and convince UKIP defectors that they've done the right thing. If he says no, he will frighten those who believe the EU is the key to millions of British jobs. And if he says neither, Labour can charge him with creating uncertainty over the country's most important economic relationship.

As it turns out, Cameron says neither, insisting that he is in favour of staying in a reformed Europe, which tells us very little.

My office, BBC Westminster

I keep checking Google. I keep checking Twitter. I keep checking my e-mail. Nothing. For weeks now I have been angsting and the BBC has been agonizing over how to respond to the complaints – and there were many of them – about my report on my bust-up with Alex Salmond a week before the Scottish referendum. The judgement was published today and endless e-mail exchanges and meetings and conference calls have been had about how to handle the fall-out. Except there hasn't been any.

The complainants say I lied when I reported that Salmond had not answered a question. The head of editorial complaints has donned his wig and delivered his verdict. I have been found partly innocent and partly guilty. There is, he concludes, no evidence of bias but the report was 'unintentionally misleading'.

I have written a column which can be placed in a Scottish paper to defend myself and explain that I'm sorry I chose my words badly. But, so far at least, no defence seems necessary. Only one of those who complained has replied. Under a company logo which proclaims that the correspondent believes in 'listening carefully and responding promptly' come the words: 'You are a pathetic piece of shit.' Not even a 'Dear sir' or a 'Yours faithfully'.

Thursday 6 November

Heathrow airport, Terminal 3

I made it and with time to spare. At eight o'clock I was giving a speech over breakfast in Covent Garden. It's now 10am and I'm at check-in. What looked like an impossible schedule was made possible thanks to my new favourite way to travel: a limo-bike. It involves sitting on the back of a big Yamaha with a rear seat while the rider up front weaves expertly through the traffic of central London. The only downside is the need to don helmet, gloves, protective jacket and wraparound blanket to keep your legs warm and hope that nobody sees you looking completely absurd.

I'm following David Cameron to Helsinki just as his dream that the media will turn on Ed Miliband appears to be coming true. The *New Statesman*, which backed Miliband for the leadership, is now decrying him as a Hampstead socialist who is out of touch with working people. Two of his MPs have told a colleague at the BBC that they've written to the chair of the parliamentary Labour party to demand a leadership contest. Numerous others have told my BBC colleagues, 'We can't carry on like this ... it's pretty hopeless . . . we're not cutting through . . . he's remote from the real world.'

What does it add up to? Not a coup. There's no alternative leader waiting in the wings, no mechanism to fell the existing leader, no one who will go on the record to complain. All of which allows Ed's spin doctors to dismiss the whole fuss as a media confection. There is something real there, though. It's a collective loss of nerve, a collapse in self-belief, a crisis of confidence from which few have an idea how they will escape.

Startup Sauna, Helsinki

We are here for the Northern Future Forum – not an event I normally ring on my calendar. It's a summit of the leaders of the eight Nordic and Baltic states, plus the man whose idea this forum was: David Cameron. His hope was to create a kind of supporters' club for the British view of Europe – pro-free trade and sceptical about Brussels. I've come to see just how supportive they really are as the PM prepares to deliver his big speech on how to curb immigration from the EU.

'Is everyone happy?' shouts the host, Finland's prime minister, Alexander Stubb, as he and his fellow leaders pose for the 'family photo'. The unspoken answer is no. My producer Chris has lined up not one, not two but three prime ministers for me to interview. Each in turn, and in perfect English, tells me how fundamental the principle of free movement within the EU is.

Stubb says it is 'rather holy'. The UK, he tells me, should be rewarded with an EU medal for opening her borders when others closed theirs. That is a medal David Cameron could do without. Sweden's prime minister is, if anything, even less helpful. He says that if one country were allowed to change rules that didn't suit it, this 'may just ruin the European Union'. The PM of Norway – a country not in the EU but which, nevertheless, chooses to allow the free movement of people from the union – thinks David Cameron would be better advised trying to reform welfare payments.

This may be a way forward for Cameron: agreeing to maintain the principle of free movement while reviewing how it works in practice.

We are the lead story on the news, relegating Ed Miliband's woes to second place. A colleague in London forwards me the texts sent by spin doctors for both parties. The Tory complains: 'You chickened out over Ed!' His Labour counterpart whinges: 'Disgraceful stuff . . . a misjudgement on the BBC's part.' There are exactly six more months of this to go before polling day.

Friday 7 November

Startup Sauna, Helsinki

Spoilsports. The PM's image-conscious minders have vetoed today's photo opportunity of the nine leaders sitting in a sauna. No one was suggesting that they sit there swathed in towels, let alone naked. There was no plan for them to sweat for the cameras or be beaten by birch twigs. The location for the picture is not, in fact, a real sauna, although with its pine benches and glass doors it certainly looks like one. This is a 'startup sauna business accelerator', a place where Finnish executives can hold meetings and hot-house ideas. Sadly, though, it seems that someone in Downing Street may have read my blog, which predicted that today's talks might get 'hot and sweaty for the prime minister', and concluded this was one theme they could do without.

Summit news conference

This morning the Finnish prime minister tries to sound conciliatory to the Brits – after all, he's married to one – using the summit's closing news conference to insist that the UK does have friends and allies. So, too, does Danish leader Helle Thorning-Schmidt, also married to a Brit. But what, I ask one of Cameron's advisers, has he got from coming here?

Understanding, is his answer. Over roast fillet of reindeer last night Cameron was able to explain that, whatever they'd read in newspaper cuttings or in their briefings, his desire to curb immigration was not simply a political reaction to one by-election defeat or the threat of another. It was a response, he said, to the public's fear that immigration on a massive scale – one sixth of the population of Lithuania has moved to the UK – is overwhelming their communities, their schools and their hospitals. Telling them that none of this matters because the British economy is growing faster than any other in the EU and unemployment is falling simply would not do.

Perhaps they did listen. Perhaps they want to help the man dubbed the 'founding father' of this summit. I wonder, though, whether they plan to agree to any changes to the EU, save a bit of tinkering, to ensure that it does not accidentally create a Europe-wide welfare state for people who choose to move but not to work.

With so many jobs being created in Britain, with English being so widely spoken, with wages being so high relative to those in many EU countries, it might be nowhere near enough to cut the numbers who want to come.

On the tarmac, Helsinki airport

I am broadcasting live on the BBC news channel from seat 27F on the Finnair flight back to London. The news of a deal over the EU budget has just broken after talks in Brussels. I have been in the wrong city. The story is in Brussels, not here.

George Osborne has emerged from a meeting with fellow EU finance ministers to proclaim that he has secured a 'great deal' for the UK by halving the £1.7 billion extra demanded to fill the coffers in Brussels, delaying the payment by almost a year and ensuring that no interest is paid on the sum owed. It all sounds too good to be true. Not one of the leaders I spoke to mentioned the possibility of the amount Britain owed being cut. Nor did officials in the commission.

As I mounted the steps of the plane the chancellor's adviser called to say they had done a deal to make sure that the full rebate would be paid on the new, larger contribution. 'Was that ever in doubt?' I asked. 'Well,' came the somewhat vague reply, 'there was conflicting legal advice.'

Something doesn't smell right here.

Labour's frontbenchers have clearly been instructed to rally round their flagging leader. I read with amusement the public statements of undying loyalty from the guy I had coffee with on Wednesday and other shadow Cabinet members who've told me of their frustration, irritation and anger with Miliband. Using quotes from anonymous sources is problematic. Party loyalists always suspect that journalists are making them up and viewers and listeners are understandably exasperated that they cannot judge for themselves who is saying what. Without them, though, you'd have to rely on the insincere guff that politicians sometimes feel they have to utter.

Saturday 8 November

A triumph of negotiation or smoke and mirrors? The row still rages about George Osborne's claim to have halved the bill from Brussels.

Every other EU finance minister is clear. There has been no change to the EU budget and therefore no cut in Britain's bill. So how is the chancellor able to insist, as he has again on this morning's *Today* programme, that he is – or rather, we are – only going to be paying £850 million instead of £1.7 billion? The answer appears to be simple. Osborne has asked for the extra rebate on our bigger bill to be applied straight away, instead of being paid to us a year later, as is the usual practice. So the total bill is the same but after that EU credit note has been taken into account the amount the Treasury has to pay up has been halved. Hey presto!

That is why the Treasury employs the cleverest civil servants in the business. They will, I suspect, all be getting an extra special Christmas thank-you from their boss.

If only the EU experts or the journalists or the opposition had factored in the rebate, the chancellor would never have been able to make his claim as everyone would have known that the amount the country has to pay was never likely to be £1.7 billion.

Andrew Lansley drops me a note pointing out that he did raise the matter of the rebate with Cameron himself at PMQs. Further proof of the adage that the best place to keep a secret is on the floor of the House of Commons.

Sunday 9 November

Things can only get worse for Ed (part 324).

The headlines in the Sunday papers are dreadful. The polls are even more dreadful: only 34 per cent of people who voted Labour at the last general election believe Ed Miliband is up to the job of prime minister, compared with 51 per cent a month ago. Forty-five per cent of Labour supporters felt he should resign.

What's still missing, though, is a single Labour MP calling on him to go. As is any obvious successor. Alan Johnson might have been the answer but he doesn't want the job. He is enjoying writing, music and life too much, and he doesn't believe he could do it properly. Twenty shadow ministers are said to be ready to quit to force Miliband out if Johnson indicates he's ready to take over. Their jobs are safe. I tell my news editor that he is more likely to become the next Labour leader than Johnson.

Look at the polls more carefully and they reveal news that is rather better for Miliband. In one he is still on course to win. What's more, all the alternative candidates for leader – Andy Burnham, Yvette Cooper, Chuka Umunna and even Johnson himself – would scarcely improve Labour's ratings. The only person who would is another man called Miliband, the man the public say they really want. There are one or two problems with that. David is in New York and he's not an MP. He might run an organization called International Rescue but this is one rescue too far, even for him.

I have picked up a rumour that Ed seriously contemplated quitting, so low was he in the aftermath of that conference speech. That would explain his curiously downbeat conversation when we had dinner together.

Short of Miliband standing down, Labour MPs can grumble, fret and panic all they like but they had better accept that Ed is their leader or hand the election to their opponents.

Monday 10 November

A radio car, behind the Grosvenor House hotel

Theresa May is making a rare appearance on the *Today* programme in an effort to sell the European arrest warrant. It's hardly a big talking point down the Dog and Duck but in the Commons tea room a certain sort of Tory speaks of little else.

The EAW unites those who twitch at the idea of anything that has the word 'European' in its name and those who worry about giving politicians rather than judges power over who gets arrested and extradited. In today's Tory party, that takes the number to well over a hundred. Teflon Theresa has been working very hard to convince them that this is not an issue about Europe at all. Dearie me, no. It's really about deporting bad foreigners and forcing other countries to send us back our own baddies so that we can lock them up for a very long time indeed.

With the help of an opinion poll that shows the public rather like the sound of this, the support of the boys in blue and the spooks and a gentle reminder from the whips that there's a jolly important by-election coming up ('We wouldn't want to give that shit Reckless a rebellion before the vote in Rochester, would we?'), Theresa has managed to squash the revolt. Those who really can't stand the idea of voting for the EAW have been told that it would be a good day for a vital visit to the dentist or a select committee trip to Ulan Bator.

All this means that the rebels are predicting there will be just thirty votes against the motion while the whips are estimating fifty. Boring, snoring. I'm going to look at a different story instead.

In fact that story has just presented itself. Asked about the Tories' promise to cut net migration to tens of thousands a year, the home secretary hesitates as the sound of the letter 'p' starts to form on her puckered lips. Sensible enough. Why repeat the word 'promise', when she knows she has as much chance of fulfilling it as she has of becoming the first woman to circumnavigate the sun? However, she succeeds only in highlighting her desperation to avoid the 'p' word by first calling the Tories' immigration target a 'comment' and then hurriedly correcting that to 'aim'.

With a little help from the CBI, whose president is going to use his speech at today's annual conference to warn against curbs on immigration, and the *Daily Mail*, I have my report for the day. The *Mail* contributes a striking front-page headline 'IS THERE NO ONE LEFT IN BRITAIN WHO CAN MAKE A SANDWICH?' to an article about the biggest sandwich-maker in the country seeking 300 workers from Hungary for its new factory because, apparently, Brits are not hungry enough for employment to take up the challenge of spreading and filling for the minimum wage.

Corrigan's restaurant, Mayfair

I have agreed to speak at the pre-conference breakfast for the CBI hierarchy. They get to hear my views about the outcome of the next election, which I sum up as a 25 per cent chance of a Tory majority, a 25 per cent chance of a Labour majority and a 25 per cent chance each for either a Tory or Labour minority outcome. Or, as my dad, a Yorkshireman, might have put it, 'Bugger knows.'

They tell me about their political worries: curbs on immigration and an exit from the EU if the Tories win; more taxes and regulation if Labour win. And indecision and uncertainty if no one really wins.

Grosvenor House hotel

The CBI is to have the pleasure of seeing all three main party leaders, who are using the conference to make their pre-election pitches.

Cameron bounces confidently on to the stage, speaks without notes (as if to say, 'Look, Ed – at least one of us can do it'), and sums up his message as 'We've got a plan – let's stick to it.' The CBI have invited me to ask a question, put me in a good seat and handed me a mic. The PM looks round the room and picks out every hand that goes up except mine.

When Miliband arrives he has to run the gauntlet made up of Messrs Crick, Ship* and Gobby, who shout variations on 'Why are you doing so badly?' at the Labour leader on behalf of Channel 4, ITV and the BBC respectively. By the time he appears on stage (clasping a full text of a script – he's not risking that again) he looks quite tense. His speech is a good one, though, and plays on what he knows is a big fear for big business: that the Tories will, perhaps unintentionally, take Britain out of Europe.

BBC studios, Millbank

Yvette Cooper calls to tell me it looks as if the speaker will rule that the government's motion on the European arrest warrant is, well, not really a motion on that at all. It's exactly what Labour and the rebels have been complaining about. I say I'll pass this on to a colleague as I'm doing another story. I'm an idiot.

I'm so busy finishing my edit that I barely notice the mayhem developing in the Commons until ministers scrape through by just nine votes and messages come in suggesting they might lose the next one.

I run over the road to find out what's been going on. The door-keepers are always the best instant source of what's happening in the

* Michael Crick, political correspondent of Channel 4 News, and Chris Ship, deputy political editor at ITV News.

chamber. 'It's chaos,' one of the men in tights tells me. 'No one knows what they're actually voting for.'

'I haven't seen anything like it for years,' says another, as the deputy prime minister races past me with a posse of flunkies, muttering sarcastically about the great strengths of our democracy.

It turns out that, sure enough, John Bercow ruled that tonight's vote 'is not, repeat not, on the EAW'. On its own this might have been seen as technical clarification but he didn't stop there. The speaker tore into the home secretary's explanation that, for technical reasons, she'd decided to hold a vote on eleven related measures but to treat it as an 'indicative vote' on the arrest warrant itself. He condemned her and the government for failing to honour their commitment to MPs, adding that the lack of 'straightforward dealing' would leave the public 'contemptuous' of ministers. Ouch.

The shadow home secretary responded by tabling her own motion, inviting MPs to decide that 'the question now not be put'. In other words, to have a debate on whether not to have a vote on a motion that wasn't really about the thing it was meant to be about. I can't see why anyone would be confused.

This has sent the Tory whips into blind panic. Their MPs were told they could head off to their meetings, dinners or secret liaisons providing they're back in time to vote at 10pm. Now the vote could happen at any moment – unless, that is, ministers and helpful backbenchers just keep on talking while search parties are sent out to round up the MPs.

As the filibuster begins I spot the chief whip negotiating with a leading Tory rebel behind the speaker's chair. The word is that the PM has just arrived, still wearing the tails, starched collar and white tie he donned this evening to address the ambassadors and dignitaries gathered at the lord mayor's banquet at the Guildhall. As Labour will delight in pointing out, it's an outfit in which he feels completely at home. Not so poor old Chris Grayling, the lord chancellor, who will now be being mocked for voting in his ceremonial breeches and white lace cuffs. Even Teflon Theresa is looking, for the first time I can remember, a little *en deshabille*.

When the motion is finally put the government has reassembled its majority, a comfortable forty-three. However, while ministers have won the vote, they have damaged their reputation, handed Nigel Farage a gift and could yet face another proper vote on the issue they have tried so desperately to avoid.

Nights like this must seem bizarre to those watching from outside but they matter – they dissolve the glue that holds governing parties together and strengthen the bonds an opposition so badly needs. If any more Tory MPs defect to UKIP after Rochester I suspect they will quote tonight's debacle as one reason they couldn't stay.

As I leave the Commons I bump into a senior minister. Surely, I say, Theresa May was winning the argument? Wouldn't you have won the vote easily if you'd actually allowed it? Oh yes, comes the reply, but we were told that any motion we put down could have been amended. Labour, he goes on, would have found any excuse to do this, arguing, say, that there hadn't been enough time for debate, and then a coalition of Labour MPs and Tory rebels would have defeated it. How, I ask naïvely, do you know this? 'Because that's what we would have done to them.'

If nobody wins the next election outright there will be many, many nights like this one. It's no way to run a country but it sure makes for adrenaline-fuelled fun.

Tuesday 11 November

Office of the leader of the opposition, House of Commons

Good timing. Ed Miliband has invited in a group of BBC editors for a background chat. He sits in shirtsleeves at one end of his long table facing the editors of *BBC News at 6*, *BBC News at 10*, *Today*, *Newsnight*, *PM*, *Daily Politics* and a host of others. Behind him a Rubik's cube appears to have been strategically placed on a shelf just over his left shoulder. Legend has it that he can solve the puzzle with one hand and his eyes closed.

He seems to have some of his old confidence back, enough at least to acknowledge self-deprecatingly that his speeches don't produce soundbites that work on TV or can be chanted on protest marches. 'What do we want?' he calls, holding up an invisible megaphone. 'Responsible capitalism! When do we want it? In the medium term!'

If Miliband does become prime minister people will say that his greatest strength during the campaign was identifying a theme and sticking to it. Labour, he says, will be turning up the heat on the NHS, warning the electorate of the twin Tory threats posed by cuts and privatization. Warming to his theme, he declares that he intends to 'weaponize' the health service – in other words, to turn it into lethal political ammunition. I glance round the room to see who else has clocked the phrase.

Being from the BBC, everyone is painfully polite and studiously avoids grabbing the bull by the horns until one colleague points out that he has smartly described the public's alienation from mainstream politics and the Westminster parties but not addressed the fact that he, of all politicians and Westminster leaders, is rated worst. This is Miliband's chance to show he gets it and has a strategy to deal with it. He doesn't take it.

Perhaps there can be no strategy, just a hope that the more people see of him, the more they'll grow to like him. Two tests of that lie ahead. I have an exclusive interview with him tomorrow and the next day he will give a speech, which are sure to be respectively dubbed his 'fightback' and 'relaunch' even though, officially at least, he has nothing to fight back against and no need to relaunch.

Wednesday 12 November

The speaker's house

I meet the speaker, who's agreed to be interviewed for a Radio 4 series I'm making on democracy and why it's going out of fashion.

John Bercow is still bursting with indignation about the events of Monday night. As so often, he's making the right stand but doing it in the wrong way. He was right to challenge ministers for trying to push the European arrest warrant through the House of Commons without having a clear and explicit motion to do it. However, he did so using language which chided, patronized and infuriated ministers and will ensure that he is driven from the chair if the Tories get any sort of majority after the next election. They loathe him so much they'll happily agree to elect a Labour speaker instead.

The sadness is that he has every right to claim to be a genuine reforming speaker who has made the Commons relevant again. Few controversies, few crises, few major government announcements are now made in television or radio studios rather than from the dispatch box. He has used his power to grant so-called 'urgent questions' to force ministers to come to the Commons to make statements when they don't want to. There were just two 'UQs' during 2008–9 and the worst financial crisis in decades. There are now dozens of them.

It's all part of Bercow's efforts to convince the public that Parliament is separate from government and to ensure that ordinary MPs are able to hold ministers to account. His problems stem almost entirely from his manner. He knows that for every admirer he has there is another who sees him as pompous and self-regarding. Yet the man known for trying to keep 'order, order' struggles to control himself.

Harlow college

'What doesn't kill you makes you stronger . . . my mettle's been tested,' Ed Miliband tells me in his 'fightback' interview before his 'relaunch' speech, which he is giving me during a visit to Harlow college.

I resist the temptation to point out that, until yesterday, his spin doctors were insisting that nothing had happened and that all the talk about his leadership was being manufactured by Labour's enemies in the media.

Perhaps they were helped to change their minds by the fact that another poll puts the party on 29 per cent, reveals that 73 per cent of voters don't see him as prime ministerial and gives him lower ratings than Nick Clegg. Here, at Harlow college, one supportive student asked him why, given that the Tories are making such a mess of things, Labour are doing so poorly.

He doesn't really have an answer but his performance is much better than it has been of late – punchy, passionate and direct. He repeats his carefully honed and market-researched lines again and again. 'I'll fight (I'm strong) for you (I'm on your side)', and 'to change Britain (things can be better than this)'.

I started my interview with policy – in particular the fact that the governor of the Bank of England has just announced statistics showing that real wages are going up for the first time in years and are expected to carry on doing so as inflation is squeezed. It could herald the beginning of the end of the 'cost-of-living crisis'. Anybody who believes that, Miliband parries, is 'totally out of touch with reality'.

On immigration – a topic he's widely criticized for ignoring, along with the threat from UKIP – I ask him what he'd say to Rochdale's Mrs Duffy, the woman Gordon Brown called a bigot. He has an answer ready: 'It's not prejudice to worry about immigration.' Labour would offer 'practical policies that will make a difference, not false promises'.

I conclude with the question: 'When you look in the mirror in the morning, do you see a prime minister?' In the past he has often paused before answering a question like that. Not today. He replies: 'Absolutely. I see someone who'll fight for people, who'll wake up every morning and think, how do we change this country so it actually works for everyday people again?'

When we've finished he looks satisfied he's done what he came to do. There's no complaint about the questions or glassy-eyed, distracted stare. In fact, he remains as friendly as ever.

Leadership is, in the end, all about displays of self-confidence. I can't help feeling that we demand inhuman levels of it from our leaders, deriding those who lack it (Brown) and attacking those who have excessive quantities of it (Thatcher and Blair) as unhinged. Any man prepared to run against his own brother cannot be that short of self-belief. Ed Miliband is driven by the conviction that he was first to understand how the rules of our economy needed to be rewritten if it was ever to work for ordinary people.

He sees himself as someone who will bring about real change, not just manage the existing settlement – another Attlee or Thatcher. Miliband's confidence dived first in Scotland and then in Manchester, after that misjudged and poorly delivered conference speech. Now he wants to be seen to have got it back.

Thursday 13 November

University of London

In the speech that follows yesterday's interview, Ed Miliband tries to rouse his party by promising to 'take apart' UKIP's policies. They have, he says, 'got away with it for too long'.

He has been helped by the release of a series of video clips of Nigel Farage speaking to his supporters and revealing what he really thinks. On the NHS, the UKIP leader was filmed telling party activists a couple of years ago: 'Frankly, I would feel more comfortable that my money would return value if I was able to do that through the marketplace of an insurance company than just us trustingly giving £100 billion a year to central government and expecting them to organize the healthcare service from cradle to grave for us.'

Up to now Farage has been able to dismiss any such stories as remnants of an old election manifesto he never bothered to read, or the ideas of colleagues that can be dismissed. Not any more. These are his words, his views and his policies.

Summarized, what they mean is 'scrap the NHS', which may be a perfectly justifiable argument. It is, however, totally at odds with UKIP's insistence that its policy is, in short, to keep the NHS.

Farage calls in the cameras to explain that his words described an idea that he 'threw out for debate' two years ago but which was rejected. He hastily produces UKIP's new official health policy. As with everything he does, he eats his own words with a good sprinkling of charm.

One of Farage's greatest strengths is the widespread public view that 'say what you like about him, he calls things as he sees them'. It is what election strategists call 'authenticity' and it is electoral gold dust.

However, seeing him say one thing on TV and then unsay it may just chip away at that view.

Friday 14 November

Colchester Avenue, London E12

A young artist from north London with a ring through her nose, a political activist from Islington sporting the sort of beard radicals used to wear, a paid official from the Fire Brigades union and I are standing outside a terraced house in east London. We're waiting for the bailiffs to arrive to evict a family with three children. They're here to stop it happening. I'm here with my radio producer to record them stopping it for my Radio 4 series on democracy. Or rather, to record them waiting to stop it.

I'm also here to speak to two local young mums who organized the resistance to this eviction. After the council turfed them out of their hostel they set up a campaign group, Focus E15, a new *cause célèbre* for Russell Brand, whose latest book *Revolution* is stirring people to fight what he calls 'a man-made system designed to serve us' which has 'gone wrong and is tyrannizing us'. Brand's book tells his hundreds of thousands of readers that 'we wouldn't tolerate that from a literal machine. If my vacuum cleaner went nuts and forced me to live in economic slavery . . . I'd fuck it off out the window.' Useful advice from a man who also tells people that, whatever they do, they shouldn't vote to change anything.

I'm keen to interview Brand but after his mauling at the hands of a series of interviewers and reviewers he's not keen, for some reason, to be interviewed by me. John, the man with the beard, reveals that he's a mate of Russell's and promises to try to get him to talk to me.

After an hour and a half we're still waiting. There's no sign of the bailiffs. No sign, either, of the local mums who, it turns out, are in the High Court waiting for the appeal against the eviction to be heard. In fact, the only people here are a bunch of nice north London folk who could have met up over a mochaccino in Highbury.

I ask John what attracts people to Brand's form of activism rather than conventional politics. A veteran of many campaigns, he tells me that political parties now exist solely to get elected. People want to get on and do things, he says.

I find myself agreeing with him until I realize that we've been standing on this street in the cold and damp for two hours and absolutely nothing has been done. I head home to, er, Highbury.

Saturday 15 November

Not Brisbane, Australia

The PM is at the G20 Summit in Australia. I'm not. He's berating Putin. I'm teaching my son to drive, which is almost as scary. I really should have gone on this trip. I could have seen an old schoolfriend who lives in Brisbane. But I feel I still haven't fully recovered from my post-party conference bug. I am, in short, knackered.

Monday 17 November

Outside the Treasury

I roll down the window and wait for the officer to approach me. He recognizes me, smiles and advises me that the next time I want to be filmed driving round and round the most prominent terrorist targets in London it might be better not to do it in a large van with blacked-out windows which has previously been stolen. I am filming a piece for tonight's news about the prime minister's warning that 'red lights are flashing on the dashboard of the global economy'. Yes, it's a bit cheesy, but television news needs pictures.

Cameron has written in the *Guardian* that recovery at home has been put at real risk by the Eurozone heading back into recession as well as a plethora of other unwelcome developments from abroad. Ministers have been angsting for some time about statistics showing that government borrowing, far from going down, may be on the way up again. On *Today* this morning I said that the prime minister is getting his excuses in early. It's a little unnerving to hear Ed Miliband use precisely the same language in the Commons. I text his office to accuse them of unhelpful plagiarism.

Miliband is definitely on better form. He denounces Cameron for going from saying that every economic problem has been fixed because of him to saying that everything has not been fixed because of everyone else.

The deputy prime minister's office

I use a catch-up coffee with Nick Clegg to try to find out how much economic trouble the Treasury is in with just under three weeks to go to the chancellor's autumn statement. I've heard George Osborne is joking that it's pretty hard to write a pre-election vote-winning budget when you've no money and no parliamentary majority for Tory-ish measures. Clegg hints that he's stopped the Conservatives doing something wacky but won't spell out what it is. The autumn statement looks like being a dull, steady-as-she-goes affair.

Nick wants David and George to commit to increasing spending on the NHS next year. He thinks that an old-fashioned crisis in the health service is the only thing that can save Ed. Ed clearly agrees.

Having checked around, I've learned that others have also heard him speak of 'weaponizing' the NHS.

Tuesday 18 November

On the sofa at home

It's Scotland versus the Auld Enemy, England, at Celtic Park tonight, which feels curiously appropriate as I've just caught up with Alex Salmond's parting shot at 'reporters from London' (er, me?) who were sent to cover the referendum by the BBC, which he accuses of acting like a 'state broadcaster'. In an interview with the *Daily Record*, the man who today becomes ex-first minister of Scotland doesn't name me but praises three BBC colleagues, all of whom just happen to be Scots.

Happily, Scotland's biggest-selling paper, the *Record*, runs an editorial defending me as 'a journalist deservedly respected right across the political spectrum for his fairness and non-partisan approach'. It goes on to explain to its readers that 'devoted followers of any political party are always reluctant to hear unhelpful questions and it is sometimes comforting – and perhaps understandable – to want to have someone to blame when you lose'. I couldn't have put it better myself.

What worries me about this is not the personal criticism – I can live with that – but the continuing effort to bully the BBC by trying to dictate who is and is not a suitable journalist to cover a story that will have an impact on people living across the UK. It's not at all far-fetched to imagine between ten and twenty SNP MPs holding the balance of power after the next election. Reporting that will be my job, and I'm determined to do it fairly and uncensored by Salmond or anyone else. What's more, if he runs for Westminster himself, as he's clearly hinting he will, and the SNP more than doubles its number of MPs, he may become a key powerbroker in the UK.

That's why it's so important that writing and reporting on Scottish politics isn't restricted to Scottish journalists who have been given Alex's public blessing.

Earlier I discussed Salmond's continuing hostility with John Pienaar, one of the BBC's wisest political heads. 'It's not personal. It's just business,' he says. 'Like Tony Soprano,' I mutter, and am rewarded with a big Pienaar smile.

Alex bows out as first minister to warm praise from all sides. It is deserved. He is the first man to quit the job at a time of his own choosing, he leaves more popular than he was when he began – an almost unique achievement for any leader of a government during these difficult times – and believes that, although he lost a battle, he may yet win the war. Scotland looks set to get more power, albeit not full independence.

Wednesday 19 November

Daily Politics *studio, Broadcasting House*

Restoring faith in politics will not be helped by the tiresome recitation of pre-prepared insults by rival leaders of failing parties who between them can scarcely muster 60 per cent of public support.

Today at PMQs, Cameron reheats every off-the-record quote from 'senior Labour figures' to attack Miliband, while Miliband attacks the PM for caring only about millionaires and not the poor. It's a puerile game. Miliband has the better arguments but Cameron is better at the theatre and more ruthless. One of his advisers has told me they believe Ed is 'in the ground in his coffin and it's just a question now of covering it with soil'.

In truth, though, their audience does not extend much beyond the few hundred people sitting on the green benches, the hundreds more of us paid to watch and the half million or so sitting in front of the telly – some genuine enthusiasts, others simply too tired or bored or ill to switch it off.

I certainly won't be putting any of it on the news.

BBC studios, Millbank

This, on the other hand, should be fun. Nigel Farage has been booked to come to the BBC Brussels studios to try to put to bed a story that UKIP has been struggling all day to contain.

Twice on TV last night his by-election candidate Mark Reckless seemed to entertain the idea that a Polish plumber who lived locally might be forced to leave, or even deported, if Britain decided to leave the EU.

The party first claimed Reckless had been 'misunderstood'. Then it was said that he'd thought he was being asked about illegal immigrants. There is no evidence for that. Besides, a Polish plumber would be here perfectly legally.

UKIP have also insisted that there is no question at all of anyone being asked to 'go home'. Ever since Enoch Powell's call in the 1970s for immigrants to be repatriated, that phrase has encapsulated one of the most controversial ideas in British politics. Its appearance now merely focuses attention on why on earth their own candidate didn't simply say that there was no chance of any deportations.

All questions I want to ask Nigel Farage. He will be expecting to do a quick 'clarification' clip with one of our Brussels team but I suggest instead that I interview him properly down the line from Westminster.

One of the things that makes Farage such a formidable campaigner is his imperturbability, and this plan doesn't throw him at all. No spin doctor complains or demands a limit to the number of questions or the duration of the interview. He is a politician who trusts his ability to perform under pressure and he may even calculate that many viewers will hope UKIP actually are in favour of deporting people.

When he tries out each of his party's 'lines to take' I point out that they're not, in fact, true and read out the questions Reckless was asked to prove it. At this the expression on Nigel's face changes from relaxed bonhomie to tense irritation. 'Look, Mr Robinson,' he spits, before attempting to blame 'the most minor confusion' on the fact that his candidate wasn't listening properly because he'd been 'doing hustings after hustings after hustings' and facing 'question after question after question'. In fact he's done three hustings during the entire campaign.

This is not the first time in recent days that UKIP has tried to unsay what they've been recorded saying. When I put it to Farage that 'you say what you think on camera, and when people notice and they don't like it, you say, "We didn't really mean it at all",' he replies vigorously: 'I think that's absolutely monstrous.'

Oh no it isn't.

UKIP are desperate to present themselves as 'telling it like it is' but they are also desperate to avoid any taint of 'extremism'.

Every row about immigration is welcome to Farage, providing it does not lead voters to conclude that the party is extreme. In an era when politicians are seen as grey and bland he lifts an otherwise dull television package, just as Boris Johnson and Alex Salmond have.

We shouldn't be such a pushover.

Thursday 20 November

Rochester station

Not long ago everyone thought they knew what a UKIP supporter looked like: an old man in a blue blazer with a golf-club tie. Then another stereotype was added: the shaven-headed, tattooed, working-class warrior. In just half an hour standing with my camera crew on Rochester's platform 2, waiting for the afternoon commuter trains from London to come in, I am reminded how partial that picture is.

It's polling day in Rochester. Team Farage is about to see off all that the formidable Tory campaign machine have thrown at them to win the by-election David Cameron said he'd throw the kitchen sink at. Not even five visits by the prime minister and hundreds by Tory MPs will have saved this once-safe Conservative seat.

First a posh-sounding City worker tells me that he's backing UKIP to force the other parties to sort out Europe and immigration. Then precisely the same point is made by a northern ex-Labour voter. Finally, I speak to a young black woman who won't utter the word UKIP but whose attitudes make it clear that, to her own surprise, she's decided to give them a try because, after all, if they don't deliver she can still vote for someone else in a few months' time.

'You want to try before you buy?' I suggest to her.

'Yes,' she replies.

It is a remarkable coalition of support.

When I catch up with Farage, he tells me this is the most important by-election in decades and that a UKIP victory will mean 'all bets are off' in the general election.

The count, Medway Park, Gillingham

Unbelievable. Extraordinary. Do they have a death wish?

Emily Thornberry, the husky-voiced shadow attorney general and close ally of Ed Miliband, has posted a tweet of a photograph taken on a campaign visit here. It shows a house decked out in three huge England flags, with a white van parked outside, captioned by a single word: 'Rochester'.

So what? was my immediate reaction, until I saw how others responded to it. They viewed the sentiment behind the picture tweeted by the MP for Islington South as: 'Oh my God, look at the sort of people who live here. How absolutely vulgar. Get me back to Ottolenghi on Upper Street pronto.' Which is a teeny bit of a problem when they're the people you want to vote for your party.

Labour could have tried to tough it out, to deny that the tweet meant anything very much at all and moved on, but, no, Team Ed tell me they've never seen him so angry and that he's demanded an apology. They ring back just before the news at ten to say he's had another conversation with Emily and she has resigned. That means she's been sacked.

I call a mate at the *Sun* who confirms what I will not have been the only one to predict. They have chucked a few quid at White Van Man, who has given them an interview accusing Emily of being a snob.

On air I say that it is as if David Cameron were at the wheel of a car heading for a brick wall at a hundred miles an hour and at the last minute Ed Miliband has thrown himself in front of it.

Friday 21 November

Rest A While café, Strood

Over a mug of strong tea (bag and spoon still in), I learn about why UKIP won their second seat last night. I'm talking to a lady who has come out for a cuppa and a natter with a friend about why she – a traditional Labour voter – backed the public-school and Oxford-educated ex-Tory MP. 'It's put Rochester and Strood on the map,' she tells me. 'Before no one knew where Strood was. They do now.'

A pensioner couple tell me that 'politicians just don't understand how we live . . . how difficult we find things'. A builder with more tattoos than teeth, but who is none the less working his way through a massive fry-up, agrees. This is the real face of this poor constituency, not Rochester's high street with its trinket shops, wide pavements and ornate lamp posts, which date back to the time Charles Dickens lived and wrote nearby.

When I offer to buy the two ladies an extra cuppa to thank them for giving up their time they look impossibly grateful. So much so that I want to weep. I think nothing of spending a couple of quid on a hot drink. For them it's a real treat. It simply highlights the gulf between the life of the 'political class' and theirs.

'ONLY HERE FOR THE SNEERS' was the headline the *Sun* ran over its interview with the Rochester resident who accuses Emily Thornberry of being a snob. I will be returning on a fast train to north London tonight, to my home just up the road from Emily Thornberry's. A host of other Labour politicians – Douglas Alexander, Tristram Hunt, Ed Balls and Yvette Cooper – all live within walking distance. In west London you can find a similar collection of Tory politicians. There is no denying it's another world.

Dickens captured it in *A Tale of Two Cities*: 'It was the best of times, it was the worst of times, it was the age of wisdom, it was the age of foolishness, it was the epoch of belief, it was the epoch of incredulity, it was the season of Light, it was the season of Darkness, it was the spring of hope, it was the winter of despair, we had everything before us, we had nothing before us . . .'

UKIP headquarters

UKIP, Nigel Farage tells me in his victory interview, can now double the number of MPs it expects to elect. He doesn't put a figure on it but that means an increase from a handful to a couple of handfuls since our first-past-the-post voting system makes it very hard for smaller parties with support evenly spread across the country to make a real breakthrough at Westminster.

However, in an election which both the Tories and Labour appear to be conspiring to lose, it may be enough to hold the balance of power, perhaps in combination with the SNP and the Ulster Unionists.

We seem to be on course for the most unpredictable election in decades, ushering in a period of real instability in which vote-by-vote, day-by-day, night-by-night haggling will be required to secure every piece of legislation. We may be heading back to the future; to a repeat of the mid-1970s when the prospect of dying MPs being carried into the Commons by ambulance drivers was seriously considered and drunks were locked into cupboards with bottles of booze simply to keep them on the premises for the latest nail-biting vote. I am too young to remember it but I know it was an exhilarating though exhausting time to be a political journalist, even if it wasn't a great period for the country.

Evening, the train to London

Just as Labour are struggling to hose down the row caused by a picture posted on Twitter, I discover that I have got myself into a similar mess.

At last night's election count I was approached by a smiley woman who asked if she could have her photograph taken with me. I'm sure as hell no rock star but at political events this happens quite a lot, and I've got pretty used to posing and beaming before trying to return as quickly as possible to whatever I was trying to do before, in this case writing a blog.

However, it turns out that the woman, who had been wearing a green fleece with a logo on it which I took to be the uniform of the workers at the leisure centre where the count was taking place, was in fact the candidate for Britain First, an unpleasant militaristic offshoot of the BNP. This group, which organizes 'mosque invasions' and other nasty stunts and is incapable of garnering much support, tends to use Facebook pictures of animals and, it transpires, naïve political editors, to draw people to its propaganda.

When I see that the image has gone viral I tweet: 'Lesson of the day. Never agree to have selfie taken without first checking who's asking. Shame but my mistake.'

Some reply that since Emily Thornberry has had to resign, I should do so, too. I draft an intemperate reply suggesting that perhaps resignation isn't enough and execution might be more appropriate. Then, thank God, I think better of it and delete the tweet. Do these people really believe that the grandson of German Jewish refugees is a closet fascist? Twitter, Facebook and other social media have unleashed the sort of bilious, judgemental anger society assumed had been wiped out when the stocks and public hangings were abolished. I must not get sucked into that.

Sunday 23 November

Home

This morning Theresa May seems to be in every paper and all over TV and radio. She's about to announce new anti-terrorism measures and new penalties for domestic abuse. She appears first on *The Andrew Marr Show* and then on *Desert Island Discs*.

Wherever she is, she does her very best to say as little as possible. On the Marr sofa she finally admits that the government will probably not meet its immigration target. Hardly a bombshell: there is as much chance of them meeting it as I have of winning Miss World.

I had warned Kirsty Young's producer on *Desert Island Discs* that the home secretary is incredibly cautious in her public utterances, let alone her private ones. But Kirsty is as skilled as ever in trying to draw out her guest. Thus, in spite of the questions that go unanswered, we learn that the home secretary has indeed got her eye on her party's leadership; that she has long been a political obsessive (she delivered leaflets for the Tories aged twelve and requests a recording of *Yes Minister* as one of her discs); that she doesn't want to be seen as another Thatcher because she doesn't believe in an -ism (other, she says, than Conservatism) and that she is very churchy (her father was a vicar and she picks two hymns to take with her on to her desert island).

She does, though, have the great merit of sounding authentic and human and could feasibly be a future prime minister.

Monday 24 November

College Green

It wasn't meant to be a sneer but I fear that's how it sounds. At the end of my news at ten two-way* about Labour's new proposals to tax private schools that don't play nice with local state schools, I point out that they've been made by the privately educated Honourable Dr Tristram Hunt. I could have added Tristram Julian William Hunt, son of the Baron Hunt, but luckily resisted that temptation.

* TV jargon for a presenter interviewing a reporter.

Worthwhile though it may well be to threaten to remove business-rates relief from a few posh schools that don't share their Latin teacher or playing field with their state-run neighbours, it is not going to transform the performance of the state sector as a whole.

The value of the announcement is political. It addresses one of the most potent questions in modern politics: 'Whose side are you on?' So there is an irony in the fact that a posh public schoolboy is aligning himself with the workers.

Team Miliband are learning from the Obama playbook. The president ruthlessly portrayed Mitt Romney, his opponent in the 2012 race, as 'on the side' of the rich and privileged. His people pounced on any comment Romney made that could be used to show how out of touch he was with ordinary 'folks'. It must be said that they had plenty of material at their disposal. In one TV appearance Romney tried to settle an argument by offering to take a $10,000 bet that he was right. Wagering half the salary of one of your potential voters isn't too astute. The Republican tried to repair the damage by talking about sports. A reporter asked him, 'Do you like football?' His reply sent his spin doctors into despair. 'Yes, two of my friends own teams.'

I'm pretty sure that, for all his Old Etonian chums, David Cameron won't be that careless or helpful to his opponent.

Over at the Royal Courts of Justice is a reminder of the hold class has over Britain. The Plebgate trial is beginning. At stake is the career, reputation and fortune of a former Cabinet minister. Bizarrely, Andrew Mitchell's defence appears to be yes, I have shouted at police officers on many occasions; yes, I have used the F-word when doing so and yes, I have patronized them by calling them 'Plod', but no, dear me no, I have absolutely never, ever labelled them 'plebs'. I'm no lawyer but I'm not sure that works for me.

Tuesday 25 November

House of Commons

The PM is presenting the report into the Woolwich killing, the savage beheading of Fusilier Lee Rigby in broad daylight by two men born and bred in London. It reveals a catalogue of mistakes and missed opportunities by the security services, though its conclusion – that none of these in themselves meant the murder was avoidable – is clear.

Look out for a mention of internet firms in the PM's speech, I've been told. Sure enough, he highlights the fact that an unnamed internet company found a message from one of the assassins expressing his desire to kill a soldier. Links to known terrorist organizations had been picked up by the firm's systems and automatically cut off but this murderous message had not been seen or passed on to the authorities.

First Cameron, then Sir Malcolm Rifkind, chairman of the Commons Intelligence and Defence Committee, and finally former home secretary Jack Straw line up to lay into the USA-based kings of the web and their 'libertarian' values. A couple of texts later I'm informed it's Facebook that is in the firing line.

Some see this as merely a convenient distraction from the failures of MI5, MI6 and GCHQ. Something else is going on, though. The security services are furious that the old understandings they had with the web giants have been blown apart by the revelations of Edward Snowden.* The Facebooks and the Googles insist that they have had to withdraw some co-operation in response to the anger of their customers. What Messrs Cameron, Rifkind and Straw are trying to do is apply some pressure in the other direction.

The shadow chancellor's office, House of Commons

Stop for a cuppa with Ed Balls, who's preparing for next week's autumn statement – a chance to crow about the fact that the chancellor will have to unveil increased forecasts for borrowing rather than the cut he promised.

I suggest to him that no one sees the link between his criticism of the cost-of-living crisis and the deficit even though there is one (lower wages means lower taxes means higher borrowing). He gets out his pen to make notes, something that always worries me as it's my job to jot down what he says, not the other way round.

The shadow home secretary pops her head round the door to

* The American computer system administrator who leaked classified information from the National Security Agency to the media.

remind him it's time to go to one of their kids' school concerts. I have no idea how Ed and Yvette juggle their lives but somehow they do, and they seem to remain remarkably cheerful the whole time, too.

Political Studies Association awards, Church House, Westminster

I've been asked to hand out the gong to the Politician of the Year as chosen by the nation's political academics. Their choice, no doubt made long before recent events, is Theresa May. I spend dinner pondering how far I can go in teasing her without spoiling the party atmosphere.

I announce that in the spirit of the recent vote on the European arrest warrant, the judges decided not to have a vote for Politician of the Year but on something entirely different, while agreeing to make that 'indicative' of who should win. It's a bit insider-y but she laughs and so do they.

In her acceptance speech – well-prepared and polished as ever – she declares that the collection of journalists, academics and political opponents in the audience is much more scary than the Police Federation annual conference. She then jokes that her aim when she became home secretary was to keep out of the news. Recent events had proved that she still had a way to go in achieving that objective.

Wednesday 26 November

Broadcasting House studio

The tide may just be turning back in Ed Miliband's favour. For months he's tried to move the NHS up the political agenda. For months David Cameron has simply responded with a litany of the failings of the Labour-run NHS in Wales. Not today, though.

In PMQs Miliband uses statistics about growing waiting times in A&E departments and the number of people who can't get to see their GP to describe an NHS 'at breaking point'. Cameron clearly knows there's something in this and chooses, for once, to answer rather than hit back.

I am increasingly hearing stories of people stuck in ambulances outside A&Es while others are being treated on trolleys, not only because of the pressure on emergency departments but because of a shortage of hospital beds to move people on to, caused by the presence of elderly patients who are, in the jargon, 'bed-blocking'. They cannot be discharged until social care is available for them outside the hospital and inadequacies with these services are creating a backlog. There hasn't yet been a single compelling human story to take this to the top of news bulletins but there soon will be.

At the last election a poster of a rosy-cheeked, airbrushed Cameron promised to cut the deficit, not the NHS. Add to that the admission the chancellor will have to make next week that he's missed his borrowing targets again, and the confirmation tomorrow from the home secretary that the Tories have missed their immigration target, too, and you have a pretty good springboard for an election-winning Labour strategy. If, that is – and it's a mighty big if – they can overcome the small matter of an unpopular leader and an economic policy seen as lacking credibility.

It doesn't help Ed that even his own MPs are now ridiculing him. Jamie Reed mocks his leader's now-infamous 'white-van' answer ('the first thing I think of when I see one is "respect"') by declaring in PMQs his first thought when he sees a white van: 'Is it my brother or my father driving it?'

Thursday 27 November

BBC studios, Millbank

David Cameron once told me that he used to tease Nick Clegg by vowing he would never have 'one of your split-screen moments' – a reference to what we TV news guys did to the Lib Dem leader when we ran his promise to cut tuition fees on one side of the screen and his U-turn on the other.

Ever since I have felt it my duty to ensure that the Tory side of the coalition suffers the same indignity for a clear pledge made and then broken. Today's the day. The latest immigration statistics show that not only has net migration (the difference between the numbers coming in and those going out of the country) not been cut to the tens of thousands promised, but the figure is now higher than when Cameron moved into Number 10. What's more, they can't even blame it on the surge of immigration from Europe. Take all those Poles and Bulgarians and Romanians and Spaniards out of the equation and they still miss their target. As I point out in my news report – gleefully, suggests one tweeter. Perhaps a bit, yes. From the day it was set it was obvious that this target couldn't be met.

All the same, I wish I was in Edinburgh reporting on the publication of the plan to give the Scottish Parliament more powers, the result of that last-minute 'vow to the people of Scotland' made by Messrs Cameron, Miliband and Clegg, and cooked up by Gordon Brown, amid the panic that the No camp might be about to lose the Scottish referendum.

I listened in despair this morning to some of the coverage of this story. 'Holyrood will be able to set the rates and bands of income tax but not the personal allowances . . .' droned one piece. Zzz. It's as if the reporters at the signing of the American constitution had begun by pointing out that in future the federal government would not have responsibility for pigswill but would have it for other agricultural products.

The proposals to give the Scottish Parliament much more power mark the beginning of a process of dramatic change and a series of arguments concerning what politics is really about – who should have control over what?

Friday 28 November

JCB headquarters, Rocester, Staffordshire

An alarm is blaring on the factory floor. The prime minister, who is standing, for no good reason, next to a digger, pretends not to have heard it and ploughs on through his big speech on immigration. He finally acknowledges it with a joke. 'The alarm bells are clearly ringing in the European Commission,' he says. He couldn't be more wrong. If alarm bells are ringing anywhere, it will be among the Eurosceptics.

This speech was billed in advance as a throwing down of the gauntlet to Brussels on freedom of movement within Europe. The talk was of insisting on a cap or a limit or an emergency brake. Yet now that proposal is nowhere to be seen. Instead the PM's speech praises freedom of movement as a vital EU principle. It has clearly been written very, very carefully to try to woo the allies in Europe he so desperately needs.

Cameron has been under mounting pressure from his sceptics to say that he would lead the campaign to leave the EU in a future referendum if he didn't get the deal he wanted. That, they argued, would show the Europeans that he meant business and eat into UKIP's support. Today he has said no such thing, merely stating the blindingly obvious: that 'nothing is ruled out' if he can't get the deal he wants. It is the rhetorical equivalent of announcing, 'If the sun doesn't come up in the morning it will be dark.' But it seems to have satisfied the Tory press, whose editors all got personal phone calls from the PM yesterday. When I downplayed the significance of this anodyne phrase on the radio earlier, Downing Street got very cross.

One other thing the Tory hardliners will surely have noticed is that although this speech is all about 'controlling immigration', what it lacks is a proposal to, er, control immigration. There's lots in it about curbing benefits, tax credits and access to housing for new arrivals – 'reducing the pull factors', as they call it in the jargon – but no new target or limit on the numbers coming in.

Perhaps David Cameron has learned his lesson after having to live with an immigration target that could never be achieved. I ask him whether he will apologize for breaking his promise, 'no ifs, no buts' (the phrase he used when he repeated the pledge a couple of years back). No, it turns out, he won't, though he will explain, he says. Explain, that is, that he hadn't foreseen the three Eurozone crises in six years that would lead to young people from all over Europe scurrying towards Blighty.

One of the reasons for the lack of trust in politicians is that they vow to control things over which voters know they have little or no control, and then have to admit that they broke their vow. At worst, this makes them look dishonest. At best impotent.

Sunday 30 November

Home

The Sunday papers have all been briefed with an Osborne promise, made three days ahead of his autumn statement, to spend another £2 billion next year on the NHS.

It is clearly his attempt to disarm the greatest threat to the Tories before Labour can 'weaponize' it. The recent news that a sixteen-year-old girl was kept in a police cell when a hospital bed could not be found for her was a warning to ministers of what might be to come. The cash Osborne has found down the back of the Treasury sofa – an underspend here, a reallocation from within the Department of Health there, with the odd bank fine thrown in – will not guarantee that there will be no more stories like it.

However, what it has already delivered is something almost as valuable politically: the endorsement of the chief executive of the NHS in England, Simon Stevens, who said it showed that ministers had 'listened' and 'responded with the funding we need'. He has even, somewhat to my surprise and Labour's horror, agreed to be filmed with George Osborne in a hospital welcoming the announcement.

I'm told that Osborne met him three times in the last week. The chancellor saw the worth of acquiring the support of a man who used to advise a Labour health secretary and later Tony Blair.

Every time the Tories are attacked on the NHS from now until election day, they will claim that they have backed the Stevens plan and he has backed them. Osborne will regard that as very good political value for a couple of billion quid.

— DECEMBER —

Monday 1 December

Train to Stevenage

As the tills ring all over Britain in the run-up to Christmas, the spend, spend, spend mood seems to have infected the nation's politicians, too. Yesterday the coalition promised cash for the NHS. Today it's roads. Tomorrow, we're told, it will be housing. Oh, and flood defences. There's just one problem: there isn't any. Money, that is. Remember that note left in the Treasury on the day of the last election, the one that read, 'Sorry, there's no money left'? At the next election the same note could be brought out, perhaps with the addition of one word, 'still'.

This is not what voters want to hear, though. People want to believe that the government can pay off Britain's debt, stop borrowing, fund better services and give tax cuts, too. That's why the parties compete to sound tough over public finances while offering a little more of what you might like.

I'm heading this morning to a factory with Ed Balls to interview him about Labour's approach. TV studios are so last year, darling. Ever since George Osborne took to donning a high-viz jacket for his every public appearance, no one can afford to be seen away from a factory floor.

Ed is, as ever, good company. He's much more worried about his Grade 4 piano exam than answering this week's autumn statement. This despite the fact that his terrible performance last year finished off any talk of him as a future Labour leader.

He tells me about a recent dinner he had with Mark Carney, who requested they go to a 'neighbourhood restaurant' rather than somewhere posh. Ed decided to try out a Vietnamese place that had been recommended to him but which he hadn't yet had time to check out.

On arrival, the governor of the Bank of England and the man who could be the next chancellor of the exchequer discovered there were no quiet tables. Indeed, there were no separate tables at all. They were obliged to squeeze into the middle of one of two long rows of diners sitting on either side of a refectory table. As they discussed quantitative easing, fiscal tightening and the role of automatic stabilizers, no one batted an eyelid.

Airbus satellite factory

I want to use my interview to tempt Ed to spell out what his real economic policy is: to spend more and borrow more for longer than the Tories on the grounds that you need to grow your way, not cut your way, out of a deficit. It's clear that he wants to do anything but spell that out. Indeed, he wants to do the opposite, stressing his willingness to say no to more spending and his resistance to uncosted promises.

His pre-planned soundbite – a pledge to be 'tough on the deficit and tough on the causes of the deficit' – does no more than hint at his real view. The causes of the deficit are, he believes, the lack of growth, the failure of real wages to rise and, therefore, the absence of a higher tax take.

World at One, *BBC Radio 4*

Sum up Gordon Brown in three minutes, they ask. He has just announced his retirement from the Commons after thirty years. I have only a moment to prepare. I write down a few words as a prompt: 'At best, brilliant, inspirational, funny. At worst, insecure, slow on his feet, furious when crossed.'

In his retirement speech Brown spoke movingly of the time he feared he'd lose his sight when he was in Number 10. People often ask me whether there are things I know but don't report. Very few, is the answer, but that was one. I saw it as first and foremost a personal and not a political matter.

Before he became prime minister I interviewed Gordon on a school rugby pitch about the accident there years earlier that left him blind in one eye and with limited vision in the other. I defended him on air when the *Sun* attacked him for misspelling the name of a dead soldier in a letter to his grieving mother. The paper got her to attack the PM's untidy scrawl in his trademark thick, black pen. She didn't know that he couldn't see to write anything smaller.

I remember his panic when I filmed him tripping over a bag blocking the aisle of a private plane taking him to Paris. I repeatedly assured him that I would not use the footage. It was then that his aides told me he was terrified of walking into places and not recognizing people who spoke to him. They always stayed close and whispered names into his ear.

All this fed a deep underlying insecurity which could turn into anger and, at times, paranoia. I found reporting on his time as PM one of the hardest things I've done. He was often rude to my face and just as frequently much ruder behind my back. I tried everything I could think of to repair a relationship that had once been good. When I met two of his closest advisers at Number 10 and poured out my frustration and despair about how bad things had got, I remember being very close to tears.

One of them is listening to my *World at One* tribute. Afterwards, he texts me. 'You nailed it,' the message reads. Knowing that he feels I captured Gordon, the good and the bad, I feel some of that old emotion come back.

10 Downing Street, pillared room

It's the lobby's annual Christmas drinks at Number 10, a chance for the nation's political hacks to boast to their news desks, wives, husbands, partners and friends, 'As the prime minister said to me the other day . . .'

When I catch up with the PM I decide to test a new theory on him. You must be a bit worried, I remark, as pretty soon Labour will be able to say, 'He broke his promise on immigration, he broke his promise on the deficit and there's a crisis in the NHS.' He pauses as if he's been giving this some thought already. He makes no attempt to deny the premise, but replies that what matters is whether you look like 'you've got a grip' on those problems. 'And we do.'

Tuesday 2 December

Downing Street

On the eve of budgets and mini-budgets, it's my job to appear all-knowing and all-seeing about what will be announced the following day.

The proper way to do this is to work your contacts for weeks in advance to winkle out what's really going on behind the scenes. The lazy way is to wait and see what scraps from the table the Treasury choose to fling in your direction. They're usually the bits and pieces no one will care about the next day when much bigger news comes along.

Sadly, the supply of even those scraps has now dried up after a super-bright, if rather politically naïve, civil servant gave a spectacularly detailed and comprehensive overview of the contents of a budget to the *Evening Standard* to help the paper prepare the front page that would hit the streets of London as soon as the chancellor began to deliver it. The news was accidentally tweeted before he'd even opened his mouth. Ever since that *Standard* front page, Treasury press officers have sounded utterly terrified whenever you ring up and say, 'Can we talk about the autumn statement?'

As a result, it is now just before 10pm and I am expected to be all-seeing and all-knowing about what the chancellor will announce tomorrow despite having seen all too little and knowing even less. No matter. This is where well-informed, calculated guesswork comes in.

The man from the *FT* told me earlier that he had a shrewd hunch as to the nature of the rabbit Osborne would pull from his budget hat. The paper's front page has just dropped, and it tentatively suggests that it might be the reform of stamp duty. This makes complete sense: tax the sale of mansions more and ordinary punters' homes less. I text people who've tried to be helpful all day. No denials follow. So I go for it, my fingers crossed, and wait to see if I – or rather, the *FT* – will be proved right.

Wednesday 3 December

The bubble, College Green

What exactly is 'masosadism'? Not a question on which I expected to have to opine on when preparing for four hours in a glass bubble with Andrew Neil and Robert Peston for BBC 2's *Autumn Statement Special*. But today's PMQs has taken on a flavour of *Fifty Shades of Grey*. The prime minister has decided to have fun with Ed Balls' 'tough on the deficit and tough on the causes of the deficit' soundbite, claiming that 'he *is* one of the causes of the deficit'. He goes on: 'I think we've all found one of the first-ever examples of political masosadism.' Some MPs are speechless. Others shout that what he means is sado-masochism. The speaker intervenes to clear it all up. 'Order, order! We all know what the prime minister meant. I understand the house gets excited.'

'I meant to say masochism,' Cameron corrects himself. 'Normally the shadow chancellor likes to dish it out but he can't take it, but after this quote I think he obviously quite likes taking it as well, so there we are.' By the time he sits down Twitter has revealed that in fact the PM was right first time round. There really is something called masosadism – apparently it describes people who like taking it more than giving it out, although they like that too. That's what an expensive private edu-cation does for you.

All this rather diverts attention from Ed Miliband's line of attack, which I predicted the other night. He reels off Cameron's broken promises one by one, first on immigration, then the deficit and finally on the NHS. The PM gets quite a spanking and gives no sign of enjoying it at all. No masosadist he, then. Why Ed wastes these lines on a day when the chancellor's announcements and not his questions are guar-anteed to make the news is a puzzle to me.

When the man with no money to spend stands up he demonstrates that he is much more interested in dishing it out than taking it. Even if George Osborne had made no statements of his own today he knew he'd still have to read out the official – and, thanks to him, independent – forecasts showing that his plan to cut the deficit is off course. So he makes a startling number of announcements designed to distract and woo target voters.

Think the Tories are friends of the rich? George has his answer. A 'Google tax' on tax-avoiding multinationals, a tax on banks who avoid tax by writing off huge losses, a higher fee on non-doms and, yes, that stamp-duty reform, which slaps a big new tax on buying what you and I might call a mansion.

For everyone else there is lower tax when you buy your house, a cut in the tax on kids' flights, a promise to freeze fuel duty and a tax-free way to inherit your partner's ISA.

The *Sun* are already calling it a Robin Hood budget. I prefer to call it a pre-election budget in all but name.

Edit suite, Millbank

Budget speeches are a nightmare to edit. The chancellor and his team try to pre-edit them for you, presenting you with well-crafted, well-delivered soundbites that make the points they want to make and keep the ones they'd rather you ignored detailed and complex and dull. So all those crowd-pleasing announcements are ready to serve whereas the reading out of the official forecasts of the deficit and what they mean is hard to follow.

They've learned from Gordon Brown, who made the mistake of allowing his obfuscations to be glaringly obvious. He would sprint breathlessly through unwelcome statistics in a way that was very easy to pick up on. By contrast, Osborne acknowledged that borrowing was going up 'slightly' this year and next but buried this nugget in the middle of a sentence claiming it would go down 'slightly' after that, so all will be fine.

This is at odds with the Office for Budget Responsibility's warning that if taxes aren't increased, the Conservatives will have to cut spending back to 1930s levels – not in cash terms, but as a share of the national cake – in order to balance the books on the timetable they've set out.

The Tories will hate that. The 1930s conjure up a powerful image of Britain before the welfare state and the birth of the NHS, of grainy black-and-white photographs of kids without shoes and queues at soup kitchens.

If today's statement had come after and not before an election everyone would have been talking of which taxes to increase and what spending to cut further. But alongside the budget deficit there is, on all sides of politics, a candour deficit.

Thursday 4 December

Home, the study

I have overslept. A series of texts reveal that a row is already raging about something Norman Smith said on the radio early this morning. In one of his characteristically vivid turns of phrase he mused that future spending cuts could take us back to the era of Orwell's *Road to Wigan Pier* territory and called it a 'terrifying' prospect.

Norman is a one-man political machine whose prodigious energy and insights drive the BBC's political journalism from dawn till dusk on Radio 4 and the news channel. Hour after hour, day after day, he calls it and calls it right. He is, though, the journalistic equivalent of that John Lewis price promise – 'never knowingly undersold' – which enrages politicians, who know that what he says first thing in the morning will shape the rest of the news day. Never more so than today.

I am sitting in my basement with a coffee and a piece of toast, listening to George Osborne's interview with John Humphrys over my headphones, the mic in front of me ready for me to go on air straight afterwards to analyze what's been said. I scribble notes of the chancellor's responses. 'Hyperbole' is one, followed by 'nonsense', 'listening to a rewind of a tape of 2010' and 'I would have thought the BBC would have learned from the last four years . . .' And so on. He has the messenger in his sights and has opened up with both barrels.

John turns to me not with a question but with an observation. 'Nick, he's very cross about the BBC . . .' My task is not to inflame the row but not to back down, either. I try as fast as I can to move the subject away from the BBC and back to the deficit and that OBR forecast.

Every battle between politicians and the BBC boils down to the same thing in the end: who controls the news agenda. That's what really underlay my spat with Salmond. Did I choose my words carefully enough? No. Did Norman? I suspect he thinks the same. Are we asking the right questions about the right things in the face of people in power who want to change the agenda? You betcha.

A pub, south of the river

It's the office Christmas party and it begins with a quiz. First, pick your team's name. Paul, the quizmaster, reads them out one by one, all chosen independently. 'The Wigan Warriors, the Wigan Piers, the Orwells . . .'

Friday 5 December

It's official. The Tories are now at war with the BBC. That's the lead story in the *Telegraph* and the splash in the *Mail*, a paper that, at times, seems blind to irony. Its double-page spread about the perfidy of Britain's state broadcaster and the history of our bloodcurdling, leftish warnings about the impact of cuts is accompanied by a straight news story: a report on the verdict of the country's leading independent think-tank, the Institute for Fiscal Studies.

'Britain faces cuts on a colossal scale,' it declares, pointing out that reductions in funding of this magnitude would mean a 'fundamental re-imagining of the role of the state'.

Pretty strong stuff. It could have been the lead story, I suppose, but why bother readers and voters with questions about cuts to the police or social care or schools when a row about what Norman Smith said is so much more important?

Saturday 6 December

Driving practice with L-plates

'Straight on . . . give the cyclist more room . . . don't look at the gear-stick when changing up . . .' My expert driving advice to my son Will is interrupted by the phone ringing. It's Gobby. He has news. Big news. The man I rely on to stand outside buildings waiting to shout at politicians has been pondering quitting himself. My fear has long been that he'd join the competition. ITV have approached him (when I joined ITV I tried to hire him myself), as have Sky. The political parties, too, have been sniffing around the guy who knows how to get things on air, chats to the snappers and has confidence to match even that of the politicians he shouts at. Downing Street talked of a role improving their events. Labour offered him a job but the money wasn't good enough and he doesn't rate Ed.

What I haven't anticipated is that he'd be hired by UKIP. His mate Nigel, the man with whom he enjoys a pint and a fag, who makes him laugh, who, above all, listens to what he thinks, has taken him on as director of communications.

Glad for him. Sad for us. Stunned by where he's ended up. But he reveals why when he tells friends that 'it's not bad for a hairy-arsed electrician from Hounslow'. And in a way that tells you everything about why Farage is reaching the parts of Britain that the others – and, yes, the BBC too – struggle to reach.

Sunday 7 December

Home

It has been the worst-kept secret in politics and now it's official. Alex Salmond is coming home. To Westminster – the Parliament where he always felt more at home than in Holyrood. In a speech today announcing that he will stand as an MP next year he says he wants to 'rumble up' Westminster to ensure that it gives Scotland a better deal.

If neither big party wins the election the Commons will become a bazaar in which the SNP, the Unionists and perhaps UKIP, too, sell their support day by day and vote by vote in return for a little of what their supporters want.

It's a prospect Salmond, a consummate Commons performer, simply couldn't resist.

Monday 8 December

National Graphene Institute, Manchester

'This is the future and you're building it,' says the man in the high-viz jacket, hard hat and heavy boots to the man next to him kitted out in exactly the same way.

The first man is the chancellor of the exchequer, George (born

Gideon) Osborne, son of a baronet, heir to a small fortune and the epitome of what his enemies would call a southern, public-school, Bullingdon club, Tory toff. The other is a builder from Ashton-under-Lyne near Manchester.

With them is a third man, the Nobel prize-winner who invented graphene at the city's university. It's a new wonder substance, a very thin (one atom thick) sheet of carbon, a hundred times stronger than steel, which conducts both heat and electricity with amazing efficiency.

A while back this scene would have exposed Osborne to scorn. The outfit would have been pronounced ridiculous, the words patronizing and the claim implausible. But not now. Somehow, this London-born, -bred and -centric politician has managed to adopt my home city of Manchester and make it his own. He's done it by a very, very simple method: flattering the city by promising to create a 'northern powerhouse', lavishing attention on it and surfing a new wave of Mancunian optimism.

Manchester Museum of Science and Industry

The way Osborne has pulled off this feat becomes obvious at his next stop, a ceremony to mark Manchester's birth as a European City of Science.

He is flanked by the Labour leader of the Manchester council, Sir Richard Leese, and TV's top scientist, Professor Brian Cox. Cox, a local lad, was a member of the band D:Ream, whose song 'Things Can Only Get Better' was Labour's anthem during the 1997 election campaign. I ask him whether he's comfortable endorsing any politician, not least a Tory southern politician, who claims to be helping Manchester. His answer is clear. I don't do politics, he tells me, but anyone who backs science and puts their money where their mouth is will have my support.

What, though, of Richard Leese, whose council, along with all its neighbours in Greater Manchester, has lost £200 million in cuts this year alone? He and the seven other Labour council leaders recently appeared in a photo-call with Osborne to endorse his vision of Manchester as the hub of his 'northern powerhouse' with its own Boris- (or Ken-) style elected mayor.

The reason, I'm told, is that George has spent hours wooing them whereas the Eds have taken their own people for granted, wavering over whether to back a high-speed rail link, hesitating over devolving more powers and spending much less time in their own political back-yard than the chancellor has.

It's an often-forgotten truism about politics that personal relation-ships are critical to success – forgotten by a variety of charismatic, impressive but aloof figures ranging from Denis Healey to Michael Portillo to David Miliband.

It is a little-known fact that George Osborne, whose public image was so bad for so long, is very good at it.

Manchester City football club

I have been far, far too generous. Team Osborne gleefully offer me a lift in the back of his car to our next and final stop: the home of the Blues. The chancellor's next assignment is to open a new Manchester City football academy, the centrepiece of a £200 million city regenera-tion project.

As a dyed-in-the-wool Red, I have never been here before. In a small and utterly childish act of defiance, I have brought my United scarf with me. I sneak it out of my bag, put it on for a quick selfie, and shove it away again.

A party in Knightsbridge

Squeezed on a balcony at a party sponsored by the *Spectator*, I come up against Nigel Farage. After berating him for stealing Gobby from the BBC, I remind him that it's not so long ago he was talking as if UKIP's role was to be less an alternative political party and more of a pressure group whose job would be done once the Tory party had been reclaimed from the 'Cameroon' modernizers. 'When did you know you could go much further?' I ask him.

He tells me that it was straight after his *Today* programme inter-view in the wake of last May's local elections, when I pointed out his relative lack of ambition. Leaving Broadcasting House, he saw a gaggle of cameramen and thought, who are they waiting for? Then he realized it was him.

A passerby whispers in my ear that if this balcony collapses, British politics would be changed for good.

Tuesday 9 December

Broadcasting House

Much mirth around the newsroom. On his first day in his new job, Gobby is handling a UKIP scandal that has it all. A parliamentary candidate who defected from the Labour party – called, appropriately enough, Ms Bolter – claims she was sexually harassed by the party's general secretary, a chap, entertainingly, going by the name of Roger Bird.

Bizarrely, Mr Bird openly admits to having sex with Ms Bolter, while she denies sleeping with him. He adds credibility to his version of events by releasing texts bearing messages along the lines of 'I love u Bird'. Suggestions of a knee-trembling encounter on a snooker table in Bird's gentlemen's club lend the story a Palmerstonesque flavour – legend has it that the Victorian prime minister and old rascal died while potting the balls on the green baize with his maid.

Wednesday 10 December

Prime Minister's Questions

Cameron is away and Clegg is filling in. A mistake. He should have found any excuse to take a day off, too. The oft-underestimated Harriet Harman begins by asking how many of his seven Cabinet appointments have been women. When he ducks the answer – which is, of course, none – she counters that Nick is normally quite forthcoming when replying to questions about himself and women. She doesn't need to say the rest. All MPs are remembering that headline about the Lib Dem leader having slept with thirty women.

Questions follow on why tax cuts help men and benefit cuts hurt women more, the gender pay gap, and so on. Nick responds with increasing defensiveness and angry anti-Labour bluster. In short, he looks and sounds like the Tory men who are cheering him on. For Harriet and Labour, who desperately need the Lib Dems not to recover, that's job done. For Nick and the Lib Dems, who have spent the last few days monstering the Tories for planning savage spending cuts, it's a strategic own goal.

Team Clegg spent no time before signing up to this coalition thinking through ways of making themselves look and sound different from the Conservatives when the Commons traditions force them to sit with the Tories and speak in front of the Tories – rendering them, in the eyes of most viewers, completely indistinguishable from the Tories.

Millbank

The new first minister is in town. Nicola Sturgeon has her first audience with the Queen. I can't help wondering how these two impressive women will handle each other. Her Majesty knows that Nicola is a closet republican. Sturgeon knows that her monarch is a unionist, scarcely a closet one, who, despite all protestations to the contrary, intervened in the independence referendum by urging her subjects to 'think carefully' about their vote.

Nicola pops into the BBC studio at Millbank for an interview and a chat first. She is conciliatory, though not uncritical of the BBC. Quite a contrast to Alex Salmond, who still exudes anger and aggression.

House of Lords bar

Over a drink, a Tory Cabinet minister tells me that he is out of the office two full days a week visiting up to five target constituencies a day. I hear that Nick Clegg now spends even more time than that touring key Lib Dem marginals. If you live in Cornwall or Somerset, you may see the deputy prime minister more often than your teenage kids.

This Parliament is crawling to an election with less to do than any in recent history and all because, at the very last minute in the negotiations that formed this coalition, George Osborne decided that a five-year fixed Parliament would be a better bet than a four-year one. Better, that is, because there would be more chance of an economic recovery and a Tory victory. In any previous era we would have had an election by now.

Thursday 11 December

Home

Just weeks after the speech that forgot the deficit comes the one that remembers it, big time. Ed Miliband knows he has a problem and can sense an opportunity. The problem is Labour's lack of economic credibility. The opportunity is the chance to paint the Tories as extreme, citing their ideological obsession with cutting spending back to – you've guessed it – 1930s levels.

University of Kent

I've come to watch the battle of the anti-'politics as usual' champions of right and left. On *Question Time*, Nigel Farage has been pitted against Russell Brand. Chatting to the audience beforehand, it is clear they relish the idea that they're seeing people who are shaking things up. One tells me that at least Brand and Farage are different from all those in the political elite who went to Oxford, studied PPE and live in Islington. 'Oh dear,' I reply. 'That's me.'

Depressingly, the audience comments slot into the usual lazy assertions: politicians are all in it for themselves (no, they're not); they're all the same (no, they're not); they all behave badly (no, they don't).

Russell Brand gets away with pretending that he didn't tell people not to vote but said merely that there was no one worth voting for. This is what's known in the trade as a lie. He wrote in the *New Statesman*: 'I will never vote and I don't think you should, either.'

He doesn't so much answer questions as stage a one-man show, reading carefully prepared lines from cue cards. Farage, he says, is 'a pound-shop Enoch Powell'. The City is what 'most of us think politicians truly work for'.

Many in the audience love it, but by no means all. One man jabs a finger at him and tells him to have the courage of his convictions and stand for Parliament. A few cheer. Lamely, Brand claims that he couldn't do that as he fears he might 'end up like them'.

Farage pursues the clever strategy of ignoring every insult. He's hoping that only those who already hate him will be stirred up by

Brand. He wants everyone else to conclude that he's being calm and reasonable in the face of extreme provocation.

After the recording, as Brand poses for photos with his fans, I wait patiently to ask him for an interview. We've had a bid in with his agent for weeks, and again and again he's told us that 'Russell may not have time'. He has plenty of time now but no, he brushes past me to pose with yet more fans. I do what I hoped I would not finish up doing: shouting questions at him, Gobby-style.

I give up and return to the departing devotees who clearly loved the Brand show. As they sing his praises I find myself angrily defending the politicians he so loves to attack. While Russell is being driven back by his chauffeur, with his PR and his personal make-up artist, to his multi-million-pound apartment, I point out, the Labour guest on the panel, Mary Creagh, will take the train, collect her bike from the station and cycle home before heading to her Wakefield constituency to hold a surgery the next day. Who, I want to know, is more in touch?

By now I am tired and coming down, I realize, with yet another cold. Most of the audience have left, but not all, as I discover – too late – when I find myself cursing Brand as 'that fucking sanctimonious twat'. I'm not sure this complies with BBC editorial standards but it feels better out than in.

No one challenges me or complains but, aware that I have been overheard, I find myself preparing my excuses. My beef is straight-forward and it is not that I know he includes me when he attacks the political establishment. Nor do I resent the fact that it has taken a stand-up comic to energize, excite and enthuse people about some of the great issues of our time where scores of politicians and, yes, commentators like me, have utterly failed. It is quite simply because I am not impartial when it comes to democracy.

The BBC pays me to leave my personal views and prejudices at the door when I report on TV, radio or online. I am not, though, required to be impartial between democracy and the alternatives. If Auntie ever asked that of me, I'd refuse and quit the job. My German Jewish grand-parents were forced to leave their country to escape the Nazis in the 1930s. They went to China, where they had to flee again, from the Communists, in 1949. If you'd told them that all politicians were the same, or that it wasn't worth voting, they'd have had a thing or two to say about it.

Saturday 13 December

Home

The Scottish Labour party has a new leader: a Glaswegian, vegetarian, teetotal street-fighter, a football fanatic and a Blairite foreign policy hawk. Yes, the man who ran David Miliband's leadership campaign now holds the key to his brother Ed's dream of becoming prime minister.

That's not all Jim Murphy has on his shoulders. If he fails to reverse the nationalist surge, it's not just his party but the union that may be doomed.

If Labour comes second to the SNP at the general election but gets the support of SNP MPs to form a government at Westminster, it will help Ed into Number 10 but end, once and for all, his party's claim at every election that the only way to keep the Tories out of power is to vote Labour. If they go on to lose the Scottish parliamentary elections it may not be long before Nicola Sturgeon calls for another independence referendum.

Murphy is a divisive figure. Len McCluskey, the general secretary of Unite, predicted that victory for a man who'd backed austerity, privatization, tuition fees and the Iraq war would be a political 'death sentence' for the party and 'all the SNP's Christmases come at once'. The new leader has himself told his friends he is 'the poison his party has to drink'.

A house in Highbury

A party at the home of one of the founder members of New Labour or, as one wag puts it, the annual convention of the Islington establishment. Delegates are in attendance not just from the New Labour era – notably Alastair Campbell and Anji Hunter – but from the post-Blair–Brown hierarchy as well: Ed Miliband, Douglas Alexander, Tristram Hunt, Rachel Reeves. So far, so unsurprising. What makes this establishment different, and attracts such loathing and suspicion, is that some of the Cameron crowd are here, too, in the shape of close aides Gabby Bertin and Ameet Gill, together with a couple of Lib Dems.

Liberal metropolitan elite? What liberal metropolitan elite? I assure myself that I, along with the few other hacks present, am a mere observer.

Ed Miliband clearly has his mojo back. Even when it is past midnight, he is keen to tell me that the Tories have made a fatal error by revealing that the cuts they're planning are deeper than necessary to cut borrowing and, therefore, ideologically driven. So keen that he passes up the chance of a dance with Justine to 'Things Can Only Get Better'.

Sunday 14 December

Home, the kitchen table

For UKIP, it never rains but it pours. Surely that UKIP councillor couldn't have been right that this is the inevitable consequence of gay marriage?*

The guy picked to fight one of their most winnable seats, South Basildon and East Thurrock, has been recorded making homophobic, racist and obscene comments. Hilariously, Kerry Smith blames the sedatives he was taking for back pain for his descriptions of gay people as 'fucking disgusting old poofters', his jokes about 'shooting peasants' in Chigwell and calling a Chinese woman a 'Chinky.'

Makes you wonder what on earth he says when the drugs aren't working.

I call UKIP's spin doctor – Gobby – to share his pain and for a little mirth at his expense but as we talk I can feel the dots joining in what had, until now, seemed to be just a week of diverting soap operas. The alleged sex scandal at UKIP head office, in which the party's chief executive did (or did not) sleep with an ambitious parliamentary candidate; the wealthy donor said to be threatening to stop funding the party if his friend is prevented from running for the Essex seat; and now today's resignation of the man who saw off the other two . . . All the separate stories are connected by one factor: a struggle for

---

* In January a UKIP councillor blamed storms and heavy floods across Britain on the government's decision to legalize gay marriage. According to David Silvester, it was the prime minister's fault that 'large swathes of the nation have been afflicted by storms and floods'. He went on to say that no man, however powerful, 'can mess with Almighty God with impunity and get away with it'.

supremacy within a party that aspires to hold the balance of power after the next election.

Kerry Smith has been forced out after a recording of him was released to the *Mail on Sunday*. A recording made not by a journalist, but by an ally of his local UKIP rival. Smith only got the seat after the favourite, Neil Hamilton, dropped out of the race. Hamilton was reacting to the leaking, by party headquarters, of expenses allegations – toxic for a man driven from Parliament by the electorate after being found guilty of taking cash for questions when he was a Tory MP. Farage does not want Hamilton as he believes his image would destroy attempts to present UKIP as a clean break from the discredited old parties.

The problem is that UKIP donor and former Tory multimillionaire Stuart Wheeler doesn't agree, and is said to be holding on to his cash in protest at the moves to block Hamilton.

And finally there's that sex scandal. The suspended UKIP chief executive Roger Bird was noticed to have been pushing candidate Natasha Bolter for every winnable seat including, you guessed it, South Basildon and East Thurrock. The man in charge of vetting UKIP's election candidates recently complained that 'half my time is spent weeding out the lunatics'. That's only one of UKIP's selection problems. The other is that they're fighting like rats in a sack for a taste of power.

Monday 15 December

Home

The *Telegraph* has an eye-catching splash this morning claiming that Labour MPs 'have been secretly ordered not to campaign on immigration because doing so could cost them the next election'. It has got hold of a private strategy document circulated by Labour HQ which advises MPs to focus on 'moving the conversation on', if voters express concerns about border controls, to subjects where Labour is stronger, such as the NHS or housing.

On a day when Miliband is venturing into UKIP territory – he's going to Great Yarmouth on the Farage-loving east coast to unveil Labour's manifesto pledge to control immigration – this is not good news. The story is a simple one: Labour have been caught saying one thing in public and another in private.

Number 19 bus

Simple, that is, until you read the document that forms the basis for the story. On my way into central London I skim through what is a long, detailed, thoughtful analysis of who votes UKIP and how likely a Labour campaigner is to persuade someone with strong views on immigration to change his or her mind.

It is based on the standard campaigning doctrine that political parties do best by raising the issues on which they're already seen as strong, rather than competing on turf chosen by their enemies. In other words, Labour are more likely to convince people that they'll deal with the low wages that uncontrolled immigration can cause, or the queues in the NHS, than they are to persuade anyone that they'll be tougher than UKIP or the Tories on curbing the numbers coming into the country.

The only thing that's stupid about the document is that someone circulated so widely something so open to being quoted out of context or misrepresented.

BBC studios, Millbank

It is not only Labour who have shot themselves in the foot. The Tories continue to do it on the deficit. Months ago, George Osborne came up with the wheeze of setting a trap for Labour. He would invite them to support a 'charter for budget responsibility' and when they refused present them as unreformed supporters of tax, spending and borrowing. It's an attempt to copy what worked so well for the Tories when they manoeuvred Labour into opposing the extraordinarily popular cap on the amount any one family could receive in benefits.

There has been a slight hitch with this strategy: Osborne has just published his charter and Ed Balls says Labour are going to vote for it. They can do so because it sets out the coalition and not the Tory approach to cutting the deficit, and has therefore been watered down by the Lib Dems. It is, Balls says, 'consistent with' his pledge.

My phone fills fast with texts and e-mails from all sides telling me why all this is a stunning victory for them and a humiliation for their opponents. This is just an absurd Westminster game that will mean nothing to anyone outside.

Tuesday 16 December

9 Grosvenor Square, Mayfair

Tony Blair strides into his office looking so much better than he does on his much-parodied Christmas card. In that photograph he appears tense, drawn, strained. Here, in the flesh, he seems relaxed, healthy and not nearly so old, or as curiously orange, as he has in recent public outings.

He has agreed to be interviewed for my democracy programme. I put it to him that he symbolizes what so many see as the problem with our politics: a politician of the left who chose to invade a country at the behest of a right-wing American president against the will of many of his own people, and who disappointed and disenfranchised Labour's traditional supporters by embracing markets and corporations with an almost Thatcherite zeal. Not surprisingly, he's having none of it.

The problem, as he sees it, is a failure of delivery, not democracy. Politics simply hasn't been good enough at delivering what voters need and want. The answer to that is stronger leadership and the taking of tough choices, not more democratic change. 'You mean,' I suggest with a smile, 'that the problem isn't too much Blair, but not enough?' He grins back as if to say, 'Quite.'

I had no intention of asking him anything about the current political battle but after he stresses the need for strong leadership for a third time I can no longer resist. What, I ask, about Ed Miliband? He'd see himself as a man with very firm convictions. The Blair brow knits. He is briefly silenced. I can almost hear the cogs in his brain whirring and the second hand on my watch ticking before he replies, 'That's a judgement for the electorate on polling day.' It's not the most ringing endorsement of his most recent successor.

House of Commons

Meanwhile William Hague, the man Blair trounced in the 2001 general election, is unveiling proposals for English votes for English laws. Or rather, when you listen hard, he proposes a series of options that haven't been agreed by all parties which might give English MPs their own exclusive say on certain stages of the parliamentary consideration of laws that may be judged to relate largely, if not exclusively, to England. In other words, after decades of politicians trying to find an answer to this problem, they still haven't come up with a simple one.

The former lord chancellor Derry Irvine once told the Cabinet he'd found the answer to dealing with the West Lothian question (that's the one about why voters in West Lothian near Edinburgh can vote on the NHS or schools in Blackburn, Lancashire but it doesn't work the other way round). He told them drily: 'Just stop asking it.'

Studio 3, BBC, Millbank

The next interview could be interesting. Alex Salmond has agreed to talk. Not face to face, sadly, but down the line from Aberdeen. Arriving late – massively so – but offering no apology, his first words to me, in response to my explanation of the basis for the series, are accompanied by sarcastic laughter. 'BBC . . . democracy . . . I could say a few things about that!' As so often, there is the sense that he's performing for an audience I cannot see.

No matter. I press on. He is as interesting as ever, even if characteristically scathing about everyone else in politics. Westminster, he says, is full of estate agents, PR-agency types and minor celebrities with no sense of their own history. To make his point, he reels off a few choice facts about Simon de Montfort's Parliament, which celebrates its 750th anniversary next year.

'Why are you so keen to come back?' I ask him. His answer is candid and direct. The SNP has the chance to hold the balance of power in a hung Parliament and to extract further concessions about the way Scotland is run.

If that happens the West Lothian question will certainly not be unasked.

Wednesday 17 December

Prime Minister's Questions

Ed Miliband is determined to follow through on the deficit. PMQs today is wittily summed up by a tweeting colleague as 'Cameron: economy all well. Miliband: economy Orwell.'

Labour's conviction that this 'back to the 1930s' thing will stick gets a boost from the latest opinion poll. The Tories have dropped below 30 per cent – that's into the electoral death zone – with 55 per cent of those surveyed saying that Osborne's deficit reduction plan is 'going too far, and imposing cuts that will endanger important public services'. Stand by for Tory jitters. They remember all too well how the warning of an 'age of austerity', delivered on the eve of the last election, was followed by a slump in Tory ratings.

10 Downing Street

I've been asked round for a cuppa and an end-of-year chat with the PM. As I am escorted into the private office, I see him sprawled out in a chair in his tracksuit. He's just back from a run, he explains. Wandering through to the den, he offers to make me a Nespresso, tells me he's in a very good mood and invites me to take a seat on the sofa.

The point he wants to get across is that things are remarkably good for the Tories going into an election year, given where they could have been a few weeks back after the defection of two of their MPs to UKIP. The message is right, he tells me (stick with the long-term economic plan and choose the best leaders); the organization is right (Lynton Crosby* is in charge and the election war chest is brimming).

But, I ask him, do you really want to win? After all, your best hope is a minority government which will have to deliver huge spending cuts and a major renegotiation of Britain's relationship with the EU, and which will be vulnerable to constant rebellions by dozens of Tory Eurosceptics who suspect you're about to betray them over Europe. The PM smiles, as if to say 'We'll worry about that once

---

* The Australian campaign consultant who masterminded Boris Johnson's successful bid to become mayor of London.

the small matter of getting re-elected is behind us.' It's clear that one way he thinks he'll do that is by scuppering plans for TV election debates.

Thursday 18 December

Studio 23, Broadcasting House

It's time for the annual *Mastermind* humiliation. *Today* fill their Christmas programmes with a series of pre-recorded features in case there's no news. In one of them, those of us with 'editor' in our job titles are subjected to a radio version of that famous black chair by John Humphrys. *Today*'s specialist subject for Messrs Peston, Robinson and Mark Easton, the home editor, is 'You and your work'.

Robert is up first and splendidly disputes an answer he is told is 'incorrect', on the grounds that the economic statistic in question was revised by the Office for National Statistics just a few days ago. Equally splendidly, when asked what it was that he described recently as the 'most important economic problem facing the country', he can't remember. Mark is dealt some horrendous questions about the exact number of Romanian migrants working in the UK in the last year.

Mine are significantly easier, which guarantees that I am declared the winner. I respond in accordance with the old dictum 'In defeat, sour grapes. In victory, smugness.'

Sunday 21 December

Home

The Sunday papers are an early Christmas present for Ed Miliband. The *Mail on Sunday* splashes on the news that the ambulance service is secretly considering extending target waiting times to deal with the growing problem of ambulances queuing up outside some A&E units for hours on end. Bed-blocking is leading to ambulance-blocking, which in turn leads to longer waits and calls to alter the targets. This is exactly the sort of evidence Labour needs if it is to do what Ed has promised (or threatened) to do: 'weaponize the NHS'.

New figures on waiting times at A&E in England are the worst in four years. Jeremy Hunt, the health secretary, has been telling colleagues that he's ready for whatever the winter might throw up, although when I bumped into him recently, he joked that he felt like the man in charge of the tiny garrison that defended Rorke's Drift against the Zulus. He knows that he faces overwhelming odds. So far he is holding out, but there is no sign yet of the Zulus.

All this at a time when the polls are beginning to show a return to a clear Labour lead and the papers are taking an interest in the Tories limbering up for the leadership battle that will follow election defeat.

Team Theresa have briefed *The Sunday Times* on her latest wheeze for cracking down on immigration: a plan to send foreign graduates home before they can apply for jobs here. Meanwhile, according to Team Boris, their boss is urging his party to champion the living wage as an answer to Labour's campaign about the cost-of-living squeeze. Over to you now, George.

The story of the next few months will not be just the battle for Number 10 but the undercover leadership scrap between the troika fighting to replace David Cameron. Labour leadership hopefuls are at it, too. I heard the other day that Andy Burnham and Yvette Cooper spent most of the recent parliamentary Labour party Christmas do standing at the bar buying drinks for all comers.

Tuesday 23 December

Home

Another *Mail* front page on the NHS. Another reason for the Tories to feel a bit queasy. The paper has photographed a long early-morning queue outside a GPs' practice of patients who have clearly concluded there's no other way to be sure of getting an appointment. The politics of the health service is very simple for them. High up the news = bad. Low down the news = good.

For the past four years it has looked as if the government might get away with something no previous government ever has: running the NHS on a virtually flat budget. After all, even in the days of Margaret Thatcher's famous 'cuts', the NHS got real-terms increases of 3 per cent year-on-year, on average.

The NHS has coped since 2010 partly due to making big efficiency savings, partly due to a succession of surprisingly warm winters and partly due to a series of emergency cash handouts from the Treasury. The question is whether this is the moment that the elastic snaps.

The irony is that money wouldn't solve the problem – not in the short term, at least. You can't simply turn on the tap and start recruiting staff at very short notice. So all that ministers and health-service executives can do is cross their fingers, fight any fires – there's a big whiteboard in Jeremy Hunt's office listing every hospital in which a crisis looms – and pray that the winter isn't as cold as the forecasters say it might be.

New economic stats bring even less Christmas cheer for ministers. Growth figures have been revised down, robbing Osborne of his favourite political claim that the UK is the fastest-growing economy in the world (the US is back in pole position). These statistical revisions are a nightmare for politicians. They find themselves not only boasting about things that are then declared not to be true, but also defending horrors that never were. Both Gordon Brown and George Osborne faced embarrassment over double-dip recessions, neither of which, it transpired once the stats were revised upwards, had ever really existed.

In other news . . . UKIP's Roger Bird has got off. But after what turns out to be a sex scandal that never was, the party's chief executive has quit anyway.

Merry Christmas.

Saturday 27 December

Home

The Times has given Nigel Farage a huge leg-up. They've made him their 'Briton of the year'. This from the paper that has done more than any other to expose the occasional wrongdoing and regular wackiness of Nigel's boys and girls. After the few weeks he's just had, Farage must scarcely believe his luck.

The Times is keen to point out that it is not endorsing UKIP, merely acknowledging the huge impact its leader has made. After all, last year their global man of the year was Vladimir Putin. None of which stops a raging debate on Twitter about the wisdom of their choice. I suspect that most of those people angrily denouncing or loudly supporting the judgement have not read a single sentence of the original article. Elsewhere in the paper, Matthew Parris has written a piece I intend to cut out, blow up and stick on my office wall. It says that Twitter and other social media have become the conduit for the modern equivalent of the eighteenth-century mob and it is the duty of journalists to stand up to them, rather than to treat the often ignorant and mindless 140-character rants of this entirely self-selecting, unrepresentative sample of the British public as the voice of the people.

Just as Farage is relishing his moment of victory comes a reminder that the real winners of 2014 and, perhaps, 2015 as well, may turn out to be Alex Salmond and Nicola Sturgeon's SNP. A new poll in the *Guardian* confirms that they have doubled their support, could take Scotland in a Westminster election for the first time and be rewarded with possession of the balance of power in a hung Parliament.

There is nothing that Salmond would relish more than dictating terms to Prime Minister Miliband. Though, of course, such a prospect will be a powerful recruiting sergeant for the Tories. Go to bed with Nigel, they'll tell voters, and you'll wake up the next day not just with Ed, but Alex and Nicola too.

Tuesday 30 December

Home

Shame. Tony Blair's real views of Miliband have been outed before my radio interview with him has been aired. He has told the *Economist* that the next election looks like being one in which 'a traditional left-wing party competes with a traditional right-wing party with the traditional result'. Asked if he meant a Tory win, Blair said: 'Yes, that is what happens.'

In one of those absurd corrections which leads people to believe that politicians can't be trusted to speak fluent English, Blair then takes to Twitter to say: 'My remarks have been misinterpreted, I fully support Ed and my party and expect a Labour victory in the election.'

Wednesday 31 December

As if to confirm the Blair critique, Team Ed decide to portray the former prime minister as a politician from a 'different era', having first, of course, noted that he is due a 'great deal of respect'.

This response is based on the assumption – for which there is remarkably little evidence – that Blair is not just unpopular but toxic. Actually, he left office with remarkably good ratings, not to mention an election-winning record that no one else in his party has got anywhere near.

Ed Miliband ran for the leadership as the anti-Blair candidate and has positioned himself as the anti-Blair leader, the man who opposed the war on Iraq, who sees Labour's role as challenging rather than cosying up to business and who wants to build an electoral coalition by combining Labour's traditional support with those who defected to the Lib Dems over Iraq and civil liberties.

The election will not just be a contest between Labour and the Tories but the Blair big tent and Miliband's rather smaller one.

— JANUARY 2015 —

Thursday 1 January

Home

I have a New Year's Day hangover, caused less by alcohol abuse (though there was a little of that last night) than by waking with a terrifying thought. What if this is the year of not just one election but two? An uncertain result followed by an attempt to get a clearer one? A repeat of 1974. The possibility has been there for ages but somehow, today, it feels real.

This could be the year the Goliaths lose and the Davids triumph. It's quite likely that neither Cameron nor Miliband will win a clear mandate to govern and one of them will need the backing of Alex (SNP) or Nigel (UKIP) or the other Nigel, the Westminster leader of Northern Ireland's Democratic Unionist party (DUP).

I've long planned my life around the vague idea that this election will be my swansong as political editor after a decade in the job. Could I really cope with two gruelling campaigns?

Friday 2 January

Home

Ed Balls is not falling into the 'Tony Blair was too right-wing and too damned popular' trap. This morning he has a skilfully written piece in the *Guardian* proclaiming that Labour are now occupying the centre ground.

He argues that the Tories have veered to the right by promising ideologically driven tax and spending cuts, thus vacating that centre ground. I can hear Blair's response to that now: you don't occupy the centre ground by default or by waiting for your opponents to make way for you.

He would be entertained, too, by an article by the *Guardian*'s Neal Lawson, a Miliband devotee, who declares that Blair attracted the 'wrong people' to back Labour, won victories that were 'too big' and thus had to pander to people who are not natural Labour supporters. Some might regard that as a quality problem to have.

None the less it remains the case that, at the start of 2015, this still looks like Miliband's election to lose. He has a poll lead, the economic data worsened before Christmas, there are growing signs of an NHS crisis and the breach on the right is no closer to being healed. No wonder both David Cameron and George Osborne took to the campaign trail today. They're painfully aware that their political careers could be over in a few months' time and long before either of them is fifty years old.

Saturday 3 January

Home

One thing I'm not looking forward to in this campaign is cutting through the crap. And the early signs are that there is going to be a lot of it to cut through.

A new Labour poster shows the airbrushed image of Cameron that glowed on thousands of billboards during the 2010 campaign, captioned with a new slogan: 'The Tories want to cut the level of public spending back to 1930s levels when there was no NHS.' Fair enough, you might think, were it not for the fact that spending will, of course, only be at 1930s levels as a share of the economy. It will be many, many times higher in cash terms. What's more, there is not the faintest suggestion from any leading Tory that they intend to abolish the NHS.

Naturally, the Tories will soon be up to the same sort of trick. They've long planned to 'cost' Labour's spending promises, allowing them to claim that the Eds will put up every imaginable tax while simultaneously borrowing enough to turn us into Greece on the North Sea.

There are fundamental truths here – Labour would spend more, the Tories less – but is it really necessary to insult our collective intelligence with warnings of plague and pestilence if the other lot get in?

Sunday 4 January

NHS drop-in centre

I queue with half a dozen other coughers, sneezers and splutterers for a doctor's appointment. If I wait till tomorrow, the first day back at work for many, I will have to sit on the phone for hours, fight through the automated answering service only to be offered, if I'm lucky, an appointment at 2pm that I can't make. We are the NHS's looming crisis made flesh, a generation that wants the kind of instant response that the health service simply isn't organized or funded to provide.

On the television in the waiting room I watch David Cameron on Andrew Marr's sofa doing what he does best: sounding prime ministerial. What he has always been much worse at is setting out and sticking to a clear vision of where he wants to take the country. Remember the era of 'let sunshine win the day'? Or the 'invitation to join the government of Britain'? Or the 'big society'? At the end of his interview I struggle to remember very much of what he said, beyond his by now very familiar insistence that the country should 'stick to the plan'.

One of his aides tells me that they've all been instructed by Lynton Crosby to hammer home the same thing relentlessly, however much journalists hate it. The Number 10 press team warned him that the more bored we got, the more likely we'd be to go off the reservation. The question, Lynton has been told, is where will the media's mischief-making take them?

Monday 5 January

Home, the study

First day back on news duty, first day proper of the election year. And yet already I feel as if I'm fighting to clear a fog of cynicism. The news bulletins and the cues on *Today* already have that world-weary he says, she says, tit-for-tat feel to them. Only 122 days of this to go . . . I struggle to overcome the ennui while broadcasting and can almost hear the nation responding, 'Nice try, but forget it.'

My office

I declined the chance of a very early-morning train trip to God's own city (Manchester, of course) to watch Ed Miliband spell out the 'choice' facing the nation. Thank goodness. Once again it turns out that the event was grotesquely over-sold and under-delivered.

Miliband, I was told, would be addressing a major rally. The pictures would be great. His team, the shadow Cabinet, everyone would be there. Instead we are given a pretty routine speech at a dull venue with a handful of the party's key faces present but scarcely visible.

When my colleague Norman Smith asks a perfectly fair question, he is booed and heckled by the party workers in the audience. Ed then places his hand over his eyes and peers into the distance, searching for reporters from ITN or Sky. None are there. Things are not going to plan.

A badly organized event without a clear news line. Oh dear.

Millbank Tower

The rival Tory attraction is, by contrast, slick and packed with journalists. Some have come to enjoy what may turn out to be a sneak preview of the hustings for the next leader of the opposition, with George Osborne and Theresa May side by side, if not shoulder to shoulder, and the young pretender, Sajid Javid, the culture secretary, present too.

They are here to flog that old election favourite, the opposition costing document. You know the sort of thing: cut and paste a few quotes from your opponent saying that cuts to libraries are bad, or we'd really like to see more cyclists, and then put a price tag on them which poor, unsuspecting voters will be told they have to pay. The Tories and Labour have pulled this stunt in every campaign since John Major knocked out Neil Kinnock in 1992 by costing his policies and claiming they would result in a tax bombshell landing on every household in the land.

To give the whole partisan propaganda exercise spurious

credibility, the Tories have made their dossier look damned near identical to the official Treasury red book. Civil servants have, they say, calculated the costings, neatly ignoring the fact that it is their political masters who have told them what to cost.

Ever so slightly bored by the whole predictable game, I ask Osborne, May and co. whether their minds aren't really on fighting each other in a few months' time, if they lose to Labour. Theresa, who has been nodding rather too often and too vigorously at everything George has been saying, now glares moodily.

A wittier colleague invites each of them to sum up in a minute why they'd be the best party leader. This is met by general laughter, even from the hand-picked Tory audience, but with a tight-lipped insistence from George Osborne that the Tories, unlike Labour, have a very good leader, thanks so much for asking.

This is the way bored hacks keep themselves entertained when spoon-fed party propaganda that insults our intelligence.

My office

No one is buying the Tories' claim that Labour have over £20 billion worth of unfunded spending promises. But the row about what Ed Miliband has dubbed the Tories' 'dodgy dossier' is making news. I am getting increasingly frantic texts and calls from Labour. Why are we falling for the Tory 'framing of the argument'? Why are we ignoring Ed's attempt to develop a detailed and thought-out presentation at the start of the campaign? The answer is as unwelcome as it is simple. The costing row is a better story. Every other news organization agrees. What's more, the BBC's competition didn't even go to the Labour event.

Another text. 'No wonder everyone hates politics . . . you've ignored a big speech about what the election is about . . . very unhappy.' Ed Miliband texts too, much more politely, in a more-in-sorrow-than-in-anger tone. Then his spin doctor Tom Baldwin calls to complain directly. I listen carefully before finally losing it, giving back as good as I've got at top volume and with a lot of choice language thrown in for good measure. Half an hour's shouting match later, I emerge from my office to the grins of colleagues who've heard every word. I feel much, much better.

Tuesday 6 January

On the tube

Just what the doctor ordered . . . for Mr Miliband, at any rate. The latest stats from the NHS front line confirm that the nation's A&E units are missing their targets and struggling to cope.

Jeremy Hunt would have made a rather reassuring doctor himself. His soothing bedside manner – 'Yes, I know this hurts, but with the hard work of the excellent staff in the health service, we'll get through it together' – is so much more effective than the standard ministerial 'line to take' in the face of bad news: 'Look, what these statistics really reveal is . . .'

Nevertheless, every day the NHS tops the news is a day closer to Labour's Andy Burnham taking his job.

BBC offices, Millbank

Three wise men – constitutional gurus – have come to brief BBC colleagues about what an election with no clear winner might look like. They provide us with a series of complex charts showing no fewer than ten alternative power permutations, a kind of political pick 'n' mix in which the Greens or the Purples or the Golds or the Yellows might help one or other of the big two parties into government. These negotiations may take many weeks, they say. That's much, much longer than what seemed an interminable five days of coalition formation in 2010. What's more, they've advised the parties not to meet where cameras can see them. Last time the opportunity to film and question the coalition negotiators as they walked up Whitehall was all I had to fill a bulletin.

God help me if in May I have to fill five weeks of post-election coverage with shots of the exterior of a building and a graphic about the ten possible governing arrangements that might emerge from the talks taking place inside.

Home, bed

A quick check on Twitter for tomorrow's front pages reveals the worst set of headlines for the Tories I can remember. 'THIRD WORLD A&E',

shouts the *Sun*. 'A&E CRISIS WORST FOR TEN YEARS', screams the *Mail*. 'HOSPITALS JUST CAN'T COPE', bemoans the *Express*. The *Mirror* doesn't hold back: 'OUR NHS IS DYING'.

Earlier, a Labour insider told me to ignore the whingeing coming from the leader's office yesterday. They feared that the Tories' costing exercise would dominate the news for days on end. It has, instead, lasted just one news cycle. George Osborne has fired one of his biggest weapons but Labour have emerged virtually unscathed.

Wednesday 7 January

Taxi to Broadcasting House

I have just finished filming at the British Museum's Germany exhibition for a piece on Angela Merkel's visit to London today.

'Are you following what's happening in Paris?' asks a text from my news desk. I wasn't, but I am now. I find video on my iPad of the assault by gunmen at the offices of the *Charlie Hebdo* satirical magazine. Twelve are dead, mainly cartoonists and journalists. Slain for what they dared to draw and write by people claiming to be acting in the name of Allah. It is sickening. And it's not over. The attackers, dressed in black military fatigues and apparently calm, calculated and ruthless, have fled.

Prime Minister's Questions

The events in Paris cast a pall over PMQs, but politics rarely stops for anything.

Miliband invites Cameron to agree that there's a crisis in the NHS. The prime minister's predictable refusal to do so allows the Labour leader to charge him with being 'in denial'. What were politicians accused of before Freud came along?

The PM looks pretty uncomfortable as Miliband lists the ways in which the government is responsible for the mess: cutting social care, the cost of a top-down reorganization and so on. Then comes the fightback – which immediately diverts my attention from surfing Twitter for the latest news from Paris.

'You told the political editor of the BBC that you wanted to "weaponize" the NHS,' declares Cameron. It is, he adds, 'disgusting' that Labour are 'playing football with the NHS'.

Ed Miliband does not deny it. He can't. Before Christmas, once I'd established that he'd been using the phrase beyond his meeting with BBC editors, I reported how he'd told his aides that this year they had to turn the problems in the health service into a weapon against the Tories.

Some Downing Street adviser clearly noted this down and stored it away for future use as armour against the weapon Ed hoped to deploy.

10 Downing Street

Chancellor Merkel's joint press conference with David Cameron is inevitably dominated by reaction to the atrocity in Paris. Having been briefed together by the heads of MI5 and MI6, and made a joint call to President Hollande, they talk of the need to stand up for common values and intelligence co-operation.

It is, though, Europe that we hacks really want to know about. Will she help him get the 'full-on treaty change' he says he needs to curb EU immigration and to recast Britain's relationship with the EU?

The chancellor responds with her usual mix of warm words of general reassurance – 'We want Britain to stay', 'We've solved other difficult problems before', 'Where there's a will there's a way' – drenched by a bucketful of cold water on the specifics. She ignores an invitation to back treaty change and hints that most adjustments to benefits for immigrants could be made by national governments or the EU without the need for it.

So, which is more important, the helpful tone or the unhelpful language? I think the former, but irritatingly I have no question today to try to find out. I'm told that if I ask one now I won't get one on next week's visit to the White House. Questions to the PM are treated like sweeties for children – they're rationed and withdrawn for bad behaviour.

At the end of the press conference the PM cracks a little joke and is rewarded with the first smile to cross Frau Merkel's face. Every time I see them together I am struck by how much he wants and needs to woo the uncrowned queen of Europe. Without her help, his hopes of defusing the Tories' EU time bomb will come to nothing.

Trafalgar Square

So much for the EU. I've switched stories to cover the international reaction to the Paris killings. I record a piece to camera in front of a silent vigil, but the signs brought by those who have gathered here, bearing the message 'Je suis Charlie', and the pens and pencils held aloft in tribute to those who died at *Charlie Hebdo*, make words unnecessary.

Thursday 8 January

Home

'Will it make an attack more likely here, Dad?' It's a question you don't want to be asked by one of your children. But on the morning after the Paris atrocity we all feel a little less safe. We all feel powerless, too, to understand, let alone combat, a mindset that accommodates slaughtering people because of what they say or write.

I try to explain that there were those desperate to kill people in London before last night and there will be those desperate to do so after it. I recall that when I was a teenager we lived with and through regular outrages by the IRA.

We will win, I predict, cheering up a little because I have absolutely no doubt that we will.

BBC Westminster

David Cameron has just said on camera, to my ITV oppo Tom Bradby, what I was told some time ago. He won't take part in televised election debates between the party leaders if the Greens are not included. I rush on to our news channel to try to explain what's going on.

Tory strategists are doing their utmost to kill the debates altogether. They fear that these are an unnecessary risk for their leader, who is ahead of all his rivals; an opportunity for Miliband, Clegg and Farage and a guarantee that the media and not they will set the agenda of the election campaign. Instead of their planned mix of 'stick to the long-term economic plan' and 'don't risk putting Ed into Number 10', they foresee endless talk about how the leaders will do or did do in the debates.

Cameron can't afford to say that he's against debates as we have copious television clips of him saying how marvellous they were last time. It would leave him open to one of those 'split-screen moments' he dreads. So instead he is backing the Green campaign for a slot, aware that if they get a place the SNP will demand the same treatment and the whole who's-in, who's-out row could get mired in lengthy legal challenges. His aim is to smash the consensus between the big broadcasters and the big opposition parties that the right solution is three debates during the campaign, with one featuring Farage.

This is now a high-stakes poker game. Do the broadcasters risk 'empty-chairing' him – in other words, threatening to go ahead without him? Does another organization fix a debate that includes Cameron and the Greens and threaten to empty-chair the other leaders if they refuse to show up?

Miliband calls to ask what I think is going on and to urge the BBC not to lose its nerve. I explain that this is a matter above my pay grade. I report on the negotiations, I don't participate in them. My hunch is that Cameron will end up doing at least one debate, but probably at a time and with a cast of his choosing. It would be a brave broadcaster who empty-chairs a sitting prime minister.

Friday 9 January

BBC Westminster

Farage has blamed the Paris killings on what he calls 'a really rather gross policy of multiculturalism' which has created a 'fifth column' of murderous jihadists in the UK as well as in France. His opponents unite to condemn him and the media aren't biting.

In part this is because all eyes are still on events across the Channel, where the gruesome drama continues with live TV coverage of two sieges. The *Charlie Hebdo* gunmen have taken a hostage in a printing works north-east of Paris. An ally has taken many more in a kosher supermarket in the Vincennes district of the capital.

Farage knows exactly what he's doing. Once this crisis is over, it will be replaced by the political debate about how to prevent more attacks. Perhaps someone will point out to him that Britain and France have taken very different approaches to their Muslim minorities. France has pursued a much more integrationist policy, including bans on burkas and Muslim schools, than the one followed in the UK. Neither has prevented isolated acts of murderous madness.

Home

I watch the sieges end live on TV. I see the explosions, hear the bullets, feel the relief as reporters tell us the attackers have all been killed. Until news emerges that four of the hostages in that Jewish supermarket are also dead.

They came for the cartoonists first, and then for the Jews, but few will see that as noteworthy. The only offence caused by these victims, like the millions who perished in Nazi concentration camps, was to be born at all. I search Twitter for messages declaring 'Je suis juif' or I am Jewish. There are a few, but not nearly enough.

Sunday 11 January

Home

It's that word again. Weaponize. Andrew Marr has just asked Ed Miliband four times whether he used it. Four times he's wriggled.

If I'd realized that reporting what Ed Miliband had indeed said he wanted to do to the NHS would have caused such a fuss I might have turned it into a proper news story. As it is, all I did was mention it at the end of the live coverage of PMQs and on a blog. I should be fired.

The interview is not a success for Miliband. Andy also pushes him repeatedly on what spending he'd cut. After a few weeks of emphasizing his hair-shirt credentials, he reverts to saying what he really believes, insisting that you can't simply cut your way to a lower deficit and that the crucial factor is raising the rate of growth.

'I couldn't have been clearer,' says the man who may be PM in less than four months. 'No, you could,' retorts the Beeb's interrogator, looking increasingly frustrated.

It's perfectly reasonable economics but much, much trickier politics.

*

Extraordinary pictures from Paris. The streets are packed with more than a million people marching in memory of and solidarity with the Paris victims. Behind bereaved relatives and friends comes a line-up of world leaders, marching together, their arms linked. Cameron is there, alongside his pal Helle Thorning-Schmidt. There is a telling gap between them and President Hollande, who strides side by side with Angela Merkel.

The Palestinian leader, Mahmoud Abbas, is present, as is Israeli prime minister Binyamin Netanyahu. But there's no Obama, no Biden, no Kerry. The Americans have sent their ambassador. Mistake. Big mistake.

At least Fox News have done their bit to enhance the image of the US. A self-proclaimed terror 'expert', interviewed about the threat of Islamic extremism in Europe on the country's favourite twenty-four-hour TV news network, describes Birmingham as 'totally Muslim' and adds, for good measure, that 'non-Muslims just simply don't go in'.

This inspires a series of hilarious 'Foxnewsfacts' on Twitter. My favourite is a photo of a building with the caption 'Typical of every Birmingham street corner.' Its name is Mecca. Mecca bingo.

Monday 12 January

The tube

The weaponizing story simply will not die. The *Telegraph* reports that Ed Miliband used the word when speaking to a group of BBC executives he'd invited in for a briefing. Given that there were more than a dozen people there, most of whom he'd never met before, it was hardly the place to say something and expect it never to be repeated. I will never forget the episode of the BBC classic *Yes Minister* in which Sir Humphrey patiently explains that if you want to leak something you should first tell a large number of people and stress to each of them that it's absolutely confidential.

Tuesday 13 January

House of Commons

George Osborne and Ed Balls are having a high old time taunting each other in the Commons. So are their cheering and baying supporters. We reporters are quite enjoying it, too. There's just one problem: the whole spectacle will be completely and utterly baffling to anyone not immersed in the political games these two are playing.

Remember George's charter for budget responsibility, which sets out his plans to cut the deficit in future years? The one he wanted to lure Ed into voting against, demonstrating that he was in favour of – wait for the drum roll – budget *ir*responsibility? Well, the vote the chancellor engineered takes place today and, as promised, Ed is not going to fall into his trap.

Ah, says, George, but if you vote for the charter you've got to spell out what you'll cut. Oh no, says Ed, your charter's based not on a firm target but a vague aim . . . blah, blah, blah.

You know what? This cannot be explained in three minutes of television and what's more I'm not bloody well going to try. They can play this game on their own.

11 Downing Street

With the words 'Je suis juif' still fresh in my mind, I dash to a reception for one of my favourite charities: the Holocaust Educational Trust. I'm introduced to the remarkable group of Holocaust survivors who tour the nation's schools to tell the next generation of their experiences in the hope it can never happen again.

They and the young people the charity sends to Auschwitz to learn the lessons of history are an inspiration to me. Paris is a reminder of why their work is so vital.

House of Commons dining room

I've been invited to speak to one of the many Commons dining clubs, little groups of like-minded MPs who meet up for a political gossip. They get to hear how I see the world. I get to hear their hopes and fears, lubricated by a few glasses of beer and wine, since they know none of them will ever be quoted.

I ask this Tory club how they'd call the election. They're more optimistic than I'd expected. Many believe it will be a repeat of 1992 – in other words, a very late swing with voters choosing at the last minute to go for the Tories rather than vote for that bloke you can't imagine in Number 10. Kinnock then, Miliband now.

I'm not entirely convinced. Yes, Ed is holding Labour back. Yes, there may be a late swing to the Tories, but Cameron is not John Major. The Blair landslide, the Tory splits, the chaos of Black Wednesday have made people forget how very popular Major was before that election in 1992. He was still a novelty, having been prime minister for less than two years and fairly obscure until then. He embodied the kindlier, gentler change people wanted after eleven years of Margaret Thatcher.

Cameron, by contrast, has been leader of the opposition or prime minister for a decade and relentlessly portrayed as an out-of-touch Tory toff. He's more popular than his party, certainly, and much more respected than his opponent. Sure, he's still capable of winning this election, but I don't foresee a dramatic swing producing a clear Tory majority.

Head home excited. I'm off to Washington DC in the morning to cover what may be the prime minister's last visit to the White House and, before that, to film Ed Balls, who just happens to be visiting DC at the same time.

Wednesday 14 January

Home

I spoke too soon. The taxi to the airport is at the door but I'm on the phone to Katy, Westminster news boss, and Jon, news editor, who think I should postpone to handle a story that's just breaking.

Late last night Messrs Miliband, Clegg and Farage formed an unprecedented alliance by releasing identical letters to David Cameron charging him with trying to block the TV election debates. Miliband will use PMQs to accuse the PM of chickening out. The story will lead the news.

Reluctantly, I agree. I'll be letting down Ed Balls, missing an enjoyable dinner and a proper sleep in DC and obliged to take a horribly early flight tomorrow, but I'm a news junkie and can't resist another fix.

Prime Minister's Questions

'Feeble . . . pathetic . . . running scared . . .' Ed is trying to be his most contemptuous of Dave.

'Frightened . . . chicken . . . why are you so scared?' Dave swaggers back defiantly.

Although it is obvious to most people paying any attention that it is the PM who, like every front-runner before him, is trying to stop these debates, he is following the old dictum that attack is the best form of defence. The mess is, he says, all Ed's fault for being too afraid to debate with the Greens.

It's a win-win for him as he knows most voters instinctively think that there's no reason to let in UKIP but not the Greens. If they are included, the broadcasters will have to admit other parties too, like the SNP and Plaid Cymru, and as all of the above are left-wing alternatives to Labour, talking them up is a good way of splitting Labour's vote.

Westminster Methodist Central Hall

Jess, my producer, has rather brilliantly found a stage with three white lecterns on it which looks just like the set for the last TV debates. It's the ideal location for my piece to camera in which I try to explain that this whole row may seem like one of those dull 'he said, she said' Westminster squabbles but is, in truth, about something much more profound. Cameron fears that if the campaign is dominated by televised debates and, in particular, one that pitches him against Farage, he'll be chucked out of Number 10. If he can water down the impact of the debates and 'split the left' by getting Ed to face the Greens and the Scots and Welsh Nationalists, he believes he might just survive.

I leave the crew to finish filming some other shots and, in one of those moments which makes TV people want to punch the air and whoop for joy, bump into a man from the *Mirror* dressed as a chicken heading back to his parked car after a photo shoot. 'Mr Chicken!' I shout. 'Do not move! I am getting my camera. You are going to be the first shot on tonight's news at ten.'

Thursday 15 January

Hay-Adams hotel, Washington DC

I made it, albeit a day later than planned. The sky is a piercing blue. The sun lights up the White House, which glows brilliantly in the distance. This is the carefully chosen backdrop for the prime minister's television interviews at the start of his two-day visit to the White House.

It's clear that the message Downing Street want viewers to take away is simply summed up as 'If Obama had a vote, he'd vote for his friend David.' So, having asked the PM about all the worthy stuff, I drop in a question prompted by one of those characteristic Cameron indiscretions in a recent newspaper interview. The man who revealed that the Queen purred when she heard the result of the Scottish referendum recently blurted out that he was on pretty chummy terms with Obama. 'Does he really call you "Bro"?' I ask. Cameron grins a tad sheepishly before replying coyly that normally it's more a case of David and Barack. It'll be interesting to see if the president's in on the joke.

Blair House, Pennsylvania Avenue, Washington DC

The travelling hacks have been invited for a briefing by the PM in the president's official guest house just across the street from the White House.

I find my attention wandering as I examine the crystal chandeliers, gilt mirrors and magnificent hand-painted wallpaper in this house, which is where every king and queen, president or prime minister you care to name has stayed over the past few decades. Then one phrase jolts me out of my reverie. David Cameron says of some policy or other, 'In a future government, hopefully led by me . . .' It is the first indication I've heard that he is aware of his own political mortality; that he knows this may be his last-ever visit to the White House as prime minister in his final weeks in the job.

*

After the PM leaves for his dinner date we learn that it was one of his predecessors, none other than Winston Churchill, who convinced the occupants of the White House that they needed a guest house.

During one of Churchill's visits to the White House, Franklin D. Roosevelt's wife Eleanor found him wandering towards the family's private quarters, cigar in hand, at three o'clock in the morning. The prime minister had to be persuaded that this was not the time to rouse the sleeping president to resume their conversation.

And if the nocturnal prowling of Britain's wartime leader wasn't bad enough, on another occasion FDR knocked on Churchill's bedroom door and was cheerily bidden to come in. The great man had just emerged from his bath and was striding around dictating letters. He was stark naked. Addressing his startled host, he said, 'You see, Mr President, I have nothing to hide from you.'

History does not record what the first lady had to say about the episode but it was after this that official guests were moved from the White House to Blair House.

Friday 16 January

The West Wing, White House

HUAW! That's the acronym that always comes to mind on these prime ministerial trips. It's used in the military and means 'Hurry Up And Wait'. The majority of a travelling journalist's time is spent either being barked at to move quickly or hanging around for long periods. Today the US and UK press corps are crammed into a White House press briefing waiting for the Obama–Cameron news conference. It looks very glamorous on *The West Wing*. In real life it's anything but. It's cramped and shabby.

I try to think of a good question to ask the two leaders. The theme is obvious: terrorism. Overnight, police in Belgium have raided a group of suspected terrorists. Secretary of state John Kerry has arrived in Paris to try to repair the damage done by the almost invisible presence of the US last weekend. Back in the UK, the police are warning that they are having to increase security for the Jewish community and their own officers.

I normally have two tests for any question I pose at a news conference. It should make the news, and it should be what people at home would ask if they had the chance. Today I self-indulgently add a third. Simply because I really want to know the answer. It's something that may interest the historians even if it doesn't get on to tonight's news.

The east room, White House

The bromance, it seems, is well and truly on. Obama opens the news conference by welcoming his 'great friend and outstanding partner' David to the White House, having teased 'commentators who've got into a tizzy' about what he'd really meant by calling him 'Bro'. Short of a hug for the cameras, Cameron could not have wished for more.

I ask first about security at home and then the question to which I really want to know the answer. Do you worry that what we are seeing may be linked to the decision of both the US and the UK to sit on the sidelines as a bloody civil war developed in Syria?

The president fixes me with a stare. It's clear he really dislikes the premise of my question. First he dismisses the idea that the violence spilling out of Syria is occurring because we're 'sitting on the sidelines'. Then he denies that that's what the US and UK have been doing. Finally, he asks me to ponder the notion that we would all have been safer if Syria had been invaded. This is, he argues, a heartache and a tragedy that cannot be confronted with weapons.

Interesting. Revealing. A tad defensive, I think. I chose this question because I know Cameron regrets that more was not done to help the Syrian rebels in the early days of their conflict with President Assad. I know, too, that Obama dates many of his political problems back to the moment he first prepared his country to take military action against Syria, in response to the use of chemical weapons, and then pulled back.

Sadly, the exchange won't make its way on to the TV bulletins. Once again Obama served up not so much an answer as a seminar, less a soundbite and more a full banquet with multiple courses. It's both a fascinating reply and hopeless telly.

Sunday 18 January

Home

I'm slumped on the sofa with jet lag, watching Nick Clegg on the Marr show. He says broadcasters should come up with new proposals for TV election debates. Only a few days ago he was insisting they should stand firm and empty-chair Cameron. Number 10 just won the first hand in the poker game.

Love the idea proposed in the *Observer* today by the king of political comedy, Armando Iannucci, the man who created *The Thick of It* and *Veep*. He's calling for a TV debate between Russell Brand and the Pub Landlord, aka comedian Al Murray, who has announced his intention to stand, in character, against Nigel Farage in South Thanet. I'd watch that, and so would millions of others.

The study

I've had a series of conversations with senior Labour folk, who all confirm a deadlock behind the scenes on how to pay for Miliband's promise to cut tuition fees. The team responsible for higher education think it's a waste of money and will undermine Labour's claim to be responsible with public spending. Ed Balls has refused to use an accounting wheeze (if fees are lower, fewer people will default on loans so the cost to the country will actually fall) to make it look as if the numbers add up. Miliband thinks the policy is a vote-winner and doesn't fancy eating his words. After all, that didn't work so well for Nick Clegg.

So the logic, I surmise, is that they might drop the policy. I put this to Team Ed in the hope they'll confirm or deny it. They deny it but won't say what they'll do or when. Something is clearly up.

Monday 19 January

Bed

Precise, elegant, deadly. No one wields the rapier quite like Peter Mandelson. On *Newsnight* he describes his party's flagship tax-raising policy as 'clobbering people with a rather sort of crude, short-term mansion tax'.

He's not the first Labour figure to attack the tax – the candidates to replace Boris as London mayor, ranging from the Blairite Tessa Jowell to lefty Diane Abbott, have been queuing up to do it – but no one makes the impact Peter does when he chooses to.

Are the Blairites making sure that if Ed loses they can say 'You should have listened to us?' If so, it's a curious policy to pick to criticize, as polls show it's hugely popular – though no doubt that is in part due to the use of the word 'mansion'. Call it a 'homes tax', as the Tories plan to do, and people suddenly get less keen on it.

Tuesday 20 January

Home, the study

On *Today* this morning, I highlight something Nigel Farage said to me in an interview. Voters' trust in politics has been shaken, he contends, by the fact that the media punish parties that have internal debates by treating them as splits. He cites his difference of opinion with the rest of the UKIP leadership over the NHS, when he tried and failed to persuade his party to back his view that what Britain needs is an insurance-based health system along the lines of those operated in many other parts of the world. I put it to him that, oddly for a man who prides himself on 'telling it like it is', he was now pretending to be one of those who love the NHS when the opposite is the case. This was, he said, 'a debate that we're all going to have to return to'.

Full marks for candour, some may say, but it poses a dilemma for those of us paid to report on politics. I, for one, won't simply report that it's party policy to invest more in the health service without pointing out that its leader is in favour of scrapping the system altogether.

When I say this on air, Ukippers take to Twitter to object to me using the word 'scrap'. Tough. That's what he means. Politicians are always trying to control the language in which their policies are described, whether it's the Tories trying to present the poll tax as a 'community charge' or the Scottish Nationalists protesting every time anyone uses the words 'separation' or 'break-up' to describe the impact of independence.

I agree with Farage that the media can stifle debate by seizing on mere expressions of contrary opinion as 'gaffes', but people are entitled to know what he thinks before they vote, not simply once he chooses to 'return to' a subject after polling day.

First minister's office, Scottish Parliament, Edinburgh

'You're popular here, aren't you? See you've not brought your body-guard,' says my cab driver.

This is my first visit to Scotland since the referendum. My first, too, since the row with Alex Salmond and the protests outside the BBC calling for me to be sacked. The Scottish *Sun* ran an interview with me recently which revealed that the BBC had hired heavies to protect their political editor from potential retribution. I've come to interview the new first minister about a change in her party's strategy and to do a little patching-up of some wounded relationships.

Holyrood's modernity and informality is in stark contrast to Westminster's gothic grandeur. It gives the Scottish Parliament precisely what many of its members wanted: the look and feel of a prosperous, modern, Scandinavian country rather than an outpost of the British empire.

Nicola Sturgeon, who has eased herself confidently into her predecessor's very large shoes, welcomes me to her office. It's clear that the first woman to lead Scotland wants to highlight that she will be a kinder, gentler, less divisive first minister of her nation than the man she has replaced.

'Smart Alec' Salmond brilliantly dominated politics in Scotland for years but his manner put off many voters, particularly women. As if to emphasize that things are different now, the SNP have arranged for me to film Sturgeon chatting to a group of women who've joined the party since the referendum and his resignation.

In future, she tells me, SNP MPs will vote on purely English mat-ters – notably the NHS, even though the Scottish government has complete control of the Scottish health service. This is necessary, she says, to protect the Scottish NHS from the knock-on effects of cuts and privatization in England. I point out that her government has cut the budget of the NHS in Scotland while it has been increased in real terms in England. With scarcely a blink, she waffles about difficulties comparing the figures (difficulties that have not stopped the independent Institute for Fiscal Studies doing it), but in a way that sounds like she has an answer.

She knows that a promise to vote in Westminster will enrage the Tory press and revive calls for English votes for English laws, all of which strengthen her position in Scotland. Simultaneously, it is designed to reassure Scots that a vote for the SNP in the general election is not, as Labour always claim, a vote for the Tories.

All this matters hugely now that the polls show the SNP on course to double their vote and potentially to treble, quadruple, quintuple or sextuple the number of MPs they have.

I'm impressed. She will not thank me for this comparison, but Nicola has the vote-winning potential to combine Angela Merkel's low-key, no-nonsense, businesslike manner with the carefully manicured image of Margaret Thatcher in her early days.

Wednesday 21 January

BBC Edinburgh, the Tun

The *Today* programme call. It's been delayed again. Until after the election. Can I talk about why the Iraq inquiry is taking so very, very long to produce?

Already the conspiracy theories are afoot, encouraged by those who want to remind people that they were right to oppose the war in the first place. Nick Clegg says some will fear that the report is being 'sexed down'.

I note that he doesn't say he has any evidence for this, or even that he thinks it himself. Just that 'some will fear it'. I text him in the hope that he might provide me with more. There's no reply.

Over breakfast I text and call a handful of civil servants and ex-ministers familiar with what's going on behind the scenes. They complain that Sir John Chilcot has missed every deadline he has been set; that the delays are nothing to do with them; that they only received his draft report just before Christmas and, given that it is ludicrously long and criticizes many more people than just Tony Blair, allowing those individuals to respond is bound to take a good deal of time.

What really held up the inquiry was an interminable row about whether Tony Blair's private correspondence with George W. Bush could be quoted at all, let alone published.

Thus the third election since the invasion of Iraq will take place without the country having been given the proper opportunity to learn and move on from what many see as one of the great foreign-policy disasters of recent times. Crazy.

Glasgow Riverside museum

Scottish Labour's new leader, Jim Murphy, and I are being filmed strolling through the snow and ice by the Clyde. I am wearing coat, scarf, gloves and a hat that comes off only when the camera's rolling. Jim insists on striding along in nothing more than a light suit. The man who campaigned against independence from the top of an Irn-Bru crate is presumably trying to send a message that he, like the old ad line for the nation's favourite non-alcoholic tipple, is 'made in Scotland from girders', unlike the soft, southern jessie beside him. I consider stripping off too but don't relish the idea of hypothermia.

Jim is tough enough and savvy enough to give Nicola a run for her money. However, he is trying to undo fifteen years of Labour mistakes in Scotland in just a few months. The party that created the Scottish Parliament went on to neglect it after the tragic death of Donald Dewar. It sent its best and brightest, including Jim, to Westminster and took the support of Scots for granted while searching for the formula that would attract middle England. Under first Blair and then, irony of ironies, Brown, the party was decaying and is now in no position to take the fight to the SNP.

We were promised pictures of a group who voted yes in the referendum but are backing Labour in the general election. Only two show up. Jim pours them tea. I whisper to Chas, my cameraman, not to take too long as the chances of us using these very dull pictures is close to zero. One-nil to the SNP.

Thursday 22 January

1 Devonshire Gardens, Glasgow

The perfect breakfast: poached eggs, bacon, haggis, gallons of coffee and four front pages with my story on the front. English front pages, that is. They are channelling what they assume will be their readers' outrage at the prospect of Scots Nats voting on English laws. The Scottish papers barely mention the story, regarding it as none too surprising.

One consequence of devolution is that it is increasingly hard to report on Scottish politics in a way that works on both sides of the border.

Dynamic Earth museum, Edinburgh

Back to Edinburgh, where the PM is unveiling plans to enact the 'vow' made to Scotland in the desperate last-minute attempt to stop the country voting for independence. Holyrood will, he tells his Scottish audience, become one of the most powerful devolved parliaments in the world. Meanwhile he addresses the English audience by promising that their MPs will get the decisive say over their laws – how, exactly, he doesn't spell out.

The team from Downing Street encourage me to put a question about Sturgeon's pledge to vote on the English NHS or the possibility of a deal between Labour and the SNP. No thanks. I ask instead why those who lost the referendum now seem to be winning the political argument in Scotland.

Cameron clearly doesn't like this suggestion one little bit. He defends what he calls his 'big, bold, audacious decision to hold a referendum, which my side won'. He sounds like a man who knows he may be out of office soon and wants to write his own version of the history of his premiership.

The problem he has is that he and others claimed victory in a referendum would stop the rise of the SNP, just as some claimed creating a Scottish Parliament would kill nationalism stone dead. It simply wasn't true.

Edit suite, BBC Edinburgh

News reaches me that the broadcasters have blinked first in the TV election debates poker game. The Greens are to be invited to take part after all – and so, too, are the SNP and Plaid Cymru. Team Cameron will be delighted. Miliband will be facing attacks from all those parties that are challenging him to his left.

The new offer is combined with a threat to empty-chair any leader (i.e. the PM) who fails to turn up. Cameron has made it clear there's no way he'll do three debates during the campaign itself so now the two sides will be staring each other out again. Will the PM back down and consent to take part? I doubt it. Or will the broadcasters or, perhaps, someone else, like YouTube or Facebook, agree to hold perhaps just one debate at a time of his choosing? I have always believed that's what will happen.

Saturday 24 January

The tube

Curious. I've been put on standby for what the Tories have obviously been regarding as a coup against their tormentors in UKIP. One of Farage's key lieutenants was due to defect back to the Conservatives, and the BBC were to get the first TV interview. Yet now I'm reading an e-mail containing the breaking news that the man in question, Amjad Bashir MEP, has been suspended from UKIP pending an investigation by the party into serious allegations. It looks and smells like a pre-emptive strike by Team Gobby at UKIP HQ.

Amjad Bashir is the sort of guy every political party would love to have: part tub-thumping, plain-speaking small businessman from Yorkshire, part proud Pakistani Muslim. I met him when he was UKIP's poster boy, posing with Nigel Farage in front of UKIP's anti-immigration billboards, just before I asked Farage about his German wife.

As allegations begin to swirl about him, are the Tories sure they know who they're embracing?

Sunday 25 January

Home, the kitchen

It's trash UKIP day. The Sunday papers have been provided with a smorgasbord of embarrassments for Farage to answer when he appears for his New Year interview with Andrew Marr.

The defector is only the start of it. The man brought in to stop the party making 'bad news' headlines – I kid you not – joked that 'people talk about UKIP being bigots. There are hundreds of thousands of bigots in the United Kingdom and they deserve representation'. A few years ago Matthew Richardson described the NHS as the biggest waste of money in Britain and dubbed it the 'Reichstag bunker of socialism'.

I'm not sure whether all the ammunition has come from the same source but I suspect it has. With the hundred-days-to-the-election milestone imminent, someone has decided it's time to throw not just the kitchen sink but all the fixtures and fittings at UKIP.

The sofa

It would be enough to have many politicians squirming and flapping like a fish caught on a hook. Not Nigel Farage. Once again, he seems able to swim through a channel full of sewage and emerge smiling and smelling of roses at the other end.

The defector? He wishes he'd got rid of him when people first told him he was dodgy.

Bigots? It was a joke made in a pub.

The NHS? UKIP had a debate about it, decided it loves it and, abracadabra, we've come up with a way to spend an extra £3 billion a year on it.

Nigel instinctively understands the first rule of success on TV: if you look and sound relaxed, those watching at home will more readily accept what you say. If you look edgy and defensive, they will smell a rat. It's why top TV presenters are worth so much. If you have the aptitude for it, it's often a pretty easy job. But it's an aptitude very, very few people have.

As for the substance of what Farage says, it may be that many voters don't care much about it as they don't expect him ever to hold power. On the other hand, it could be that these stories will accumulate like snow before an avalanche until, suddenly, something gives way.

Monday 26 January

BBC offices, Millbank

A hoax caller pretending to be the head of GCHQ in Cheltenham has got through to the PM on his mobile phone. Some report this as a serious security breach, others, including David Cameron himself, as a harmless joke. What I thought was, oh God, maybe that's where my stolen mobile got to. It wasn't. My phone was never found but was replaced by the BBC with a much more secure one.

Tuesday 27 January

Home, the kitchen

Put up your souvenir wall chart. Start counting the days. Yes, there are now exactly a hundred to go to the election. Yippee! The media can never resist a countdown or an anniversary, and the party PR men know it. So this entirely meaningless date has been imbued with utterly artificial significance. Some bright spark has come up with a campaign countdown graphic that has even me screaming at the telly, 'Wake me up when it's all over!'

The study

David Cameron is doing live interviews on the morning shows from the Cabinet room. He wants to talk about the economy; his interviewers want to ask him whether he'll agree to TV debates. His answer is very Vicky Pollard – yeah but, no but. Yeah but he does want to come, no but he won't unless the Northern Irish parties are included and the election debates are not held during the, er, election.

I follow him on to the *Today* programme to try to explain what I think he's up to. He knows he may need the support of the DUP's nine MPs in a hung Parliament so he's very happy to be seen fighting their corner. He also knows that his call will delay negotiations again and strengthen his hand for what my guess is he plans to do next.

My hunch is that he'll keep the debates about debates going until the last possible minute, at which point he'll offer to take part in one of them, with all comers, just before the campaign begins.

He'll claim the media's obsession with the story has proved him right in warning that debates during the campaign would crowd out the real issues.

He'll calculate that, while this strategy will lead many voters to view him as, well, a little bit chicken, it won't bother them enough to change how they vote.

We shall see.

The consequence of all this pre-packaged election blah is that everyone is searching for what's unplanned and off-message.

Ed Miliband does his interviews from the first NHS hospital, in Trafford, unaware that Labour's former health secretary, Alan Milburn, has chosen the day his party launches its ten-year health plan to warn his old colleagues not to make a 'fatal mistake' by running a 'pale imitation' of its losing 1992 general election campaign and promising cash for the NHS but no reform.

I hear that Milburn was invited to the Labour health launch but turned it down on the grounds it was his birthday. Perhaps this was his idea of a birthday treat. And was this message his alone? After all, he used to employ a bright young political adviser by the name of Simon Stevens – a great believer in the health service but someone who saw the value of and, indeed, earned quite a few bucks from the private sector, too. He just happens to be the new chief executive of the NHS.

Wednesday 28 January

Home, my sick-bed

'If you come in, we won't put you on air.' That tells me. Katy and Jon, who run my life at the BBC, are fed up with my continuing coughing, spluttering and whingeing and order me to take a day or two off to get better. 'And don't look at texts and e-mails either.' Of course, I obey – until it's time for Prime Minister's Questions.

Once again Ed Miliband tries to get the NHS to the top of the news. Once again David Cameron responds by asking him to deny that he's spoken of 'weaponizing' the NHS. This time, though, he takes a slightly different tack. The PM decides to 'weaponize' me, or at least try to use me as a shield against Labour's attacks.

He not only reads out the original report in which I wrote about Miliband talking of weaponizing the NHS, he names me and then praises me as 'one of the most respected journalists in Britain'. A few of those watching sweetly message me or tweet to say that this is a great compliment. It isn't. It is, as Miliband observes, a smokescreen to avoid answering difficult questions.

The 'weaponizing' tactic works for Cameron partly because he's using it to suggest that Labour's motives for talking about health are cynical and political rather than caring and compassionate, but mainly because Miliband has none of Nigel Farage's TV skills. Again and again he has wriggled about whether he used the word 'weaponize'. So much so that every interviewer has another go at it. Viewers and listeners can sense his discomfort.

For him to deny saying it would be risky, given that I had not, contrary to what many people believe, reported a private conversation between the two of us but something I knew he'd said to a large roomful of journalists and on other occasions as well.

Admitting it would be risky, too, but he could have turned it to his advantage by saying something like, 'You know what? I do want to use what the Tories have done to our great NHS to damage them, and make sure they don't get the chance to destroy it altogether. I do want to make sure that they pay the political price for all those people who are waiting in pain for so long at A&E . . .'

Doing neither is not clever politics.

In the meantime, Cameron is hurting rather than helping me by encouraging Labour supporters to think I'm on his side, and turning 'weaponization' into a big story, when he is well aware that I only mentioned Miliband's use of the word once, way back in November, and then only in passing.

Matt's cartoon in the *Telegraph* got it right this morning. A man in despair at the thought of ninety-nine more days' electioneering looks at his wife and declares, 'I'm going to weaponize my apathy.'

Thursday 29 January

Home

The team back at the office clearly enjoyed my brief absence. They've run a caption competition for an image created by the Huffington Post website of a 'weaponized' Nick Robinson. It consists of my head photoshopped on to Rambo's body, complete with rippling biceps. The figure shoulders a rocket-launcher and is surrounded by the bodies of his enemies.

The winner is: 'What do you mean, Robert Peston's the lead story?' Struggle as I might, I've simply no clue what they're talking about. No, really.

One colleague sends me a favourite Rambo quote. The all-action hero is asked, 'Who are you?' His reply is: 'Your worst nightmare.' Are they trying to tell me something?

Members' dining room, House of Commons

Curious place, Westminster. By day the press – or at least, large parts of it – compete to make Ed Miliband look nerdy, dangerous and unfit to be prime minister. By night here they are, dressed in black tie, sipping champagne and introducing their wives (or, albeit only occasionally in this male-dominated world, their husbands) to the guest of honour at the Westminster correspondents' dinner: none other than the Labour leader himself.

The dinner is modelled on its glamorous, lavish, star-studded White House equivalent. Except that, as Ed observes wittily, the host, my BBC deputy James Landale, is not quite George Clooney and the guest speaker is no Obama.

Politics barely features at these dos. They're a mixture of mutual back-slapping and teasing from people forced to spend inordinate amounts of time in each other's not always very appealing company.

Last year it was the PM who spoke. Recalling a recent visit to China, during which I'd complained loudly that he and his Communist hosts were scared to take journalists' questions, he joked that he'd been delighted 'to accompany Nick Robinson on his trip to China'.

This year James introduces Ed with a good-natured collection of jokes at his expense (bacon sandwiches, nerds, Rubik's cubes and forgotten speech lines all get a mention) and a nice self-deprecating pay-off. Looking ahead to the election debates, he notes that this may not be the last time Ed gets 'to stand next to an Old Etonian who's patronizing you'. (James bears lightly the burden of having gone to that school.)

Having shown that he's more than capable of laughing at himself, Ed turns characteristically serious. The real significance of this week, he says, is not the hundred days to the election, but the seventieth anniversary of the liberation of Auschwitz. He speaks emotionally about his discovery earlier this year that his grandfather died in a German concentration camp and recalls the small family candle-lighting ceremony the Milibands held in his memory.

Few have seen him speak this way. Many look moved. I was filming with him in Israel just hours after he was handed the file that revealed his grandfather's fate. I recall him telling me that he would have to ring his mother to break the news to her before I asked him about it on camera. It's clear that he's been absorbing it ever since. It is a real irony that Ed is finally reconnecting with his Jewish roots just as the Jewish community at home have pretty much written him off.

He ends with a skilful reminder that everyone in the room is, like it or not, seen as part of the Westminster establishment. 'We,' he tells his tormentors, 'are custodians of politics and its reputation.' As he sits down I look over and give him a thumbs-up.

Last year, when David Cameron effortlessly teased and charmed the room, few, including a nervous-looking Ed Miliband, believed he could do the same. Sensibly, he has focused instead on delivering a message that can't be repeated often enough, and one that we have always agreed on: the need for all of us, whatever our jobs, and whatever our views, to make the case that politics can and should be a force for good.

Friday 30 January

Mothers' Union headquarters, Tufton Street, SW1

I've been asked to give the troops a pep talk before they head into the campaign. BBC Westminster's finest have gathered in the unlikely setting of the Mothers' Union offices to discuss how we can make the election exciting. After an hour on Google with Harry helping me to find pictures of people yawning or bursting with enthusiasm, I have my PowerPoint presentation ready to motivate them for the battle ahead.

This, I tell them, will be thrilling! It's a once-in-five-years moment of decision. It's extraordinarily unpredictable. The stakes are very high, I conclude, not entirely sure I've convinced even myself.

I can't help noticing all the stories that really engage journalists are about the day after the election: what deals or pacts or coalitions might be formed and who will run for the leadership in whichever party is defeated.

— FEBRUARY —

Sunday 1 February

The Macclesfield 'alps'

Azure sky, sparkling white snow, air so clear you can taste it. Why did I ever leave this place to go to London? A family walk in the Peak District is a glorious but painful reminder that there is another life I could have had. It's also much needed to recover from the trauma of the 'Murray meltdown', Andy Murray's at first brilliant and then calamitous attempt to defeat Novak Djokovic in the final of the Australian Open.

When I eventually get round to reading the Sunday papers, it's clear they've decided to do their best to generate the political equivalent of the beating dished out to Murray on that court in Melbourne, or what the *Sun on Sunday* calls the 'Edache'. The *Mail on Sunday*'s splash is 'LABOUR KNIVES OUT FOR "LOSER" RED ED'. The *Sunday Telegraph* leads with 'BOOTS CHIEF – LABOUR WIN WOULD CAUSE "CATASTROPHE"'.

Not since the days of Neil Kinnock have we seen a personal campaign quite like it. To be fair to the papers, most of the stories in the Tory press are based on self-inflicted Labour wounds. It is Messrs Blair, Mandelson and Milburn who have been most devastating in their critique of Miliband. It is a book written by the former Labour mayor of Doncaster in Ed's own constituency that has given the *Mail on Sunday* three weeks of unalloyed Labour-bashing joy. The most excoriating commentary pieces have been written by former Labour advisers, namely Damian McBride, Gordon Brown's former spin doctor, Jason Cowley, editor of the Labour-supporting *New Statesman*, and journalist Dan Hodges, a former Labour party and GMB trade-union official.

No wonder Ed's advisers want to focus on the fight with the boss of Boots, a Tory-backing, tax-avoiding resident of Monaco. That way they can portray all his problems as a plot by the rich and powerful to stop a man who's ready to stand up to them. Bet the Tories can hardly believe their luck.

Monday 2 February

Home, the study

I tee up an Ed Balls interview on *Today* by talking about a letter in *The Times* from university vice-chancellors warning bosses that they could lose billions of pounds if Miliband sticks to his stated ambition of cutting fees by £3,000 per year.

Labour, I say, has a £2 billion problem to solve – that's the annual cost of cutting fees, which will have to come from somewhere. The universities are determined it won't come from them. The shadow business secretary, Chuka Umunna, is equally adamant it won't come from him. So where will it come from? No one can tell. Or are Labour still considering watering down, phasing in or postponing delivery of the promise to cut the costs? Ed Balls won't say.

Kingsmead school, Enfield

A school gym. A backdrop spelling out a series of 'commitments' (nobody believes politicians' 'promises' any more). An invited audience of party activists. The PM has come here to unveil the 'protection' the Tories will give to the budgets of English schools if they are in power after the election. He didn't have much choice: a few weeks ago a photograph emerged of a secret briefing note which advised ministers not to say anything about school budgets beyond 'Of course, there will be difficult decisions in the education budget in the next Parliament . . .' It was an invitation to their opponents to predict just how difficult (cue accusations about 'massive cuts').

The formula Cameron announces is carefully worded. Very carefully. 'The amount of money following your child into the school will not be cut,' he states, explaining that 'in Treasury speak, that's flat cash per pupil'. When it's my turn to ask a question, I point out that, as any economics student at the school would know, 'flat cash' equals cuts in real terms, as spending will not be increasing in line with inflation. Somewhat to my surprise, he doesn't make any attempt to deny or deflect this.

As a result, Tory cuts to school budgets becomes the lead story on the six and ten o'clock news.

I show the latest brilliant Matt cartoon to Tory strategist Craig Oliver. A man with a clipboard talking to a snowman is saying, 'David Cameron would like you to take part in the TV election debates.' My contact beams. 'He's got it!' They'll invite anyone to take part if it screws up the whole thing.

College Green

My final assignment of the day is to interview eleven-year-old Fran from Lewisham, who has just won an election at her school to become head for a week and will be appearing in a BBC children's documentary. What was her most attractive election-clinching promise? I ask her. Free candy floss for all, is her reply. Not forgetting a new playground sweet-shop and a visit to a funfair. The producers have urged me to grill her like someone with real power. I point out that parents may object to their kids' teeth being rotted at school. She has a plan for smaller portions for smaller kids. Under pressure, she concedes that parents might be allowed to stop their children participating. 'Ha!' I say. 'You've just broken your election promise to those who actually voted for you!'

Fran looks unimpressed. She tells me she wants to become mayor of Lewisham and has a plan to stop knife crime. Then she'd like to be an MP. 'What about prime minister?' Oh yes, she replies, and I'll do it by the time I'm thirty.

I wonder if in 2035 someone will dig out this tape, as they did the kids' programme Margaret Thatcher appeared on in the early 1970s, in which she predicted there wouldn't be a woman prime minister in her lifetime.

Tuesday 3 February

Home

'Have you tried xxxx?' A series of texts arrive from Team Cameron,

helpfully suggesting the names of business leaders who just might –
'nothing to do with us, of course' – want to join the chorus of criticism
of Ed Miliband's attitude to business. After Ed's fight with the boss
of Boots, the Tory press can't get enough of it. Stuart Rose, once
the executive chairman of Marks and Spencer, has accused him of
being a '1970s throwback' who has wrecked Britain's pro-business
consensus.

Labour seem split over how to handle this. Team Ed are itching to
come out with all guns blazing, proclaiming that their guy is 'on your
side', but the other Ed and Chuka Umunna seem keen to avoid risking
further damage to their relationship with corporate Britain.

A Westminster restaurant

A memorable lunch with one of the next possible leaders of the Labour
party, who does nothing to mask the fear of defeat ('I can name six
seats we can take from the Tories, but not the ten we need'), or the fact
that many minds have already turned to the leadership campaign that
will inevitably follow if they lose. In a few weeks' time my guest will
either be a senior minister hailing the triumph of Ed Miliband or a
candidate to succeed him explaining why he was a failure. Funny
business, politics.

BBC offices, Westminster

Fresh from having saved the United Kingdom, Gordon Brown re-
emerges to take on a much tougher task: saving Scottish Labour from
imminent catastrophe. The author of the last-minute eve-of-referendum
all-party 'vow' to give fresh powers to the Scottish Parliament is now
proposing a Labour-only 'vow plus', an offer to hand Scotland more
control over the cash it spends on benefits. It's an attempt to wrestle
back from the Nats the claim to be Scotland's party of social justice.

Meanwhile, William Hague has presented his English votes for
English laws plan which, to most of those who care about such things,
feels like an obscure and complex parliamentary fudge. Scottish, as
well as Welsh and Irish, votes will still be cast for English laws, but
English MPs alone will debate the details and get a veto. Though none
of this excites folk south of the border, Gordon attacks Cameron for
'blowing the UK apart'.

Wednesday 4 February

Home, bed

'Did you catch Ed and Bill?' queries a late-night e-mail I read on waking. I didn't, but Twitter is full of Ed Balls' struggle on *Newsnight* last night to come up with a single business leader who is backing Labour. Asked to name one, Balls said he'd just been at a dinner with 'a number of business-supporting Labour figures'. The best questions in journalism are the simplest. 'Who were they?' inquired Emily Maitlis. 'Well, erm, Bill. The former chief executive of EDS, who I was just talking to . . .'

Emily scented his uncertainty and pressed on. 'What was his name?'

Balls candidly admitted that the name had 'just gone from my head, which is a bit annoying at this time of night'. Emily smiled and moved in for the kill. 'OK. So, frankly, you've got Bill somebody. Have we got anyone else?'

Balls had taken to the airwaves to try to reassure voters that Labour is the centre-ground, pro-business party, but instead he has accidentally offered up what the media can never resist: a memorable gaffe that risks doing precisely the opposite.

A text pings up from the *Today* programme. 'Can you come on to talk about Bill Somebody?' It is, of course, a phrase Balls never used, but it's going to stick.

Prime Minister's Questions

Ed Miliband chooses to march towards the sound of Tory gunfire at PMQs. He knows that if he dares to raise anything about the economy today he will face a barrage of 'Bill Somebody' taunts. But he takes the risk.

The reason becomes clear in his final, carefully polished sound-bite, which brands the Tories 'the party of Mayfair hedge funds and Monaco tax-avoiders'. It's a none-too-subtle message to voters that he is 'on their side' and comes on the day the *Mirror* splashes on the news that the company Samantha Cameron works for – Smythson, the makers of posh stationery and handbags – is, you guessed it, avoiding tax.

Her husband has a pretty good soundbite of his own prepared. 'Bill Somebody isn't a person,' he jokes. 'Bill Somebody is Labour's policy!' He employs this gag after ignoring Miliband's posing of the same question – on why hedge funds have been given a tax break – a total of six times. Cameron's refusal to answer outrages many watching live, but he knows the 'Bill Somebody' clip will make the TV news, along with the hedge-fund attack – a score draw is his best hope. It's cynical but a reminder of his ruthless determination to hold on to power.

To move the story on from Bill Somebody, I want to find a business leader who will highlight in public what I'm hearing about in private: business anxiety that David Cameron could end up steering Britain out of the EU. I call a couple of well-connected contacts. Both tell me the same thing. There are plenty of bosses who are very nervous about what may follow a Tory victory, but as almost all of them are more worried by the idea of Ed Miliband reaching Number 10, they're keeping quiet.

BBC office, Millbank

Third time lucky? Perhaps. The home secretary has finally made her third choice of chair for the inquiry into child sex abuse. In her search for someone, anyone, who can't possibly be accused of being part of the establishment, she's travelled over 11,000 miles to New Zealand and picked one of their judges. Surely there is no way that, unlike the last two appointments, Lowell Goddard can have lived down the road from a former home secretary or be related to a former attorney general. Can she? Watch this space.

We were given a glimpse this morning of where this might all end up when the chair of the Iraq inquiry, Sir John Chilcot, told MPs he still didn't have a schedule for publication and it wouldn't be in the foreseeable future. It took less time to mount the London Olympics than this inquiry has taken and I can predict with perfect accuracy that when it reports many will say there has still been a cover-up – just as they will after a child-abuse inquiry that costs millions, takes years and quite probably solves very little.

Friday 6 February

Home

'Where is Britain? Where is Cameron? He is clearly a bit player. Nobody is taking any notice of him. He is now a foreign-policy irrelevance.'

With François Hollande and Angela Merkel in Ukraine and about to head to Moscow, these are the questions being asked by a former top NATO commander, Sir Richard Shirreff.

It comes a day after the Defence Select Committee described Britain's role in fighting Islamic State as 'strikingly modest', the RAF having carried out just 6 per cent of coalition air strikes.

The committee's chairman said that it would be a real pity if Britain lurched from engagement to isolation. The boast years ago by one foreign secretary, Douglas Hurd, that Britain punched above its weight is not a claim I can imagine being made by the current occupant of that once-great office. Come to think of it, I'm not sure most people could name the current foreign secretary.

Post-Iraq, and in this age of austerity, many may feel relieved to see Britain shrink on the world stage. But shouldn't we have a debate about it? Or are we happy to be, as President Putin's spokesman put it, 'a small island no one cares about'?

Chest consultant's clinic

I've been coughing and wheezing on and off since the party-conference season. No huge surprise there. I've been an asthmatic all my life, I'm over fifty, I work stupid hours and three weeks of early mornings and very late nights trapped in the company of thousands of perspiring, plotting political activists would be enough to make the fittest person ill.

And yet and yet . . . what began as a routine review of my asthma treatment has turned into something rather different. My consultant, Mike Beckles, has done all the usual stuff – listening to my chest, getting me to blow into a tube, asking me how I feel – and we are almost done when I drop in that I've lost weight. Actually, I've gone down a whole belt size. 'In fact, you know what?' I remark to the elegantly dressed guy behind the desk, 'I've just treated myself to a slim-fit Paul Smith suit for the election, which I really didn't expect to get into.' No, I haven't dieted. No, I'm not exercising any more than usual. I've just lost weight.

In the short pause that follows it feels as if a klaxon has gone off and red lights are flashing.

'I'm sending you for a CT scan. Now,' he says. Oh.

Under the scanner

I lie flat on a hard bed and am told not to move. It slides silently into a giant white tube which takes images of my lungs. What the hell is hiding there?

Sunday 8 February

Home, the kitchen table

Curious. If my memory's correct, the country still has no money. The age of austerity still has a good while to go. The cuts will continue for at least another three years, whoever's in power.

Yet I could swear that's the chancellor of the exchequer on *The Andrew Marr Show*, promising to give older people (who've been most protected from those cuts) with money to save (who are, therefore, far from poor) an incentive (handout from taxpayers) to save. But hurry, folks, this offer must end by May. Funny, that.

The Tories are not the only ones flourishing pre-election bungs. Labour are unveiling plans for longer paternity leave.

Perhaps every report we do between now and polling day should end with a cautionary reminder, like the ones telling you that shares can go down as well as up. This one should say: 'Every election in recent times has been followed by major tax rises.'

Sofa

The late news includes a gift for Labour: a preview of tomorrow's *Panorama*, which has evidence that HSBC was involved in aiding and abetting tax avoidance (legal) and evasion (illegal) on a massive scale. The man in charge at the time, Lord Green, was given his peerage and the job of trade minister by David Cameron after the authorities first got wind that something was up.

Monday 9 February

Home, the study

'He started it.'
   'Did not.'
   'Did so.'
   'Liar.'
   'Pants on fire.'
This is not a verbatim summary of the texts that have bombarded my phone from the moment I woke but it isn't that far off.

The fact that more than a thousand wealthy Brits hid their money in HSBC's Swiss bank accounts and were advised by the bank how to dodge tax was not, apparently, the fault of them or their bankers but all the fault of (delete as applicable) a) Ed Balls, who was the City minister at the time of the offences, or b) David Cameron, for rewarding the bank's boss with a peerage and a ministerial red box.

Every story I report on has now become a contest between Craig Oliver and Tom Baldwin – Team Cameron and Team Miliband – over whose narrative wins. Every broadcast and tweet is followed by a stream of complaints that I've ignored this or not emphasized that or simply not understood what the other lot are up to.

Edit suite, Millbank

Texts continue to pour in from the rival spin doctors. Why am I letting the Tories/Labour off the hook? Why am I ignoring X or Y? Can I guarantee that A or B will be in that night's news report?

I've had enough. I tell Tom that if he really wants to decide what the BBC broadcasts he should apply for a job here and Craig that if he wants to know what I'll be saying he can watch the news at ten like everyone else.

After a day weighing up claim and counter-claim, I conclude that while it's perfectly understandable to want Ed Balls to take his fair share of the blame for lax regulation of the banks (indeed, he's apologized for it), it is absurd to blame him for corruption at a bank whose own bosses and regulator did not know about it.

Less clear is whether David Cameron could or should have known before giving Lord Green a peerage and the job of his trade minister.

Certainly the Revenue had already been tipped off – though they may not have told the Treasury, never mind Number 10 – and natural caution would have made most people wary of promoting a banker, almost any banker, after the scandals of 2007 and 2008.

On the other hand, Lord Green, a priest, is a trusted adviser to the Church of England. So if the prime minister got it wrong, so, too, did the archbishop of Canterbury, who sat on a commission into banking standards.

Tuesday 10 February

QE2 conference centre

David Cameron is channelling his inner Kinnock in an effort to stir up the nation's boss class. Addressing the British Chambers of Commerce conference he self-consciously echoes a speech that will be familiar to anyone his age or older (though a mystery to anyone else).

'I warn you not to grow your business, because they'll come after you. I warn you not to take people on, because they'll slap taxes on you. I warn you not to create wealth, as they'll demonize you.'

Before the 1983 election, Neil Kinnock tried to rouse the country with the words: 'I warn you not to be young. I warn you not to fall ill. I warn you not to get old.'

I want to ask Cameron whether business shouldn't be as worried about his stance on Europe as they are about Labour. I put it to him that perhaps he should have told his business audience, 'I warn you that I may not get a better deal in Europe, I warn you that I might not do it on the timetable I've set out and I warn you that we may leave the EU by mistake.'

Barely pausing for breath, he replies: 'That's not quite how I'd put it,' prompting gales of laughter from his audience.

Tellingly, Ed Balls got barely a titter when he tried a series of self-deprecating jokes about forgetting businessmen's names.

Edit suite, Millbank

As I edit my news piece, intercutting the Cameron and Kinnock warning speeches, I start to worry that I am doing exactly what some

Tory strategist wants: reminding the older voters being targeted by the Tories about Neil Kinnock. Is Cameron's unstated message, 'You rejected one left-wing loser, now it's time . . . ?'

Conservative hopes of victory now rest on a repeat of the last-minute 'hold your nose and vote Tory' swing that kept Kinnock out of Downing Street when he ran against John Major in 1992.

Osteria dell'Angolo, Westminster

We have been invited to visit the court of Queen Nicola to hear of her plans not just for Scotland but for the rest of the UK, too, if – as so many now expect – the SNP keep a minority Labour government in power.

My oppos at Channel 4, Sky, *Newsnight* and ITV have gathered in the basement of an Italian restaurant to break bread and sup wine with the first minister, her deputy and the leader of the SNP colleague in Westminster. All are on their best behaviour. One mutters to me, 'Why are we being so extraordinarily polite?' The answer is simple. They matter now. We know it and, boy, so do they.

Nicola's aims are not modest: an end to Treasury-imposed austerity; the postponement, if not the cancellation, of the renewal of Trident; and another independence referendum within a decade. We would have scoffed at her a while back. Not now.

We are all kept entertained by the splendidly irrepressible Jon Snow, presenter of *Channel 4 News* and anti-establishment pin-up. Jon tells us that Westminster is dead, British politics is moribund and radical change is coming. After a glass or three I start my riposte. This has the makings of a memorable dinner-party joust – until I remember what we've come for.

'Jon,' I remind him, 'we're here to hear from the first minister, not you.' On the way out I suggest to him that we should have our debate on a stage at a literary festival. 'Let's do it, old boy,' he replies, Tigger-like. Snow has what so few in my trade possess: a never-ending supply of curiosity and excitement. Whatever it is he takes, I want some of it.

Wednesday 11 February

Victoria line tube

The newsroom want me to cover Sturgeon's speech but I've got a hunch that we haven't seen the end of the tax-avoidance row.

I text someone in Ed Miliband's office: 'Help me out – where's this story going next?' In response I learn that *Guardian* online are about to publish a list of seven Tory donors, including the former party treasurer Lord Fink, who had those secretive HSBC Swiss accounts. Ed will challenge Cameron on this at PMQs.

Damn. Damn. Damn. The BBC has the bloody files but they're all locked in a safe in Belfast. Having made the original big splash with *Panorama*, we're now letting the *Guardian* make all the running. I bash out a string of e-mails asking whether there's any chance we can get our own version of the story ready to go asap.

New Palace Yard, Palace of Westminster

When I'm finally able to make a phone call I discover that the researcher who knows where everything is in the HSBC files has the day off; the chap at BBC Belfast says Stanley Fink's name isn't there; the lawyer is worried about implying that anyone with a Swiss bank account (which is perfectly legal) is a tax-dodger and the guys in the BBC Editorial Policy Unit, who try to keep us on the straight and narrow, are concerned about breaching people's confidentiality.

I am immensely proud to work for the biggest news organization anywhere but every so often it can be a curse as well as a blessing. It is at times like this that I want to raze Broadcasting House to the ground. It is full of brilliant, hard-working, dedicated journalists who make sense of the world day in, day out but just occasionally it can feel as if it is equally full of very clever people who see it as their job to tell you why you shouldn't do something or why things are more complicated than they might at first appear. Infuriatingly, sometimes they are right.

BBC offices, Millbank

There's nothing my news editor Jon likes better than breaking news, and there's nothing he's better at than making the BBC machine work. 'Tell me what you need,' he says. I bark out a series of orders. 'Get the guys in Belfast/the duty lawyer/Editorial Policy on the line and tell them it's bloody well urgent!'

The place starts to move. The *Panorama* team dig out the information I need. The lawyer approves a form of words. Editorial Policy agree that the situation has materially changed since their last ruling.

'Get me on air!' I scream, running to the newsroom camera for a hit on the news channel. I put in my earpiece and hear not the voice of a producer or a studio director but a boss. He says we should put the allegations to the individuals concerned in order to give them the right of reply. Normally I'd agree, but as all those concerned are about to be named by the *Guardian*, whose report will be picked up and repeated by all other media outlets, I think we are being a tad too rule-bound.

You can only report what the *Guardian* says, not what our own work has revealed, the voice in my ear tells me. 'Are you absolutely sure?' I reply. Or words to that effect but possibly less polite and slightly more direct.

When told that he is, indeed, totally sure, I write my silent verdict on the back of my notes in large block capitals. It involves several F-words and a T-word, too. I stand up and shout: 'I am not bloody well paid to report second-hand journalism! Someone else can tell the world what the *Guardian* has found because we were too bloody useless to do it ourselves!'

A while later the decision changes and I run round one outlet after another with the news of the Tory donors with Swiss bank accounts.

Before I can get near a camera, Jon grabs my notes, pointing out that if I pick them up I might easily accidentally display my abusive message for the entire world to see on screen. Instead he briefly pins it up above his desk to entertain the troops. It isn't there long because he soon realizes there is a risk of some visitor taking a picture of it and posting it on Twitter.

Prime Minister's Questions

Sure enough, Ed Miliband comes to PMQs ready to fire the ammunition provided for him by the *Guardian*. Its report and my broadcasts are scrupulous about pointing out that having a Swiss bank account is not illegal and neither is so-called tax avoidance, or legally minimizing your tax bill, as millions do. What is illegal is tax evasion but, as yet, no one on the donor's list, and certainly not Lord Fink, has been accused of that, never mind found guilty of it.

Miliband's language is carefully chosen to blur this distinction and to imply wrongdoing, if not criminality. David Cameron, 'a dodgy prime minister surrounded by dodgy donors', is 'up to his neck in it'. He is much, much more circumspect when he asks Cameron what he'll do to tackle Lord Fink's 'tax-avoidance activities'. M'learned friends have clearly been consulted.

Most voters neither know nor care about the distinction between avoidance and evasion, having nowhere near enough money for it to make any difference to them. They will merely conclude that the rich are getting away with it again.

Chinese restaurant down the road from the office

Lunch with Tom Baldwin to discuss a pre-election soft-focus feature we want to make with Ed Miliband. Dealing with the other party leaders has been a doddle in comparison. Farage wants us to come with him on a day trip to First World War battle sites while Cameron has invited us to film him making the family Sunday lunch.

The Labour spin doctor is, understandably, still buzzing after PMQs. This moment, he tells me, is like the moment when the story broke about the hacking of the murdered teenager Milly Dowler's phone. What he means is that they are both balance-tipping moments, the point where an issue that hasn't previously excited most people – in one case phone-hacking within the Murdoch empire, in the other tax avoidance – suddenly galvanizes the public. This is a moment when Ed can show he's 'doing the right thing' and standing up to the rich and powerful.

My office

Lord Fink appears on his doorstep to read out a letter he's written. Its message, roughly summed up, is 'I dare you to step outside and say that again.' MPs can say what they like in the Commons (they enjoy so-called 'parliamentary privilege') without fear of ending up in court.

But if Ed Miliband repeats the comments he made today, Fink is promising to sue him.

Radio studio 3

I've only just finished my report for *BBC News at 6*. Now radio want a piece, too. They've agreed to take it at the end of the bulletin as they know I won't start writing it until after the news is on air.

My WDIAM, 'What Does It All Mean?', focuses on why Miliband is pursuing tax avoidance so aggressively. Remembering my lunchtime conversation with Tom, I write that Ed's advisers see it as a 'Milly Dowler moment', run into the studio, file the report and think no more about it.

My office

A moment to close my office door, to breathe, to pause. I've been playing phone tag all day with my chest consultant. Finally we get to speak. Mike has the results of my scan. There is a shadow on my lung. I'm no medic but I know that's not good. Hold on, he tells me, it might be a bad infection. It could be inflammation. After all, I inhaled a lot of smoke in the car crash I was in when I was eighteen. Yes, he agrees, it could be cancer, but that's not at the top of his list. The only way to be sure is to have another scan.

Oh.

Thursday 12 February

Home

I may have thought no more about that Milly Dowler moment but others on Twitter certainly have. The Tory press, nudged by Tory HQ, are suggesting that this was an outrageous misuse of the memory of a murdered schoolgirl. It was, of course, nothing of the sort. At worst it was a slightly clumsy and insensitive shorthand.

Tom Baldwin texts in something of a panic. He and Ed are heading to Ed's old school to launch Labour's education policies. They're happy for this to be overshadowed by questions about yesterday's row on tax avoidance. Indeed, they're positively encouraging it. Ed is planning to take up Lord Fink's challenge by repeating what he said in the Commons. What they really don't want questions about, though, is whether they see this as a 'Milly Dowler moment'.

Tom wants me to 'clear things up'. In other words, he wants me to say that no Labour figure – and in particular not him – used the phrase. This is awkward as I'm certain he did say it.

Haverstock school

When I arrive for the speech the scale of the problem becomes clear. Virtually every hack there asks me who it was who said 'Milly Dowler moment'. I have absolutely no desire to be involved in a media witch-hunt about the language people use or a repeat of the 'weaponizing' saga. So I tell them, and I tweet, that neither my blog nor my radio report contained a direct quotation. This has the benefit of being both true and ambiguous, as it leaves open the matter of whether the phrase was ever uttered. Time to move on to the substance. Could we? Please?

As soon as I do so, a much better story is dropped at our feet. Lord Fink has performed a spectacular and humiliating U-turn in an interview for the *Evening Standard*. Not only has he told them he doesn't want to sue the Labour leader, he has also admitted to tax avoidance, albeit of the 'vanilla' variety. Game, set and match to Ed, who duly repeats his calls on the PM to explain how he'll deal with this. Nowhere in his speech, though, does he repeat the word 'dodgy'.

I ask him whether he is now saying that Fink is not dodgy. To my amazement, he replies that indeed he is accusing him of no such thing. He appears to read his words as if they've been dictated by lawyers.

So, two U-turns – the first and biggest by Fink, but Ed has made one, too.

My question is heard in stony silence by the invited audience of party supporters and teachers. As every other journalist asks about the same subject they are booed and heckled. Why, the audience wants to know, aren't you asking about education? The blunt response is because it's not as newsworthy. A blunter one is that we'll ask what we like, thank you very much.

The real answer is that the spin doctors – in all parties – should abandon these hybrid party rallies–news conferences. They annoy everyone who goes to them.

Car home

It's only on the way home that I properly catch up with the rest of what has been a frantic news day. Only then that a lightbulb comes on above my head: so that's why George Osborne has given yet another handout to pensioners.

The governor of the Bank of England has announced that the price of oil is dropping so fast inflation may soon become deflation. Prices won't be going up, they'll be going down. This might sound good but in fact it's a nightmare, not least for those with savings. Mark Carney explains that it may lead to further cuts to already low interest rates, which in turn means that pensioners' savings will continue to wither. This is surely why the chancellor began the week with his act of apparently spontaneous generosity.

Friday 13 February

Home, the kitchen

Good grief. For a long time the 'Tory press' label seemed to have lost its meaning as the *Telegraph*, *Mail* and *Sun* made life hell for the leader of the party they were supposed to be backing. Post-Leveson they gave Cameron a regular kicking. Not any more. Not since the days of Neil Kinnock – remember the *Sun*'s election-day headline in 1992: 'IF KINNOCK WINS TODAY WILL THE LAST PERSON TO LEAVE BRITAIN PLEASE TURN OUT THE LIGHTS'? – have I seen coverage so personal and so politically motivated.

The *Mail*'s front page is dominated by the headline: 'RED ED THE TAX AVOIDER'. Beside it is a photo of Milly Dowler and the words '. . . and now Labour drags Milly into election battle'. The *Telegraph* front page includes the story of the 'Dowler family's dismay at Miliband'. No mention of Fink. No attempt at balance. No context or perspective. Papers that regularly attack the BBC are now using my name to try to give extra credibility to their attacks on Labour.

I text Ed Miliband and those I know best on his team to say that I don't much like being used by the *Mail* and *Telegraph* in this way. As ever they are polite, but it's pretty clear they blame me for providing the bullets the Tory press have fired. It's not just the Milly salvo. The tax-avoider headline comes from the answer to another question I asked Miliband, about how his father's will was designed to limit inheritance tax. It's an old story but it was a fair question, I thought, on a day when he was accusing others of doing exactly that. The question never made it into my reports, just as the Milly line was only a brief reference in a low-key radio piece and blog.

The complaints are already rolling in. Many allege that I made up the reference to Milly or raised her name first. This despite the fact that Tom Baldwin told *The Times*, among others, how Milly Dowler had 'crystallized' public concern over phone hacking, just as the HSBC revelations had crystallized concerns about tax avoidance.

I am going on a half-term holiday tomorrow and I have another scan this afternoon. I could really, really do without this.

I rattle off a response to the complainants and a blog explaining what did and did not happen. Up to a point. It does not say what I'd like to say, which is, 'He bloody said it. All I did was report it. And no, I don't agree with the Tories and the Tory press that he is exploiting the death of a teenage girl.'

Instead I conclude that this will not be the last time my reports are used by others to attack someone else.

A radiology clinic

I am still dealing with texts and e-mails and calls about a story that threatens to go radioactive as I prepare to have radioactivity injected into my own veins. If it glows on the scan, it's bad.

The nice Irish nurse says I need to lie still for an hour in an empty room, with no phone or iPad or papers or books or music. I must clear my mind and relax my body as stress and exertion can interfere with the scan results.

'I bloody well can't!' I want to scream. 'I might have cancer and I'm having another row I didn't want to have and don't you know there's *an election coming*?' Instead I smile, attempt to go into Zen mode and try not, repeat not, to think about cancer.

Under the scanner

Lie flat. Don't move. Try to clear your mind. Another hard, flat bed glides into another white tube. To my surprise, I find myself dozing off and daydreaming of snow and blue skies and sunshine on the slopes of Italy.

Saturday 14 February

The runway, Turin airport

Half-term. A week's skiing. An escape, but old habits die hard. The second the plane's wheels touch the tarmac I switch on my phone. There's a message from my consultant. Can I call him? I wasn't expecting the results of the scan for a day or two. Oh, God. I'm nervous. Very nervous.

The luggage hall

'Can you help Mum get the bags?' I ask the boys. 'I've got to take a call.' They look at me as if to say, 'What? Work? On a Saturday morning? On holiday? *Again*?'

Mike is, as he's always been, calm, clear and reassuring. The scans show what looks like a tumour. There is some 'activity' in my lymph glands, too. It still may not be cancer. May not. The balance of probability has clearly changed. Only a biopsy will tell. No, I don't need to fly home but I should have a test as soon as I do.

As I listen and concentrate and take notes, I lean on the exit door, setting off an alarm. Seeing me edge away from the scene of the crime, the boys and their friends burst out laughing.

My mind is racing. Soon I will have to tell them and their mum news that will stop those smiles. Your dad's ill. It's not good but it could be a lot worse. We just don't know. But we're not going to let it spoil our holiday.

I wave at Pippa to come over. She looks a tad irritated. She, too, thinks I've put work first. Again. I take her to one side and do what I do every day of my working life: summarize a stream of complex information on a subject I know very little about as simply as I can.

But there's a crucial difference. This time it's about me. And us.

She looks numb. She leaves much unsaid of what she must be thinking. For now the priority is to keep going. Don't scare Will and Harry. Don't spoil the holiday. Don't assume the worst.

Bus to the slopes

Pippa and I sit quietly holding hands. I turn the music on my iPod up loud and stare out of the window, looking for snow.

I text anxious colleagues at work who are waiting for news. 'Not good – BUT – and I really mean this – not yet bad.' I've lived with uncertainty before, I tell them. I'll just have to do it again. I – we – need a holiday . . .

Friday 20 February

Cervinia, chairlift

Lift the bar, lower skis, come to a stop. I can hear Jim Naughtie filling in through my earpiece before he says, 'And joining us now is our political editor, Nick Robinson.'

It is the first time – and I suspect it will be the last – I've ever broadcast from a ski slope. I couldn't resist it. The Labour and tuition fees story I've been chasing is taking yet another twist. Peter Mandelson, who was once the minister responsible for universities, has been on the programme to warn his party that universities must be fully compensated if they lose money because Labour cuts tuition fees.

A couple of texts at the bottom of the chairlift revealed that there is still no agreement behind the scenes about how the policy will be funded. So here I am, 'live from the Alps' (though sensibly, *Today*'s producer has not mentioned to Jim where I am in case he tells those listening), revealing that Labour has not yet agreed on where to find the £1.7 billion a year they need to pay for Ed's promised fee cut.

It might seem like a busman's holiday but it sure as hell beats phoning hospitals about appointments for next week.

Sunday 22 February

Home

The holiday over, reality returns. I have my next test first thing tomorrow morning. In the meantime, here we go again. Hidden cameras, journalists posing as company executives keen to get their views heard in Whitehall and Westminster and former ministers who should know better boasting about who they know and what they can find out – for the right fee.

Channel 4's *Dispatches* have teamed up with the *Telegraph* to expose the murky world of lobbying, or 'cash for access', as everyone prefers to call it. No money changes hands, no access is secured, no secrets are revealed but the prospect of all three taking place is there for everyone to see.

Messrs Hoon and Byers fell for it five years ago. This time it's Labour's Jack Straw and the Tories' Malcolm Rifkind. The best clips have been released in time for *BBC News at 10* to ensure a full news cycle of outrage. Just like the expenses scandal, which was drip-fed to television night after night and which, whisper who dares, we – I, damn it – did too little to question or to contextualize.

Monday 23 February

Piccadilly line tube

'Scandal? Really?' I e-mail the newsroom.

En route to the test that should confirm whether or not I have cancer I am distracting myself. Keep busy. Keep focused. Don't worry about what you can't control. So it's back to the 'cash-for-access' scandal.

I have yet to hear Rifkind's and Straw's defence of themselves detailed on the *Today* programme but I have had a thorough read of the *Telegraph*'s story, which reveals that Straw, who is retiring as an MP in a few weeks' time, told a firm he would not be able to work for them now but could once he'd left the Commons. He did boast to the 'Chinese company executives' he was meeting about how he'd helped companies to change policy 'under the radar', but that was in Brussels and Kiev, not Westminster or Whitehall.

Rifkind bragged that he knew all the ambassadors in London and went on to talk of all the things he could find out about. None of them, though, was really private.

Not much of a scandal there. What is outraging people is that two ex-foreign secretaries should be naïve enough to meet representatives of a business they did nothing to check out, even though it purported to be Chinese and should, therefore, have rung alarm bells; to talk of how they could earn £5,000 a day, well over two months' wages for the average earner, and to show off about who they knew and what they could do.

In short, they may not be guilty of breaching any rules but they look bang to rights.

So what should we report? The impression or the reality? Not my problem today. I'm not on duty.

Clinic

A man is sticking a tube down my throat to take a closer look at the nasties lurking in my lung. You'll be sedated, they told me. You might even sleep through it. Hardly. Instead I find myself gagging horribly, desperate to sit up and pull the damn thing out. I know this is in my interests but I feel as if I'm being waterboarded.

Tuesday 24 February

Home, the kitchen

Will he stay or will he go? Malcolm Rifkind tried anger and defiance where Jack Straw deployed contrition and regret. A scan of this morning's papers makes it absolutely clear which has worked best.

Every interview Rifkind did yesterday was another nail in the coffin of a forty-year political career. One line in particular stands out: his insistence that he is 'entitled' to earn more than his MP's salary to keep his earnings in line with other similarly qualified professionals.

I text a well-placed Tory for guidance on what might happen next. The reply is redolent of a party that still thinks of itself as being of the officer class: 'He'll be handed a tumbler of whisky and a revolver and invited to do the honourable thing.'

Victoria Line tube

As my train rolls into Oxford Circus a message flashes up on the iPad. Sir Malcolm has drunk the whisky and fired the revolver. He has resigned as chairman of the Intelligence and Security Committee, due to meet today, and won't stand again for his seat.

A Westminster eatery

It is one thing to pull off a murder. The art, though, is to make it look like suicide. So says my lunchtime guest from Team Cameron. Rifkind has taken his own political life after being given the clearest possible hint that the PM planned to finish him off, using a party disciplinary inquiry to administer the fatal blow.

Though one faction at Number 10 worried that all this was mightily unfair on a man with four decades of public service, another argued that it was better to act brutally now than to hang on day after day, trying in vain to head off the inevitable. We did that with Maria Miller*, I was told.

As I emerge from lunch Sir Malcolm is emerging from his ISC meeting. 'Did you do anything wrong?' he's asked.

'No,' he replies, before admitting 'errors of judgement'. You can say that again.

My office

'Have you heard it?'

'She's done it again!'

The newsroom huddles around a PC to hear the latest car-crash interview with the leader of the Greens. Natalie Bennett proves completely incapable of explaining how much her policy to build 500,000 new homes will cost or where the money will come from. She sounds

---

* The ex-culture secretary fought an ultimately losing battle to defend her use of parliamentary expenses to pay, at least in part, for a home in which her elderly parents lived.

close to tears as she realizes how hopeless her performance is. Only a couple of weeks ago she was shown to know less about her own party's policies than Andrew Neil. He brilliantly revealed that the Greens were just £270 billion – that's almost treble the budget of the NHS – short of the money required to pay for their promise of a national citizen's income and had a policy of making it legal for people to join ISIS or Al-Qaeda.

In her defence Bennett admits to giving an 'excruciating' radio interview, which she blames on a new concept that looks certain to catch on: a 'mind blank' or 'brain fade'.

You know what? I think many will sympathize with her. Few people have any expectation that the Greens will ever get a chance to implement any of their policies and therefore it will make very little difference to how many votes they get.

Wednesday 25 February

Daily Politics *studio*

It would have been easy for Ed Miliband to have shied away from raising the issue of lobbying. After all, one of his own has been caught in the latest media sting. However, he sees it as another chance to define himself as the champion of a new kind of politics.

Six times in all he invites David Cameron to join him in the lobbies tonight in voting for a proposal to ban MPs from having second jobs. Six times Cameron tries but fails to hide behind the suggestion that Miliband will only ban certain second jobs (Tory ones) and not positions as trade-union officials. Problem one with this line of argument is that there are no MPs who are also trade-union officials. Problem two is that Miliband instantly offers to include such jobs in the ban Labour are proposing.

But it is clear where Cameron's real sympathies lie when he effectively endorses the warning by Sir Peter Tapsell, the father of the house (its longest-serving member) and a Tory grandee with a fine aristocratic lisp, that imposing restrictions on outside earnings would limit membership of the Commons to 'inhewitors of substantial fortunes or to wich spouses or to obsessive cwackpots or to those who are unemployable anywhere else'.

Chest consultant's clinic

Dread. There is only one word to describe how I feel waiting to hear what my consultant has to say about my lungs. I have a growing feeling I've been kidding myself that an infection or inflammation or even TB are as likely as cancer.

I have decided to face the news alone. Pippa offered to come with me and I feel a little guilty that I asked her not to. I said I wanted to be able to focus on the detail of what I was being told but the truth is I am trying to shield myself from emotion and approach this as just another briefing to be listened to, noted down and subbed for passing on to others. That way, perhaps it won't really seem to be about me, my life. My possible early death.

'I've got as long as you need,' says Mike. So much for this being good news. It is, of course, cancer. Cancer in the lungs but not, he insists, your everyday killer. Not, then, the disease that claimed the life of my father, a smoker, and my father-in-law, a doctor who never touched fags.

It is, apparently, a slower-growing, nicer sort of tumour which very few people get: a bronchial carcinoid tumour. And it is 'fixable'. Mike is, by lucky chance, a bit of a specialist in these little blighters and says he recommends a 'radical approach', swift surgery to cut out the tumour along with all my lung lymph glands. He says it'll be possible to get me back to work within three weeks – in other words, in time for the election campaign. I sense that he has set himself this goal as a personal challenge. It is now mine, too.

In the taxi home, I phone Pippa, who is with her brother, Hugh, a doctor, and cling to the facts like a drowning man grasping for a piece of driftwood. Then I call my big sister, Debbie, another doctor. She's not only my emotional prop; she's also my unofficial medical adviser.

Home

Pippa and I hug but make an unspoken pact to hide from what we don't want to confront by sticking to the facts we have, the arrangements we must make and thinking about how to tell the family what they need to know.

Thursday 26 February

Home

This will be a day for breaking the news. Last night Pippa and I agreed a plan. There is much comfort in drawing up plans. We'll tell the boys over dinner tonight, go and see Alice at Oxford tomorrow and visit my mum the next day.

I have already texted the team at work. The response from my producer, Chris, brings the first smile to my face. 'I know you like *Borgen,*' he writes. 'Remember the statsminister had her own health scare during the election campaign . . . she went on to win the balance of power. Not a bad precedent.'

His next text prompts a much-needed guffaw. The other comparison that sprang to mind, he tells me, was with Madonna (who took a tumble off the stage at the Brit awards last night) as she's 'a decorated but ageing superstar who embarrassingly falls on her arse but gets back up and keeps singing'. Apparently, it was the image of me in fishnets that made Chris plump for the *Borgen* metaphor.

A room near Broadcasting House

One of my former producers used to say that I was only happy when I knew that someone was 'flying the plane'; that somebody was in control and that there was a plan.

I've asked Sue and Katy, my BBC bosses at Westminster, to meet me to discuss my flightplan now I've discovered, on the eve of a general election, that I have a cancerous tumour.

I explain to them that my timing's lousy but the prognosis is fine. I spell out my ludicrously simple agenda: I will have the tumour and any other nasties cut out and get back to work three weeks later. This can all be fixed, I tell them, quoting my consultant.

Then I pause and think and cry, hot, shoulder-shaking tears. If I don't believe what I'm saying, what on earth can they be thinking?

No one else must know yet, I insist. I have not told the kids or my mother. I want them to hear it face to face from me when they have the time and space to digest what I'm telling them.

Home, the kitchen

Over dinner with the boys Pippa and I work hard to make normal conversation; to laugh before we break the serious news. Will and Harry listen and seem to take it all in. They don't say a lot – they are teenage boys, after all. Kids take their lead from their parents, I think. If we deal with it calmly and rationally then, I hope, they'll deal with it calmly and rationally, too. There'll be no avoiding the 'C' word, no silly euphemisms, no secrets but equally no panic, no self-pity, no funereal tones. I have an illness. My doctors say it can be cured. I need an operation. It's a bore and a challenge but many people have been through far, far worse.

Friday 27 February

By the river, Oxford

Last night went well, so why am I this bloody terrified about today? We're in Oxford, about to buy lunch for Alice and tell her my news. But first Pippa is having coffee with an old schoolfriend. I lie down on a bench by the river and stare into the sky. What will I do if Alice cries? What will I do if she asks questions I can't or don't want to answer? 'So, Dad, you might be cured, but what if you're not?' Am I kidding everyone else that I'm going to be fine because I'm kidding myself?

St Peter's college

I text Pippa: 'Black Dog has come.' She arrives to hold my hand and cheer me up before we meet Alice. And guess what? It goes just as well as last night. No tears. No unanswerable questions. Concern, sympathy, smiles and then the gossip about college life. Just what the doctor ordered.

Encouraged, I call my big brother Mark, who also says all the right things.

The real world

Meanwhile Ed Miliband has finally done it. He's made the promise which, for so long, he's been under such pressure from his own shadow Cabinet to abandon – the promise to cut tuition fees from £9,000 a year to £6,000. Having covered every twist and turn of the build-up to this moment, I have missed it.

I haven't had the chance to ask the question I've always wanted to ask: why is a man who has repeatedly made it clear that he will have to cut spending if he becomes prime minister, who has talked of the overwhelming priority to fight inequality, who has struggled to find the money needed to invest in the NHS, decided to spend 3 billion quid a year, a huge sum of money, subsidizing wealthy kids, including my own, to go to university? It's not the low-paid who will benefit. Even now they don't have to pay back their fees.

Ed has his answers, of course. Higher fees have been, he says, a 'betrayal of an entire generation'. What's more, since many loans will never be repaid, this will add to the nation's debts. And he'll increase the cost of the loans to higher-paid graduates.

And yet that wasn't enough to convince his own shadow ministers in private. Not enough to persuade former Labour university ministers. Not enough to win the backing of those who run universities.

I have a hunch as to the real reason. Miliband doesn't want to be accused of 'doing a Clegg'. He first talked of cutting fees way back in 2011 – before, incidentally, he had any idea that the deficit would remain as big as it is now. The giveaway is what he has said about Clegg's U-turn, which left 'a whole generation doubting politics; doubting anyone can be believed or trusted'. He went on: 'I made you a promise on tuition fees. I will keep my promise.'

It's the same reason Cameron refused to cut or tax or means-test benefits to wealthy pensioners, giving my mum not just a free bus pass but a free TV licence and an annual contribution towards her heating bill she simply doesn't need. He is desperate to avoid one of those split-screen moments.

This is how we end up with politicians giving large amounts of cash to people who don't need it as well as to those who do. It's not fear of the pain they'll inflict on those they'll disappoint but fear of the damage they'll do to their own reputations if they back down.

Saturday 28 February

Train to Macclesfield

I'm on my way home to tell my mum I've got cancer. Thank God she hasn't heard it first from somewhere else. My great worry has been that the news would leak out. Already the questions are mounting in the Westminster bubble. 'Why did Nick suddenly pull out of covering the tuition fees story?' 'Why isn't he doing that filming next week after we spent weeks setting it up?' 'When will he back?'

Today is going to be a very curious day. First comes family: coffee with Mark and his wife, Andrea, then home to my mum's. Debbie and her husband Wayne, also a doctor, will be there for support. Finally, a press release. My agent and adviser and friend Mary will issue a statement to explain why I'm suddenly disappearing from the airwaves in the run-up to the most unpredictable and exciting election in a generation. I've spent days agonizing about what we should say. The minimum – I'm unwell or dealing with a family issue – will merely provoke speculation. The partial – I have cancer – will raise unnecessary alarm. So we've decided to go for the full monty and spell it out.

I feel that dread again. How will my mum react?

Mum's house

Today is my late dad's birthday. Mum is sitting in the chair he always sat in when I break the news. She says almost nothing. It's not lack of care or concern, let alone love. It's shock. Not for the first time she's having to face the possibility that I might die before she does.

The village pub

As Pippa and Debbie try to cheer Mum up over lunch my brother-in-law Wayne is having a quiet word. Wearing his medical hat, he's concerned that I might really believe what I'm saying about being back at work, doing fifteen- and sixteen-hour days covering an election, within three weeks. He urges me to put my health before my job, to appreciate the value of rest, to be realistic. This op on your lung is a biggie, he tells me, with a reassuring smile, over a pint. Even if it's as successful as your doctors hope, you'll have to recover from the equivalent of being repeatedly stabbed in the back. Can't wait.

The train home

Relief. Huge relief. Everyone knows who needs to know. What's more, it was lovely to see my family before going under the surgeon's knife. Now for everybody else.

We're barely on the train before a text arrives from *The Sunday Times*. The press release has not yet been issued and already they know every detail. So, my worry about word leaking out was not paranoia. It's a quiet news day, apparently, and this story is going to lead page 3. Bloody hell.

Another text instructs me to turn on my iPad and watch the news channel. I should be breaking the news. Instead I *am* breaking news. My God, this is surreal.

The boys start to follow it all from home. Harry texts to tell me to check Twitter. I can't bring myself to do it. I am afraid it will be filled with the normal bile – 'Good for the tumour', 'Won't be missed', 'Now at least we'll get some straight reporting', and so on. There is a bit of that after the prime minister tweets his good wishes but then Ed Miliband follows suit and so does Nicola Sturgeon. Now that is a nice surprise. If you work for the BBC you get impartial sympathy.

A friend texts to commiserate over the breach of my privacy. I explain that we have chosen to do things this way and I've no regrets. The response is both overwhelming and a real source of comfort. And it is a weight off my mind to be able to avoid the debilitating chore of having to have the same conversation about my illness again and again. The news has done it for me.

Home, the sofa

Texts continue to pour in. The messages I've had from Robert Peston, whose beloved wife Siân died of lung cancer, have been among the nicest and the most supportive. Few people call. One who does is Ed Miliband. He is kind, generous and thoughtful and sounds genuinely shocked.

— MARCH —

Sunday 1 March

Home, the kitchen

'Jihadi John', the ISIS executioner with the British accent, has been unmasked. A Russian politician has been shot dead in broad daylight near the Kremlin. Sophie Raworth is reading out the newspaper headlines from the Marr sofa. She turns to *The Sunday Times*. 'And in other news . . . Nick Robinson says he's having "a quick cancer op and will be back to cover the election".' *The Sunday Times* have done me proud. A lovely piece and a flattering picture from their archives.

Messages from Pesto and the prime minister are no match for a text that leaves the boys almost speechless. 'It's from Fergie!' they gasp. Perhaps Sir Alex remembers that I described him as 'the greatest living Briton' when he retired from Old Trafford. I pretend to be cool about it but I'm not. Given that we barely know each other, I am hugely touched that he made the effort.

Will and Harry agree that only a message from the Queen could top this.

Monday 2 March

The Crown and Sceptre, near Broadcasting House

It's the eve of my big day and I'm having a kind of pre-operation stag night. Friends from the BBC, plus four pints of Doom Bar, a few bags of crisps and a bowlful of pistachios. What more could a man facing major surgery want? It might feel like a stag night but it's a curious metaphor, really, considering I'm planning to divorce my tumour rather than to live with it for ever in sickness and in health.

I'm overwhelmed by the good wishes I've had. The support I am enjoying as a result of being in the public eye brings it home to me how very, very lonely so many people must feel as they face the horrors of illness on their own.

Everyone keeps telling me how well I look. Note to self: when this is all over I must find a way to keep my weight down without relying on rapidly multiplying, potentially fatal cells to do it.

Tuesday 3 March

Royal Brompton hospital

I am waiting to be called down to the operating theatre. I feel as if I am standing at the top of a black run at a ski resort. The sky is blue, the sun is shining, the steep slope stretches out below me. I'm scared, aware that I may fall and hurt myself badly, but overriding that is a sense of anticipation. I'm looking forward to the feeling of exhilaration I will get if I make it down the run in one piece.

Or almost in one piece. Today, as well as saying goodbye to my tumour, which I first met only six days ago, and the cancerous bits of my lymph glands, I will be parting with a third of my right lung. Apparently, I don't need it.

See you at the bottom.

High dependency unit

So far this has proved easier than I feared.

I'd expected to come to in a morphine-filled, pain-obsessed trance. Instead I am sitting up in bed, smiling, chatting and texting. I'm even well enough to have my photo taken to be posted on Facebook, to reassure friends who may fear I'm doomed. These surgeons are miracle-workers. Perhaps they weren't having me on when they said I could be back at work in three weeks' time.

Wednesday 4 March

High dependency unit

Or then again, maybe they were.

The operation was, I'm told, a great success in removing the cancer from both my right lung and my lymph glands. But, but, but . . . it also seems to have stopped my vocal cords working. I can barely speak above a whisper.

My surgeon, Eric Lim, warned me that he might not be able to get rid of every last bit of nasty cancerous stuff from the inaccessible bits of lung near my main airway and a critical artery. He was delighted to find that he could. It was, I gather, the surgical equivalent of removing a shelled, soft-boiled egg from an eggcup into which it has been glued – without touching the inside of the eggcup. Some feat. Unfortunately, the nerve to a vocal cord took a bit of a battering in the process.

I am assured – and a quick search of the internet confirms – that this sort of complication is far from unheard of with this sort of surgery. It is, though, for me, a disaster for which I am totally unprepared.

Everything else I had thought through. The possibility that the cancer might have spread, or that the tumour would turn out to be bigger and meaner than hoped, or of a complication during the operation (that 1 per cent risk of mortality which had stared at me from the information sheet).

But not this.

Mr Lim brings with him an ear, nose and throat man – the guy rock stars and opera singers call for when they get a pre-performance sore throat – who says that, given enough time, the body may recover on its own. But time is something I haven't bloody well got or, at least, I don't have right now. He adds that he can try to fix the problem with an injection or another small op. It will certainly give me a voice back, though it may not be the one I used to have or one I want. My new voice could be hoarse and raspy and it might tire easily, but it will be a voice.

It's funny how you can take for granted something as fundamental as your ability to make yourself heard, thanks to what are, it seems, just a couple of vibrating folds of mucous membrane stretched across your larynx and the nerves that send them electrical signals. One of my folds ain't twanging any more, which means that while I might well be able to get myself fit enough to go back to work in time for the election, no one will be able to hear a word I say. Just an awful lot of airy breath.

Everyone keeps telling me that my health is more important than the election, than any story. Of course it is. But it was the prospect of fighting my way back for this election that was keeping me going. Now I am confronting the possibility not just of missing it, but of never broadcasting again.

My pathetic, thin reed of a voice and the further unwelcome news that my slowest-growing, nicest form of cancer may be a little less slow-growing and less nice than I'd hoped leaves me feeling low. Very, very low.

Thursday 5 March

Royal Brompton hospital

In the middle of the night, unable to sleep and with my morale at rock-bottom, I find a new source of strength. The calculated cynicism, machiavellian scheming and southern drawl raise the spirits. I speak, of course, of Francis Underwood, the star of the TV drama *House of Cards* which, until now, I have not had a chance to watch.

Underwood is a great distraction from the emptiness of long nights where all you have for company are your symptoms and your fear. The aphorisms he utters in his trademark asides to the viewer delight me. 'There are two kinds of pain. The sort of pain that makes you strong, or useless pain. The sort of pain that's only suffering. I have no patience for useless things.' Me neither, Frank. Me neither.

Chelsea embankment

I've escaped. Boy, it feels good.

I'm looking out over the river Thames. Pippa was encouraged to get me walking and we made it all the way here. It took just fifteen minutes but a few hours ago I wouldn't have believed it was possible.

Hospital shrinks your world alarmingly. Its micro-population of nurses, doctors, physios and support staff; its daily routine, which reduces your life to a never-ending cycle of being measured – temperature, blood pressure, oxygen levels – and filled with drugs, to lessen the pain and to counteract the side-effects of the drugs to kill the pain, and asked constant questions. Does it hurt? How much on a scale of one to ten? Can you cough? And apparently the most crucial one of all: have you moved your bowels?

After that a stroll down the King's Road feels like taking a first step on the moon.

Watching the news in my hospital bed

News from the real world has done surprisingly little to offer a distraction. Until now. David Cameron has finally done what I long ago predicted he would. He (or rather his spin doctor, Craig Oliver) has thrown his hands in the air and, more in sorrow than in anger, you understand, declared that the debate about TV debates has gone on for so long and is still so inconclusive that somebody – and, shucks, it might as well be him – has to 'break the logjam'.

So, in a gesture of generosity and goodwill to all, he's prepared to take part in any debate you care to mention – except that it has to be on a date of his choosing and not during the election itself, and it must involve at least six other party leaders.

Few politicians can be quite as spectacularly disingenuous as David Cameron when he wants to be. His real position, simply stated, is: I think debates are good for democracy. I promised I would take part in them. I even said I thought a head-to-head with Ed Miliband was a good idea, but my advisers have pointed out that I have nothing to gain and everything to lose by taking part, and that calling me chicken may excite the media but it will convince few if any voters to actually change their minds. So I've decided to take some pain now for the undoubted gain of enabling the Tory campaign machine and the Tory press to dictate the agenda, and not the bloody broadcasters.

Rather unhelpfully, I text Sue, my boss, who is in charge of negotiating the debates for the BBC to say, 'Told you so.' The question now, I add, is whether one of the broadcasters will cave in and offer Cameron the debate on the terms he wants.

Friday 6 March

The real world

Well, they're not caving in. Publicly, at least. The broadcasters – Sky, ITV and Channel 4, as well as the Beeb – are officially rejecting Cameron's 'final offer' and simply repeating their invitation to the three debates they've already dreamed up. From all I hear, the guys in the news divisions are holding firm. I wonder whether their bosses, who will not relish the prospect of a stand-up row with the prime minister, will do likewise.

There are many strengths in the British system of broadcasting. One of its weaknesses, though, is that, for all the theory about politicians being kept at arm's length from decisions about what appears on our screens (unlike in many other countries, where the government directly appoints television executives), broadcasting companies always need regulatory favours from politicians. Think of the battles over the take-overs of ITV and Sky, and the future of the BBC licence fee. So no senior executive of a big media company has much of an appetite for falling out with someone who could directly affect its business.

If you were running Sky, who, as things stand, face having to air a head-to-head debate with only the one head, you might be tempted to make Number 10 a different offer. If you were Archie Norman, former Tory MP and now ITV chairman, holding out for a ratings-killer of a debate with six leaders and no PM might not look so attractive.

Revealingly, a new poll shows that just 4 per cent of people listed this row – which has led TV bulletins and newspaper front pages – as among the ten most-noticed news stories of the past week.

Royal Brompton hospital

A bottle of wine, a tube of Pringles and a movie. Bliss. It's one of those rare Friday nights in. In hospital, that is, but Pippa and I try to pretend for just a moment that life is normal. And in fact it feels so normal that I duly fall asleep during the film and get laughed at by the kids who, when we Skype them at home, take one look at my bloated neck and face – a by-product of lung surgery – and declare that I look as if I am using the FatBooth app, which digitally converts a picture of a regular face into an obese one. Ridicule is the perfect cure for self-pity.

Saturday 7 March

Royal Brompton hospital

Eee. Ooo. Rrr. I'm damn well trying but nothing more than a faint, husky whisper emerges from my flaccid vocal cords.

The idea of these exercises is to rouse them from their post-operative slumber. The vocal gymnastics have been set for me by Julia Selby, my speech therapist. The moment I met Julia I sensed she got it. She understood the enormity of what's at stake for me: not just the chance to cover one election but an entire career as a broadcaster. We'd been acquainted for only a few minutes before Pippa confided something she knew I hadn't dared reveal to anyone else: I was more scared to be told I'd lost my voice than that I had cancer. My voice is no mere tool. It is who I am. Without words, spoken words, I am nothing.

This morning, though, I am feeling positive. Julia and Guri Sandhu, the ENT surgeon, have convinced me that I will get my voice back. Rest plus these exercises might do the trick. If they don't, the little op he suggested will help. It involves cutting a slot in my neck and inserting a small prop to shift my vocal cords closer together and reduce the size of the hole through which all that breath is passing. It's all done under local anaesthetic so that they can 'tune' the sound by getting me to talk as they adjust the size and position of the prop. Isn't medicine marvellous? I hope.

Confirmation that today is going to be a good day comes when I play Scrabble with Pippa and use all my letters in one go to make the word 'idolatry'. A fifty-point bonus. Who needs a bloody voice?

Sunday 8 March

Royal Brompton hospital

This will be my last night in hospital. I will be allowed home tomorrow. That's the cheering news brought to me by Mr Lim.

Before I first met him I feared he would fit the mould of the stereo-typical surgeon: long on self-belief, short on empathy. It's a combination that is probably necessary to instil the confidence required to slice away at someone else's innards in a way that could very easily leave them worse off than they were before, if not dead.

My fears were groundless. It's not just that I've seen Mr Lim's vulnerability – how his delight at successfully excising every last visible cancerous cell from my body was tempered by his obvious frustration at the collateral damage to my vocal cords – or that he has taken the time to patiently talk me through what doctors can and cannot tell me about what's happening in my body. It is also that I have got to know what makes him tick.

Today he has brought in a chart showing the number of his patients with lung cancer who are non-smokers. It has doubled in seven years. He is working on a blood test designed to increase the chances of detecting the disease early enough to do something about it. He wants my help to get this some attention. It's the least I can do.

The real world

Yesterday Ken Baker was on the radio musing about a grand coalition after the next election bringing together Labour and the Tories. After all, they've got something similar in Germany. His point is that although this might sound madly implausible, it may be the only way to save the UK from being broken up by the SNP.

The Tories have produced the first memorable poster of this long, long election campaign. A tiny Ed Miliband is shown sitting in the breast pocket of a giant Alex Salmond. It is cleverly designed to fuel the twin fears of those who believe that the Scottish Nationalists could dictate policy to England after a close election and sense that Miliband is too weak a leader to do very much about it.

Will it convert many people? It doesn't need to. If it motivates Tories to get out and vote and not to defect to UKIP, it will have done its job.

Monday 9 March

Home

It's been less than a week since I was at home but it feels like a lifetime. I have returned, as planned, without my tumour and a third of my right lung, but also, as not planned, without my voice. If I can just get that back again I might one day be able to dismiss the last extraordinary fortnight as 'a little local difficulty', the phrase used by Harold Macmillan when shrugging off the resignation of his entire ministerial Treasury team.

What is needed now, I've been told, is rest. Lots of it.

The real world

The year began with Tory ministers lining up to tell us that Labour's sums didn't add up. Now Ed Balls has unveiled his shock analysis that it is the Tories' sums that are dodgy. I have much the same reaction today as I did then. Yes, but . . .

Ed's claim today is that the Conservatives' commitment to cutting £70 billion over the next five years is unachievable without plans to reduce spending or raise taxes, which they won't admit to. This whole 'costing' exercise is nothing more than an elaborate justification for a crude propaganda campaign asserting, no doubt, that the Tories will cut the NHS and hike VAT. Just as the Tories will assert that Labour will put up taxes and bankrupt the country.

I'm tempted to pay for some election posters of my own. These would point out that whoever you vote for will have to cut spending and raise taxes in ways they've not yet told you; that they will struggle to find the money the NHS needs and will face a huge budget deficit and debt, which is still rising. The bottom line would read: 'Labour will spend more, the Tories less. Exactly how much will depend on the circumstances. So vote for whichever seems fairest and most sensible.'

I'm not sure the BBC would approve.

Tuesday 10 March

Clissold Park, north London

Beautiful. Wife, dog, ducks on the pond, deer in their enclosure, a steaming cup of fresh coffee in the sunshine. It may be just a small, urban park. You might be able to see the cars, hear the traffic; you might never quite forget that you are in one of the least green areas in London. But today it's bloody beautiful.

The real world

If I wasn't in my parallel universe I would have been in an edit suite looking at last night's filming *chez* Miliband. After weeks and weeks of negotiations, the boss (Katy) and I persuaded Team Miliband that they should give us a glimpse through the keyhole. They agreed to let us film at home with Ed and Justine and the kids. My deputy, James Landale, has filled in for me – as he may be doing for some time to come.

Predictably, Justine is the star of the show. She tells James: 'I think over the next couple of months it's going to get really vicious, really personal, but I'm totally up for this fight.' She comes over as the Justine I've got to know: clever, passionate, likeable.

Equally predictably, and frustratingly, Ed fails to seize the opportunity. I'm told that his interview lasted a staggering twenty-eight minutes – and still, it seems, lacked a single clear, compelling message.

What I didn't foresee was how interesting it would be to eye up the Miliband home. Hmm. Not sure I like that brown sofa, and the kitchen where the two of them are self-consciously sipping mugs of tea looks a bit spartan.

Superficial, I know, but . . .

Wednesday 11 March

The real world

'Speaking as a friend of the BBC, can I say . . .' This is how it always starts. Politicians know that Auntie is simply too popular, and they are too mistrusted, to justify the risk of opening up with both barrels. So instead they seek to persuade those who are seen as cheerleaders for the Beeb, but who are also sympathetic to them, to do their fighting for them.

This morning Michael Grade, former BBC executive and chairman and now a Tory peer, has written in *The Times* and taken to the airwaves warning that there is 'no divine right' to election debates. Democracy, he says, resides with Parliament, not with broadcasters, and threatening to empty-chair a political leader would be 'completely unacceptable' and 'risk breaching their duty of impartiality'.

I have no idea if Lord Grade, who has earned the right to be listened to, has been lobbied by Team Cameron. I do note, however, that a common theme is emerging in recent commentary in the Tory press. A few days ago, in an op-ed in the *Mail*, Dominic Lawson, 'speaking as a friend of the BBC – and one who treasures much of its political output', begged the corporation 'not to endanger its own future, and for such a petulant gesture'.

The message from Team Cameron couldn't be clearer. Empty-chair our guy and he might just be tempted to empty your coffers.

Royal Brompton hospital

Back to Chelsea for some speech therapy. Julia tries to show me how to differentiate between my noisy, airy whispering and the purer, quieter sound of my real voice. She has me manhandling my voice box, filling my cheeks with air and clenching my body as if fighting constipation. The spectacle would be hilarious if it wasn't so pathetic.

On the way in to see her I catch sight of PMQs on the TV in the waiting room. So self-absorbed have I become so quickly that I hadn't even registered today was Wednesday, let alone that I was therefore missing my weekly ritual. And ritual it has become. Ed taunts David for changing his mind on debates. David taunts Ed for being in Alex Salmond's pocket. Backbenchers jeer and cheer.

The sound is down but there are onscreen subtitles. One has John Bercow being addressed as 'Mr Squeaker'.

Thursday 12 March

A room above King's Cross station

My speech therapist and I eee and ooo and rrr together in a room hired for the purpose. She makes beautiful sounds. I gurgle unattractively until, quite suddenly, there it is! The faintest echo of the voice I once had. Not loud, not pure, not clear, but a little hint that, buried away somewhere in my throat, is the means to make the sounds I used to make. We call Pippa to see if she notices the difference. She does – instantly. I phone Katy at work, and she can hear it too.

And then, just as quickly, it's gone. I don't know where, or why, or how, and I have no idea what I did to summon it up in the first place. But boy, am I going to keep on trying.

Friday 13 March

The real world

Hold the front page! Ed Miliband has two kitchens! That's right, two! And he chose to be filmed in the one that looks a bit grotty!

This is what passes for news just a few weeks before the country decides whether to make Ed their leader for the next five years. Many people now know more about his tea-making facilities than about what he might actually do in office, and all because of that 'at home' feature James Landale did on the news the other night.

It is a story of our times, one that should be used as an example in future media studies classes. James never mentioned the kitchen. It featured in his piece for just a few seconds and took not much longer than that to film. The shot – of Ed and Justine standing drinking tea together – was arranged at the last minute, I hear, to link one sequence recorded in the house to another. It was given almost no thought by the TV crew or Ed's spin doctors.

It did, however, catch the eye and earn the contempt of Sarah Vine, the *Daily Mail* columnist who happens to be Mrs Michael Gove. Sarah managed to write an entire page about a room 'devoid of colour or character' except for the 'hideous lime green laundry basket', comparing the 'mirthless Milibands', to 'aliens' with a vision for a Britain 'about as much fun to live in as a communist housing block in Minsk'.

This provoked another columnist, who happens to be a friend of Ed Miliband's, to rush on to Twitter to defend him. Jenni Russell of *The Times* writes that 'Ed Miliband's kitchen is lovely. Daily Mail pix: the functional kitchenette by sitting room for tea and quick snacks.'

So he has two kitchens!

On the basis of a single fact and a single image, thousands and thousands of words have been written about the meaning of all this. It has almost none. But it does show why the Tories' spin doctors obsess about every detail in every shot in every piece they do.

Under the scanner again

I'm lying on another cold, hard slab wearing nothing more than one of those paper dressing gowns. I am rolled slowly into another vast white tube and every minute or so I'm told to stop breathing. If I move the scanner won't be able to focus on any rogue cancerous cells in my liver. I struggle to make myself heard above the banging and whirring sound. With my glasses off I can't see much further than the end of my nose. I have that feeling again. Pure dread.

At this point a cheery radiologist says, 'Funny thing is, you remind me of someone on the news.' I smile, and only just stop myself replying, 'Yes, it is a funny thing. That someone on the news used to be me.'

Oncologist's consulting room

The oncologist beams. Your scan, he says, is completely normal. The cancer has not spread. What's more, all that can be seen even under a microscope has been removed from your lung. It's possible, he continues, that you have been cured and that you will never have cancer again. We'll have to keep checking you for the next couple of years, but I'm not inclined to give you any further treatment.

No chemo, then. No debilitating sickness, no loss of the little hair I have left.

Pippa and I look at each other, waiting for the 'but'. We test his reassurances.

There can be no certainties, no guarantees, no way of knowing for sure whether cancer may return, in the lung or elsewhere, but this is the best possible outcome. Our joy is unalloyed and overwhelming.

Home

When this is all a distant memory one thing above all others will stay in the mind: the relief on the faces of the children when we tell them the good news.

Sunday 15 March

Home, sitting in bed

We journalists like nothing more than seeing politicians wriggle on being repeatedly asked a question they have decided not to answer but which those viewing think they should address. This morning sees both Ed Balls and George Osborne squirming on Andrew Marr's sofa.

There is a row going on in Labour about what they should and shouldn't say about the SNP – categorically excluding a deal would be popular in England but very unpopular in Scotland – whereas no senior Tory anywhere thinks it makes sense to flirt with UKIP.

Again and again Andy invites Ed to rule out forming a post-election pact with the SNP. Again and again he refuses, sticking to his leader's formula that there's no intention, no plan, no need for any such deal while echoing Miliband's evasive refusal to rule one out. George Osborne does the same when it comes to a Tory deal with UKIP, although he looks a lot less uncomfortable.

Both sides fear the same thing, though. Once you answer one 'what if' question you will end up facing a deluge of them. So, Ed, you rule out a coalition with the SNP, but what about a deal on different lines with the Lib Dems/ Democratic Unionists/whoever?

It is a sign of the times that, at the start of budget week, what sticks in the mind from the big, scene-setting interviews with the chancellor and shadow chancellor is their synchronized wriggling over deals they might do after an inconclusive election.

None of this, though, seems to matter very much to a media obsessing about the future of Jeremy Clarkson. The star of *Top Gear* has been suspended after a 'fracas' in which he allegedly punched a producer who had failed to provide a hot meal after a long day's filming.

A BBC executive has made the huge error of telling a reporter what he was really thinking, giving the *Mail on Sunday* the headline, 'ASTONISHING REMARKS ON TOP GEAR AFFAIR AS SENIOR BBC BOSS CLAIMS "CLARKSON IS LIKE SAVILE".' It should be clear to anyone paying close attention what the unnamed exec meant. Savile became too big a star to handle. He gained the backing of the establishment and people were frightened to confront him. But uttering the name of a disgusting serial child-abuser in the same sentence as that of one of your biggest, best-loved household names is not just offensive. It's madness.

I text one of those involved to warn that we are in danger of falling into a trap being set for us by the press. They are looking for the chance to present this as a culture war between the liberal, metropolitan, politically correct BBC luvvies and an un-PC, tells-it-like-it-is man of the people.

I don't add, though perhaps I should have, that we should learn a lesson from David Cameron, who stopped dismissing UKIP as a bunch of 'fruitcakes, loonies and racists' once he realized that such contempt for the views of a sizeable chunk of the electorate was doing a lot more damage to him than it was to Nigel Farage.

Of course, if Clarkson did attack a member of his team he'll rightly be disciplined. Still, I know how demanding I am when I'm on the road. My producer Jess provides regular supplies of hot drinks, snacks and, above all, packets of Percy Pigs. Maybe she is afraid that if she doesn't I might do a Clarkson.

Monday 16 March

Thirteen. Unlucky for some. The number of times Ed Balls refused yesterday to rule out a deal with the SNP has been counted up and it was evidently far too many, because the other Ed has now announced that, after all, there will be no SNP ministers in any government he leads.

This is jolly interesting but completely beside the point. There was never, ever the slightest prospect of a formal coalition between Labour and the Scottish Nationalists. What could be in prospect is the need for a governing arrangement, some kind of deal to secure SNP votes and allow Labour to stay in power.

The declaration is, though, the clearest possible indication that the ad showing Ed Miliband in Alex's pocket has been working for the Tories. It is also an illustration of the difference between being leader and being the poor sod who has his interview about the economy ruined by being forced to repeat thirteen times an utterly unsustainable line.

A room above King's Cross

Eee. Ooo. Uh-oh. What on earth does the guy in the hired room next door think of the sounds I am making? Or, rather, struggling to make.

Julia and I practise the exercises meant to stimulate some noise, any bloody noise at all, from my vocal cords. Last week when we met here, there seemed to be some hope. There was something there. Now there's nothing.

So it's down to my surgeon to see what he can do. The op he has proposed may need to be followed by days of total silence then weeks of slowly, carefully, cautiously coaxing my cords to produce a voice I can rely on. I know I'm being ungrateful. I know I'm being self-pitying. I know it is pathetic, but I feel bloody miserable.

Tuesday 17 March

Home, bed

I always feel more positive after a good night's sleep. This psychological rollercoaster is much harder to deal with than any pain or discomfort. And it's even worse, I fear, for friends and family.

My spirits are raised every morning by the lovely cards, letters and messages I receive. It is heartening to be reminded that for every Twitter troll there are dozens of nice, decent people who emerge from their silence only when something really bad happens.

Today's post includes a very kind note from Gordon Brown – as unexpected as it is appreciated. I know only too well that during his time as prime minister my reporting often made him feel pretty sick. It is one of the biggest regrets of my career that my relationship with him broke down. Not, it must be said, that I was the only one, as a read of any of Alistair Darling's or Peter Mandelson's memoirs makes very clear.

Front door

Alice is home from university. Hooray! She always cheers me up.

Royal Free hospital

Medicine is a team game these days. I am having my first meeting with the guy who's taking over as team captain, an expert in my type of rare tumour. I would have met Professor Martyn Caplin sooner but he was off last week presenting his research at the annual European Neuroendocrine Tumor Society conference. He takes time, a lot of time – much of his evening, in fact – to explain his thinking.

He's a tad more downbeat than I'd hoped. My tumour, he tells me, is at the more aggressive end of the least aggressive kind you can get. Although all the cancer that can be seen even under the micro-scope, let alone with the naked eye, has been removed, it still could come back. I could do nothing but, to try to reduce the chance of a recurrence, he recommends, just as a belt-and-braces option, a course of the dreaded chemotherapy. Is deliberately poisoning my body a price worth paying? I ask myself. The answer is instant. Yes. The crushing disappointment is just as immediate.

Car home

I turn on the radio. The news is full of budget speculation. How odd. Normally I would be desperately trying to find a leak or get a steer or make a clever guess about what's in that red box. I would be pumping with adrenaline if I succeeded. Yet tonight I see no reason why it can't wait until tomorrow. Is this how other people feel about the news?

Wednesday 18 March

Home, the sofa

And there it is. The red box is being held up for the cameras outside the door of Number 11 as George Osborne follows a tradition so old that most people, including me, have never asked why chancellors do it. My friend Danny Finkelstein informs me that it's because a Victorian predecessor forgot his speech one year and the next wanted to prove he hadn't made the same mistake.

For the past fifteen years or so I have sat in a studio giving instant analysis of the budget. Now I am just sitting and watching and twitching. Pesto and Huw Edwards send me cheering messages saying they're missing me.

Just because I'm not there, it doesn't mean my brain isn't still filling with the same 'Aha, so that's what he's done'-type thoughts. I simply can't resist sending them to the boss. Katy gets a stream of e-mails detailing what I would have said if I weren't 'resting'. Sad, I know.

I tell her that Osborne is trying to correct the huge mistake he made in his autumn statement, in which his promise of more austerity to come conjured up images of soup kitchens and rickets and gloom for years to come. In other words, this is meant to be the Norman Smith memorial budget.

Osborne boasts of choosing to spend the 'windfall' from lower than expected borrowing responsibly. Don't try this at home – 'Darling, we have a windfall! Our overdraft is only £94,000 and not £100,000, as we thought a few weeks ago.' (Multiply that by a million and you get the nation's overdraft.) The chancellor uses this cash to curb the cuts he set out only a few months ago in a speech sprinkled with upbeat rhetoric about Britain being 'the comeback country . . . walking tall again' and 'the sun starting to shine'.

He reveals an official measure that 'proves' living standards are now higher than at the last election (many other stats tell a very different story, of course); insists that spending is down to the level it was under Gordon Brown in 2000 (ditto); declares that debt will now fall as a share of GDP before the election, which means he won't have broken his promise at the last election; reduces his planned budget surplus, so that Ed Balls can no longer claim the Tories are committed to cutting £70 billion more than Labour; spends £600 million of the money Labour planned to raid from pensions on cutting tuition fees and nicks their policy of giving councils more of the cash they raise from business rates.

He takes a penny off a pint, freezes petrol duty and cuts income tax for 27 million people and tax on savings for 17 million. It's a confident performance, free of the anxious, dry-throated spluttering of previous budgets.

Ed Miliband is equally confident and just as slick, though. He condemns a budget people won't believe from a government that is 'not on your side'. If the budget had contained anything that wrong-footed him, you'd see notes being hurriedly passed to him, hear it in his voice and smell his fear. There is no sign of any of that. Nothing announced today will stop him running a campaign that claims the Tories have presided over a decline in living standards; that they will, indeed, take us back to the 1930s, and that they have secret plans to slash the NHS and/or to put up VAT again.

Just as nothing will stop the Tories boasting that no one should risk handing the keys back to the guys who drove the economy into a ditch and warning that Labour offer a guaranteed double whammy of higher tax and higher interest rates.

The Brownswood pub

On the eve of the op that's meant to get me talking again, I need a dose of normality: a pint or two, a bag of crisps and a bit of banter. Any patient will tell you that sympathy and concern, though very welcome, can become a tad wearying. You also need the relaxing distraction and laughter of good friends, a few beers and having the piss taken out of you.

Thursday 19 March

Home, the kitchen

I cook myself a comforting pre-operation slap-up breakfast. The post-budget front pages will please the Tories much more than the broadcast news. The BBC focuses on arguments about cuts to come whereas many papers pick up the promise of sunshine. Cue more muttering at Tory HQ about BBC bias.

Hospital waiting room

Ping! It's a family WhatsApp message – a photo of an envelope marked 'Special Delivery', 'Private and Confidential' and 'Buckingham Palace'. Open it, I tell the kids, and send me a photo of what's inside. It turns out to be a letter from Prince Charles, whom I met once and only briefly, but he told me then that he was a regular viewer of *BBC News at 10*. It is warm, generous and personal. I can hear his voice in the words and yes, see the black, spidery writing. It is, above all, very kind.

A curious by-product of an illness like this is the chance it gives you to read your own obituaries – but with all the nasty bits left out, since people know you're still around to read them.

Operating theatre

I am to be awake, though sedated, as my ENT surgeon Guri Sandhu cuts a hole in my neck and inserts a prop for my floppy vocal cord. Awake but, sadly, unable to watch Sweeney Todd at work as my eyes have to be protected from the bright lights that illuminate my throat. My speech therapist is there, too, to ask me to say a few eees and ooos so that they can add or take away bits from the prop to fine-tune the sound of my voice.

I have waited excitedly for this, deluding myself that it would be a Eureka moment; that I would be punching the air and celebrating the instant return of my normal, full-strength voice. Instead all I can hear is a gravelly, husky rasping. This is not at all how it was meant to be.

Recovery room

Julia explains that the op went as well as it could have done but, but, but it was not a total success. Despite the surgeon's best efforts, there is still a gap at the back of the vocal cords. Any gap allows air to get through and makes the voice breathy rather than sharp and clear. He has other tools in his surgeon's box. I might, for example, have an injection to plump up the cord that isn't working. Otherwise it's therapy. Lots and lots of it. Julia senses my crushing disappointment and does her best – and her best is as good as it gets – to make me feel positive and to remind me that I promised her I was a stubborn bugger and that we'd crack this together. I wish I could believe her. I really do.

Home, the kitchen

I arrive home, facing three days of enforced silence, feeling morose. I cheer myself up by getting my iPad to convert anything I type into a Stephen Hawking voice. Over dinner with the family I'm reduced to pleading with them to stop me from giggling as it might dislodge my newly installed prop. What got me going was typing 'Ho, ho, ho' so that my iPad Hawking laughs for me, and then getting him to read 'Romeo, Romeo,' followed by a few favourite chants from the terraces at Old Trafford.

Friday 20 March

Home, the kitchen

The morning after the op I am sitting in the kitchen surrounded by a pile of signs made for me by a friend and a small hand bell for summoning assistance. Each sign has a request written on it – 'A cup of tea, please', 'I need a beer', 'Pass the remote control' and even 'I need a cuddle'. I write an additional sign demanding dumb obedience. I can't see that one lasting the morning.

Nigel Farage must wish that his election candidates could be forced to stay silent and issued with signs reading 'I am not permitted to speak if I'm going to make a fool of myself'. UKIP has had to suspend one of its star candidates, Janice Atkinson MEP. The *Sun* has published a secret recording that appears to show her chief of staff asking a restaurant manager for a receipt for much more than the bill she has actually paid. She is heard explaining, 'The idea is we overcharge them [the EU] slightly, because that's the way we repatriate it.' This is no mere chicken-in-a-basket. The receipt handed over and accepted gratefully is for more than three grand.

Saturday 21 March

Home

And lo, it came to pass that he said, 'Let there be a deal,' and it was so.

Cameron has finally got his way. It has just been announced that there will be just one election debate, weeks before polling day, featuring seven political leaders, a number of whom many viewers will not even recognize, let alone have the option to vote for. There will be no head-to-head with Miliband but the Labour leader will have to face a line-up of his enemies – the Greens, UKIP and the

Scottish Nationalists – without the comforting presence of Cameron.

Ed, Nick, Nigel, Nicola and co. all feel that the broadcasters have succumbed to bullying from Number 10. The broadcasters, on the other hand, hail a victory. The principle of leaders' debates at election time has been upheld. Mmm. Just.

I text the Number 10 communications director, Craig Oliver, to suggest that, given his role in screwing the whole thing up, he's owed at least a pay rise if not a peerage.

Next time we need to do a whole lot better than this.

Sunday 22 March

Home, on the sofa

Just when you thought it was safe ... My old friend Alex is frightening the English again in his characteristically low-key, unassuming way.

The man who lost the referendum is relishing the prospect of the SNP gaining dozens of seats at the election and with them the balance of power at Westminster. From the comfort of the Marr sofa he declares, 'If you hold the balance, then you hold the power.'

Though this will not win them bums on the seats of ministerial Rovers, it will, Salmond says, give them leverage over those who do hold office. Whether it's a question of the route of HS2, the recommissioning of Trident or the pace of austerity, ministers in a minority Labour government would be forced to negotiate with the SNP, vote by precarious vote. And Alex knows exactly how this is done. He ran an extraordinarily successful minority Scottish government when he originally became first minister. Not, of course, that Holyrood controls the really big things – peace and war or the major decisions on tax and spending.

The Tories are looking about as pleased with him as he is with himself. They've released a campaign cartoon video showing Miliband dancing a jig as Mr Salmond 'calls the tune'.

The rise of the SNP is a win-win for the Tories. Almost every seat they gain will be one off Labour's total and they scare the living daylights out of precisely the sort of English voter David Cameron needs to woo back. It's a win-win for the SNP, too. Either they will get a minority Labour government they can harry or a Tory one they can angrily reject as an alien impost.

Monday 23 March

Royal Brompton hospital

They'd look pretty good on an episode of *Doctor Who*. Two wobbly, damp hunks of pulsating pink flesh that first open, then shut. I am watching the bits of my insides that are meant to make a noise when I speak. Julia has passed a tiny camera down my nose so we can see what is – and more importantly what is not – happening.

The key to it all is two tiny white strips in that pink mass: my vocal cords. If they close together I will make a proper sound. The good news is that, post-op, they're much nearer one another than they were before. But there is still that little gap at the back that is making my voice so weak and breathy. The question now is whether the exercises I do with Julia – mum, mum, mum and mee, mee, mee have now been added to my repertoire – will be enough to close the cords.

I pop in to see my lung surgeon, Eric Lim. The cancer's completely gone, he tells me, and I'm fit enough to fly, cycle or swim. When he promised me that a few weeks ago I didn't really believe him, and it's great news. But unspoken between us is the knowledge that though I may be able to fly, cycle or swim, I'm not ready to take to the airwaves.

Royal Free hospital

The next stop on my psychological big dipper is an unpalatable conversation about chemo with another oncologist, Professor Tim Meyer. Tim is everything I want in a doctor: clear, direct and a good listener. My personal chemo cocktail – there are, I've learned, dozens of different recipes – is described as 'rather punchy'. In other words, side-effects are pretty much guaranteed. The one I fear the most is not becoming hairless (what do you mean, what hair?), not nausea, but what's known as 'chemo head', a sort of fuzziness that blunts your mental sharpness. I have a horror of appearing on live television and finding I simply can't remember a name or find the word I need.

The real world

One happier side-effect of my illness is that it has given my deputy the space he's been denied for too long. His series of pre-election features should become known as *James's Kitchen Nightmares*. First Ed, now David have come to regret inviting the BBC, now in the shape of my understudy, Mr Landale, to join them 'at home'.

After the 'scandal' of Ed's two kitchens we have the 'shock' of Dave's curious resignation 'announcement'. As James and Dave stood chopping carrots together, chatting amiably about how long the PM wanted to stay in the top job, he took a new, radical and unsettling approach to a journalist's question. He answered it fully and, it would appear, honestly: 'I've said I'll stand for a full second term, but I think after that it will be time for new leadership . . . Terms are like Shredded Wheat – two are wonderful but three might just be too many.'

My phone lights up with myriad versions of the same question: what on earth did he mean by that? Doesn't he realize it will make him look a lame duck and/or trigger a leadership beauty contest and/or make it appear that he's taking an election win for granted?

In vain I try arguing that his answer is not terribly surprising. He could hardly have said he would quit sooner or that he intended, like Mrs T., to go 'on and on and on'. He probably felt he might as well answer the question now as later, since he's bound to be asked it again. Perhaps being at home is softening my brain but I can't see many people down the Dog and Duck saying, 'I can't bloomin' well vote Tory now I know there'll be a Tory leadership contest in 2020.'

But leaders rarely acknowledge their own political mortality except when in a weak position. Cameron might well have wanted to head off a post-election coup by his own backbenchers and any attempt to turn the referendum on the EU into a referendum on his continued leadership. However, musing about your retirement ain't a great way of convincing people of your hunger for the top job.

Tuesday 24 March

Royal Brompton hospital

Stop talking. Just stop. Unless it's absolutely necessary. These are my new instructions from Julia. She says I'm like an athlete who's had the plaster taken off a broken leg and tries on day one to run a marathon. She's worried we're rushing things by targeting a return to work next week. Of course she's right, but it is not what I want to hear. When I was originally told I'd be back at work within three weeks I thought the doctors were being absurdly optimistic. Now, though, I realize it would have been possible – if it hadn't been for losing my bloody voice.

I'm terrified that someone will print a story about me being unable to speak. I'm pretty sure that it would be written sympathetically ('Brave cancer Nick's fight to recover voice'), but I'm also pretty sure that it would result in people beginning to write me off.

I feel like that reporter featured years ago on the TV out-takes programme *It'll be Alright on the Night*. 'Nick Robinson, BBC News, sad, sick, married, several children, pissed off, really dreadfully pissed off.' Except if I said that nobody would hear a bloody word.

Carluccio's, Fulham Road

I'm wallowing in self-pity when the waitress who has struggled for two days to hear my order comes up to my table with something I haven't asked for. It is, she explains, her secret hot honey and mint concoction for curing sore throats. It brings a big smile back to my face.

The real world

So what am I missing? Today I should have been in Birmingham to see Ed Balls launch a new Labour election poster featuring big, swinging 'VAT'-shaped concrete blocks with the warning, 'Don't let the Tories hit you with this'.

His message is simple. Don't forget that the coalition increased VAT when it first came in. Don't forget that every Conservative administration for forty years has raised this tax or that 'the only way the Tories can make their sums add up on their extreme plans is to raise VAT again after the election'.

I'm quite glad I stayed in London.

Wednesday 25 March

Carluccio's, Fulham Road

Another voice therapy session – my 'mum mum mums' and 'many many manys' are getting stronger – followed by another hot honey and mint brew. I haven't the heart to tell the waitress that I don't actually have a sore throat or to explain to her why she can't hear me, let alone what 'vocal fold palsy' is. This morning is different, though. I have company: a friend on the inside of the Tory campaign who can be relied on not only to have some good gossip but not to gossip in turn about my difficulties. We make a bizarre spectacle as I scribble questions and comments on a whiteboard.

Apparently, Dave's kitchen resignation statement took the whole Tory campaign by surprise as the minders who accompanied the PM failed to spot that he'd said anything remarkable. Cameron's rare interview mistakes tend to happen on the road or, whenever they've happened with me, on a train, when he relaxes a little. After two trips with yours truly led to news stories he stopped me at the ticket barrier of the station where we next met to say, 'I'm not sure this is a good idea.'

Prime Minister's Questions

Never, ever, ever ask a question to which you don't already know the answer, or to which you are not ready to get either a yes or a no. That has been one of my golden rules since my earliest days as a researcher, after I prepared a plan for a twenty-minute TV interview with a government minister based on the premise that he would say no to our opening question. There was no way he wouldn't. He always had in the past and it would make no sense if he did anything else. That, at least, is what I tried to explain to Jonathan Dimbleby, having watched him struggle to recover from the answer I insisted could never be.

So it is today at the last PMQs of this Parliament. Picture the scene in the opposition leader's office beforehand. 'Let's ask him to rule out a rise to VAT. Can't fail. Every Tory government for years has put it up. Osborne was asked repeatedly only yesterday and kept using weasel words about "not having any plans" to increase it.'

So ask Ed Miliband does – prefacing his question with a nice gag in which he quotes the explanation Cameron gave for announcing his 'retirement plans': that he believed in 'giving straight answers to straight questions'.

The PM's answer does not, however, follow the script. 'Yes,' he says.

Miliband looks outraged. Having demanded a straight answer, the last thing he expected was to actually get one.

Tory MPs howl. Labour MPs sit grim-faced. Eleven-year-old Nancy Cameron, in the gallery for what might be Daddy's swansong PMQs, is no doubt shouting, 'You've been poned!' (Ask a child what it means.)

But there is more. 'Now that I have ruled out VAT,' says a gleeful Cameron, 'will he rule out National Insurance contributions? Yes or no?' Miliband has been so thrown by what has just happened, he has failed to realize that his opponent was about to use the same manoeuvre on him.

This might be the final PMQs of this kind we see. Again and again Ed Miliband has told me of his desire to do something – anything – to end the spectacle of half an hour a week of parliamentary bear-baiting. Today's session will leave him more determined than ever to do so.

Change on another front comes immediately. A few hours after one Ed has refused to do it, the other Ed rushes over to our Millbank studios to make it clear that a future Labour government not only has no intention of raising National Insurance, no plans to raise it and no need to raise it, but would actually rule out entirely any increase. Why on earth would anyone think anything different? Well, perhaps it might have something to do with the fact that, just as the tax rise of choice for Tory chancellors is VAT (they hate taxes on incomes), the tax rise favoured by Labour occupants of Number 11 has been National Insurance (because people wrongly believe that it is spent on their pensions or the NHS when, in truth, it is just another tax destined for the national coffers).

The Treasury mandarins will be furious. We still have one of the highest budget deficits in our history and in the developed world. NI and VAT are two of the biggest revenue-raisers available to ministers and, at a stroke, they've both been ruled out by both major parties of government. This is no way to make tax policy.

Thursday 26 March

A restaurant near Broadcasting House

Lunch with James Harding, head of BBC News, and Sue Inglish, head of BBC Westminster. Having originally told them, along with everyone else, that I had the nicest, kindest, gentlest, never-comes-back sort of cancer and that, once it had been whipped out, I'd be back at work in three weeks, I now have to reveal that one small part of it turned out to be a tad more like its host – loud, aggressive, the type you fear you'll never hear the end of. So I'll be having chemo. Added to which I am missing a voice, a rather fundamental problem for a man employed in broadcasting.

James and Sue have a plan: a slow, phased return to work, starting with blogging, followed by the occasional bit of radio, then some telly, building up to the big match itself: election week and what may turn out to be the real story – the messy aftermath.

James tells me he's more interested in my next ten years at the BBC than the next ten weeks, and I believe he means it. It all makes sense and it's presented with real generosity. And yet I have a sense of mounting panic.

I think for the first time I am being confronted with the stark reality that I am not halfway through a short sprint but instead at the starting line of a marathon that may involve reporting on the election but, if things go wrong again, may not.

The real world

Meanwhile, just down the road, it is the last day of this Parliament; the day when many of the biggest names in politics, people I've known all my professional life, are bowing out. I'm sad not to be there to say farewell to Beith, Blears, Blunkett, Brown, Campbell, Darling, Dobson, Dorrell, Hague, Hain, Jowell, Straw, Young and many more. Not to mention those who don't know they're saying farewell today but will find in six weeks' time that the electorate have taken that decision for them.

It is not the happiest of last days for William Hague. His final act as leader of the Commons is to try to change the rules governing how the next speaker is chosen by introducing the shockingly radical idea of a secret ballot. The reality, and everyone knows it, is that this is a last-ditch attempt to make it easier to dump John Bercow, the man most Tories love to hate, after the election.

Most, but not all. Bercow is saved by the support of twenty-three Conservative MPs. One of them, Charles Walker, chairman of the Commons Procedure Committee, is tearful as he berates ministers for not consulting him: 'I have been played as a fool and when I go home tonight I will look in the mirror and see an honourable fool looking back at me and I would much rather be an honourable fool in this and any other matter than a clever man.'

Labour MPs get to their feet to applaud. The speaker smiles and can't resist adding (when has he ever resisted?), 'I'm not going anywhere.'

Home, the sofa

Cameron looks terrified as he faces Jeremy Paxman tonight in the first TV leaders' debate that is not a debate. Instead first he, then Miliband will be separately scratched, mauled and toyed with by the ageing king of the TV jungle.

The PM's fear is rooted in the fact that he swore never to be interviewed by Paxo again, having spectacularly turned the tables on him in their first confrontation a decade ago during the Tory leadership contest.

You can see that he is waiting for the retaliatory killer blow. He dodges and squirms when asked how many food banks there are and whether he could live on a zero-hours contract. I suspect his calculation is that this is better than getting the answer wrong and becoming tomorrow's YouTube sensation.

Miliband wriggles awkwardly, too, under sustained assault on Labour's record on borrowing and immigration, and when he's asked about his brother it's almost too painful to watch. He comes alive, though, when challenged on whether he's tough enough to stand up to the likes of Putin. I stood up to Obama over Syria, he claims – which is one version of history – before lighting the fuse on the night's planned verbal firework: 'Am I tough enough? Hell, yes, I'm tough enough.'

An instant poll has Cameron as the narrow winner. This raises the question of what it actually means to 'win' a TV debate. All that really matters is whether people might be more likely to switch their vote as a result of watching a debate or the coverage that follows. Headline polling doesn't tell us that. I've no doubt that Ed will have made some people take another look at him. That's the advantage of being the challenger. That's why Labour was desperate for debates and the Tories did everything in their power to scupper them.

Saturday 28 March

Home

'Morning, Harry.'

My son looks at me, startled and a little emotional: 'That was your voice, Dad!'

And you know what? It bloody well was. Having stayed as silent as I could yesterday, and given it as much of a rest as possible, there it was. A bit thinner, a bit quieter, a bit hoarser but unmistakably my voice. I wasn't sure I'd ever hear it again.

Sunday 29 March

It's not every day that politicians say in public what you know they're thinking but don't want people to know they're thinking. Alex Salmond, however, has just told the SNP conference he doesn't believe what he calls 'the broadcasting issue' will be 'properly resolved until we have broadcasting under the remit of our democratic Parliament in Scotland'.

To be fair, Salmond only craves what so many politicians crave: control. What a lot of politicians forget is that what makes our system of broadcasting the envy of the world is that it is not controlled by them. Sure, they try. They threaten to cut the licence fee and they attempt to bully us, but they don't control who broadcasts or what is broadcast. Never have, never will.

The former first minister tells SNP delegates that 'some of the experience of the referendum has scarred the BBC and there has been some gain from it already from our perspective'.

This from a man who is known to have taken the closest interest in appointments to jobs in the arts. I have never had the chance to check it for myself but people I trust tell me the word went out that if you did not share the first minister's political outlook, you might as well not bother applying. People in universities and businesses are also worried about the consequences if they don't mind their language.

Perhaps that's why I don't find talk of the BBC being 'scarred' and 'some gain from our perspective' terribly reassuring.

But perhaps the fact that I have my first session of chemotherapy tomorrow is fuelling my irritation.

Monday 30 March

Hampstead Heath

The condemned man's last request is a walk on the heath. The Westminster world might be watching the PM's visit to Buckingham Palace to ask the Queen to dissolve Parliament, but on the day the election campaigns begin in earnest, the day I'd planned to be back at work, I'll be in the chemo clinic.

A tweet from Gyles Brandreth cheers me up: 'Remember Balfour's line: "Nothing matters very much & most things don't matter at all".'

Royal Free hospital

I have a cappuccino, my laptop and a rather nice view. If chemo is hell they have yet to turn up the heat. I feel curiously relaxed as a nurse hangs up a bag of cell poison and turns on a tap to pump it through my wrist into my bloodstream.

No one knows for sure if it will do me any good, in other words, kill off any cell that dares even to think of becoming cancerous. Equally, no one can know whether it will knock me for six, inducing nausea, fatigue, diarrhoea, constipation (quite how it can do both at the same time I have yet to discover) and a plague of locusts. On the plus side, I'm told my hair might thin but it won't all fall out.

Now there is nothing I can do but wait and wait and wait. Drip, drip, drip. Just eight hours to go. And then more waiting to see if and when and what side-effects will kick in.

The real world

The PM has come back from seeing Her Majesty. Since the date of the next election has been fixed for years it was a trip without purpose, beyond nostalgic symbolism and providing the TV news with pictures to build up the drama.

Outside Number 10 Cameron's pitch is an interesting one: 'We must see this through together,' he says, as if running the country has been a shared national endeavour. His key message is that there is a 'stark choice': either he or Ed Miliband will walk through that door in thirty-eight days' time.

He's counting on enough people who've deserted him having the John McEnroe response to his opponent ('You *cannot* be serious!') and voting, perhaps with a heavy heart, for the Tories.

Gather two or more Conservatives together and they will convince themselves this is bound to happen. Remember Kinnock, they say. I always reply: 'Remember Thatcher.' Much less popular than Callaghan in 1979, but she won nevertheless.

— APRIL —

Wednesday 1 April

Chemoland

I can't say I wasn't warned. What poisons the cancer will, of course, poison the rest of you, they said. You may feel nauseous, tired and have a metallic taste in your mouth. Yeah, right. Nothing prepared me for this.

I feel as if every normal function of my body has been disrupted: tasting, smelling, digesting, breathing are all unspeakably unpleasant. I could fight pain. I could focus on the enemy and defy it. Not this. My body is being taken over and I have no means of restoring control.

The bloody irony of it all is that I have been declared cancer-free. This is a mere precaution. It feels worse than having the disease, the surgery and even losing my voice.

I hate it, hate it, hate it.

The real world

There is one organ the chemo hasn't hit. Not yet, at least. My brain. So I will carry on writing until someone tells me it looks as if the chemicals are scrambling my thought processes.

I write a blog on who will win tomorrow's TV leaders' debate and what on earth that really means. With the inclusion of both the Welsh and Scottish Nationalists, there is not a single voter who will have the chance to vote for all the parties on show. The polls will test the views of people who have already largely made up their minds. Twitter or Facebook merely lend a loudhailer to the committed, the partisan and the organized, and the verdict of the commentariat, who will be packed together in the 'spin room', will be no more than a reflection of the political classes talking to themselves and producing their own instant brand of not particularly reliable conventional wisdom.

Thursday 2 April

The road to nowhere

We can't go forward. We can't go back. We can't turn left or right. It's gridlock. The car taking me to voice therapy has driven straight to the location of a major fire. One glance at Twitter shows that the blaze started last night. It was a headline story but the little god satnav told my driver to head into a major emergency, so head there he did. All knowledge, judgement and experience has been binned in favour of a bloody screen with an annoying voice which instructs us where to go but almost always gets it wrong.

The tube

Don't get on the tube straight after chemo, I was told. You're vulnerable to infection. You need to avoid crowds with coughs and colds. But here I am. I will get to my session and say those eees and ooos and woops and nyaas if it bloody well kills me.

Royal Brompton hospital

'What do you think will happen tonight?' a senior Tory texts me. 'What do you think?' I reply in a text equivalent of 'I'll show you mine if you show me yours.'

His response is telling. I wouldn't be surprised if Sturgeon does well. Some Labour supporters might even say she's the best leader we never had.

The spin has begun. The Tories won't try claiming their guy won but they will try to show that Ed lost – and to the woman who, they'll say, will wear the political trousers when Labour and the SNP cosy up after 7 May.

Home, the sofa

It's a curious sight. Seven party leaders lined up in a row. Three are women, two of whom are not even standing in this election. One is almost completely unknown in most of the UK.

Nicola Sturgeon, Natalie Bennett and Plaid Cymru's Leanne Wood catch the eye and set the tone for a leaders' debate which symbolizes the fact that we now live in a multi-party political world. They have been given equal billing with the prime minister, deputy prime minister and the leader of the opposition. It's a status they and their predecessors have craved for decades and which, until now, has always been denied them. They make the anti-austerity case with a passion rarely heard from Westminster's men in suits these past five years.

Cameron performs like a competent but inspired batsman relieved to reach teatime with his wicket still standing and not too bothered that he's scored few runs. He has come to see debates as all risk and no opportunity, and now they are over – for him, at least.

Miliband has some good lines, if obviously heavily scripted and rehearsed, and delivers them well. Once again he will have defied the ridiculously low expectations many have of him but Cameron's relief will be his disappointment.

Clegg is by far the most natural, as he was five years ago. He makes a powerful case for the need for someone to stop either of the other two going OTT but looks like a man who knows many voters don't want that someone to be him.

Farage is pure Farage: the political street trader who insists that all the others are trying to sell you dodgy gear and he is the only one you can possibly trust. The man who feeds off controversy and condemnation holds up a political hand-grenade labelled 'HIV-carrying immigrants' and gleefully pulls out the pin. Some of his opponents give him exactly what he wants: a 'how dare you?' row about it.

After two hours there has been, though, no real game-changing moment. No zinger. No gaffe. No clear winner.

I am left wondering if the damage Labour will suffer from seeing their vote split could be limited by a change in the terms of political trade. Could Ed Miliband's position now be seen as more moderate, more centrist, more – dare I say it – Blair-ishly 'Third Way' in comparison with those of the women he's up against?

Friday 3 April

Home, the kitchen

Over the years in the trade, I have come to know and even at times love our rude, raucous and rumbustious press. Its blatant partisanship is a healthy and necessary counterbalance to the careful, cautious, conventional wisdom that we 'impartial' broadcasters serve up. There are, though, moments when even I am stupefied by the willingness of papers to print nonsense to promote their political chums.

The *Sun*'s splash showing a gloomy Ed Miliband under the headline 'OOPS, I JUST LOST MY ELECTION' will surely be a candidate for the first picture on the wall of the new prime minister if Labour win.

My Tory source was right, though. On the morning after the debate, Sturgeon is the person everyone's talking about and that is bad news for Miliband.

Saturday 4 April

Suffolk

Sun, clear skies, sea air. The chemo horror is starting to lift a little. When I have a pint of Adnams in my hand I will know that it has finally passed.

In the real world, this election has its first whodunnit. Or what some wag on Twitter has already dubbed the 'Nicileak affair'. Who leaked the Whitehall mandarin's memo recording what the French ambassador was allegedly told in private by the first minister of Scotland?

The bombshell revelation is that Nicola Sturgeon is said to have confided over coffee and croissants that she'd rather see David Cameron remain as PM and doubts Ed Miliband is up to the job.

The story keeps Sturgeon in the news, which will suit the Tories, but its underlying narrative works for Labour, who have always asserted that the SNP are so obsessed with securing independence that they secretly lust for another Thatcherite government to drive Scots voters into their arms. On the other hand, the Lib Dems run the Scottish Office and they face a Scottish wipe-out at the hands of the SNP. My money would be on them having leaked it.

So great is the paranoia about an establishment plot to deny the SNP their rightful gains that Twitter is awash with rumours it may be a Zinoviev-style forgery.

Few spoil a good tale by addressing the small matter that Sturgeon and the ambo deny she ever professed a preference and that the memo conceded there may have been glitches in translation.

Much more interesting and surprising to me is the realization that what is said to foreign diplomats is subsequently conveyed to government officials. I used to enjoy gossipy lunches with a former French ambassador. The splendid food and wine served by flunkeys in blue tailcoats, red waistcoats and white gloves was matched by the quality of the insights into British and EU politics.

On the eve of a rather vital EU summit I recall him unsheathing an elegant fountain pen to jot down my prediction of the prime minister's negotiating position. It was a reminder to me that there is, as they always say, no such thing as a free lunch.

Sunday 5 April

Suffolk

A breathless text from a Tory spinner last night told me to stand by for a scoop in the *Sun on Sunday* which, I was assured, the BBC would want to follow.

It's Easter Sunday. I paint my morning egg with a smiling face, dip in my toast soldiers, finish off breakfast by beheading Harry (my cute chocolate rabbit, not my son) and then turn to the papers to see what all the fuss was about.

The *Sun on Sunday* has got hold of the handwritten crib sheets Ed used and binned after the leaders' debate, in which he reminds himself to be a 'happy warrior', 'calm, never agitated' and to accentuate the positive. It's a good scoop and a great tale but it has almost no wider consequence or news value. The *Sun* does its best to create one by claiming the notes explain the Labour leader's 'robotic performance'. It's a talking point rather than a story for a BBC news broadcast. What strikes me as extraordinary is that the Tories seriously think voters will care a damn about this. Could they be getting just a little bit desperate?

Tuesday 7 April

Home

Blair is back again. Back on the election trail, back in Sedgefield, supporting Ed Miliband '100 per cent'. Not so long ago he was telling me it was up to the voters to decide whether Ed would make a strong leader.

With his usual skill he has identified the one major issue on which they do see eye-to-eye: Europe. The two men are, though, 200 miles apart so that no camera can focus on them as they're asked about all the other tensions and contradictions between them.

Blair knows that Miliband came under sustained pressure to match the Tory promise of an EU referendum and resisted. He knows what that pressure is like because he faced it himself as prime minister, when there were proposals for a new EU constitution. Blair executed a humiliating U-turn on the question, saying no for months before finally conceding defeat. I remember filming a rather cheesy piece to camera in a blue Jag making repeated U-turns outside the gates of Downing Street.

Blair was told then, as Miliband has been since, that you can't afford to oppose giving people a say . . . you'll never face down the pressure from the press . . . a referendum is inevitable . . . and more besides. Even some pro-Europeans joined in, arguing this was a chance to close the gaping wound that had been suppurating for decades by settling Britain's place in the EU once and for all.

Where Blair conceded Miliband has, so far, resisted, and, in that one respect, if in no other, I suspect he *is* backing the Labour leader 100 per cent.

Wednesday 8 April

Home

'Whose side are you on?' is one of the most powerful questions in politics. Ed Miliband has always believed his response would propel him into Number 10, hence his promise today to scrap the special tax status enjoyed by so-called 'non-doms'.

They're very rich and they're often foreign or based abroad. They enjoy a lifestyle that stirs the resentment of anyone who's struggled to make ends meet in recent years. Which is why George Osborne targeted them to pay more when he was looking for a way to fund a promise to cut inheritance tax way back in 2009, and why he has increased the annual tax charge they do pay on more than one occasion.

It was this question that helped Barack Obama secure a second term in the White House despite being far from popular and seen as less economically competent than Mitt Romney, a man so fantastically wealthy he thought nothing of having an elevator installed in his seaside house – for his car.

Labour's best day so far turns briefly sour when an enterprising BBC local radio reporter remembers that he asked Ed Balls about this idea a few weeks ago only to be told that it would cost the country money. Today he seems to be saying that it would raise hundreds of millions.

How can this be? The headlines Labour wanted, and got, today give the impression they would scrap non-dom status altogether (which was what Balls was saying would lose the country cash). In fact their policy preserves a special tax status for those who live here temporarily.

The muddle will take a bit of the gloss off Labour's day, but not much. The news is filled with pictures of fat cats, their mansions and luxury cars and Ed Miliband arguing they should pay the same tax as everyone else.

If you asked viewers and readers whose side they are on, I think the answer would be obvious.

Thursday 9 April

In my bath

I can't quite believe what's coming out of my radio. The defence secretary of the United Kingdom is seriously inviting listeners to ponder on what he says is the most important question facing the nation: if Ed Miliband was prepared to stab his brother in the back to become leader, surely he'd be prepared to stab the country in the back to get his hands on power? This, Michael Fallon tells us, would involve

Miliband abandoning Britain's defences – in particular our nuclear deterrent – as part of a 'grubby deal' with the SNP to get him to Downing Street.

The politics underlying this smear are clear for all to see. The story is designed to raise the so-called 'character issue' ('is Ed up to it?'), to keep the threat of the SNP alive in English voters' minds and to focus them on a matter – the renewal of Trident – that the Labour leadership are desperate not to discuss because it upsets many of their own MPs and supporters, not to mention boosting their rivals in the SNP, Plaid and the Greens.

I reach for the soap and feel the need to scrub a little harder. Then Jim Naughtie comes up with a clever question. Surely standing against his brother demonstrated that Miliband is strong enough to defend Britain?

ENT clinic

It is the question I haven't dared to ask directly before but it is time to ask it. Guri has taken a look at my vocal cords and declares that they are recovering nicely.

'So have I got a future as a broadcaster?'

'Oh, yes,' he says, unaware, it seems, of the significance of what he has just said. He adds that a full recovery may take a few months. Who cares? I once thought it would never happen.

Home, the sofa

I now understand the rationale behind the back-stabber attack. It turns out that this is what Lynton Crosby calls the 'dead cat' strategy. The idea is simple. If you're irrevocably losing an argument – on, to pick an example at random, taxing non-doms – you need a distraction. That's where the dead cat comes in. People may be outraged, alarmed, disgusted but, says Lynton, everyone will shout, 'Jeez, mate, there's a dead cat on the table!' They will then be talking about what you want them to talk about and not the argument you were losing.

My local Italian

Dinner out. The first post-chemo glass of wine, the first cup of coffee, the first time in ten days I've been able to relish every sip, every mouthful and every taste.

Friday 10 April

Home

So you thought there was no money? You thought that tens of billions of pounds of extra cuts were still needed to balance the books? You thought the age of austerity still had years to run?

Well, stop fussing about all that. The Conservatives have found £8 billion a year more to pay for the NHS. How have they found it? Well, of course, the answer's simple – by sticking to the long-term economic plan. Yes, but where is it actually coming from? More borrowing, higher tax, more spending cuts elsewhere? Answer comes there none. This is what used to be condemned as an unfunded spending commitment.

It's the clearest possible confirmation that the focus groups are telling the politicians voters don't want more candour about cuts. What they want are promises to spend, spend, spend.

Sunday 12 April

Broadcasting House

Roll up! Roll up! See a man with only half a voice broadcasting to the nation!

I'm bored watching the election from home, but still don't have enough of a voice to risk going out on the road. So Katy and I have hatched a plan to allow me to do some election reporting. I'll just do the 'lives' on the TV news – except they won't be live and they won't be outside. They'll be recorded in a nice, quiet studio with a specially sensitive microphone.

I record one video as a test and another to tweet tomorrow morning. The aim is to get out of the way as soon as I can – and before I say anything that actually matters – the inevitable reaction to my scratchy voice. I can hear people now: 'What's wrong with him? Why does he sound funny? Oh, cancer, is it? I thought he was just taking a holiday. What was that he just said?'

Key to the decision about what to do next are two women who are not natural soul-mates. Julia is a softly spoken, calming, mint-tea drinking sort of girl. Katy is assertive, passionate and fully caffeinated. Therapy and news journalism are not an easy fit.

Julia, my therapist, is worried. She winces when she sees me chatter in the newsroom. She fears I'm using up my very limited 'voice minutes' and could hinder my recovery. She'd prefer me to wait a couple of weeks. Katy, my news editor, wants what's best for me, too, but she knows a big part of that is being on the front line doing my job, and she's as desperate as I am to get me back there.

Unwittingly, George Osborne adds his own contribution to the debate when I bump into him in the newsroom. 'Don't worry about rushing back to cover the campaign,' he says. 'The time your judgement will be needed is on election night and in the days that follow.'

But I've never been much of a one for caution. So sod it, let's give it a shot this week, as the parties launch their manifestos.

Monday 13 April

Home, the kitchen

Too late now. It's out there. No more secret worrying about how people will react. We're about to find out. I've just tweeted a video of me explaining that I'm taking another step back to work, but that my voice is still recovering and has a way to go yet.

Labour manifesto launch

Can he pass the blink test? That's what really matters to Ed Miliband today, not the document he's waving or the list of policies he's pushing. Can he change people's views of him so that when voters shut their eyes for a moment and are told he's their next prime minister they don't guffaw or weep but think, maybe – why not?

He arrives in Manchester determined to address the nation's doubts, to confront his weaknesses and to tackle them head on. It can all be summed up in three soundbites: 'I am ready', 'I will always stand up for you' and 'We are the party of responsibility'.

The deficit – forgotten entirely just a few weeks ago in this same city – is now the centrepiece of the speech and the front cover of the manifesto.

Studio C, Broadcasting House

It is, I say in my first recorded broadcast since my surgery, one of the most powerful speeches I've seen him make but voters must now decide whether they think he *is* ready and whether Labour *is* the party of responsibility. If so, he'll be standing on the steps of Number 10 as our prime minister in four weeks' time. It's a statement of the obvious, and yet for years now I've been struck by just how many people – even Labour backers – have never believed it possible.

Behind the camera stands Julia, my conductor. She points upwards to warn me not to drop my voice so that it becomes hoarser, holds up her hands to remind me to take a breath before the next sentence and spreads them out to indicate that I should slow down. What I used to do without a moment's thought now involves training, concentration, stress and lots of time.

After a couple of takes we all agree: we've got one that can go on air.

Edit suite

A total of six BBC news managers line up for my very own version of the blink test. If you shut your eyes for a moment, do I sound like someone who ought to be on air? They watch my tape, with its apology for the 'croaky voice'. Like a bloodied gladiator, I await the thumbs-up or the thumbs-down. We have only minutes before the six o'clock news goes out.

I sense that the decision has in fact already been taken but James, the head of news, is inviting all to air their worries: am I risking my recovery? Are the BBC exercising their duty of care? Will viewers find it totally distracting? With Julia's loyal support, I try to reassure on all fronts.

The studio gallery, BBC News at 6

'Five, four, three, two, one . . . run titles.' Soon Sophie Raworth is introducing my report with a warm smile and the explanation that after my op I 'sound a bit different at the moment'. I haven't been this nervous since my very first broadcast on the old *Nine O'Clock News*.

Taxi home

The nice texts roll in but I turn to Twitter for a more candid verdict. Lots of lovely 'welcome backs' there, too. My new hushed tones remind some of snooker's legendary commentator, Ted Lowe; others recall 'Whispering' Bob Harris on *The Old Grey Whistle Test*. Only one viewer suggests that my new voice is 'very 0898 & am sure a couple of million people are ready for some late night erotic action'. The cybernats are almost silent. Almost. One writes candidly, if not charmingly, that 'I genuinely hope Nick Robinson gets better. Then immediately gets run over by a bin lorry.' Nice.

Tuesday 14 April

Conservative manifesto launch

The political cross-dressing goes on.

At his manifesto launch David Cameron tries to rebrand the Conservatives the 'workers' party' and promises the 'good life' instead of all that dispiriting talk of the 'age of austerity' and red flashing lights on the dashboard. The Tories are trying to inject some optimism and positivity into a campaign that has been condemned as dull and negative.

In a vain attempt to stop the fifty-somethings who appear on our screens searching for archive footage of Tom and Barbara in the 1970s Surbiton sitcom, a pedant from Downing Street texts me to insist that the PM was referring to 'a' good life and not 'the'. I resist replying, 'Too late. Should have thought of that before.' Robert Peston has already dug out some clips.

Studio C, Broadcasting House

Today I've abandoned the studio desk and my special sensitive microphone – part CNN's Larry King, part the wartime BBC's Alvar Lidell – in favour of standing. The voice sounds better and I look more, well, like me.

I end my broadcast tonight with a parallel question to the one I posed last night. 'Do you really see David Cameron as leader of the workers' party? Do you believe that the Tories can deliver the good life?'

Just as I did yesterday, I can't help feeling that this attempt at rebranding feels mighty late. Rhetoric alone can only achieve so much.

Wednesday 15 April

Liberal Democrat manifesto launch

It's quite a contrast with the Cleggmania of five years ago. The most unloved leader in British politics in effect tells the nation today, 'If you don't like me, have you thought about the alternatives?'

Who do you want to be calling the shots, to have the power to hold the next government to ransom? he is asking. Salmond? Farage? With the political classes obsessing about an SNP–Labour deal, Clegg is desperate to raise the spectre of what he calls Blukip – the Tories, UKIP and the DUP.

It's a struggle. In large part because many voters have written him off and simply stopped listening, partly out of anger, partly because they wrongly think he's finished.

But the Lib Dems are, I point out in my broadcast, likely to be much more significant players in the next Parliament than the new kids on the political block, UKIP and the Greens. They could have between twenty and forty MPs, compared with at best a handful or two between the other two parties.

Don't, I conclude, be at all surprised if after 7 May Mr Clegg is still sitting smiling at the Cabinet table.

Earlier UKIP, too, launched their manifesto, proving that there's more to the party than Nigel Farage. There was a super-slick performance from its author, Suzanne Evans, who emphasized again and again that theirs is the only fully costed manifesto. They got a think-tank to do it for them.

While I confess that I haven't gone through it line by line, I am a tad sceptical that it would really prove possible to pay for extra spending on the NHS, defence, police and multiple tax cuts worth £32 billion simply by cutting cash to foreigners of one sort or another – the EU, aid recipients, oh, and the Scots – with the only pain felt by the English being the cancellation of HS2.

As Alistair Darling once told me, he'd learned when being given advice as chancellor of the exchequer, if it sounds too good to be true, it probably is.

Thursday 16 April

Some of the leaders' debate

If the first debate was odd, this looks odder still. It's not just that it is dominated once again by a woman who isn't even running in this election. It's also that two of the coalition leaders, Cameron and Clegg, aren't there at all. If you want to know what a mess multi-party negotiations can produce you need look no further than the so-called 'challengers' debate' – part of the deal made with broadcasters to ensure debates went ahead at all. I very much doubt we will ever see another like it. It will be remembered as the Ed and Nicola show.

Miliband uses the absence of the prime minister to make himself look more like one, responding to attacks from the left (on austerity and Trident) as well as from the right (Europe and immigration) to portray himself as statesmanlike.

Sturgeon, with a little help from her chums, Plaid Cymru's Leanne Wood and the Greens' Natalie Bennett, taunts the Labour leader for being 'Tory lite', letting the Conservatives off the hook and not being bold enough.

David Cameron was berated for refusing to take part in this debate. My hunch is that he will think that tonight has gone pretty much as he hoped it would. Conservative HQ and the Tory press will delight in using clips of the Ed and Nicola show to stamp the election with the image of a weak minority Labour government being forced to deal with and placate a rampant SNP.

Sunday 19 April

On the sofa watching the sofa

The bags under his eyes are the first thing you notice. The next is the tetchiness. David Cameron is not enjoying himself one little bit on the Marr show. This is not how it was meant to be.

By now the polls should have turned. The electorate is supposed to have acknowleged that the 'plan is working' and, therefore, that it is not 'time for a change'; to have compared him with the other guy and decided that they are not ready to take the risk. But the polls aren't budging. The Tories are neck-and-neck with Labour and that points only to one thing: Ed Miliband will walk through the door of Number 10 in a little over two weeks unless something shifts fast (or, of course, if the polls are wrong).

The one hope Team Cameron still has is that the Nats will do their job for them by robbing Labour of enough seats in Scotland while terrifying enough voters in England into returning to the Tory fold. Cameron declares it's 'a frightening prospect' that for the 'first time in our history nationalists would be altering the direction of our country'. The man with a first in PPE from Oxford surely knows that the Irish Nationalists held the balance of power between 1910 and 1914, but we know what he's saying.

On the sofa watching the news

Grim. Truly grim. Another tragedy in the Med. Hundreds are feared drowned after a boat just 70ft long, but carrying up to 700 migrants, capsized in Libyan waters en route to the safety and freedom of Italy.

I can hear ringing in my ears the words of that minister who insisted that if there were fewer attempts to rescue people there would be fewer attempts to cross the waters and therefore fewer deaths.

I think back, too, to words I heard twenty-odd years ago in a *Panorama* film I was making about the future causes of warfare. A rather scary Israeli military analyst predicted that the Italian navy would one day sink a boatful of migrants in an effort to stop the human tide coming from North Africa. We thought he was crazy. I wonder.

Monday 20 April

SNP manifesto launch

I am watching on screen the undoubted and unexpected star of this election. Five years ago everyone seemed to want to agree with Nick. Now they are lining up to agree with Nicola – even though no one anywhere can actually vote for her in this election. She is not even a candidate. Yet when she declares that her inbox is full of e-mails from people outside Scotland who want the chance to vote SNP, nobody dismisses it as spin.

Her backdrop promises to build a 'stronger Scotland' but her message is that she will build a fairer Britain, with less austerity and, above all, more spending on the NHS.

This makes me pause. Last time I interviewed the first minister I pointed out the conclusion of the tax and spending gurus at the Institute for Fiscal Studies that the budget of NHS Scotland had been cut even as the wicked Tory-led coalition were increasing NHS spending in real terms. I remember the very convoluted, waffly answer she gave, which convinced me the number-crunchers were on to something.

If I could be in Edinburgh rather than stuck in London I would have asked the question again. Instead I text and e-mail the SNP spinners and the civil servants in the Scottish health department. In reply I get answers, but they're dressed up in an awful lot more waffle and obfuscation. Something doesn't add up here.

The Cabinet office

Here he is: the man of whom David Cameron is said to have once joked: 'Remind me, Jeremy, do you work for me or do I work for you?' He's the country's top civil servant, the Cabinet secretary, the official who has whispered in the ear of three prime ministers: Blair, Brown and Cameron. I've asked to see Sir Jeremy Heywood to discuss how he'll handle what now looks to be a racing certainty – an uncertain election result. We run through the what ifs and the maybes. We discuss the constitutional duties of the PM and of the Queen, who must be advised on whom to summon to form the next government.

The morning after election night will be when the fun could really start. Exhausted, disappointed, confused politicians may spend days traipsing between Whitehall and Parliament, wondering what deal they can do with whom to get into government. The master of ceremonies will be a man few have ever heard of who has wielded immense power as prime ministers and their parties have come and gone.

There is one scenario to which Sir Jeremy has clearly given a bit of thought: the one that would trigger a battle over legitimacy. If the Tories should win the most seats but can't assemble a majority, even with allies, and, at the same time, Labour refuse to talk to the SNP, whose votes they would need to be sure of a majority, Cameron could legitimately claim that he should remain prime minister while Miliband would insist he should quit. The constitutional 'bible', the Cabinet manual, which sets out the rules, leaves it to the prime minister to exercise his judgement. That's what journalists call 'good for trade'.

Sir Jeremy points out with a smile that David Cameron won't even get the chance of a good night's sleep at Number 10. Just as the votes stop being counted, a three-day celebration of the seventieth anniversary of VE Day will begin. It includes a late-night concert on Horse Guards Parade, just outside the windows of the Camerons' flat.

Broadcasting House

I still don't know the bloody answer. I'm determined to find out before I do my piece for the six o'clock news whether or not the SNP has cut the health budget. I call the IFS and ask for their help. Do they still think what they used to think? Well, comes the reply from an earnest number-cruncher, the Scottish government has changed the way they organize health, inflation came in lower than expected and the calculations aren't as easy as they were. Yes, yes, yes, I say, as politely as I can, but there's an election on, and this really, really matters. Can't they do their calculation again? I'll try, comes the faint reply.

Minutes before I have to record my broadcast he comes up with the answer. Nicola Sturgeon, who is promising to spend more than any other politician on the NHS, did actually end up increasing health spending but much less quickly in Scotland than David Cameron did in England.

I say so on the news, confident that it won't make a blind bit of difference to the debate. Voters think Sturgeon looks and sounds like someone who believes in the NHS whereas the Tories' reorganization and history of ambivalence towards the health service mean they don't.

Tuesday 21 April

Royal Free hospital

Drip, drip, drip. The poison works its way slowly into my veins. It feels fine now. It did the first time. The chemo horror began afterwards. I'm told that this time it should be better. One nausea-inducing drug has been swapped for another which is ever so slightly less so. All I can do is wait and hope.

Wednesday 22 April

Bed

My post-chemo slumber is interrupted by texts from Tory high command. Have I seen the video? It's a 'big, big moment . . . like the Romney footage'. A quick search of Twitter reveals the Tories see this as such a big moment that Cameron himself has posted a shaky clip of Alex Salmond declaring at an SNP meeting how he'll write Labour's first budget.

Frustrated to be sitting on the sidelines, I tweet out the question on my mind: 'Are you scared or amused?' In other words, was Salmond boasting or just joking? The partisan answers pour in thick and fast.

My view crystallizes once I realize the obvious: it's both a joke and a boast. Salmond was mocking Tory press headlines which used what he said in a recent interview to claim that he, not Ed Balls, would be deciding what went into the chancellor's red box. They were only able to do so, though, because of his proclamation that 'if you hold the balance, then you hold the power' and his talk of amending the budget to help Scotland.

A poll drops into my inbox that gives some insight into why the Tories can't leave this alone. One in twelve voters think a Labour–SNP deal is likely and would be a bad thing and that a Tory government would be preferable, but are not planning to vote Tory. Woo just a fraction of those and Cameron keeps his job.

Thursday 23 April

Home, the kitchen

I'm eating breakfast. I feel pretty weary and a bit nauseous, but not, thankfully, as if every cell in my body has been invaded by hostile forces. I slept; I can think reasonably clearly. I dare to allow myself the hope that perhaps Chemo 2 – The Sequel is going to be a little less scary than the original blockbuster.

The study

One man has been on the telly more often than most politicians in this campaign. He's become the nation's unofficial stats watchdog, the broadcaster's bullshit-detector of choice. Let's hear it for the head honcho of the Institute for Fiscal Studies, Paul Johnson.

The IFS has drawn a big crowd to hear them spell out the differences between the big parties' tax and spending plans. Hacks are poised with their notepads and tablets and laptops to note down a dizzying list of millions, billions and percentages. Party spinners are primed to issue press releases claiming that 'we've spelled out our plans' and 'it's the other lot whose numbers simply don't add up'. I watch on a livestream at home as Paul and his team of clever folk patiently explain the facts we have and highlight the detail we're not being told by those pesky politicians.

Yet something is missing from all this. We're all getting sucked into the weeds. It is the scale of the choice the electorate are facing – a choice that has been masked by deliberate evasiveness and obfuscation on all sides, by vague ambitions dressed up to sound hard and specific and, above all, by the poaching of political territory by the two big parties.

First Labour tried to convince voters that the deficit, which Ed Miliband had forgotten to mention in his party conference speech, was in truth the first thing on his mind at all times.

Then the Conservatives, who've endlessly warned of the risks of unfunded tax and spending promises, splashed the cash on pledges to fund the NHS, an inheritance tax cut, additional childcare places and more besides.

What's more, the choice is very simple to understand and pretty much what you'd expect. The Tories will spend less than their opponents and should be rewarded by borrowing less, too. Labour will spend and borrow more unless they can do what few governments have ever successfully done and increase the speed at which the economy grows. And the Lib Dems are – and, again, there's no surprise here – somewhere in the middle.

So, put aside the rhetoric and the evasions and the cross-dressing, and the differences aren't hard to see. You don't need an institute to tell you the answer. Or a number-cruncher. Or a statistic. You have to make a judgement based on whose values you share and who you trust.

And that, of course, is precisely what so many voters find so difficult.

ENT clinic

'Say "hey",' instructs Guri, thrusting a metal stick with a camera attached to it towards the back of my throat. It's time for yet another look at that vocal cord. I'm finding it increasingly hard to reconcile myself to the fact that it's not cancer, it's not major lung surgery, it's not even the dreaded chemotherapy that is stopping me working but a bit of my body which was working perfectly well before and on which I am hopelessly dependent.

Guri points to the movie of my vocal cords. 'That's what's causing it to sound raspy,' he says. The gap is still there.

Our target was always to be ready for election night: eight hours of live broadcasting, followed by a day, maybe many more, analyzing the fall-out. We agree a revised plan for how to give it our best shot but as I leave I have a sinking feeling. It simply isn't going to happen. I'm going to miss my Cup final. Think Paul Scholes and Roy Keane in 1999. Oh, all right, maybe not.

Friday 24 April

Home, the kitchen

The PM has just got back from an emergency EU summit in Brussels on how to avert yet more tragedies in the Med. A staggering 3,500 people are estimated to have died last year. The position he has adopted is telling: yes to a warship, military support and more money to patrol the waters between North Africa and Italy; no to taking in any refugees. With soaring immigration the key to the rise of UKIP, he doesn't dare.

Is Ed Miliband now accusing him of having blood on his hands? Is he holding him responsible for the drownings in the Med? That's certainly how it sounds on the early-morning news bulletins. Yet I detect uncertainty in what I'm hearing. The headlines and the news-reader's words are much stronger than those of the report that follows. The story scarcely features in the morning papers. I sense a row brewing. A huge row.

I go online to see what precisely the Labour leader is and is not saying. The overnight press briefing is pretty clear: 'He will say the refugee crisis and tragic scenes this week in the Mediterranean are in part a direct result of the failure of post-conflict planning for Libya', a failure Miliband will blame on David Cameron.

It's becoming clear that this isn't how Miliband's one big foreign policy speech was meant to go. A message from a grown-up in Team Ed reads: 'I'm properly annoyed . . . this is an unsustainable inference.'

I reply that all people have done is 'join the dots'. The speech attributes the tragedy to Cameron and other world leaders having 'walked away' after the war and failed to plan for what might follow. The finger of blame has been pointed and the Tories have reacted with outrage. Within a couple of weeks Miliband could be taking decisions on whether to send British troops to their deaths, yet this row obscures almost everything else he had to say.

I e-mail asking for evidence that Ed had worried and warned about this before, despite having supported the bombing of Libya itself. Back comes a list of quotes from the Commons showing that he raised it repeatedly at the time – in 2011 – and then again in February 2015. So not once in 2012, 2013 or 2014, I reply. Silence.

The garden

Uh-oh, uh-oh, I intone, like a demented parrot who's just had the blanket removed from his cage. Julia says it's great news that I can make this absurd sound. I'm not sure the neighbours agree.

Saturday 25 April

Oh dear, oh dear, oh dear. But should it matter? In an election in which almost nothing unexpected, nothing unplanned, nothing unmanaged has happened, it will. David Cameron has made himself a laughing stock among football fans – in other words, 90 per cent of the male population of Britain, not counting the women – by appearing to forget which team he supports.

In a speech about the multiple identities of Britain's ethnically diverse population, he has declared: 'You can support Man United, the Windies and Team GB all at the same time. Of course, I'd rather you supported West Ham.'

Fine. Except that he is a fan of Aston Villa, who just happen to play in the same colours as West Ham. The PM puts it down to a dose of what Natalie Bennett called 'brain fade'. Many won't be so kind. They will simply not be able to imagine forgetting which team they support. They'll assume he has never been a football fan at all; that he's just a posh bloke who loves shooting and hunting and has been pretending all along. That it's another example of inauthenticity, just like the official car that once drove behind him carrying his papers and his shoes as he rode to work on his bike.

#Villagate is soon trending. Alastair Campbell, who can't spot a Tory solar plexus without wanting to punch it, tries to get #phoney-cameron going. On *Match of the Day*, Gary Lineker introduces the highlights of Manchester City v West Ham before theatrically correcting himself, 'Sorry, Aston Villa.'

The irony is that the leader of the people's party knows nothing about football at all. Ed Miliband is a baseball obsessive. There again, he's never pretended to be anything else.

Sunday 26 April

Home, the kitchen

It's official. It's Wobble Weekend. The Sunday papers have decreed it. There was always going to be one: there is in every campaign.

They always begin the same way. A party donor or a backbench MP or an anonymous 'senior' party member who's not being listened to by his own side vents his frustration to a pathetically grateful hack bored with the carefully choreographed, pre-scripted, sanitized election campaign.

The source describes the campaign of his own party as lacklustre, or failing to cut through, or unduly negative. More often than not, he says the leader is being given the wrong advice. Then he concludes that if only they would heed *his* advice, victory would follow.

So it is that David Cameron is being told to fetch John Major's soapbox from the attic, get out among the real people and show some passion. This, I hear, is being strongly resisted by the architects of his campaign – Lynton Crosby and Craig Oliver – who have obsessively controlled not only what their leader says (it's the long-term economic plan, stupid), but where he is seen saying it: on factory floors or building sites. How on earth would it help, they've demanded to know, if the prime minister were seen being heckled or egged not just on TV news but on a clip that would be watched again and again and again on YouTube, Facebook and Twitter?

I've witnessed real election wobbles – Margaret Thatcher, for instance, smuggling in a new ad agency via the back door of Number 10 midway through the 1987 campaign, which she went on to win by a landslide. Compared with that, today's Tory angst is a mere tremor.

On the sofa watching the sofa

Every campaign wobble story needs one other element: calls for the party to unleash its 'secret weapon'. And so it is that the blond bombshell is sitting on the TV sofa. This is Boris's chance to demonstrate what he could do if he were Tory leader, not just as a solo act but head-to-head with Ed Miliband, who's there next to him.

The Boris and Ed Show is universally hailed as the best bit of political television of the campaign so far. It's unscripted, it's unpredictable and it's funny.

And yet Boris blew it. He's unfocused, he's self-indulgent and he gives Miliband another opportunity to look calm and statesmanlike in comparison.

This was not, as someone once said, his finest hour.

Monday 27 April

He's 'pumped up'. He's 'bloody lively'. He's desperate to win. Meet the new, improved, turbo-charged, non-chillaxing, three-Shredded-Wheat-a-day David Cameron.

There's no soapbox, no opportunities for egg-throwing or heckling. There is, though, one new prescription to counter what was in danger of becoming a narcolepsy-inducing campaign: prime ministerial passion.

This can, of course, have nothing to do with the polls indicating that only a quarter of voters think he's the leader who wants to win the most, or the focus groups unnerved by the fact that he began this campaign in a kitchen telling James Landale about his retirement plans.

All this as Ed Miliband is successfully rolling out populist policies – first rent controls, then the scrapping of stamp duty for first-time buyers.

Downing Street

'Welcome back, sir,' says the policewoman on security. The guy with the machine gun gives me a smile and a thumbs-up. I'm back on the street that over the years has become almost as familiar as the one where I live.

I've come to give my voice another road test, to see if it can cope beyond the peace and quiet of a studio. Hell, yes, it can! My God, I might actually be able to report on this election before it's all over. I'll try to film a piece tomorrow. It will be my first in over two months.

As I limber up my vocal cords, a fearsome quartet strides up to the front door of Number 10: Lynton Crosby, the Tories' Aussie hardman and campaign chief; Mark Textor, his equally tough American sidekick, who uses Twitter aliases to troll and wind up his political enemies; Ed Llewellyn, the PM's old schoolfriend and chief of staff; and Stephen Gilbert, the Conservatives' political director. They inquire generously about my health and then stonewall infuriatingly when I inquire in turn about the health of the Tory campaign.

If appearances can tell you anything, they look pretty chilled, whereas the messages I'm getting from Team Ed seem increasingly frantic.

Tuesday 28 April

On the bank of the Thames by Lambeth Bridge

I've come down to the river to interview the owner of the finest set of mutton-chop whiskers in Westminster. He's the man Speaker Bercow loved to hate, the man who for years was the custodian of our constitution and the grand panjandrum of parliamentary tradition. He is, of course, the ex-clerk of the Commons, formerly Sir Robert Rogers, now Baron Lisvane.

He has joined me to answer a key question about what could happen on the morning after election night. How could the party who comes second still win? If the Queen doesn't decide, who does?

This is a political trainspotter's dream but it may prove to be a living nightmare for people with other things to worry about, such as working or getting a life.

The Bailey room, BBC Millbank

'Uh-oh . . . Jzzz . . . Eee . . .'

Julia is putting me through my paces to get the voice working before I record my commentary.

'One, two, three . . .'

What is that sound? No roughness. No raspiness. No breathiness. Something clicks in my brain. That's my voice. My old voice, the one I had before all this happened. It is like meeting the ghost of the man I used to be. Will I hear him again? Hot tears start to flow. Cancer didn't make me cry. Nor has surgery or chemotherapy. Losing my voice and struggling to get it back has proved to be much more traumatic. It's not about illness. It's not about pain. It's about who I am.

Edit suite, BBC Millbank

My producer, Chris, has dug out some delicious archive footage to try to inject some life into tonight's report. A ticker-tape in Piccadilly Circus broadcasts the election results in 1923. First is 'Mr Baldwin', the sitting Tory PM; second 'Mr MacDonald', who went on to become Labour's first-ever prime minister with the help of 'Mr Asquith', whose Liberal party comes third. There's also Pathé newsreel of the removal men calling for Baldwin, the last PM who 'won' but lost.

Next is the dramatic night in 1979 when the difference of one vote spelled the end for Jim Callaghan's Labour government. And then there's that moment five years ago when David Dimbleby and I unveiled the exit poll on *Election Night* – the poll we didn't believe but which almost perfectly predicted the result that would produce the coalition.

Will I be able to take my place in the *Election Night* studio next week? I simply do not know. Now I need it, I cannot get my voice to sound as it did just a few moments ago.

Wednesday 29 April

Home

Late last night Ed Miliband was snapped making a visit chez Russell Brand. 'MONSTER RAVING LABOUR PARTY', screams the *Sun*. 'DO YOU REALLY WANT THIS CLOWN RULING US?' shouts the *Mail* over a picture of the two men. I am, as is probably now clear, no fan of Brand's insistence that people shouldn't vote. I'm also aware that older voters will not regard cosying up to someone they see as a hairy, trouble-making anarchist as prime ministerial. But the fact remains that Brand reaches the parts of Britain that others cannot reach and provided Ed holds his own, this may prove to be a risk worth taking.

David Cameron, meanwhile, is promising a new law to stop himself or any future government increasing the three taxes that together account for two thirds of what the Treasury raises: VAT, income tax and national insurance.

Have they learned nothing? Do they not remember 'Read my lips – no new taxes' or 'No more boom and bust'? Surely they know that history is littered with politicians promising – or appearing to promise – that they can rewrite the rules of economics and then being forced to gag on their own words?

No doubt the PM's hired hands have told him that in order to deal with the public's lack of trust he needs the equivalent of a supermarket price-war pledge. If only voters would instead demand that politicians are more honest about the limits of what they can promise and deliver, given the sheer unpredictability of the world. Not that a pledge to 'do our best but keep our options open if circumstances change' has much of a ring to it.

Daily Politics *studio*

All my oohing and aahing has been a build-up to this moment: the first time I risk appearing live with no chance of a retake. If it goes well, I'll do my first live on the *BBC News at 10* tomorrow night.

After the first few sentences I realize that I am thinking about what I am saying rather than how I say it, or whether it will come out at all. Job done.

Train from King's Cross to Leeds

A journey that would normally be routine suddenly feels like a great adventure. It's my first trip away from the safety of home, hospital or office since my operation. Tomorrow sees the last big TV election moment in the series of un-debates: *Question Time* live from Leeds. I want to be there to taste a little of what I've been missing on the campaign trail.

Thursday 30 April

Conservative battle bus, *en route from Leeds to somewhere*

The PM, who has been criticized for not meeting real people, is, we're told, going to do a 'walkabout'. Real people, as opposed to hand-picked party activists or invited local notables, will be there. But where is there?

'Where are we going?' asks one reporter.

'It's near,' replies a Tory press officer.

'How far's that?'

'Not far.'

Apparently, this counts as one of the more useful and informative exchanges between journalists and their political minders on the Tory battle bus. My fellow hacks have the glazed looks of men and women who have been travelling for hour after hour, day after day, only to see and hear nothing that is remotely unplanned, unscripted or unexpected. They've eaten too many bags of the free crisps and popcorn on board while being starved of journalistic nourishment.

And it's not only journalists, I gather, who've been getting irritable. The hack pack have grown weary of what is described to me as a never-ending stream of complaints about the BBC's election coverage. The website and morning radio reports are objects of particular loathing.

Wetherby, Yorkshire

The secret is out. We are now officially allowed to know (though not report) where we're going. Our coach pulls up near a Morrisons. Credit to Cameron, I think, he really is going to meet the people. But no. We are marched, like a party of schoolchildren, past the supermarket to the location that has been chosen for the PM's brave foray into the real world. It's Church Street, home to everyday convenience stores such C'est Chocolat, Art & Frames and the Artisan Cheese Company. The PM confidently glad-hands the sort of people who might regard Waitrose as a bit downmarket. He mounts some steps in the market-place and delivers a punchy and effective stump speech, shorn of the 'I'm pumped' rhetoric regarded by many as faintly risible. Although I'm told the PM was delighted when he watched Gogglebox and discovered that the sofa-sitters loved it.

Malmaison hotel, Leeds

I catch the PM for a quick word before he heads to his hotel room to prepare for *Question Time*. He looks and sounds remarkably relaxed. Gone are the bags under his eyes and the tetchiness on display on the Marr sofa a couple of Sundays ago.

The Tory high command think they've turned a corner. Not that any of them are talking, except in public, about winning a majority. In private they are preparing for the argument about who's really won that will ensue if they end election night as the biggest party, but with Labour ready to claim that they should govern as they could form a majority with the backing of the SNP, Plaid, the Greens and others. There's no doubt, though, that they believe they'll still be in their jobs by the end of the week.

Leeds town hall

As the son of a Yorkshireman I know you can always depend on the people of God's own county to speak plainly. Once again the audience are the real stars of *Question Time*, prodding and probing Cameron over benefit cuts, the bedroom tax, food banks and the morality of his policies, then confronting Ed Miliband on Labour's record on spending and borrowing.

The difference is in how the two men respond. Cameron has his best evening yet, Miliband his worst. In part that's down to how they handle their interrogators. The Tory leader doesn't seek to connect with people who are clearly never going to vote for him. He ignores hostile questions and uses them as a jumping-off point for what he wants to say to the audience at home. His opponent deploys a technique that has worked for him with the crowds of sympathizers he is used to addressing but which is disastrous here. He asks questioners their names, what they do and then tries to engage with them directly. Handing the floor to your critics is not a good idea, particularly if they want to know why Labour has spent too much money.

When Ed loses his footing as he leaves the stage he supplies an obvious metaphor for a bad night.

On the Question Time set

Now it's my turn. I only have to speak for a minute and a half and I won't face any tough questions. I've done it thousands of times with hardly a thought, but, boy, am I scared now. I just don't know if I can rely on my voice to hold up, not least when I feel under pressure to call this big moment right.

My news editor, Jon, and speech therapist Julia have come to help. They both know that the more tense I feel, the worse I will sound. Jon fields all editorial calls, giving me space to work with Julia, who gets me to take deep breaths, shrug my shoulders up and down and exercise my vocal cords. I must look and sound ridiculous to the workmen dismantling the set around me, but it works. Until a voice from London says down my earpiece: 'With you in thirty.'

My heart starts to pound and my brow starts to furrow. 'Tell me a joke,' I bark to Jon, who instantly obliges. I barely crack a smile. My brain is focused on one thought and one alone: you're not ready for this. Not since my earliest days in broadcasting have I had this feeling of looking down on myself talking and thinking, 'Screw this up and you're finished.'

'Huw,' I plough on, 'this was not a game-changer – few things ever are – but it has come at a time when, according to one poll, ten million people have yet to make up their minds how to vote.' I say that this was the night Ed stumbled and, for balance, that it was also a night when Cameron dodged. I am in no doubt, though, that there was one clear winner. Cameron will leave Leeds a much happier man than Miliband.

As I pull out my earpiece Jon and Julia are smiling. One of the crew who've been watching our elaborate warm-up for this routine bit of TV work comes up and says, 'That's one of the bravest things I've ever seen anyone do in this job.' He is being absurdly generous but I really appreciate it. I feel that I've conquered my greatest enemy. Fear.

Pizzeria, Leeds

Post-match elation turns all too quickly into late-night angst. Will I be up to taking my seat on *Election Night* and, if so, for how long? Even if I can, will it wreck my voice for the day or days of drama that will follow?

David Dimbleby and my news bosses quiz Julia and me. One peak has been climbed, but another lies ahead.

— MAY —

Friday 1 May

Home

Damn, damn, damn. A day of worry, of BBC confusion, of anger as I finally face up to reality. There's no real choice. There's no way I can broadcast throughout *Election Night* and all the next day, too. I'll start the programme, then bow out and return at breakfast time. I will have to sit in bed and watch the results come in like everybody else.

Sunday 3 May

Triton showers, Nuneaton

Funny business, politics. Gone are the days when prime ministers wanted to look, well, prime ministerial. Their advisers always used to insist on interviews being filmed in front of oak-panelled walls or the Cabinet table.

Today I have been asked to come all the way to Nuneaton to a shower factory. The PM and I are to sit on an empty production line, surrounded by shower heads and thermostats. There are no workers here for him to talk to, except for the MD and a security guard. No showers are being made. In fact, there is no purpose at all in being here save one. The backdrop is meant to scream the Crosby message to casual viewers, 'It's the long-term economic plan, stupid!'

In this interview, and in one I have lined up next week with the Labour leader, I'm determined to ask something neither man has already been asked to try to ensure I don't get answers from the political jukebox. You know the ones I mean. The interviewer puts a question about, say, welfare cuts, and the politician effectively presses a button in his brain that produces a response as familiar as a tune you're sick of hearing on the radio.

Any well-trained political leader has hundreds of these stock answer buttons and 'lines to take', ranging from A1 (spending cuts) to Z8 (post-election deals). The only way to trick the machine is to ask it for a record it doesn't have. The telltale sign that this has worked is when the person in front of you pauses, or swallows, or frowns.

My first question today is on Europe. Cameron has warned that Labour will create chaos, but doesn't his pledge to reopen the issue of Britain's membership of the EU do just that? The Tory jukebox really should have this record by now as I've put this question before, but there are some questions to which there isn't an answer.

'And if you don't get the deal, and if you don't win the referendum, what's plan B for Britain?' I ask.

'Well, I'm confident we will get the deal.'

'What's plan B?'

'Well, I've demonstrated. People said you'll never cut the EU budget. I cut it. People said you'll never veto a treaty. I vetoed a treaty. So people know, with me, I have a strong record of negotiating in Europe.'

'But what is plan B?'

'Well, plan B is to hold a referendum. And for the British people to choose—'

Ah, yes. Repeating yourself is a giveaway. 'Plan B is you don't know,' I persist.

'I do know.'

'You may have a negotiation you can't succeed in and a vote that you lose and Britain will be out of the EU.'

'The only thing you have to be clear about is to have a plan for the changes you want, which I've been clear about.'

So that's clear, then. You need a plan for what you want but not a plan B in case you don't get it.

Next up is Scotland. I put it to him that he has encouraged and exploited the advance of the SNP as they hold the key to his hopes of retaining power. 'Isn't it the case that without the rise of Nicola Sturgeon you'd already be packing your bags?' Unsurprisingly, he does not say, 'Hell yes, you've got a point there,' but takes this as an invitation to warn against a weak Labour government propped up by the SNP.

An old boss of mine once told me that sometimes the questions matter more than the answers. 'Isn't that just arrogance on our part?' I countered.

'Not,' she replied, 'if you're pointing out something that's true that they're refusing to acknowledge.'

Not that any of this flusters Cameron. At the end he is as relaxed as when he first arrived. He can scarcely conceal his delight at Ed Miliband's latest ill-conceived photo opportunity, which the PM says reminds him that *The Thick of It* is as much political documentary as political satire. Calling target voters the 'Quiet Bat People' (you need to have seen that episode) is as nothing compared to the idea that the leader of Her Majesty's opposition should be filmed standing in front of an 8ft piece of limestone into which Labour's six election promises have been engraved. Carved in stone! Geddit? The stone in question has of course instantly been dubbed the 'Edstone'.

Cameron has the air of a man who is confident that he won't, after all, be packing his bags in a few days' time. Or perhaps he has just come to terms with the fact that he's not in control of his own destiny.

To test how much he's been preparing for an uncertain result and a row about legitimacy I ask him whether he's up to speed with the Baldwin precedent.* Of course, he says, I studied it with Vernon. He means constitutional expert Professor Bogdanor. He's ready, all right.

Flaming Grill, Nuneaton

I've been struck by the curse of the spinning egg-timer. On a day when the BBC science editor's report has made it from the middle of an ice floe in the Arctic, mine seems to be stuck in the ether somewhere between Nuneaton and Broadcasting House. An exclusive interview with the PM, my first of this campaign; hours of work lost.

I escape to the beer garden and text the team to say, 'It's only telly. No one died. The drinks are on me.' One upside of having been ill is that it might have given me a little bit of perspective.

---

* Stanley Baldwin tried to hang on as prime minister after winning the most seats in the 1923 general election but failing to gain a majority.

My tranquillity is quickly disrupted by incoming fire from Team Cameron. Given just a few moments to work out how to fill the top five minutes of the six o'clock news, the newsroom decided to run the first long chunk of the interview they could find on their unedited footage. So all viewers saw was the PM getting a hammering on lack of a plan B for Europe. I explain that it was a technical cock-up and not an editorial conspiracy. With seventy-two hours to go before polling day, I sense that the PM is now anything but relaxed. He's obviously not that confident of victory.

I assure them that a proper version of the interview will run at ten o'clock.

Driving home

The story of the Edstone gets better and better. Miliband has promised to erect it in the garden of Number 10 'where we can see it every day as a reminder of our duty to keep Labour's promises'. Some enterprising hack has got a source at Westminster Council to say they'll never give planning permission for it.

Rumour has it that it's having to be driven around the M25 because it's too big to fit through the door of Labour HQ. It was made so large because someone seriously argued that if it was 8ft tall no one would compare it to a gravestone. No, really.

What few seem to have pointed out is that the 'promises' that have been carved in stone are so broad they may as well have been written in butter and left in the sunshine. My test of how meaningful a political statement may be is whether anyone would ever argue for the opposite. So stand up all those in favour of weak economic foundations, lower living standards, a health service that doesn't have time to care and no controls on immigration.

Bank holiday Monday, 4 May

Home

It may be a bank holiday. It may be that the only news most people care about is the birth of a new princess. It may be that I am not on duty today as I am rehearsing for general election night.

Nevertheless the complaints are coming thick and fast. From the Tories. They are outraged that the news is leading on something the prime minister allegedly told his deputy, even though David Cameron has denied it and, so far at least, Nick Clegg has refused to confirm what a friend of his claims was said not long ago.

What the PM is alleged to have told the DPM is that he knew the Conservatives couldn't win a majority at the election. The Lib Dem subtext, of course, is that if they can't win you might as well vote for us to keep them honest.

News reaches me from the Tory campaign bus that the PM marched on board and called the story 'rubbish'. When one hack jokingly muttered 'Bloody BBC,' the PM responded, 'I'm going to close them down after the election!' Joke? Expression of frustration? Threat? All three? No one could be sure. In a few weeks' time working out which it was could really, really matter.

In the meantime, Ed Balls has been warning Scots that normally it is the party that wins the most seats that forms a government. He's saying, in other words, that if Labour comes second on Friday, you can't assume they'll get into power just because the SNP would back them against the Tories.

Even Nigel Farage is preparing the way for disappointment. He is telling people that a vote for UKIP is a vote for changing the electoral system. Decoded, this means 'I know I'll get a lot of votes but we might not get many seats.'

Defeatism, it seems, is the theme of the day.

BBC election studio, Elstree

I'm finally here, on the bridge of the BBC's equivalent of the *Starship Enterprise*, sitting alongside David Dimbleby at the centre of the *Election Night* studio for a rehearsal. We are all preparing to boldly go where no election has gone before.

Here with us is Jeremy Vine, plus his virtual maps and graphs and swingometers, the Dr McCoy of the operation taking the temperature of the nation. On our other side is Emily Maitlis (Uhura) with her touch analysis of every result. Above our heads in the engine room is Andrew Neil (Scotty), putting politicians through their paces.

Behind the scenes are the people who process the results, crunch the numbers and analyze the trends. Add the technical staff who man cameras and mics and comms, those who generate the graphics, the dozens involved in outside broadcasts and you end up with 600 staff working on this night alone. The sheer scale of it is exhilarating.

We begin by rehearsing the biggest moment of the night: the unveiling of the exit poll. David reveals that we're heading for a hung Parliament and reads out the key numbers: Conservative 280, Labour 261, SNP 54, Lib Dem 31, UKIP 1.

I stare into camera 5 and declare that this is a moment of 'exquisite torture' for our two main political leaders as the result is close enough to give them both hope but grants them absolutely no certainty.

If the real result is anything like this, it should be quite a night.

Car home

Here comes that rollercoaster again. Just as things are going well with my voice, my body's not feeling too clever. I'm cold. I'm starting to shiver and shake. Damn it, I'm getting a temperature. Not good if you're on chemo.

Accident and Emergency, Royal Free hospital

They've taken my temperature, measured my pulse, checked my blood pressure, sent my blood for tests, hooked me up to an ECG and X-rayed my chest. Nothing is left to chance.

The bad news is they want me to stay in overnight. The good news is that the Prof, Tim Meyer, is coming early in the morning in the hope of being able to give me the all-clear to head off and interview Ed Miliband.

Tuesday 5 May

Royal Free hospital

The Prof did come early, but not to wave me goodbye. He wants me to remain in hospital under his supervision. I've spent days planning an interview with Miliband and now I have to text to explain I can't make it.

I was going to start by asking him how many friends he has who run businesses and what experience he has of making a profit before putting it to him that his remedy for many of the country's ills is instructing or regulating or taxing businesses into doing what he thinks is right.

Even his close allies say that Ed Miliband, unlike, say Ed Balls or Chuka Umunna, treats businesspeople as if they are talking in a foreign language. What motivates them is a total mystery to him. It is an attitude that underlies his belief in a bigger role for government and another illustration of the fact that the gulf between the two big parties is wider than most voters recognize.

It's not a question I'll ever get to put now. Once again, my deputy James steps in to save the day.

I need something to bring a smile to my face. A good old-fashioned gaffe does it.

It's about the Edstone.

One of Miliband's closest advisers, Lucy Powell, has told *Radio 5 Live*: 'I don't think anyone is suggesting that the fact that he's carved them in stone means he's absolutely not going to break them or anything like that.'

Translated this seems to mean that the promises carved in stone are not really, er, carved in stone.

Lucy calls to tell me this is terribly unfair. She's been quoted out of context. It's not what she meant. She was trying to say that she knew the stone alone wouldn't convince people, but Ed had shown he was to be trusted.

Laugh it off, I advise her, pointing out that I've no doubt David Cameron felt hard done by when people banged on about him mixing up Aston Villa with West Ham. I resist the temptation to add, 'Sorry, it's your turn.'

Wednesday 6 May

Royal Free hospital

I'm still here. Worse, I have just been told I will have to spend a third night in hospital. So much for returning to report on the final week before the election.

To think that not long ago I really believed I'd be fully back at work three weeks after surgery and would cover the whole campaign.

It has, though, given me an opportunity to see this election as many voters do and to stand back from it, rather than getting bogged down in the daily minutiae and rows that make up any campaign.

I settle down to write my last blog before polling day tomorrow:

Both Labour and the Tories originally planned for this campaign believing that if they were neck-and-neck on polling day Ed Miliband would walk into Number 10 . . . But the loss of, perhaps, dozens of seats in Labour's former Scottish stronghold is what makes this election too close to call.

. . . If the campaign has often felt narrow and introverted the arguments that will follow an uncertain result could raise some of the biggest issues in our country: the future of the UK, our membership of the EU and the fairness of our democracy.

Not only that, but it may raise the prospect of another election coming along sooner than we originally thought.

That may give me the chance to do what I've been unable to do for a lot of this campaign as I've had to follow much of it from my sickbed. I'm all too aware, though, that the thought of another few weeks like the last few may be enough to make most people feel pretty unwell.

An uncertain result is what everyone is preparing for as a call from Charlie (Lord) Falconer, the former Labour lord chancellor, makes plain.

'Have you read paragraph 2.12?'

Yes, I tell Charlie, I have read not just that one, but all the relevant paragraphs in the nearest thing Britain has to an election rule book: the so-called Cabinet manual, written by the Cabinet secretary and signed off by the prime minister.

Charlie wants me – and all the other editors and commentators he's calling round – to understand that even if the Tories come first tomorrow Cameron can only stay on as prime minister if he can find enough allies to form a majority government. If he can't, says the nation's former top lawyer, he has a duty to resign and let Miliband take over and have a go himself.

Not so fast, I say, showing off that I know my Baldwin precedent and have spoken to the head people in Whitehall about what it means now. Paragraph 2.12 also suggests, I point out, that Cameron need only quit if he's confident that his opponent can form a majority government. Given that Miliband has said he won't even talk to the SNP, let alone do a deal with them, surely he couldn't be confident? In other words, 2.12 has been written ambiguously enough to let the PM do what he wants.

When I suggest that the Tories could even go so far as tabling a Queen's speech in the hope that the odd maverick in other parties might vote for it, Charlie suggests that this would be constitutional Micawberism – in other words, planning a government in the hope that something or, rather, someone will turn up to support it.

I call Craig Oliver to get the Tories' take on paragraph 2.12. He seems to know surprisingly little about it and certainly a lot less than me. He is, though, sure of one thing: if the Tories 'win', no one will get away with claiming they really 'lost'. I put it to him that 'winning' means crossing the finishing line, i.e. getting a parliamentary majority, not simply being ahead of the other guy.

At the end of my calls what's abundantly clear is that both sides are preparing for a hung Parliament and the likelihood that the Tories will be the biggest party in it.

What's also clear is that this result would be heaven for pundits like me and hell for pretty much everyone else.

BBC election studio, Elstree

The Prof has given me a 'pass' for two hours to appear on the eve-of-poll *BBC News at 10*. I'm warmly greeted by old colleagues and friends. I don't tell anybody that an hour ago I was in bed having antibiotics fed into a vein. I look normal; in fact, some say slimmer, and more tanned than usual. I sound pretty normal. I feel anything but. The fear has returned. The old me did this in his sleep, but can the new me hack it? The answer is yes . . . up to a point. Close colleagues and family note extra tension in the face. Viewers send mainly kind messages. One Twitter exchange makes me laugh out loud: 'poor @bbcnickrobinson losing his voice at the worst possible time for him.'

To which someone replies: 'Um you know he's survived lung cancer don't you? I imagine the rough voice is a mere detail :).'

A very valuable reminder not to lose sight of the fact that what Tony Blair used to call the 'big picture' is good.

Thursday 7 May

Polling station

A pencil in your hand. A ballot paper in front of you. A box waiting to receive your vote – worth as much as that of any other man or woman in the land. This is the joy of democracy. I've never felt it more than today when I walked to the polling station with my eighteen-year-old son Will, who is casting his first-ever vote.

Make-up, BBC Elstree

I can't find my tie . . . I can't find my bloody tie! Where is it?

I've found my tie, but now look. There's a thin white line going straight down it and nothing will remove it.

And I've forgotten to charge my iPad.

Damn, damn, damn. Nothing's going to plan.

Deep breaths, now. It's going to be all right.

Election Night *studio*

'It's always better live,' David grumbles as he stumbles during pre-recording the opening for *Election Night 2015*. The same words have caught him out a couple of times. They are 'Ed Miliband'. Before he opens his mouth for another go, a voice rings out from somewhere in the studio: 'He'll never be prime minister.'

Meeting room

'Are you sitting down?' says the voice emerging from the speaker of a mobile phone held by the *Election Night* editor, Sam Woodhouse. This sounds ominous. I look around the room at the handful of others – among them David Dimbleby and Jeremy Vine – to be trusted with the information that everyone else, from the prime minister down, is desperate to hear.

Sam rehearsed everything yesterday, including having a meeting in this room. Security had to be called to let him out after he got locked in.

'Conservatives: three hundred and sixteen,' says the voice on the phone.

Bloody hell. That's nine seats more than they've got now.

'Labour: two hundred and thirty-nine.'

That's nineteen down. I swallow hard.

'Liberal Democrats: ten.'

Ten! That's a massacre.

'SNP: fifty-eight.'

All but one Scottish MP. A tidal wave.

Jeremy quips: 'So Scotland will go independent and the BBC will be shut down.'

Wisely, no one reacts. Sam says 'Fuck!' repeatedly. On the TV screen in the corner of the room a shark is devouring a small fish.

I want to shout, '*Really*? Labour go backwards and the Lib Dems collapse? Why the hell haven't the polls shown that happening?'

Mine is to be the first voice on air after David reads out the raw numbers. What on earth should I say? I don't want to treat the exit poll the way I did five years ago, like a man holding up a rotting piece of fish. That poll turned out to be absolutely spot-on. It doesn't necessarily mean, of course, that this one will be right, and if isn't, we all know that it will be us and not the number-crunchers who feature on the endlessly repeated YouTube clips. We are all scarred by memories of 1992, when the exit poll led Neil Kinnock to crack open the bubbly on an evening when John Major was about to clock up a historic victory.

Election Night *studio, 10pm*

I am looking down the lens of camera 5 when Big Ben strikes.

Bong, bong, bong...'Ten o'clock and we're saying the Conservatives are the largest party...' begins David, pausing ever so briefly, but for what must seem like hours to those anxiously waiting for the numbers to be displayed under holograms of each leader standing and staring into the distance.

I notice something I didn't register in the rehearsals. The Miliband hologram blinks repeatedly. Not so Cameron, who simply stares straight ahead.

David finishes reading out the figures and turns to me. 'Sensational, Nick?'

'Sensational, David, an extraordinary night – if that exit poll is right . . .'

The emphasis is all on the 'if' and two more follow. It will, I add, be a source of joy for the Tories, gloom for Labour, ecstasy for the SNP and misery for the Lib Dems.

I have no way of knowing, and yet I do know. I may be closeted within the walls of a TV studio, but I can smell the emotions from here.

Just before midnight

Ignore or attack. That's the standard political approach when inconvenient facts emerge.

The early big-name guests behave as if the exit poll hasn't happened. They trot out pre-cooked 'lines to take'. Michael Gove repeatedly says, 'We won', which is what you do when you fear that people might conclude that you haven't actually won, i.e. by securing a majority. Ed Balls dismisses rumours that he may have lost his own seat and declares that David Cameron's ability to remain in Downing Street is 'on a knife edge'. He seems to be saying that Labour could and should form the government, even if they're fifty or more seats behind. I describe that on air as 'quite a claim', which is BBC impartiality code for 'You've got to be kidding'.

Captain Ashdown takes on the mission of launching Operation Rubbish the Exit Poll. Paddy tells Andrew Neil he's so confident the Lib Dems are on course to win thirty seats that 'I will publicly eat my hat on your programme' if the poll is right. Alastair Campbell joins in the culinary fun by promising to eat his kilt. Nicola Sturgeon is wise enough not to promise to dine on any of her apparel but tweets to express her scepticism about the idea that the SNP will sweep the board. As ever, though, it is Peter Mandelson who wins the prize for the most barbed putdown of the night as he attacks Jeremy Vine for presenting 'hyperbole heaped on speculation heaped on hypothesis'.

David, Jeremy and I are powerless to rebut what they say as we have no more idea than they do whether the exit poll is right. I cautiously point out that if it is ten seats wrong either way it could dramatically change the outcome.

It falls to John Curtice to appear, godlike, on the balcony overlooking the studio to do the job. He is still struggling with his microphone as David introduces him. His arrival has been delayed by producers, who could not persuade him to wear make-up but did insist that he tuck in his shirt. The Prof explains that the early results in the north-east, all good for Labour, were all as predicted by his poll. So, far from disproving it, they suggest he's on course to enjoy watching Paddy eat his hat and Alastair his kilt.

Friday 8 May

Election Night *studio, just before 1am*

I need to get off. I'm exhausted, my voice is getting worse and the end-less supply of peppermint tea and chocolate isn't clearing it. Neither is the odd snatched mum-mum-mum whenever voice therapist Julia can dash on to the set.

I am about to hand over to my pundit tag-team partner, Andrew Marr. There is something rather comic about a man full of antibiotics and chemo poison with half a voice being replaced by someone still recovering from a stroke on a programme anchored by a seventy-six-year-old. Even though Andy and David remain the best in the business you can see why some of our bosses were so bloody nervous.

As I walk off the set my final, rather needy, tweet reads: 'Hope voice didn't distract too much and thanks for all tips & recipes.' The replies are extraordinarily generous. To my surprise and pleasure they're led by Gary Lineker, who replies: 'Well played @bbcnickrobinson. Don't worry about the voice. It's what you say not the volume that counts and you're on top of your game.'

Thank you, Gary. That is the nicest thing you could possibly have said. Instead of leaving the studio niggled by regret and frustration, I've a sense that I've climbed my personal Mount Everest. It feels bloody marvellous.

A hotel down the road

Rest. Both the body and the voice. Then return to broadcast at breakfast time. That's the theory. I watch a little, doze a little, watch and
doze, but can't quite get to sleep. There is no taking your eyes off the
extraordinary drama.

Nuneaton becomes the Basildon of this election. Back in 1992 I was
the producer in the home of Essex Man. I vividly remember the moment
I was told by local Lib Dems that the Tories would win the seat,
confounding the polls. 'That's it. It's over. John Major is heading back
to Number Ten,' I told anyone who would listen. No one did listen –
why would they? – until, that is, the result was confirmed. Nuneaton
shows that not only were the day-to-day polls wrong, the exit poll was
actually an underestimate of the Tories' success. It predicted a 1 per
cent swing to Labour here but in fact the swing is 3 per cent to the
Tories.

Finally the news starts to sink in at the top of the big parties. One
of David Cameron's inner circle texts a colleague to say simply, 'Fuck
me!' Earlier, the prime minister and his closest advisers ate beef pie
and salad at the kitchen table of his constituency home in Dean, near
Chipping Norton. In the hours before ten o'clock, they still feared that
their time in government could come to an end, if only through Labour
being able to carry out what they would regard as a constitutional
'coup' by claiming power even if they came second. Some insiders,
such as Jim Messina, the man hired from Obama's White House,
predicted a result almost identical to that forecast by the exit poll but a
sceptical George Osborne is said to have promised to snog Lynton
Crosby if the Tories got a majority.

Ed Miliband is in the kitchen of his cottage in his Doncaster constituency with his wife Justine, his closest advisers, Stewart Wood and
Bob Roberts, and his university friend and speechwriter Marc Stears.
It is now becoming clear to him which of the two speeches they've
prepared will have to be delivered at his Doncaster count in a few
hours' time. Earlier, before the polls closed, they'd worked on the
'long' speech he hoped to give, setting out the moral case for Labour
governing even if the party came a close second and spelling out
the plan for Britain he'd pursue if he did become prime minister. In the
event that the Tories got fewer than 283 seats, Labour would dub
Cameron a squatter in Downing Street if he tried to hold on to power.

Miliband's team had been buoyant. Labour HQ had detected no late swing to the Tories and they felt that their ground operation was going well, whereas they'd heard that their rivals 'get out the vote' software programme wasn't working.

Just in case they were wrong, they also prepared a 'short' speech. That's the one the world will hear.

At just after 2am the long-forecast SNP tsunami hits land for the first time. Labour lose Kilmarnock and Loudoun to a virtually unheard of 26 per cent swing. Soon afterwards Paisley follows, knocking off his feet the man who not only ran Labour's election campaign and was earmarked as 'our next foreign secretary' but an MP of the old-fashioned kind, a son of the manse who grew up to represent his own town. Douglas Alexander has been beaten by a twenty-year-old politics student who has tweeted about her love of vodka and hatred of Celtic.

An hour later comes confirmation that Labour's failure is as much an English as a Scottish phenomenon. North Warwickshire, their number one target seat, began the night with a wafer-thin Tory majority of just 54 votes and ends it with a comfortable margin for the Conservatives of almost 2,000.

Sophie Raworth is outside Broadcasting House filling in a giant electoral map of Britain. SNP yellow is surging across Scotland. Alex Salmond greets his return to Westminster by declaring that 'the Scottish lion has roared'. It has, but with the Tories now heading for a majority, his hope of real influence is at an end.

Orange disappears from the map as fast as yellow spreads, with Lib Dem big names falling one after the other. Davey has gone. Laws, Alexander and Hughes have gone. Finally, just after 4.30am, the Tory candidate in Twickenham smiles as she removes a speech from her handbag. Vince Cable has gone, too.

The Conservatives have systematically and ruthlessly strangled their coalition partners over these past five years. Almost to make matters worse, they ensured that one big name was kept alive. Tories in Nick Clegg's seat were advised to vote tactically to make sure the Lib Dem leader was available just in case another deal with Cameron was necessary.

At around 5am a visibly shell-shocked Clegg speaks from his count in Sheffield of 'a cruel and punishing night for the Liberal Democrats'. The soon to be ex-leader of the Lib Dems now has a parliamentary party that can fit into a couple of black cabs with the odd seat to spare. Day after day he will be confronted by the legacy of his leadership. It will be a form of living hell.

Next to face the public torture of admitting defeat is Ed Miliband who, at 5.23am, delivers his short speech in Doncaster looking tired and despondent. Labour is forecast to be 77 seats behind the Tories after what he concedes has been 'a very disappointing and difficult night for the Labour party'. They have been 'overwhelmed by a surge of nationalism in Scotland' and failed to make the gains they'd hoped for in England.

Twenty minutes later a beaming David Cameron stands up at Windrush leisure centre in Witney to hail 'a very strong night for the Conservative party' and pledges to lead a 'one-nation' government. On stage with him, watching this moment in political history, are a man dressed as a giant furry red Muppet, the candidate for the Give Me Back Elmo party, and a fake sheikh, standing for the Land party, which proposes bulldozing the hamlet in which Cameron lives in order to make way for the HS2 train link. Only in Britain.

It is time for me to get up – in truth I never really went to sleep – and head back to the election studio.

BBC Elstree, radio booth, 6.30am

My first morning broadcast is on the *Today* programme.

Not, I say, since the fall of Thatcher or the Blair landslide has there been a political moment quite like this one. Personal triumphs for the prime minister and for Scotland's first minister will not just reshape British politics but could perhaps reshape the future of the United Kingdom itself. Bitter disappointment for Ed Miliband and a political disaster for Nick Clegg will lead to months of soul-searching for their parties as they mourn the loss of some of their most famous faces, felled by a brutal electoral firing squad.

BBC election studio, 7am

I return to the studio I left six hours ago. As I arrive the master of ceremonies is leaving. The man who's been at the helm not just for every election I've covered but every one I can remember, nine in all, has announced his last-ever result.

I've scarcely time to mutter a 'well done' to David Dimbleby as he vacates his chair for Huw Edwards and the crew clear away his glasses of jelly babies and nuts, chocolate and bananas.

It is the TV equivalent of being at Sir Alex Ferguson's last game. What I should have said was that no one will ever match what he has achieved, though I know Huw will give it a damn good try.

BBC Elstree, radio booth, 8.16am

Back on the *Today* programme, John Humphrys is beginning to ask me a question when Julia holds up her phone for me to read. On it is a high-priority text she's been urged to show me. It's from our local reporter watching the count in Ed Balls' constituency. I tell John that however interesting what he just asked me might be, it's not half so interesting as the news I've just been handed.

Twenty-four hours ago Ed Balls believed he might be delivering a budget within weeks. He spent all that day, and most of the preceding weeks, visiting other constituencies around the country. Ten hours ago his adviser told me that a rumour he might be about to lose his seat was nonsense. But I can now break the news that not only will Balls not be our next chancellor, he will not even be an MP. His defeat will be the emblem of Labour's night of disaster and the Tories' new dawn.

BBC election studio

I run back on to the TV set just as Balls is finishing his concession speech. Huw turns to me for a comment. This, I say, is Labour's equivalent of the 'were you up for Portillo?' moment that symbolized Tony Blair's landslide in 1997. And, I add, I am going to make an unpopular prediction that Balls, who is widely loathed just as Portillo was, will, like him, go on to be a much more popular figure out of office than he was in.

A Westminster hotel

Sleep. Glorious, desperately needed sleep. Two and a half hours before the PM heads to the Palace. Zzzz.

Whitehall, 12.25pm

You know how it is – you wait for one leader to resign and then three resign at once. First it was a sullen Farage (who quit as soon as he learned that he hadn't been elected in South Thanet – his seventh attempt to get into Parliament), then an emotional Clegg and now a disbelieving Miliband.

I walk up Whitehall listening in my earphones as Ed delivers a speech that is generous ('I take total and absolute responsibility for our defeat') and self-deprecating (he thanks the public for 'the most unlikely cult of the twentieth century: Milifandom') and yet devoid of any insight into what has happened: 'While we may have lost the election, the argument of our campaign will not go away.'

That sounds awfully like telling the electorate: 'We were right, and one day you'll understand that.'

This on a day when Labour was almost wiped out in Scotland, went into reverse in England and when the two men who hoped to be our next chancellor and foreign secretary have joined the unemployment register.

Downing Street, 12.50pm

I have a front-row seat for the making of history: a folding chair under a camera pointing at the most famous front door in the world.

David Cameron strides up to the lectern placed in front of Number 10 and utters the words he never thought he'd say: 'I will now form a Conservative majority government.' After all, governing parties don't gain seats, do they? Especially parties promising two more years of painful cuts. But he just has, achieving what had seemed to be Mission Impossible.

This is David Cameron's day. But he knows it is another leader's, too; the woman who dominated an election in which she didn't even run: Scotland's first minister Nicola Sturgeon.

That's why his pledge to work to show 'respect' to the people of Scotland and ensure that the country remains 'one nation, one United Kingdom' will define his legacy.

What remains to be seen is how – whether – they can learn to live together or if he will become the last-ever prime minister of a United Kingdom and she the first-ever leader of an independent Scotland.

Downing Street, 10pm

So this is it. It's over. There will be no days of uncertainty, no negotiations, no need for deals or rows about legitimacy.

The final tally is: Conservatives 331, Labour 232, SNP 56, Liberal Democrats 8, UKIP 1, Greens 1, Plaid Cymru 3 and 18 others. So even the exit poll underestimated the scale of the Tories' triumph and Labour and Lib Dem woes.

It is, I say on BBC News at 10, what almost no one expected to happen. Not the pundits or the pollsters or the politicians. Not David Cameron himself. Not the nation's top civil servant who picked the officials, booked the rooms and even ordered the sandwiches for days, if not weeks, of haggling over who governed Britain.

What I don't say, but is already obvious, is that an inquest is sure to follow. Why did the opinion polls get it so wrong? Did the media allow them, rather than the choice facing the country, to shape too much of the coverage? Or were they/we right until many voters made a last-minute decision? All this is, though, for another day.

In my eyeline Julia is still conducting me, trying to ensure that my by now very husky voice sounds as good as it can. It has a long way to go but it is so much better than it was just a couple of weeks ago. All the signs are that it will keep improving steadily.

So much has happened, so much has changed since we filmed David Cameron here in the flat above the shop exactly a year ago. So much that could never have been predicted.

Looking back, there is, perhaps, one simple lesson I've learned: you can never know what lies around the corner, you can never control everything but you must never, ever give up hope.

Index

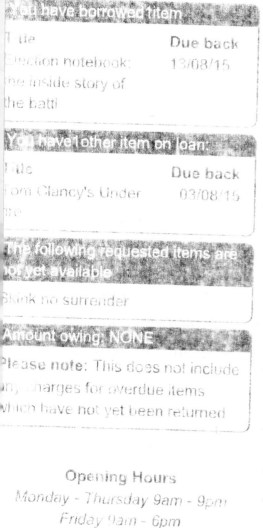

ABOUT THE AUTHOR

Nick Robinson has been Political Editor of BBC News for a decade. Before that he was Political Editor of ITV News. He's the only person to have held both posts. He studied Politics, Philosophy and Economics at Oxford before joining the BBC in 1986. After ten years working behind the cameras – as a producer on programmes ranging from *Crimewatch* to *On the Record* and *Panorama* – he became a reporter and presenter. His first book, *Live from Downing Street*, was published in 2012. Nick lives in North London with his wife and three children.